The Films of John Carpenter

The Films of John Carpenter

by JOHN KENNETH MUIR

McFarland & Company, Inc., Publishers
Jefferson, North Carolina, and London

The present work is a reprint of the illustrated case bound edition of The Films of John Carpenter, first published in 2000 by McFarland.

LIBRARY OF CONGRESS CATALOGUING-IN-PUBLICATION DATA

Muir, John Kenneth, 1969–
    The films of John Carpenter / by John Kenneth Muir.
        p.   cm.
    Includes bibliographical references and index.

    ISBN-13: 978-0-7864-2269-2
    (softcover : 50# alkaline paper)∞

    1. Carpenter, John, 1948–   — Criticism and interpretation.
    I. Title.
PN1998.3.C38M85   2005
791.43'0233'092 — dc21   99-88930

British Library cataloguing data are available

Front cover, from top: John Carpenter directs then-wife Adrienne Barbeau in
Escape from New York (1981). Nancy Loomis in Halloween (1978). Kurt Rus-
sell in Escape from New York (1981). Malcolm Danare in Christine (1983).
Karen Allen and Jeff Bridges in Starman (1984).

Manufactured in the United States of America

McFarland & Company, Inc., Publishers
    Box 611, Jefferson, North Carolina 28640
        www.mcfarlandpub.com

To Allan Lindsey and Chris O'Brien,
friends from *Halloween* to *They Live*.
And to *The Thing*—
the best science-fiction film of 1982

Acknowledgments

The author would like to acknowledge Kurt Russell, Jamie Lee Curtis, Peter Jason, Sandy King, and all the other members of the "John Carpenter Repertory Company" who for more than two decades have consistently worked with Carpenter to create a body of film art which merits debate, discussion, and analysis. Of course, special appreciation must go to the auteur himself, John Carpenter, an artist who, despite his protestations to the contrary, is no bum.

Contents

Introduction

Long-time John Carpenter action hero and silver screen icon Kurt Russell once commented that there are only ten directors in the world whose films he can identify as "theirs" right off the bat. Importantly, his friend and frequent collaborator John Carpenter is one of that select ten.

Russell's remark is particularly insightful because John Carpenter is arguably the most consistent of all the film directors working today. In style, in composition, in technique, in sound, and even in mood and texture, he rarely strays from his own personal ethos. His films inevitably feature martial-sounding, pulse-pounding soundtracks, slow-moving (but elegant) camera-work, and hair-raising jolts galore as the forces of evil pop into the foreground with an unexpected intensity, causing the audience's adrenaline to skyrocket.

Beyond the jolts, John Carpenter's movies commonly appear to derive from the same source because the director is an outspoken proponent of the auteur theory: the belief that a film's director is its primary and most important player, and thus responsible for generating the film's overall "vision." In keeping with this once-cherished theory of filmmaking, Carpenter exerts total control over the filmmaking process, from the composition of the musical score to the final editing. He also tends to work with the same group of performers, artists and technicians over and over again, whether it be the director of photography (Dean Cundey, Gary B. Kibbe), lead actor (Kurt Russell, Donald Pleasence, Sam Neill, Jamie Lee Curtis), costume designer (Robin Michel Bush) or even the gaffer (Mark Walthour).

With this support, Carpenter consistently delivers films that easily fit under one umbrella and present a coherent body of work, a remarkable whole. If he requires a solid, capable actor to come in and nail a difficult supporting role, he calls on Peter Jason (*Prince of Darkness* [1987], *They Live* [1988], *In the Mouth of Madness* [1995], *Village of the Damned* [1995], *Escape from L.A.* [1996]). If he needs a powerful and charismatic action hero, he recruits Kurt Russell (*Escape from New York* [1981], *The Thing* [1982], *Big Trouble in Little China* [1986], *Escape from L.A.* [1996]). If he needs a cold-hearted doctor with evil undertones, he selects David Warner (*John Carpenter Presents Body Bags* [1993], *In the Mouth of Madness*). These performers represent different sides of Carpenter the storyteller, and he deploys them again and again, in film after film, to express certain facets of his vision.

1

Like his auteur hero and filmmaking role model, Howard Hawks (1896–1977), John Carpenter ambitiously seeks to impose his personal filmmaking vision on not just one movie genre, but all. Thus he has explored horror and suspense (*Halloween* [1978], *Someone's Watching Me!* [1978], *The Fog* [1980], *Prince of Darkness* [1987]), action (*Assault on Precinct 13* [1976], *Escape from New York* [1981]), science fiction (*Dark Star* [1975], *The Thing* [1982]), comedy (*Memoirs of an Invisible Man* [1992]), and even pointed political satire (*They Live* [1988], *Escape from L.A.* [1996]).

As the contemporary king of all film genres, John Carpenter has also generated some significant box office sizzle by artfully mixing and matching his subject matter in unexpected ways. *Starman* (1984) is a remarkable blend of the Hollywood road picture *It Happened One Night* (1934) and the science fiction "alien visitation" movie *The Day The Earth Stood Still* (1951). *Vampires* (1998) is simultaneously a vampire "horror" picture and a modern-day, Sam Peckinpah western. *Big Trouble in Little China* is an amalgam of martial arts/kung-fu/John Wayne/action/fantasy tropes served up in one glossy and delicious nonstop package. Though to the untrained eye many of these genre blenders may seem less than significant in thematic complexity, each one loudly and cogently represents John Carpenter's career agenda. Specifically, each one dramatizes his ability to work artfully in a genre outside the traditional horror venue.

Importantly, Carpenter envisions himself not as a "personal" director who directs "individual" message films for limited audiences. He is a studio director, like Howard Hawks or Alfred Hitchcock, who directs stylish films designed solely to entertain mass audiences. His desire is not necessarily to connect with the viewer on an independent, "small" scale (like the cinema of Ed Burns, Woody Allen, or Jim Jarmusch), but rather to entertain and manipulate the masses in the manner of the Hitchcock or Hawks blockbusters he remembers from his own youth. But, like Hawks before him, Carpenter's taste also tends to be the audience's taste. Carpenter dramatizes the stories he personally wants to tell, yet he is uncannily skilled at luring audiences to his way of thinking.

There is yet another side to John Carpenter and his motion pictures: His films frequently reflect the mischievous side of the director's personality. For John Carpenter is surely the last maverick standing in Hollywood — a director who does what he wants, when he wants, and for wholly personal reasons. This anti-authoritarian streak, this rampant individualism, has resulted in Carpenter turning down directorial assignments on films as diverse as *Top Gun* (1985), *Fatal Attraction* (1987) and even *H20* (1998), the twentieth anniversary sequel to his own horror masterpiece *Halloween*. Simply stated, he is not at all interested in directing films that do not stimulate his creative juices.

Carpenter not only makes the films he wants, he infuses each project with his own strong anti-authoritarian, laconic bent. In *Assault on Precinct 13*, *Escape from New York*, and *Escape from L.A.*, Carpenter's protagonists are convicted criminals, anti-heroes who loathe society's repressive laws and institutions. In *The Thing*, the officially appointed leader of the Antarctic research team is removed from authority early on in the picture and replaced by the more individual common man, MacReady. In *They Live*, *Village of the Damned* (1995) and *Memoirs of an Invisible Man*, Carpenter's heroes find themselves aligned not with the "national interest," but against the government, the police, scientists, and other groups that have traditionally been dramatized in films as almost innately heroic. This tactic is not a result of Carpenter's specific dislike of any of the above-listed organizations; it only reflects his total displeasure with authority, and the establishment as a whole. Censorship is the issue of *In the Mouth of Madness*; lack of religious freedom is the theme of *Escape from L.A.*; the inherent greed of the Reagan era is the dynamite that causes *They Live* to explode into violence, etc. In each of these films, Carpenter sees the state working against its people, and he shoots it as he sees it, often lampooning such American pillars as Jerry Falwell (*Escape from L.A.*), Ronald Reagan (*They Live*), Stephen King (*In the Mouth of Madness*) and even TV film critics Gene Siskel and Roger Ebert (*They Live*).

Beyond being an auteur concerned with poking holes in figures of authority, John Carpenter is an artist obsessed with both mankind's failings and his strengths. His pictures enunciate the importance of self-sacrifice (*The Thing, Prince of Darkness, They Live, Village of the Damned*), individuality (*Christine* [1983], *Big Trouble in Little China, They Live, Escape from L.A.*) and even love (*Starman, Prince of Darkness, Memoirs of an Invisible Man*). Some Carpenter scholars who would prefer to see him as an unrepentant and cynical nihilist, perhaps because of the godless, purposeless worlds so successfully dramatized in Carpenter epics such as *Dark Star* and *In the Mouth of Madness*, but a close viewing of Carpenter's work reveals a romantic streak beneath the skepticism: a belief down deep — far below the anti-establishment hatred — that a single committed and idealistic person can make a difference, even if society does not recognize that person as valuable or good. The Snake Plisskens, the Napoleon Wilsons, the MacReadys, and the John Nadas of the worlds are out of step with their times because, underneath the machismo, they are essentially romantics who "still believe in America" (per *They Live*) and the nation's stated ideals of liberty and opportunity. Their beliefs put them in constant opposition with the law and current "the forces that be" but nonetheless secure their position as true patriots.

When Snake Plissken plunges the world into darkness in the finale of *Escape from L.A.*, he is striking a blow not for anarchy, but for freedom and liberty. Snake points out that freedom in America "died a long time ago," and thus he spawns a reparation and renewal of those sleeping ideals. When John Nada destroys the alien hypno-transmitter in *They Live*, he is likewise restoring, not destroying, America by delivering a wake-up call for freedom. Despite the authority-bashing nature of his heroes, the belief in American ideals and in man himself is inherent to the work of John Carpenter. He believes that man can do better, and his heroes consistently prove that worthy goals (such as saving the Earth from malevolent shape-shifters) can be accomplished, but only through individuality.

The mission of this turn-of-the-millennium John Carpenter retrospective is to spotlight the developments of the director's 20-year career, both as an auteur with an ongoing repertory company, and as a straight-faced genre-blender who often delights in homages to his favorite films, directors and writers. At the same time, Carpenter's unique status as Hollywood's last maverick will be detailed.

In *Big Trouble in Little China*, Wang bemoans the fact that his "mind and his spirit are going north and south," a problem that could never be attributed to the film's atypical director. Though his steadfast consistency has often irked critics who wish he would take a new tack, John Carpenter remains admirable in his devotion to being the latter-day Howard Hawks. Auteur, anti-authoritarian, and consummate entertainer, director John Carpenter is a supernova of talent, and Hollywood's most tenacious "Dark Star."

I

A History and Overview of John Carpenter's Career

Beginnings

As the year 1948 marched to an end, America's major Hollywood studios unveiled a parade of new cinematic westerns, films noirs, and suspense-thrillers from notable directors such as Howard Hawks (*Red River*), John Ford (*Fort Apache*), John Huston (*The Treasure of the Sierra Madre, Key Largo*), and the master of suspense himself, Alfred Hitchcock (*Rope*). Like their films, these directing talents would one day be idolized and honored by generations of film fans the world over. They would become the modern legends, and the role models of new cinema-loving artists like François Truffaut, Jean-Luc Godard and Brian DePalma. Unnoticed in those long ago days, but perhaps equally important in the annals of twentieth century genre filmmaking, a new cinematic "dark" star named John Howard Carpenter was born in January of 1948 in Carthage, New York.

Not surprisingly, the artist who would one day entertain moviegoers with contemporary, "stylized" westerns (*Assault on Precinct 13* [1976], *Vampires* [1998]), *outré* films noirs

(*In the Mouth of Madness* [1994]) and tension-filled suspense-thrillers (*Halloween* [1978], *Eyes of Laura Mars* [1978], *Someone's Watching Me* [1978]) was first a determined and impressionable little boy who knew exactly what he wanted to do with his life. At four years old, John Carpenter saw his first movie in a theater in Bowling Green, Kentucky: John Huston's adventure flick *The African Queen* (1952), starring Humphrey Bogart. After the end credits rolled, Carpenter was a changed person. He became obsessed with film and the notion that he too could contribute to the stream of images he watched unfold on the silver screen. Although Carpenter also followed in his father's footsteps and studied the piano and violin, he longed to create moving film portraits and compositions like those conceived by Hawks, Ford, Huston, Hitchcock, Capra and the other filmmaking luminaries of the time. He wanted to be a movie director.

John Carpenter's early cinematic influences included not just westerns such as the Howard Hawks classic *Rio Bravo* (1959), but also science fiction productions focusing on the possibility of life from other worlds. Among his favorites were Ray Bradbury and Jack Arnold's *It Came from Outer Space* (1953), the quasi–Shakespearean outer space version of *The Tempest, Forbidden Planet* (1956), Roger Corman's low budget *It Conquered The World* (1956), Nigel Kneale's Quatermass adventure *Enemy from Space* (1957), and the grandaddy of all monster movies, *King Kong* (1933).

By age eight, John Carpenter was inspired to realize his fantasies and produce his own films. Equipped with an 8mm camera and ingenuity to spare, Carpenter began directing his schoolyard buddies through intense cinematic paces in the Carpenter family back yard. Through age 14, John continued producing and directing 40-minute genre shorts with evocative 1950s exploitation titles like *Revenge of the Colossal Beasts, Terror from Space, Gorgo vs. Godzilla,* and even *Gorgon the Space Monster.* All the while, the young director experimented with his craft by employing stop-motion photography (*à la* Willis O'Brien or Ray Harryhausen), rear projection, forced perspective, and other special effects uncommonly seen in homemade movies. At the same time, Carpenter indulged his desire to dramatize entertaining and often frightening adventures.

Clearly John Carpenter was no ordinary child. His precocious nature may have come from his father and mother, also highly creative individuals. His father, Howard Ralph Carpenter, had earned a Ph.D. in music and had attended the Eastman School of Music in Rochester, New York. Howard Carpenter later played in sessions with celebrity musicians Johnny Cash, Frank Sinatra, Roy Orbison and Brenda Lee. Often, young John Carpenter would ride with his father to Nashville, Tennessee, to watch his dad perform with these icons, and so Carpenter Junior was exposed not only to a universe of creativity, but the world of celebrity as well. Desire and determination are two of the most important factors in forging a successful life in Hollywood, and Carpenter learned

early on from his father's career that the stars were within his reach, whether they shone on the world of music or the world of cinema.

As he grew, John Carpenter continued to find inspiration not only in motion pictures, but on the printed page as well. He was an avid reader of science fiction and horror stories, and he was exposed to the works of Edgar Allan Poe and H.P. Lovecraft through a book entitled *Tales of Terror and the Supernatural.* A teenage Carpenter also fueled his imagination on a regular diet of '50s pulps, from *Weird Science* and *Weird Fantasy* to the behind-the-scenes magazine *Famous Monsters of Filmland.* As he matured, John Carpenter also made a stab at producing his own genre fanzines, devoted to *King Kong* and the universe of "fantastic" films. These endeavors established that John Carpenter's talent extended beyond the realms of music and film: He was a skilled artist, and his aptitude for drawing would later serve him well in the story-boarding process of his earliest films, *Dark Star, Assault on Precinct 13,* and in part, *Halloween.* The developing medium of television also played a role in his growth as an artist, and in the late '50s and early '60s John Carpenter often stayed up late on Saturday evenings to view the local *Shock Theater* presentations.

After attending Western Kentucky University, John Carpenter prevailed upon his parents to send him to U.S.C, the foremost film school in the United States. There, Carpenter gained the practical experience he needed to become a filmmaker, while at the same time investigating the artistic side of film. At U.S.C. Carpenter learned how to be comfortable and adept with the mechanical and technological nature of filmmaking, and the school also presented him with the opportunity to watch the films of John Ford, Orson Welles, Luis Buñuel, Sergio Leone, and Howard Hawks, Carpenter's favorite director. At U.S.C., Roman Polanski and Howard Hawks visited and addressed Carpenter's class. For John, to be in the presence of his idols was a dream come true.

Film school also stressed the importance of making personal films, an in-vogue idea of the day expressed in unique cinema like *Easy Rider* (1969) and *Five Easy Pieces* (1970). Demonstrating his maverick qualities, Carpenter did not completely buy into the party. Instead, he saw it as important to bring his own personality to big, entertaining films like those of Hawks or Hitchcock.

In 1969, John Carpenter earned his first official credit, serving as co-writer, editor, and composer — and, uncredited, as co-director — on a 15-minute short subject entitled *The Resurrection of Bronco Billy* (1970). The 16mm production, which concerned a young man who fancied himself a modern cowboy, gave Carpenter valuable experience in cutting film and scoring film music. It also turned out to be a prestigious assignment: *The Resurrection of Bronco Billy* won the Academy Award for best short subject in 1970. The award went to producer John Longenecker, but there was no doubt that John Carpenter's contributions to the project were important and considerable.

John Carpenter's life and career even reflect the main character of *Bronco Billy* in some intriguing ways. John Carpenter too often is a "man out of a time," an artist who would rather make Howard Hawks westerns and "big" entertainments than the personal but non-commercial visions of the late sixties and early seventies such as *The Graduate* (1967) or *The Last Picture Show* (1971). Although there is always a danger of reading too deeply into film, John Carpenter's desire to be a "retro" director like Hawks, Hitchcock or Ford is a theme that reappears throughout his career. He acknowledged this goal in an interview with *Films in Review* in 1980:

> I want to make westerns and comedies and detective films.... I'd love to be the Howard Hawks of the '80s.... Hawks ... influenced me the most stylistically

> ... but also in terms of control. He always talked about how much control he had over his films. And Hawks was a dedicated commercial filmmaker.... That's where I relate myself. In terms of telling good stories, working with good people, making films that make money.[1]

To some of the academic minded at U.S.C., Carpenter's approach was unthinkable. Here was a talented young student who saw film not only as art, but also as (gasp!) entertainment. This retrograde desire to make fun movies rather than "important" ones often left Carpenter feeling out of step with his colleagues, but it would become part and parcel of his choices as a filmmaker.

When You Wish Upon a Dark Star

Although John Carpenter had made a name for himself in the early 1970s with his work on *The Resurrection of Bronco Billy*, he still wanted to be a director, even an auteur. He wanted to be the one to call the shots and to forge his vision on the screen. So, unlike many students, as well as his hero, Howard Hawks (who had worked his way up the filmmaking roster after beginning in the unglamorous role of assistant propman), Carpenter started not at the bottom of a long credits list, but at the top, as a director.

With a friend from U.S.C. whom he had met in 1965, John Carpenter set out to make a very special student film for his Master's thesis project. In August of 1970, John Carpenter and Dan O'Bannon met to discuss the production of a very low budget sci-fi film that Carpenter was calling *The Electric Dutchman*. The duo labored on the screenplay together throughout the fall semester, and the film changed titles. Now it was *Planetfall*. Despite the changing title, the essence of the outer-space story remained the same. Carpenter and O'Bannon wanted to make a response to Stanley Kubrick's *2001: A Space Odyssey* (1968), as well as a film that would look at the nuts and bolts of space travel in a completely different and unique way.

What eventually came out of the script was an unusual science fiction piece entitled *Dark Star*. It concerned the lives of four "slacker" astronauts who were doomed to spend eternity on an endless, absurd space mission. Their spaceship was a wreck, the astronauts did not get along well with one another, and the meaning of their existence was more than just a tad obscure. Years later, John Carpenter aptly described *Dark Star* as *Waiting for Godot...in Space*. As Dan O'Bannon characterized the unusual setting and non-traditional protagonists of *Dark Star*, it was obvious that the film reflected the slightly off-kilter sensibilities of its two creators:

> The characters and their spacebound living conditions became a reflection of the way we ourselves were living our lives: young alienated males forced together in communal poverty.... Astronauts' days aboard the Dark Star resembled the days and nights of our lives ... inspiring, sad, ridiculous.[2]

The *Dark Star* screenplay was ambitious from a technical perspective, filled with miniature effects, seemingly expensive opticals, zero-g effects, and all the other bells and whistles associated with space travel movies in the post–*2001* film era. Despite the challenges, principal photography on *Dark Star* began in the spring of 1971. As it was a low-low-budget production funded solely by Carpenter and O'Bannon, no professional actors were utilized on the project. Instead, friends from U.S.C. were enlisted to play roles, and Dan O'Bannon himself essayed the important role of Sergeant Pinback, the spaceship know-it-all and resolute idiot.

Sets were constructed by O'Bannon and Carpenter, and the complex instrumentation and control panels of the Dark Star were created through many nights of rummaging through garbage and picking up Styrofoam forms, appliance knobs, and cast-off machine parts that might fit the bill. *Dark Star* was then filmed in basements, in rented soundstages, and even the Producers Studio. Amazingly, only about 10 percent of the film was actually lensed on the U.S.C. campus.[3] The *Dark Star* production crew was small, too, consisting mostly of O'Bannon and Carpenter again. Still, there were times when as many as five or six people were contributing time and energy behind the scenes of the unusual project.

Contributing special effects to the Carpenter-O'Bannon affair were some notable technical artists who would go on to become the greatest of such talents in the industry. Jim Danforth (*When Dinosaurs Ruled the Earth* [1970], *The Day Time Ended* [1978], *Clash of the Titans* [1981], *They Live* [1988]) contributed matte paintings of starscapes and planets, and Greg Jein (*Star Trek V: The Final Frontier* [1989]) constructed the miniature of the *Dark Star* spaceship based on the utilitarian design sketches of Ron Cobb (*Star Wars* [1977], *Close Encounters of the Third Kind* [1978], *Alien* [1979], *Blade Runner* [1982], *Conan the Barbarian* [1982], *Leviathan* [1989], *Total Recall* [1990]). Cobb was a friend of Dan O'Bannon's from the Los Angeles Free Press Cartooning Association. When he learned that O'Bannon needed a spaceship blueprint, Cobb devised a unique exterior shell, the projectile-shaped craft of the title. According to Cobb, it was a good conjunction of talent:

> We shared an enthusiasm for films, science fiction and filmmaking.... I started scribbling out things on napkins at an all-night coffee shop. They [Carpenter and O'Bannon] liked it, I drew up the plans, and it appeared in the film as a model built by Greg Jein.[4]

By spring of 1972, *Dark Star* was substantively complete. The only problem facing

Carpenter and O'Bannon was that the final cut came in at a length of just under 50 minutes. Thus John Carpenter's debut film was too long to qualify as a short picture, like *The Resurrection of Bronco Billy*, and far too short to qualify as a marketable, releasable feature film. Broke and despondent, Carpenter and O'Bannon realized that they needed an investor to provide additional cash to beef up the production and pave the way for new shooting. In response to this exigency, Jonathan Kaplan, a Canadian money man, put up $10,000 to extend *Dark Star* to an acceptable length of 80 minutes. Excited about the chance to improve their student/professional film, Carpenter and O'Bannon prepared a great deal of additional footage in 1972, much of it improvised.

Interestingly, much of the newly lensed footage tended to be rather humorous, pushing *Dark Star* from a semi-serious science fiction film with some moments of way-out humor to a full-scale *2001* satire filled with broad comedy and edgy repartee. An alien resembling a beachball was added to the cast to vex Dan O'Bannon's Pinback, and an extended comedic scene in an elevator shaft also emerged. This latter set-piece was very reminiscent of the silent film era, particularly the work of Charlie Chaplin and Buster Keaton. Designer Ron Cobb explained the change in *Dark Star*'s thematic thrust this way:

> When they got a chance for theatrical release, extra footage was shot. They brought people back and the extra footage was down-right slapstick. It was added to the body of the student film which was kind of solemn…. The slapstick scenes, the elevator, and the alien make the rest of the scenes look funnier than they did originally when that was *all* the humor there was, Pinback griping and all that. They did a number of re-edits.[5]

So with Kaplan's cash providing the impetus, *Dark Star*, Mark II, was completed — at least until it was time for the important post-production work to come together. John Carpenter and Dan O'Bannon realized they would require at least another $35,000 to assemble all the opticals, do the sound recording, and create a professional film worthy of national distribution.

Entrepreneur and frequent film backer Jack H. Harris (*The Blob* [1958], *Beware! The Blob* [1971], *Eyes of Laura Mars* [1978]) swooped into the picture in 1973 and bought all rights to *Dark Star* outright, while demanding even more reshoots. By this time, all of the actors involved in *Dark Star* had changed haircuts several times, and some had aged dramatically in the intervening two years since the recording of the original footage. Still, the reshoots were conducted, with some actors wearing unconvincing hairpieces, and *Dark Star*, Mark III, was completed in February of 1974.

By this late date, more than four full years since the inception of the project, John Carpenter and Dan O'Bannon were often getting on each other's frayed nerves. Each one was exhausted, and each felt that he had contributed more to the picture than the other. Additionally, the two men had become irritated by the micro-management style of Harris, who is rumored to have been quite a tyrant. What finally resulted for pals Dan O'Bannon and John Carpenter was a parting of the ways that, fortunately, would be rectified in 1976 when the duo would rediscover each other as friends, if not as co-workers.

After six years at U.S.C., John Carpenter dropped out of the film program, but *Dark Star* was finally completed — at a total cost of $60,000, including $10–12,000 of Carpenter's own money. *Dark Star* premiered in a wide multiple theater in Los Angeles in January of 1975, and the black comedy almost immediately earned Carpenter a reputation as a clever underground director. *Dark Star* was also warmly received by science fiction critics and given considerable nationwide attention, even meriting a review by *Time* magazine.

From a financial standpoint, things did not look so cheery. Carpenter and O'Bannon were paid only $5,000 apiece for their years of hard work. That amount did not even begin to recoup the money each man had contributed to *Dark Star*.

In addition, *Dark Star* failed as a calling card. It did not inspire the all-important decision-makers in the big Hollywood studios. John Carpenter quickly learned that the average moviegoer had not really understood or even liked *Dark Star*, and that there was very little chance of Paramount, 20th Century–Fox, Columbia or any other Hollywood organization plucking him from obscurity and handing him the reins on a major new movie. Instead, Carpenter found that he had to earn his living as a writer, which he considered a poor substitute for directing. Still, Carpenter found success in this alternate venue. He penned a suspense thriller called *Eyes*, which was eventually filmed as *Eyes of Laura Mars* in 1978; a Western called *Blood River*, which was intended to match screen and music legends John Wayne and Elvis Presley; and a crime-thriller called *Black Moon Rising*, filmed in 1985 with Tommy Lee Jones. The other project he framed during this period was the unusually titled *Escape from New York City*, a futuristic gang action picture designed to cash in on all of the *Death Wish* hoopla of 1975. In 1981, John Carpenter directed this screenplay, retitled *Escape from New York*, with Kurt Russell as his star.

Under Seige:
Assault on Precinct 13

Though *Dark Star* had failed to secure a directing career for him, John Carpenter came back with a vengeance with the production of his second independent feature, *Assault on Precinct 13* (1976). An investor from Philadelphia, the C K K Corporation, took a gamble on Carpenter and put up the money for a new exploitation picture he was planning. More importantly to John Carpenter, his backers offered him free rein to make any kind of picture he desired.

What he desired to make was a Howard Hawks–style western in the tradition of *Rio Bravo* (1959), *El Dorado* (1967) and *Rio Lobo* (1970), but there was simply not enough money in his $100,000 budget to sponsor a full scale Old West adventure. Instead, John Carpenter planned a stylized updating of the classic *Rio Bravo* scenario, replete with the stereotypical Howard Hawks woman and much macho dialogue. He cleverly substituted modern urban gangs for Indians, and beleaguered cops for the cowboys. A rotting station house, Precinct 9 Division 13, became the equivalent of the Alamo.

Even more than *Dark Star*, *Assault on Precinct 13* indicated the path of John Carpenter's career. A true "auteur" merits that title by, among other things, working with the same actors and same settings again and again. Appropriately then, *Assault on Precinct 13* found John Carpenter carefully selecting the foundations of his repertory company, the people who would populate his movies, as well as a group of behind-the-scenes personnel who would follow him from picture to picture.

After an open casting call, a group of talented actors was selected to star in the production. Charles Cyphers (*Halloween, Someone's Watching Me! The Fog, Escape from New York, Halloween II, Buffy the Vampire Slayer:* "Go Fish" [1998]), Darwin Joston (*The Fog*) and Nancy Loomis (*Halloween, The Fog, Halloween II, Halloween III: Season of the Witch*) all began their long association with John Carpenter on this film, and in the lead role of Lieutenant Bishop the African-American thespian Austin Stoker (*Battle for the Planet of the Apes* [1973], *Time Walker* [1982]) was excellent.

Behind the scenes, Carpenter continued to work with art director Tommy Wallace (*Halloween, Dark Star, Halloween III*), Craig Stearns (*Dark Star*) and a young new talent,

Debra Hill. A graduate of Temple University, with a bachelor's degree in sociology, Hill had cut her teeth editing and producing documentaries for an East Coast outfit called Adventure Film Limited. She relocated to Los Angeles and quickly landed work as script-supervisor on *Goodbye, Norma Jean*. After that assignment, she served as John Carpenter's script supervisor on *Assault on Precinct 13*. A year later, Debra Hill was Carpenter's co-writer and producer, in fact a full partner. With Carpenter, Hill co-wrote and produced *Halloween* and *The Fog*, and produced *Escape from New York* (1981) and *Escape from L.A.* (1996).

As he had with *Dark Star* and would do again with *Halloween* and later pictures, John Carpenter wrote the riveting musical score for *Assault on Precinct 13*. He was assisted in the effort by Dan Wyman. The final result was a unique, synthetic sound that is still quite catchy, even after 20 years.

The script John Carpenter had fashioned for *Assault on Precinct 13* told of a diverse trio of heroes caught in a siege as an urban Los Angeles prison house is attacked by rampaging gang members. Although that premise may sound like a typical 1970s action picture, it was quintessential Carpenter in execution — which meant it was really quintessential Howard Hawks. Of primary importance was not the bloodshed or action, but rather the developing friendship and respect in evidence between white convict Napoleon Wilson and black cop Lt. Bishop. As writer Leigh Brackett, the author of *Rio Bravo*, *El Dorado* and *Rio Lobo*, once described the men of Hawks films:

> There were certain basic themes which were very important to Hawks: the relationship between two men, which was actually a love story; the obligations of friendship — what a friend is required to do for a friend. If you examine his films carefully, there are great parallels among the character relationships.[6]

The same could easily be said of the characters Bishop and Wilson in *Assault on Precinct 13*. Though originally the two are on opposite sides of the law, cop Bishop quickly gains convict Wilson's respect and trust by saving his life, twice. In return, Wilson becomes loyal to Bishop, saving *his* life. Their dialogue, bordering on flirtatious at points, artfully highlights both their differences and similarities.

Also important to *Assault on Precinct 13*'s homage to director Hawks was the unforgettable presence of actress Laurie Zimmer as a prototypical "Hawksian woman," i.e., a female who gives as good as she gets and is both tough and feminine at the same time. As Robin Woods wrote of Angie Dickinson's character in *Rio Bravo*:

> Dickinson's marvelous performance gives us the perfect embodiment of the Hawksian woman, intelligent, resilient and responsive. There is a continual sense of a woman who really grasps what is important to her... It is not so much a matter of characterization as the communication of a life quality.[7]

Zimmer, relatively inexperienced, managed to convey the same emotions and life quality as Angie Dickinson, Lauren Bacall, and other classic Hawks women. She was solid, calm, and passionate at all the right moments. And, in the best tradition of Howard Hawks films, she was always ready to share "a smoke" with the male who caught her eye, Napoleon Wilson.

Further cementing the homage to Hawks in general and *Rio Bravo* in particular, Carpenter spiced his *Assault on Precinct 13* screenplay with a variety of nice in-jokes. Laurie Zimmer's character was named "Leigh" after *Rio Bravo* scribe Leigh Brackett. And Carpenter even edited the picture under the pseudonym John T. Chance — the name of John Wayne's sheriff in *Rio Bravo*.

Because John Carpenter was able to wield total control on the set of his *Assault on Precinct 13*, as well as pay loving homage to his favorite director without interference, the film has become his favorite, and he often refers to its creation as the most fun he has ever had directing a film. With all of the interiors shot inside a studio, it would have been easy for a young Carpenter to imagine that he was continuing in the Hawks Hollywood western tradition. The details may have been updated, but *Assault on Precinct 13* emerged as a great western.

Unfortunately, nobody got it. At the same time that Carpenter had taken such caution to infuse his project with Hawksian humor and characters, he added his own unique touch: contemporary graphic violence along the lines of urban action flicks like *The Warriors* (1979) or *Death Wish* (1974). This explicit violence resulted in a serious misreading of the film's intentions, first and foremost by that self-proclaimed guardian of cinematic morality, the MPAA. The organization demanded that Carpenter cut out a crucial scene wherein a young blond girl named Kathy gets shot down in cold blood while asking politely for vanilla twist ice cream. The anti-authoritarian Carpenter, who has hated censorship all his life, pulled a fast one in response to this request. He cut the sequence all right, but *only* in the print sent to the MPAA. The rest of the *Assault on Precinct 13* prints went released untouched and uncensored.[8]

When the film was released in 1976 by distributor Turtle Releasing, other factions joined the MPAA in their misinterpretation of this strange, stylized western. When it was not being ignored by critics and the public, the film was being marketed mostly as a blaxploitation picture. Europe, however, was a different story. There, *Assault on Precinct 13* was recognized as the genre-buster it was. It emerged as the surprise hit of the 1977 London Film Festival, and its warm reception overseas did much to cement Carpenter's reputation as an auteur there.

Although financial success was still a year or so away, *Assault on Precinct 13* built much of the John Carpenter mystique that would

come to dominate his career. It was a stylish, audacious film, like *Dark Star*, but it showed his versatility in tackling a very different genre from sci-fi. Carpenter revisited "siege" film territory in 1987 with *Prince of Darkness*, another movie set in a rotting L.A. structure, this time a church. And Darwin Joston and Austin Stoker, so powerful and charismatic together in *Assault on Precinct*, were reunited briefly in a rather dopey 1982 Mummy flick called *Time Walker* that also starred Ben Murphy (*The Gemini Man* [1974]), James Karen (*Poltergeist* [1982], *Return of the Living Dead* [1985]), and Shari Belafonte (*Beyond Reality* [1991-93]).

After *Assault on Precinct 13*, John Carpenter had an interesting offer in 1976. Like George Lucas and Steven Spielberg before him, Carpenter was approached by Paramount Studios to write the movie version of the classic sci-fi TV series, *Star Trek*. Feeling that he could not do anything creative with the material, Carpenter turned the job down. Considering the budget, scheduling and special effects problems to emerge from *Star Trek: The Motion Picture* (1979), this was probably a wise decision. Still, one has to wonder how the 23rd century (and film history) might have been different with John Carpenter at the helm of the Starship *Enterprise*.

The Tricks and Treats of Halloween

Although John Carpenter had in many senses already mastered the technical requirements of filmmaking in *Dark Star* and *Assault on Precinct 13*, he found that he was still not being called to active service by the studio system he hoped so much to work within. All that changed after 1978, the most important year, perhaps, in the director's career.

In late 1977, Carpenter was recruited by Irwin Yablans, a producer for Compass

International Ltd., who had a compelling idea for a new exploitation picture:

> I was in Milan and suddenly I thought we should do something with a baby-sitter. Put some nubile girls together and terrorize them. There's a common denominator there, I thought, everybody's been a babysitter, or had one. So I called John and he was enthusiastic.[9]

John Carpenter later recalled the same conversation, as well as his own lack of enthusiasm about the original idea. It was not until Yablans came up with a second marketable movie notion that Carpenter realized that the new project had some real potential:

> It started with a distributor saying to me: "I would like to do a movie about a guy killing babysitters. We'll call it *The Babysitter Murders*." Being unemployed ... I said "OK, fine, I'll do it." ... Then he said, "Let's set the movie on Halloween night because Halloween is such a good time — the Bogeyman." I thought that was a great idea.[10]

Carpenter then agreed to write the *Halloween* screenplay with Debra Hill. Additionally, he would direct the picture and Hill would produce it. Carpenter, however, had three conditions before committing himself to the film. First, he wanted complete autonomy on the film, a status he had enjoyed so much on *Assault on Precinct 13*. Secondly, he wanted to write the musical score as he had done on both of his earlier feature films. His last demand was a corollary of his first: Not only did he want complete control on *Halloween*, he also wanted a promise of no interference from the money men, perhaps remembering his experiences with Jack H. Harris on *Dark Star* in 1973. Yablans and financier Moustapha Akkad agreed to Carpenter's terms, and production on *Halloween* was set to commence with a budget of $300,000 dollars.

Debra Hill and John Carpenter fashioned the entire *Halloween* screenplay, about an escaped mental patient named Michael Myers who breaks free from an asylum and terrorizes babysitters in his home town on All Hallow's Eve, in just 10 days. Debra Hill wrote the first draft, focusing on the sections involving the teenage babysitters. Carpenter wrote a second pass, including all the material that had to do with the psychologist who would hunt down pure "evil" in Haddonfield.

At the behest of his daughters, who were fans of *Assault on Precinct 13*, Donald Pleasence [*Fantastic Voyage* [1966], *THX-1138* [1974], *The Freakmaker* [1974],) joined the cast after Christopher Lee turned down the role. (Pleasence would become a regular contributor to Carpenter's films, appearing in *Halloween II* [1981], *Escape from New York* [1981], and *Prince of Darkness* [1987].) Just as *Assault on Precinct 13* had been designed as a Howard Hawks tribute, Carpenter and Hill envisioned *Halloween* as an Alfred Hitchcock–style film, and so named Pleasence's character Dr. Sam Loomis after John Gavin's character in *Psycho* (1960). Additionally, Loomis's partner in many sequences was a nurse (played by Nancy Stephens) named "Marion" — Janet Leigh's character name in *Psycho*. So entrenched in modern slasher lore was Donald Pleasence's *Halloween* character (reprised in *Halloween IV: The Return of Michael Myers* [1988], *Halloween V: The Revenge of Michael Myers* [1989] and *Halloween VI: The Curse of Michael Myers* [1996]) that scribe Kevin Williamson named a character in the crossover hit *Scream* "Loomis" as well — thus referencing an earlier film reference of an earlier film!

Cast in the lead role of Laurie Strode was 19-year-old Jamie Lee Curtis, the beautiful daughter of Janet Leigh (*Psycho*, *Night of the Lepus* [1972].) Before *Halloween* catapulted her to stardom, Jamie Lee Curtis had appeared only on the *Operation Petticoat* (1977–79) series as the regular character Lt. Barbara Duran. Following *Halloween*,

Curtis became horror's favorite star and was dubbed "The Scream Queen" for her appearances in *The Fog* (1980), *Halloween II* (1981), *Prom Night* (1980), *Terror Train* (1980), and *Road Games* (1982). Curtis traded horror for comedy in 1983's *Trading Places*, but returned to the genre in *Halloween: H20* (1998), the 20-year anniversary sequel to John Carpenter's original picture.

Another horror veteran in *Halloween* was the delightful P.J. Soles, one of the nasty high school girls in DePalma's *Carrie* (1976), as Laurie's doomed friend Lynda. After *Halloween*, Soles went on to do another cult classic, *Rock 'n' Roll High School*, in 1979. Nick Castle, the man who played the Shape, Michael Myers, graduated from horror movies to direct such notable pictures as *The Last Starfighter* (1983). According to the documentary film *Halloween: Unmasked*, directed by Mark Cerulli, the name Michael Myers came from a real source. The real Michael Myers was a film distributor in London who brought Akkad, Yablans, Carpenter and Hill together after *Assault on Precinct 13*.

Rounding out the *Halloween* cast were Carpenter repertory regulars Charles Cyphers (of the *Bette White Show* [1977-78]) as Sheriff Leigh Brackett (another reference to the Hawks collaborator) and Nancy Loomis as Annie. Both of these actors had appeared in *Assault on Precinct 13*.

Behind the scenes of *Halloween*, one of the most important John Carpenter film contributors joined the team: cinematographer Dean Cundey, the man responsible for the look of Carpenter films *Halloween*, *The Fog*, *Escape from New York*, *Halloween II*, *Halloween III*, *The Thing* (1982), and *Big Trouble in Little China* (1986), as well as big non–Carpenter flicks such as *Romancing the Stone* (1984), *Back to the Future* (1985) and *The Flintstones* (1995). A graduate of U.C.L.A. Film School, Cundey had worked his way up in the business, starting as a makeup artist on a low-low-budget Roger Corman flick called *Gas-s-s-s* (a.k.a. *It May*

Become Necessary to Destroy the World in Order to Save It) in 1971. He also lensed certain scenes on *Beware! The Blob* before becoming director of photography on such pictures as the lurid-sounding *Satan's Cheerleaders* (1976), *Without Warning* (1980), and *Galaxina* (1980). With much of the *Halloween* story occurring during the impenetrable night, Cundey's lighting and photography were crucial to the success and look of the suspense film.

After three weeks of preproduction planning, principal photography on *Halloween* began in spring of 1978. Starting in March, production ran for a scant 22 days. Donald Pleasence, in America for only a short time, was available for only five days of shooting. Exterior daytime scenes were shot in Pasadena, an unlikely location to represent the mythical town of Haddonfield, Illinois. Although the residents of Pasadena were cooperative with the film company, a continuing headache for John Carpenter during the exterior sequences was keeping the ubiquitous California palm trees out of the frame. Night scenes and interiors for *Halloween* were shot in and around Hollywood, and Carpenter and Cundey lensed the film in Panavision, making extensive use of Panaglide technology, the precursor to the popular Steadicam.

The props which made *Halloween* so memorable also caused some difficulties. Since the production was lensed in the spring, there were no pumpkins to be found anywhere. The crew's creative answer to this dilemma was to spray paint squashes orange for the sequences requiring jack-o-lanterns! The mask that Michael Myers wore throughout the flick also had a unique origin. John Carpenter and Debra Hill had originally intended their psycho-killer to wear a frightening clown mask, but instead they settled on a William Shatner Captain Kirk mask from Don Post Studios. The eyeholes were enlarged, the pointed *Star Trek* sideburns were cut off, and the face was painted a stark white. Although the creators of the film could not have anticipated it, this bizarre mask became one of the most effective scare images in film history. At many points throughout *Halloween* (and even *Halloween II*) there is total darkness in the frame until the blank, chalky mask appears suddenly out of the shadows. Still, it is strange to realize that the cast of various *Halloween* movies have been offed by none other James T. Kirk. (It gives new meaning to the catchphrase, "He's dead, Jim.")

Halloween completed production on time, on schedule, with no overtime whatsoever. It was the first of his films not completely storyboarded by Carpenter, although he did storyboard the conclusion of the film following Laurie's discovery of her dead friends in the upstairs bedroom of the Wallace house.

Satisfied with his efforts, Carpenter screened the film, minus its musical score, for studio executives around Hollywood — and the unanimous conclusion was that *Halloween* was not scary. Alarmed by the reaction, John Carpenter devoted two weeks to writing and performing the musical score. Using the work of Ennio Morricone and Bernard Herrmann as his guide, Carpenter created what is perhaps the most memorable theme song in horror movie history, except perhaps for the screeching melody of *Psycho*.

When Carpenter rescreened the film complete with its score, the same executives who had claimed the film was not frightening raved that *Halloween* was in fact the most terrifying movie they had ever seen. Moustapha Akkad and Irwin Yablans saw the first reel in a mixing room at Goldwyn Studios and knew they had a winner on their hands. With a budget of $24,000 devoted to advertising, *Halloween* was set to take America by storm.

Halloween, which featured the ad line "The Night *He* Came Home," opened in John Carpenter's hometown of Bowling Green, Kentucky, on October 25, 1978. Its sub-distributor in the New York and Philadelphia market was Aquarius Releasing, and

the film played at the Rivoli Theater in the Big Apple. It also opened in Los Angeles, where it played for four weeks on 232 screens.

Strangely, critics hated the picture until Tom Allen of the *Village Voice* picked up on its finer points and afforded it a rave review. Soon, other critics, including Gene Siskel and Roger Ebert, followed suit and called *Halloween* a four-star film in the tradition of Alfred Hitchcock. Boosted by strong word-of-mouth and critical support, *Halloween* became a cult sensation.

Realizing that they had a crossover hit on their hands, the producers of *Halloween* and Aquarius mastermind Terry Levene pulled it abruptly from release. Aquarius Releasing representative Ron Harvey explained the unique strategy to *Fangoria*:

> The film was doing great business ... and it would be smart not to blow it, to instead take the film out of release and do it up right the next year. They booked it ... in Greenwich Village ... before it disappeared ... creating "cult" status.... A year later, word of mouth had spread like wildfire.... People that had seen it ... were really talking up this film. This marketing ploy paid off in spades.... We had teaser trailers ... running weeks ahead of time hyping how "*Halloween* is back" and that sort of thing.[11]

The ploy worked, and *Halloween* quickly went on to gross more than 50 million dollars, making it the most profitable independent movie in film history, even edging out George Romero's runaway horror hit *Dawn of the Dead* (1979). By 1990, when *Halloween* lost the title of most profitable independent film to *Teenage Mutant Ninja Turtles*, the picture had generated more than $80 million in the United States alone. On a budget of $300,000, such a return was unprecedented, but most welcome.

At the same time that *Halloween* made a killing at the box office and transformed director John Carpenter into a horror celebrity (thanks in part to articles in the *New York Times* by Vincent Canby and a positive review in *Newsweek* by David Ansen), *Halloween* also prompted a spate of imitator "slasher" films, most of them clearly lacking in the style that made Carpenter's film so successful. Among the myriad imitators were *Friday the 13th* (1980), *Prom Night* (1980), *Mother's Day* (1980), *Christmas Evil* (1980), *My Bloody Valentine* (1981), *Graduation Day* (1981), *New Year's Evil* (1982), *Silent Night, Deadly Night* (1984), *April Fool's Day* (1986), and *Bloody New Year* (1987). Each one of these knock-offs matched a mad slasher with some lesser holiday. Lacking the explicit holiday connection were numerous other slasher films that imitated the *Halloween* story and "stalker" aspects. These included *He Knows You're Alone* (a.k.a. *Blood Wedding*) (1980) starring a young Tom Hanks; *Visiting Hours* (1981) with William Shatner; *Hell Night* (1982) with Linda Blair; *The Driller Killer* (1979), directed by Abel Ferrara; *The Toolbox Murders* (1979); and the terrifying *When a Stranger Calls* (1979) with Charles Durning and Carol Kane. (For a complete list of post–*Halloween* slashfests, see Appendix B.)

Carpenter and Debra Hill were quick to insist there would be no sequel to *Halloween*, but the financial success of the film dictated otherwise, and the pair found themselves aboard a sequel project in early 1981. And the sequels were to continue: To date, there have been seven *Halloween* films.

In 1980, NBC-TV bought the rights to air *Halloween* on network television for a whopping $3 million. New footage with Jamie Lee Curtis, Donald Pleasence and other cast members was shot for the TV version when the original was found to be too short for its time slot. One of the new scenes included a hearing wherein Dr. Loomis attempted to keep Michael Myers incarcerated. This second version only succeeded in causing confusion, because it was this extended (but less violent) version that was mistakenly released

on videotape in 1981 rather than the original—at least until the distributor pulled it off the market.

Halloween, for all intents and purposes, signaled the real start of John Carpenter's career. He was examined by critics not just as a good director, but as part of a "school" of young Hitchcock-inspired directors which included Steven Spielberg (*Night Gallery* [1970-73], *Duel* [1971], *Jaws* [1975]), and Brian DePalma (*Carrie*, *The Fury* [1978], *Dressed to Kill* [1980], *Body Double* [1984].) More a fan of classic Hollywood in general and Howard Hawks in particular, Carpenter did not find the comparison to Hitchcock particularly apt:

> Critics compare me to Hitchcock, but I know that's bullshit. If I start taking myself seriously that's bullshit too. I'm just out to make a good film.... I try my best with each one, and then go on to the next one. If people don't like it, I will have failed, but there are worse things in life than failing.[12]

Three Big Deals: Eyes of Laura Mars, Someone's Watching Me! *and* Elvis

Perhaps the reason so many critics compared John Carpenter to Alfred Hitchcock had more to do with the cumulative result of his many 1978 projects than his overall career. For *Halloween* was not the only prestigious project to sport his name on the credits that year. Remarkably, there were two others as well, both of which actually preceded the production of *Halloween*. Both were suspense-thrillers which involved a stalker pursuing lovely young women.

The first was a major motion picture, *Eyes of Laura Mars*, based on John Carpenter's screenplay *Eyes*. Jack H. Harris, the final backer on *Dark Star*, contacted Carpenter in 1977 and was interested in making a film based on one of his scripts. Soon producer

Jon Peters was on board too, and ready to do an "A" budget film. For a time Barbra Streisand was to star in the picture, but this was a span in her career when her name was attached to many projects, including Universal Studios' unmade remake *The Legend of King Kong* in 1976.

Before Streisand left the project, Carpenter was assigned to direct the film, which concerned a Hollywood resident who had a psychic link with a skid row psycho. Because Streisand, a major star, was interested, Carpenter was asked by producer Peters to make significant changes in his screenplay to take advantage of her audience and abilities. Although Carpenter had hoped to make the psycho killer another of his "faceless" evil villains, like the blank-faced Michael Myers or the roving, unstoppable gang members of *Assault on Precinct 13*, the producer wanted the killer of *Eyes of Laura Mars* to be someone with whom the main character was in love. In addition, the setting was changed to New York, and the main character became a glamorous celebrity photographer rather than just a workaday protagonist. Eager to please, Carpenter made the changes, but Streisand soon dropped out nonetheless. When Carpenter's screenplay was rewritten with all new dialogue, he left the project, too, but retained screenwriter and story credit. After his departure, nine other writers took a shot at the script, and Dave Goodman did the final rewrite.

Eyes of Laura Mars was made into a big, glossy $8 million feature film. It starred Academy Award Best Actress winner Faye Dunaway (*Bonnie & Clyde* [1968], *Network* [1976], *The Wicked Lady* [1983], *Supergirl* [1984]) as Laura Mars, a woman who photographed a dazzling and "hip" combination of fashion and violence. Also in the cast was a delightful group of character actors who would go on to be major voices in the horror and science fiction genres. Brad Dourif (*Child's Play* [1988], *Spontaneous Combustion* [1989], *Dead Certain* [1990], *Exorcist III* [1990], *Alien Resurrection* [1997], *Urban*

Legend [1998]), Rene Auberjonois (*Night Gallery:* "Camera Obscura" [1971], *King Kong* [1976], *Star Trek: Deep Space Nine* [1993–1999]), Raul Julia (*Overdrawn at the Memory Bank* [1983], *Presumed Innocent* [1990], *The Addams Family* [1991]), and Tommy Lee Jones (*Black Moon Rising* [1985], *The Fugitive* [1993], *Men in Black* [1997], *U.S. Marshals* [1998]) all made terrific murder suspects in *Eyes of Laura Mars*, and the picture was helmed adeptly by veteran genre director Irvin Kershner (*The Empire Strikes Back* [1980], *Never Say Never Again* [1983], *RoboCop II* [1990]). Still, the picture took a critical drubbing when it came out. And, importantly, John Carpenter hated the final product, feeling that his original story had gotten lost in the Hollywood rewrite shuffle. Still, John Carpenter's name on an $8 million movie starring Faye Dunaway gave him a certain respectability in Hollywood, and he knew it.

The year 1978 also saw John Carpenter responsible for one other suspense thriller, the TV movie first known as *High Rise* and finally as *Someone's Watching Me!* This Carpenter teleplay was about another faceless slasher stalking a woman in a high-tech apartment building. Carpenter originally wrote *High Rise* as a theatrical movie for Warner Bros., but the studio wanted it to be a TV movie instead. As a result, John Carpenter joined forces with producer Richard Kobritz (*'Salem's Lot* [1979], *Christine* [1983]) to make an exciting and very Hitchcockian thriller. Reminiscent of *Rear Window* and *North by Northwest*, with its Saul Bass–like opening credit sequence, *High Rise* moved fast, and Carpenter was afforded only 15 days to complete principal photography. The film starred Lauren Hutton (*Once Bitten* [1985]) and a woman who would become very special to John Carpenter: Adrienne Barbeau (*Maude* [1972–78], *Swamp Thing* [1982]). After completing work on the film, Carpenter and Barbeau were married on January 1, 1979. Barbeau later appeared in *The Fog* and *Escape from New York*.

With Harry Sukman writing the music, and director of photography Robert Hauser ensuring that the film met Carpenter's artistic standard, John Carpenter's first union shoot went smoothly, and *Someone's Watching Me!* gained Carpenter his Directors Guild of America card. Although he had a little trouble with the Network Standards and Practices Department about the level of violence he was allowed to depict in his television venture, Carpenter was pleased with the final results.

Someone's Watching Me! aired on November 29, 1979, and earned solid ratings. Still, there could be no denying that by making three intense thrillers like *Halloween, Eyes of Laura Mars,* and *Someone's Watching Me!* in one year, Carpenter was providing the critics with plenty of fodder for their "son of Hitchcock" theories. Interestingly, Brian DePalma would stage a virtual re-make of *Someone's Watching Me!* in 1984, this one entitled *Body Double* and starring Craig Wasson and Melanie Griffith.

Though 1978 was seen primarily as the year of horror (and success) for John Carpenter, it ended on a determinedly different note. The sky was truly the limit, and the young director who so deeply loved westerns, film noir and all of Hollywood's classic genres was intent on exploring his abilities outside the slasher craze his film had ignited. Carpenter selected his next project, and surprisingly it was another television movie, this time a three hour mini-series documenting the life of rock 'n' roll idol Elvis Presley. Since Carpenter had once written a western for Elvis Presley called *Blood River,* the project was perfect. Carpenter also took it as a sign of good karma that Elvis had once played a character named "Dr. John Carpenter" in a 1969 film entitled *Change of Habit* starring Mary Tyler Moore.[13] Determined to make the "biography" of his hero absolutely accurate, John Carpenter enlisted the aid of a Presley bodyguard named Charlie Hodges, and he approached his new project with glee and a sense of fun.

Elvis was written by producer Anthony Lawrence, and John Carpenter found that ABC TV gave him carte blanche on the product, again a situation that Carpenter found irresistible. Disney teen idol and former *Lost in Space* guest-star Kurt Russell was cast as "the King," and Russell soon became a part of Carpenter's repertory company, later to appear in the director's *Escape from New York, The Thing, Big Trouble in Little China* and *Escape from L.A.* Kurt Russell's then-wife, Season Hubley, was cast as Priscilla Presley.

Elvis was shot in a fast 30 days, commencing production in the September of 1978. Carpenter recreated the look and sound of Elvis's musical numbers with the help of the talented Russell and a sound-alike singer. When it premiered in 1979, Carpenter's *Elvis* bio-pic handily won it's time slot, outgunning *Gone with the Wind* and *One Flew Over the Cuckoo's Nest.*[14] The picture was a success through and through, and Kurt Russell revealed charisma, wit and screen presence unseen in his Disney years. Both Carpenter and Russell were well on their way to greater stardom.

In 1979, John Carpenter and Adrienne Barbeau formed their own production company, Hye White Bread Productions. Enjoying the spotlight, Carpenter found that his success allowed him to select any project he wanted. Although he toyed with writing *Fangs* (1978)—a "revenge of nature picture" featuring rattlesnakes and apparently inspired by *Kingdom of the Spiders* (1976), *Frogs* (1972) and *Empire of the Ants* (1976)—he did not, in the end, do the picture. His nuclear "accident" musical comedy, *The Prometheus Crisis,* and *El Diablo,* his long delayed western, were also bandied about as future projects, but again, neither film was made. At this time, Carpenter also expressed his desire to film an adaptation of Alfred Bester's science fiction novel, *The Stars, My Destination.* That too, failed to come off. In fact, one of the many interesting facets of John Carpenter's career is that he has as many interesting *unmade* projects as he does filmed projects attached to his name. Through the years, he came to be associated with these titles, and many others, though they never came to fruition.

Despite the fact that these projects never materialized, Carpenter received a high honor for the exemplary film work he had completed. In late 1979, he won the "New Generation Director" award from the Los Angeles Film Critics Association.

Caught in The Fog

The film Carpenter finally decided to make in 1979 is one that is usually unheralded in his filmography. Although *The Fog*, co-written and produced by Debra Hill, was a huge hit at the box office, it goes unfairly unremembered today as one of Carpenter's best films.

The Fog is a disturbing and beautifully filmed ghost story that harkens back to the "town in jeopardy" subgenre represented by films such as *The Blob* (1958) and Alfred Hitchcock's *The Birds* (1960). In this case, the menace is not a pack of flying sparrows, or a malevolent ball of protoplasm, but rather a deadly fog bank that cloaks vengeful spirits in its murky insides. Like *Assault on Precinct* and *Halloween*, *The Fog* also dramatizes another of John Carpenter's "faceless evils": an encroaching shroud of fog that envelopes its victims and spits out cadavers. And, delightfully, the film ends with yet another reference to a Howard Hawks film, this time *The Thing from Another World* (1951). At the climax of that picture (which was already referenced by Carpenter in *Halloween* when youngsters Tommy Doyle and Lindsey watch it on TV), a worried news reporter warns the world to "watch the skies!" for further extra-terrestrial menace. In *The Fog*, Carpenter and Hill's screenplay culminates with Adrienne Barbeau's disk jockey sound-alike warning to ships at sea to "look out for THE FOG!"

The visual aspects of his unusual villain in *The Fog* were also motivations for Carpenter to do this creepy supernatural film:

> The idea of fog provides a framework in which I've always wanted to work. There are opportunities to do certain cinematic things with ghosts that can only be done in the movies. You don't really see the ghosts in *The Fog* as much as you think you do. The fog moves around, it glows, it comes through windowpanes…. I think that audiences are going to have fun with it.[15]

Halloween graduates Tommy Wallace, Charles Bornstein, Dean Cundey, Ray Stella and Debra Hill all reteamed with John Carpenter and his executive producer Charles B. Block for production of *The Fog*, which was budgeted at $1 million. The cast of the film came primarily from Carpenter's repertory company, with Jamie Lee Curtis, Adrienne Barbeau, Charles Cyphers, Darwin Joston, and Nancy Loomis playing critical roles. New to the mix, but no less welcome, was the cool Tom Atkins, a laconic and underrated actor who would later act for John Carpenter in *Escape from New York* and *Halloween III: Season of the Witch* (1982). And an additional *Fog* casting coup saw the wonderful Janet Leigh herself essay a major role. George "Buck" Flower also joined the Carpenter Club as one of *The Fog*'s first victims. He too returned for more scares in the director's *Escape from New York*, *Starman* (1984), *They Live* (1988), *John Carpenter Presents Body Bags* (1993) and *Village of the Damned* (1995), as well as non–Carpenter horror such as *Wes Craven Presents Wishmaster* (1997). The great John Houseman of *The Paper Chase* opened the picture in stylish fashion as a crusty old sailor recounting a haunting ghost story around a campfire at midnight.

The Fog was John Carpenter's tribute to the E.C. Comics of the 1950s (an inspiration also for fellow horror director George A. Romero's and writer Stephen King's *Creepshow* in 1981). The ghost story of *The Fog* was frightening and wonderfully conceived, and just as *Halloween* had done with slashers, *The Fog* initiated a slew of new "ghost" stories on the silver screen, including Peter Medak's *The Changeling* (1981), Peter Straub's *Ghost Story* (1981) and Sidney Furie's *The Entity* (1983).

Like his *Halloween* script, John Carpenter's teleplay for *The Fog* was also packed with delightful in-jokes. Characters were named "O'Bannon" after Carpenter's *Dark Star* collaborator, "Nick Castle" after the *Dark Star* camera assistant (who also played the masked Michael Myers in *Halloween*), and even "Kobritz" after the producer who had given Carpenter so much creative leeway on *Someone's Watching Me!*

Lending immeasurably to the eerie look of *The Fog*, Carpenter and Hill opted to shoot at an isolated, century-old lighthouse at Point Reyes in beautiful Marin County. The picturesque lighthouse could only be reached by a tremendous staircase carved into the side of the mountain. The 640 steps seemed to stretch on forever, and one of the many atmospheric moments in the film saw an isolated Barbeau traversing the neverending staircase alone as fierce winds whipped all about her. Other fine moments included a poltergeist disturbance at midnight in the scenic Marin County town Antonio Bay, and a night scene involving a haunted clipper ship, the *Elizabeth Dane*.

The look of "the fog" was engineered by Dick Albain, Jr., of L.A. Special Effects Film and A&A effects. With the help of dry ice vapors, fog filters, optical tricks, and a naturally foggy locale, the malevolent fog was able to move convincingly across the landscape, claiming victim after victim in stylish and suspenseful fashion.

The Fog opened in early 1980 to rave reviews. Tom Allen of *The Village Voice*, the critic who had championed *Halloween*, called it "classy looking," while Bruce Williamson of *Playboy* referred to it as "edge-of-your seat terror." The horror picture opened in a relatively dry season, facing competition only

from forgettable fare like *Hero at Large* starring *Three's Company* star John Ritter, *Foxes* starring Jodie Foster and directed by Adrian Lyne, and Marshall Brickman's *Simon*. Not surprisingly, the film made a financial killing.

Despite the positive reviews and the financial success at its release, *The Fog* later fell prey to much critical second-guessing in what might be termed the first anti–Carpenter backlash. Since *The Fog* remains one of the best and most stylish ghost stories ever put to film, the perception that *The Fog* failed in some way is difficult to understand. In the late '80s, for instance, an interviewer once asserted to star Janet Leigh that *The Fog* was a very "slick and good-looking film," but one that really didn't come off well. Rather than echo the reporter's own perception, Leigh replied diplomatically:

> I too thought it was *done* well…. The special effects came across and everything; maybe it was just a little too farfetched. *Halloween* had a more understandable, basic kind of menace, whereas in *The Fog*, they were really *reaching.*[16]

What John Carpenter had been reaching for, of course, was another fascinating but faceless representation of evil. If *The Fog* failed to connect with some viewers, it is, as Janet Leigh suggests, because people were not ready to accept a more intellectual style of horror than that of the knife-wielding psycho popularized by *Halloween*. Still, John Carpenter was not dissuaded from his goals, and many years later he would try again to create an intellectual brand of horror with the unique *In the Mouth of Madness* (1994). Sadly, his efforts on that account failed both with the critics and at the box office. Though currently out of critical favor, *The Fog* remains a beautifully done film that deserves to be remembered as one of Carpenter's best and most unusual features.

Taking a Bite
out of the Big Apple:
Escape from New York

After *The Fog* cleaned up at the box office, John Carpenter was eager to shift to his dream project. Back in the mid–1970s he had written a script for a movie called *Escape from New York City*. It was a futuristic yarn about a hero turned convict (shades of Napoleon Wilson in *Assault on Precinct 13*) assigned to rescue a kidnapped American president from the island of Manhattan, which in the 1990s had been transformed into a maximum security prison. Below, Carpenter describes his inspiration for this bizarre futuristic adventure story:

> I wrote *Escape from New York* way back in 1974; I believe I was inspired by the movie *Death Wish*, that was very popular at the time. I didn't agree with the philosophy of it, taking the law into one's own hands, but the film came across with the sense of New York as a kind of jungle, and I wanted to make an SF film along those lines.[17]

Also critical to the shaping of the story was the talent of co-writer Nick Castle, a friend of Carpenter's from U.S.C. and the actor who had played Michael Myers in the first *Halloween* picture. Castle took Carpenter's grim action-adventure, a reaction originally to the era of Watergate, and added what Carpenter later referred to as a "skewed" sense of humor. Thus the story's hero encountered not just thugs and convicts, but crooks singing a Broadway musical. (After Castle's contributions to *Escape from New York*, he went on to direct *The Last Starfighter* in 1983.)

Avco-Embassy, aware of John Carpenter's record for transforming low budgets into huge profits and thrilled with the success of *The Fog*, greenlighted a budget of $7 million for the film. With his largest budget yet, Carpenter and partner Debra Hill embarked on

the creation of the pessimistic, fascist world of 1997. Although Avco-Embassy wanted either Charles Bronson or Clint Eastwood as anti-hero Snake Plissken, Carpenter prevailed in his desire to see *Elvis* star Kurt Russell essay the important part. His perseverance paid off, and *Escape from New York* was the first action picture to headline Kurt Russell.

After working for John Carpenter again in *The Thing* and *Big Trouble in Little China*, Russell would become a mainstream action star in Hollywood, appearing in films such as *Tango and Cash* (1989), *Stargate* (1994), *Executive Decision* (1996), *Breakdown* (1997) and *Soldier* (1998). For all intents and purposes, *Escape from New York* was really Russell's big break. Before working on the film, Russell turned down the opportunity to star in Dino De Laurentiis's remake of *Flash Gordon* (1980). That role instead went to Sam J. Jones, but Russell made the right decision, and was grateful to Carpenter for standing by him during the casting process. Just as John Wayne and Howard Hawks had forged a very close actor-director rapport through the '50s, '60s and early '70s, so did Kurt Russell and John Carpenter begin to explore a similar relationship in the '80s. For his part, Russell knew he was in the hands of a master:

> I'd be not only contented but *honored* to work with John on as many more films as possible. Apart from being a really nice guy and, I feel, a very good friend ... he's also very talented. To me that's the best of both worlds. I've seen lots of movies, and I think he's on top of the hill. He's fearless, he's got a great visual sense, and he's got a wonderful imagination.[18]

Another long-time John Carpenter fan and performer, Donald Pleasence, also returned to the States to play in *Escape from New York* after appearing in a dreadful low-budget *Superman* knock-off entitled *The Pumaman* (1980). This time, however, Pleasence was cast against type, playing an

American president. Pleasence characterized his character as the unholy union of Ronald Reagan and Margaret Thatcher.

The larger budget of *Escape from New York* also made available to John Carpenter a cast of well-known character actors. Ernest Borgnine (*The Devil's Rain* [1975], *The Black Hole* [1979], *Deadly Blessing* [1981]), Harry Dean Stanton (*Alien* [1979]), music legend Isaac Hayes, and Carpenter's childhood hero from *It Conquered the World*, Lee Van Cleef, were welcomed aboard. Also returning from the Carpenter repertory company were George "Buck" Flower, Adrienne Barbeau, Tom Atkins, and Charles Cyphers.

Behind the scenes, Dean Cundey was back to lens the film, and Carpenter selected Joe Alves (*Night Gallery*, *Jaws* [1975], *Close Encounters of the Third Kind* [1978], *Jaws III* [1983]) as his production designer. Carpenter was especially thrilled to work with Alves when he learned that the artist had animated the infamous "Monster from the Id" sequence of Disney's *Forbidden Planet*, another of his favorite childhood films.

The most difficult task for Alves and director Carpenter on *Escape from New York* was to find a city that could double for the Big Apple. New York itself was out of the question for the shoot, because it was too expensive to film there. Alves and Carpenter embarked on a trek across the country to find the right city, and they eventually settled on St. Louis. Alves explained to *Starlog* why St. Louis proved to be such a good double for New York City:

> Around the turn of the century, New York City and St. Louis were very much the same.... New York began to change radically in the 1930s, but St. Louis has kept many of the old qualities.... John and I ... came here [St. Louis] to inspect a bridge and started walking the streets; we looked around at the old buildings and thought they were fantastic. These were structures that exist in NY now, and have that seedy run-down quality that we're looking for.[19]

Also noteworthy in the *Escape from New York* crew was an unknown matte-painter who would one day become an Academy Award winning director: James Cameron. A young Cameron (*Galaxy of Terror* [1981]) was in charge of painting a glass matte that would double for a decaying Central Park near the film's finale. Of course, Cameron, like John Carpenter, later became a genre icon, directing such notable films as *The Terminator* (1984), *Aliens* (1986), *The Abyss* (1989), and *Terminator 2* (1991), not to mention his nongenre megahits such as *True Lies* (with Jamie Lee Curtis) and the unsinkable *Titanic* (1997).

With its cast, crew and locations settled, John Carpenter started principal photography on a film that was Avco-Embassy's most expensive and complex production in years. The *Escape from New York* shoot lasted two and a half months and stretched through a hot, humid summer. Making it even more taxing, virtually all of *Escape from New York* was a night shoot, with shooting "days" lasting from 9:00 P.M. all the way through 7:00 A.M. It was an exhausting schedule, but as was typical for Carpenter, he brought the film in on time and on budget. Outside St. Louis, additional footage was lensed in Atlanta at the Metro Atlanta Rapid Transit System, although the scene at the subway was eventually cut from the film. Finally, there was a brief location shoot conducted on Liberty Island off of Manhattan, so Carpenter could work the Statue of Liberty into his action flick.

Escape from New York premiered in the summer of 1981 against such blockbusters as Steven Spielberg's *Raiders of the Lost Ark* (1981), and it more than held its own against the competition. In fact, *Escape* was another monster hit, earning Avco-Embassy more than $50 million. On an investment of $7 million, that huge revenue was terrific news for all involved. As the icing on the cake, the film garnered great notices, with critics engaged by the unusual premise and the clever New York jibes, as well as by the film

On the set of *Escape from New York* (1981), John Carpenter directs then-wife Adrienne Barbeau.

noir style and production values. *Escape from New York* was John Carpenter's third blockbuster in a row, and the director was rapidly becoming known to everyone as one of the hottest and best directors around.

The Nightmare Isn't Over: Halloween II

Next up for John Carpenter was a film that for him represented more of a business transaction than a creative endeavor: *Halloween II*. Neither John Carpenter nor Debra Hill had expressed any real interest in creating a sequel to their 1978 stalker film, but financiers Moustapha Akkad and Irwin Yablans understood that a *Halloween* sequel could be very profitable. When faced with the possibility that the film was going to be made with or without them, Carpenter and Hill elected to write the sequel so it would have at least a chance of being a good film. Also, John Carpenter has readily admitted that one motive for doing a sequel to *Halloween* was financial. He and Debra Hill had not shared in the original film's enormous profits, and *Halloween II* was an opportunity for re-negotiation, and a piece of the franchise's box office pie.

So Carpenter and Hill agreed to produce *Halloween II* as well, overseeing the production and assuring that it met their high standards for quality. The film's story would take place on the same Halloween night as the first film (October 31, 1978), and it would feature Myers's ongoing attempts to kill Laurie Strode, who is revealed in the course of the picture to be his younger sister. To recreate the distinctive look of the already classic *Halloween*, director of photography Dean Cundey returned to the camp along with stars Jamie Lee Curtis, Donald Pleasence, and Charles Cyphers. In one incredibly well-done moment of continuity, Nancy Loomis even appeared in the *Halloween* sequel — as a corpse. Directing *Halloween II* in Carpenter's stead was a young new director, Rick Rosenthal (*Darkroom* [1981]), who put the cast through its paces in Pasadena. Dick Warlock replaced Nick Castle as Michael Myers (known now and forever as "the Shape") and shooting for the most part was uneventful and easy.

However, when Rosenthal delivered his final cut of *Halloween II*, John Carpenter was not at all pleased with what he saw. He felt the film was neither suspenseful nor scary, and a controversy soon erupted. Additional shots of intense gore were shot to buttress the film's box office potential. Rick Rosenthal claimed that the gore only ruined his vision, and that it made the film a target for critics who had grown tired of the "inventive" murders of films like *Friday the 13th* (1980) and *Prom Night*. Carpenter, who admits to "fixing" a film which he once described as "about as frightening as an episode of *Quincy*," asserts that he did not shoot any additional gore, and that Rosenthal's cut was gory, but not scary.

Regardless of the specifics of the case, it was obvious upon release that *Halloween II* was not the great film its predecessor was. However, it was not at all the terrible sequel that some pundits have suggested. In fact, it is better than all the *Friday the 13th* films, which is something, at least. Reaction to *Halloween II* also depends heavily on which version a person sees. In the television version, there are altered sequences, particularly the ending of the film which sees Laurie's paramedic boyfriend (actor Lance Guest of *The Last Starfighter* [1983]) survive the massacre.

Despite all the controversy, *Halloween II* opened well against Michael Crichton's *Looker*, *Mommie Dearest* and Neil Simon's *Only When I Laugh* in the final week of October 1981. The film generated more than enough money for the producers to greenlight a further sequel: 1982's *Season of the Witch*. And many critics, perhaps ashamed of missing the boat on *Halloween* in 1978, were even quick to praise the sequel as a worthy heir to Carpenter's classic.

After *Halloween II*, Rick Rosenthal went on to direct episodes of television programs such as *Life Goes On* (1987), *Early Edition* (1996) and *Dellaventura* (1997). He also directed another sequel to a horror classic, *Birds II: Land's End* (as Alan Smithee).

The Play's The Thing

John Carpenter's next directing assignment after *Escape from New York* resulted in a movie that forever changed the tenor of his career. Although he had toyed with many projects since completion of *The Fog* and *Escape from New York*, John Carpenter signed on with Universal Studios to helm a remake of the Howard Hawks horror–science fiction classic, *The Thing from Another World* (1951). *The Texas Chainsaw Massacre* director Tobe Hooper and his *Massacre* writer Kim Henkel had been ensconced on the project first, but the duo left after being unable to create a script with a satisfying and unique monster. When John Carpenter became connected with *The Thing*, he surprisingly opted *not* to remake the Hawks picture he so revered, but rather to reshoot the original short story, "Who Goes There," written by John W. Campbell, Jr. (as Don Stuart) in the 1940s:

> I'm only doing it because of the story. Hawks didn't do the story, and nobody else has either. If I had to remake it just in terms of the movie I wouldn't dare because it's so well done it wouldn't be worth it. But there's this element of the story which is so fine and interesting and unique, and that's what I'm going to concentrate on.[20]

Howard Hawks's 1951 version (starring Kenneth Tobey, James Arness, Margaret Sheridan and Robert Cornthwaite and directed by Christian Nyby) concerned the staff of a U.S. Arctic base who excavated a crashed flying saucer from the ice and then encountered a deadly alien "thing," a living humanoid "vegetable" that fed off the blood of humans and was intent on breeding. By contrast, John W. Campbell's source material was about an Antarctic team that encountered a deadly, malevolent alien capable of changing shapes and, by absorption, assuming the identities of human team members. Thus *Who Goes There* was not just the title of the novella, it was the central issue of the chilling story. None of the characters could be sure *who* was the alien, and so the short story took on the eerie and demented air of a paranoid nightmare. Today, "Who Goes There" is considered to be the inspiration not just for both versions of *The Thing*, but for *Invasion of the Body Snatchers* (another story wherein people's identities are absorbed by aliens) and *Alien* (with the alien hiding inside people's bellies).

What appealed to John Carpenter about *The Thing* was the chance to make a horror film about issues of trust, as well as the occasion to dramatize a formless, insidious evil. Carpenter had been a fan of monster movies like *Gorgo* (1961) since childhood, and this was his opportunity to make perhaps the ultimate monster film. He was inspired to do so by the work of 22-year-old Rob Bottin, a talented special effects guru who assured Carpenter that in 1982, unlike in 1951, it was possible to believably portray a shape-shifting alien monstrosity. As Carpenter told Steve Swires, a reporter for *Starlog*:

> Rob's concept was that the "thing" could do anything. It doesn't look like any one particular entity, and has no respect for what it imitates. It can look like a million life-forms from a million different planets.... That gave me the opportunity to do things that have never been done in a movie, because

there's been no excuse to do them before. The audience isn't going to expect this ... they'll never be ahead of us.[21]

To write the film, Bill Lancaster, author of *The Bad News Bears*, was selected. Before and after *The Thing* premiered, Lancaster was lambasted by the science fiction community for his script, and many prominent "authorities" vocally wondered how the writer of *The Bad News Bears* could possibly have been selected to rewrite a classic genre film. Of course, everyone who has worked in Hollywood realizes that there are times when one accepts assignments on sub-par material. After all, James Cameron directed *Piranha II: The Spawning* (1985), Wes Craven began his film career in the New York 1970s porno industry, and so forth. It was unfair of the critical community to lambaste Lancaster because he had worked on a kids' movie (which was a hit, after all). In fact, Lancaster wrote a brilliant script for John Carpenter's *The Thing*, and he was extraordinarily faithful to the details of the Campbell story not just in the recreation of scenes like "the blood test" and the names of characters, but in Campbell's intent to create an atmosphere of paranoia as well. Bill Lancaster did add considerable action and carnage to the project, but such was necessary for an audience weaned on *Star Wars*, *Halloween* and *Alien*.

John Carpenter and Bill Lancaster met half a dozen times in preproduction to iron out the details of the *The Thing* script, and the collaboration was a very positive one. Lancaster wrote the first 40 pages of the script, which John Carpenter loved, and then he went back to finish it up on his own.[22] *The Thing* was the first film directed by John Carpenter that he did not write himself, but that was fine with the director. He was just as happy visualizing another's work.

Universal's *The Thing* was budgeted at $10 million, and the film ended up being the most difficult shoot of John Carpenter's career. Many of the film exteriors were shot in

Stewart, British Columbia, a small mining town accessible to the film crew only by a 27 mile dirt road. It was there, on the side of a huge glacier, that the American Antarctic base was constructed. (So believable was this installation that stock footage of it was utilized in the first season *X-Files* episode "Ice.") The interiors of the base were shot entirely on the Universal Studios lot in Los Angeles, but it was necessary to refrigerate the shooting stages so that the breath of the actors could be seen on film. To create this effect, the stages were brought down to a temperature of 40 degrees in the heat of the summer.

Special effects presented incredible difficulties, and Bottin led a crew of 35 artists and technicians, each one responsible for the care and feeding of the Thing. Because most of these special effects were tricks that had never even been attempted, let alone captured on film, John Carpenter and his team shot for 14 hours a day, seven days a week for weeks on end in 1982. As Carpenter remembers it, the special effects sequences, which added up to $1.5 million of the $10 million budget, were the most grueling element of his ultimate monster movie:

> They go on-and-on-and-on-and-on-and-on-and-on…. You do one shot in a day, or two shots in a day. They are a pain in the neck if you try to do 'em in the first unit, and try to do 'em all at the same time.[23]

Still, Carpenter and his team persevered through over a hundred complex special effects set-ups with the assistance of exquisitely detailed storyboards from Marvel Comics illustrator Michael Ploog (*Planet of the Apes*), art director John Lloyd, and Carpenter's reliable director of photography, Dean Cundey, who labored on *The Thing* for 13 months and even shot special effects insert shots when necessary. Despite the multiple hardships, production of *The Thing* remained a highly creative and inventive time for both Carpenter and Cundey. Though stretched to the point

of exhaustion, both men did the best work of their careers on the picture.

Dean Cundey recalled how his own input helped to make the final film an unforgettable cinematic exercise in white-knuckle horror and nearly unbearable paranoia:

> I suggested putting ceilings on all the sets and bringing the pipes into the frame line, to increase the claustrophobia…. I suggested using practical lights to make it look realistic, so we lit whole scenes with just the flares the actors carried…. We ended up using color selectively, with the 'thing' … the most colorful object…. We painted the … Arctic station in shades of gray…. Even the wardrobe was coordinated to be in somber colors of dark blue, gray and brown.[24]

These decisions ended up giving *The Thing* an almost documentary-style texture throughout its 100 minute running time. The film was also very realistic in art design and execution, and Carpenter opted for believability and restraint over flashy camerawork. His work in *The Thing* was smooth and efficient, but not showy. Since he was dealing with a rather fantastic alien creature, Carpenter's decision to infuse the film with a kind of "you are there" feeling, from actors' performances to *mise en scène*, dramatically increased the realism of the entire venture.

Although Howard Hawks had told his version of *The Thing* with overlapping, rather theatrical dialogue, Carpenter applied a different tenet to his masterpiece. All the actors, from Kurt Russell in the lead to actors Keith David, Donald Moffatt and Wilford Brimley (who filled in for Carpenter veteran Donald Pleasence when the British thespian became unavailable), were understated in their approach. They were "real" people, dealing with every nuance of human behavior, from long stretches of boredom to instants of intense fear and anxiety.

But because "the thing" was to be such a horrible creature, literally erupting and bursting out of human flesh throughout the picture, John Carpenter and his technicians knew that they had to stray into the terrain of the unbelievable if they were to avoid the dreaded X rating from the MPAA. Special effects architect Rob Bottin understood that he could not use "human" flesh tones and torrents of blood in the picture, for fear that audiences would run vomiting from auditoriums, and so instead he concentrated on making the alien's internal physiology more withdrawn from the audience's everyday reality:

> I thought, "This movie could be really terrible to watch"; I mean, not only are there five transformations ... it couldn't help but be bloody.... I suggested we play it more fantasy. In other words, when something bursts open, or changes, the insides don't look like they really should. So, we ended up using these wild colors. Blood makes you turn away, almost as a reflex, but the colors sort of draw your attention.[25]

Everybody involved had high hopes for *The Thing*. It boasted a terrific look, the most frightening monster in film history, a pulse-pounding soundtrack from Ennio Morricone, an overall air of believability courtesy of Carpenter's restrained direction, and a sympathetic, attractive lead in Kurt Russell. Astonishingly, the film bombed upon its release in the summer of 1982. Facing cutthroat competition from Steven Spielberg's *E.T.*, Nick Meyer's *Star Trek II: The Wrath of Khan*, Tobe Hooper's *Poltergeist*, Clint Eastwood's *Firefox*, and Ridley Scott's *Blade Runner*, the progressive Carpenter film quickly disappeared from theaters. After three full weeks, *The Thing* had grossed only $13.8 million. With a budget of $10 million (not counting advertising costs), that tally was more deadly than the creature dramatized in the film. For the first time in his illustrious career, John Carpenter was riding a box office bomb. Worse than that, critics responded not just negatively, but hatefully. From Siskel and

Ebert to *Newsweek* and *Time*, *The Thing* was trashed by critics as a pointless gore-fest. Science fiction critics, who should have known better, were equally caustic. Harlan Ellison called the film "dreck," and writing for *Starlog*, Alan Spencer reported that John Carpenter was more suited to directing "traffic accidents, train wrecks and public floggings" than science fiction films.

The Thing's critical and box office reception remains bewildering. The film is a successful horror picture not only because it masterfully depicts a new kind of alien threat (above and beyond anything seen in *Alien*) and spins an engrossing web of paranoia, but because it makes audiences acutely aware of how fragile the human body really is. At the core of *The Thing* is fear and loathing of the flesh and an awareness of its true vulnerability. Like some kind of sick cancer or tumor, the malevolent alien in *The Thing* twists and boils human flesh, corrupting the very thing that is our contact with the world outside ourselves.

One gets the feeling from reading the reviews of *The Thing* that critics had been waiting for a very long time to take their potshots at the *wunderkind*, John Carpenter. Ahead of its time by at least fifteen years, *The Thing* gave them that opportunity. They wanted to take John Carpenter, a critical and box office sensation for five years running, down a notch or two, and so they did. Additionally, bad timing surely played a part in the film's poor reception. Audiences around the country were busy loving the story of that cute alien, *E.T.*, and *The Thing*, which espoused an opposite and rather frightening philosophy about life on other planets, was not welcomed in the slightest. So strong was the backlash against *The Thing* that even cast member Wilford Brimley came out and said that it "stunk."[26] Although it is within any person's rights not to like or enjoy *The Thing* as cinema, it seems beyond the pale for so many critics to attack John Carpenter personally for the film, and sadly, that is exactly what happened after the release of *The Thing*:

I was called a "*pornographer of violence*." I had *no* idea it would be received that way. I knew what a *great* film I had made.... *The Thing* was just too strong for that time. I knew it was going to be strong, but I didn't think it would be *too* strong. I made it as strong as I thought it *should* be.[27]

Though Carpenter was the target of vitriolic commentary on all sides, something surprising began to happen as the 1980s slipped by. People began to defend *The Thing*—loudly in many cases. Peter Nicholls, editor of *The Encyclopedia of Science Fiction*, named John Carpenter's *The Thing* as one of the top ten science fiction films of all time. Acclaimed author Alan Dean Foster noted that John W. Campbell himself would have loved the remake because Carpenter went back and filmed his story faithfully, rather than attempting to duplicate the story and effects of the Hawks film.[28]

Then, in 1991, *Terminator 2: Judgment Day* premiered, featuring a shape-shifting automaton from the future. The CGI transformations of the T-100 were highly reminiscent of (though less visceral than) those seen in *The Thing*, and the shape-shifter's death scene was almost identical. Dying, the T-100 began to assume all the shapes it had assumed during the course of the film, just as the final appearance of the *Thing* was a combination of dog, human and alien when Kurt Russell blew it to pieces.

The tide really turned in the 1992 when a comic book continuation of *The Thing* was written by Chuck Pfarrer and published by Dark Horse Comics.[29] The adaptation picked up at the conclusion of the Carpenter film, and featured all new adventures with hero MacReady and the nightmare monster from Carpenter's film. Then, in a first season *X-Files* story called "Ice," John Carpenter's *The Thing* was referenced not just with stock footage of the base constructed for the film, but thematically as well. The story involved an Arctic team who had drilled deep into the ice and pulled up a prehistoric but extra-terres-

trial life-form that invaded the human bloodstream. As the people of the base became infected, their identities were altered by the entity. "We're not who we are," one paranoid researcher realized, echoing the "Who Goes There" plotline in surprising detail.

And, in 1995, the television series *Star Trek: Deep Space Nine* ("The Adversary," "Way of the Warrior") went where John Carpenter had gone before by introducing a "new" enemy: a race of alien shapeshifters (like *The Thing*) who could only be detected through, you guessed it, blood tests. So while Carpenter's *The Thing* was reviled in the Reagan era, it was ground zero for a new generation of science fiction productions in the 1990s.

Still, for John Carpenter all the attention and backtracking must seem like too little too late. After *The Thing* was booed off screens by audiences and critics alike, *he* was probably the one feeling paranoid. Carpenter's career path forever changed at this point: He had gone from being genre filmmaking's golden boy to its whipping boy in just one year.

Kurt Russell, who also weathered some nasty attacks after the release of *The Thing*, was one of the few commentators who really understood how relevant and important a film *The Thing* was:

> In terms of the human condition, it certainly has a recognizable theme. People today are experiencing ... paranoia in their daily lives. You read a headline about a murder and, the next day, you begin looking at the person walking next to you a bit more carefully. This movie takes that underlying feeling and lets it grow.[30]

It is no coincidence that as the '80s progressed, and the paranoia about "random violence" grew in the United States, the critical estimation of *The Thing* also improved. Perhaps one day it will be recognized as not only the best science fiction film of 1982 (a field which includes the revered Ridley Scott feature *Blade Runner* and *E.T.*), but perhaps the best and, in the long run, most influential science fiction and horror film of the entire decade.

Today, John Carpenter counts *The Thing* as his best film, and hopes for the opportunity to some day prepare a sequel.

Season of the Witch: *Something Old, Something New*

In the year 1982 also saw the release of the third installment in the ongoing *Halloween* franchise. John Carpenter and Debra Hill produced the second sequel, which they had decided early on would send the film series in a bold new direction. Carpenter and Hill both felt that the slasher formula had been done to death (so to speak), and that it was better to move the *Halloween* series into an exploration of other horror stories, all of which would revolve around the "trick or treat" aspects of Halloween night.

The new *Halloween*, ultimately titled *Season of the Witch*, started off promisingly when John Carpenter enlisted a seasoned science fiction writer to pen the screenplay. While on a trip to England to discuss horror and sci-fi on a BBC program, John Carpenter had the opportunity to meet Nigel Kneale, the respected author of the BBC *Quatermass* TV series and films. Kneale was interested in working with Carpenter, and so he began to toil away on a screenplay for *Halloween III*.

He penned a script that was a sort of high-tech, high-concept combination of *Invasion of the Body Snatchers* (1956), *The Stepford Wives* (1975) and *Village of the Damned* (1960). His script was ambitious and determinedly different from the previous *Halloween* "Michael Myers" concept. Unfortunately, the money end of *Halloween III* did not like what was happening. Kneale later explained the situation in an interview:

> I got drawn into writing *Halloween III* for John Carpenter.... I wrote an original, large-scale screenplay with a lot black humor in it debunking sentimental "Irishry".... The front office ... demanded that *Halloween III* should be *exactly* the same as *Halloween I and II*.... So my screenplay was cut down to B-picture size, and had eye-gougings and electric-drillings added.... It bore no resemblance to what I had written.[31]

What happened was that the backers of *Halloween III* became worried when they realized that the latest installment would diverge from the popular (and profitable) formula. They did not want a science fiction scenario with humor and intelligence; they wanted a horror flick with lots of violence and gore — elements that had made money in the *Halloween* series before. Kneale left the project in disgust, and Tommy Lee Wallace, frequent Carpenter contributor and writer of *Amityville II: The Possession* (1982), fashioned his own screenplay based on Kneale's work. He was then given the assignment of directing the film.

Halloween series stars Jamie Lee Curtis and Donald Pleasence were not involved in the second sequel, and Tom Atkins, star of *The Fog* and later *Night of the Creeps* (1986), took center stage. Instead of the faceless evil of Michael Myers, Dan O'Herlihy (*The Last Starfighter* [1983], *RoboCop* [1987]) played Conal Cochran, the technology-minded warlock of the film. Lensed by Dean Cundey, the film retained the creepy nighttime look that distinguished the earlier *Halloween* pictures. Unfortunately, however, Cundey and Carpenter had an undisclosed problem on the set of *Halloween III* that resulted in the duo not working together again until 1986 and *Big Trouble in Little China*. Still, all was not lost. With Carpenter and frequent co-composer Alan Howarth doing the music for the film, *Season of the Witch* not only looked, but also sounded very much like the first two franchise pictures.

Halloween III: Season of the Witch premiered near Halloween, 1982, and it was a dismal failure at the box office, satisfying neither critics nor audiences. The die-hard series fans missed Michael Myers, Jamie Lee Curtis and Donald Pleasence (whose character had died at the end of *Halloween II*), and in the final analysis the film was not very good, despite a solid performance by Atkins and an interesting central concept. Tommy Lee Wallace did a fine job directing the picture, mimicking Carpenter's use of foreground "jolts" in his compositions to a high degree, but it was hard to reconcile the intellectual sci-fi nature of the premise (technology and superstition blend in modern witchcraft) with the very graphic, very gory murders. An attempt to do something noble and different, *Halloween III* ended up a hodgepodge of ideas that did not really fit together well. The weak nature of the sequel resulted in the collapse of the *Halloween* film series. Another sequel was not prepared for six years, until 1988's *The Return of Michael Myers*. As the title indicates, that film chose not to be a meditation on the Halloween ethos, but rather an extension of the first two *Halloween* pictures.

Exhausted by the rigors of maintaining a franchise he had no real interest in perpetuating, John Carpenter departed the *Halloween* universe after *Season of the Witch*, and never looked back. Tommy Lee Wallace continued to work in the horror genre, directing *Twilight Zone* revival episodes in 1985, *Fright Night II* in 1989, and the TV miniseries *It* (based on Stephen King's novel) in 1990.

Driving Christine

Following the disastrous reception to *The Thing*, John Carpenter was left to reassess his career and his filmmaking skill. This difficult period of introspection led him to accept a job as a director on the only film of his career which he maintains he did as a hired gun, purely for the money: *Christine* (1983).

Stephen King's novel about a 1958 Chevrolet Fury haunted by the spirit of a deceased owner was delivered in manuscript form to producer Richard Kobritz (of *Someone's Watching Me!*) in the summer of 1982 by America's favorite horror author. Interested in adapting the property to film, Kobritz took the *Christine* manuscript to Mark Tarlov of Polar Film, and together they made a bid on the material.[32] The bid was accepted, and Kobritz selected a director for the project: his old friend Carpenter, who quickly agreed to take his shot at adapting Stephen King.

As Stephen King's novel hit the market to record sales, principal photography on the $10 million film began in earnest on April 15, 1983. The shoot lasted for five weeks; twenty-three 1958 Furies were purchased (and destroyed) by the film crew to simulate the villainous moves of the haunted Christine, and a highlight of the shoot involved the blowing up of a full-scale gas-station mock-up near Valencia, California, with special effects accomplished by Roy Arbogast.

Although John Carpenter always liked to work with his repertory company in front of and behind the scenes, *Christine* represented a bit of a departure for him since Dean Cundey did not shoot the picture. Filling in was cinematographer Donald M. Morgan. The cast was also filled with new talents, with Harry Dean Stanton (*Escape from New York*) being the only familiar face. In the lead role of Arnie Cunningham was Keith Gordon of *Dressed to Kill*. The hero of the film was played by John Stockwell (*My Science Project* [1985], *Stag* [1997]), and the beautiful Leigh was essayed by Alexandra Paul, later a star of *Baywatch*. In the character role of Darnell was Robert Prosky of *The Keep* (1983) and *Gremlins 2* (1990).

John Carpenter also wrote the musical score for *Christine* and peppered the King adaptation with his favorite rock 'n' roll and bebop music from the late '50s and early '60s. Songs such as *Bad to the Bone* and *Keep a Knockin'* were expertly used in the motion picture to sometimes humorous, sometimes menacing, effect. Overall, *Christine* revealed a more humorous side of Carpenter, and many scenes involving the interplay among the teen stars were dynamic, interesting and realistic. Also of real dramatic impact was the opening "flashback" to Christine's manufacture in a Detroit assembly line. Shot on Fuji film stock to give it the appearance of being old, the scene graphically depicted how *Christine* was bad from birth.

Because of the negative reception of *The Thing*, John Carpenter did not speak to the press during or after the shooting of *Christine*. He hoped that the work he did would be judged for itself, rather than as an opportunity to take personal potshots at him.

Despite the press blackout, *Christine* opened to good reviews throughout the country, with many critics noting John Carpenter's satiric and humorous touches. *Christine* was a light film to be sure, but Carpenter carried it off with distinction, style, and wit, and the critics acknowledged the finer touches. Audiences also liked the picture, though it was only a moderate success in the final analysis, competing with other King adaptations *The Dead Zone* and *Cujo*. Despite the nice reception, John Carpenter considered *Christine* distinctly unscary, and today counts it as his worst film.

As far as Stephen King adaptations go, *Christine* is probably somewhere in the top third of a very large pack (at this point over 36 films and mini-series). While perhaps not as good as *Carrie, The Dead Zone* (1981), *Misery* (1990) or *The Shining* (1980), it is undeniably better, funnier, and a lot more stylish than most of the King film adaptations that have come down the pike (including *Firestarter* [1984], *Maximum Overdrive* [1985], *Silver Bullet* [1985], *The Dark Half* [1991], *Graveyard Shift* [1991], *Sleepwalkers* [1992], *The Mangler* [1995], and *Thinner* [1996]).

Aiming for Heaven: Starman

Although *Christine* had been only a mild success, John Carpenter found himself at the helm of a large-budget science fiction adventure in 1984. Originally written by Bruce A. Evans and Raynold Gideon, *Starman* had been a troubled project for several years when Carpenter arrived. Columbia Pictures had originally turned down Steven Spielberg's *E.T.* to do the picture, but then abruptly shelved *Starman* after *E.T.* made a killing, fearing that the two projects were too similar in tone and story. Still, executive producer Michael Douglas (*Romancing the Stone* [1984], *Black Rain* [1989], *The Game* [1997]) was determined to make the movie. After several writers took a shot at rewriting the screenplay, and directing luminaries such as Tony Scott, John Badham, Adrian Lyne and Mark Rydell came and went, John Carpenter, at age 36, committed to the picture.

A new draft by Hollywood script doctor Dean Riesner (*Play Misty for Me*) proved to be just the story Carpenter was looking for. The tale of a Christ-like alien who has but three days to learn about humanity before ascending to the Heavens, *Starman* was a more intimate and personal effort than most of Carpenter's earlier film work. It was also appealing to Carpenter, ever the film buff, because it was something of a genre buster, artfully combining Frank Capra's road picture *It Happened One Night* (1934) with Robert Wise's science fiction masterpiece, *The Day the Earth Stood Still* (1951). Although Carpenter had been pigeonholed as a horror genre director by 1984, he was still able to make the movies he wanted to make by turning action pictures into modern westerns (*Assault on Precinct 13*) and science fiction blockbusters into comedy-romances (*Starman*).

As John Carpenter began to assemble his team — including Joe Alves (*Escape from New York*), Daniel Lomino, Roy Arbogast, Donald Morgan (*Christine*) and producer Larry Franco — authorship of the *Starman* screenplay became a bone of contention. Though Carpenter planned to shoot the revised draft by Dean Riesner, the Writer's Guild determined that writers Evans and Gideon, associate producers on the project, should receive sole screenplay credit. Miffed, Carpenter acknowledged Riesner's contributions to *Starman* by adding the line "For Dean Riesner" in the film's closing credits.

Working with a budget of $23 million, Carpenter's largest budget yet (more than twice the budget of *The Thing*), Carpenter spent much of the shooting schedule in Tennessee, location of the Starman's crash early in the film. Because of rain and humidity there, special effects were slow in coming off, and the schedule was delayed. Overcoming these technical difficulties, Carpenter once more established his ability to direct actors in his experience with stars Jeff Bridges (*King Kong* [1976], *The Big Lebowksi* [1998]), Karen Allen (*Raiders of the Lost Ark* [1981]), Richard Jaeckel (*Black Moon Rising* [1985]) and Charles Martin Smith (*Never Cry Wolf* [1983]).

Jeff Bridges's challenge was to create a fully grown, adult alien life-form that lacked experience not only with the human condition, but even the human body. The actor rehearsed with a dancer and observed the movements of his young children for weeks in preparation for his role in *Starman*:

> For me, the toughest part of the picture was in the beginning when I get inside this fellow's body and start it up. I am not at home in this body. I don't know how it works. I had to try to imagine I was sitting inside my head operating the control center…. I worked with dancer Russell Clark to figure out the right moves.[33]

It may have been tough for Bridges to create this unique character, but his diligence paid off. He turned in a marvelous performance, brimming with childlike innocence and pure goodness. Bridges was rewarded with an Academy Award nomination for best actor of 1984.

His acting partner, Karen Allen, had a less flashy but equally difficult role to tackle in *Starman*. She was playing a tragic woman who had lost her husband in an accident. At times suicidal and depressed, Allen's character,

Jenny Hayden, was forced to undergo a transformation in the film. She was caretaker, lover, teacher and example to Bridges's Starman. Predictably, the talented actress was remarkable in the role.

According to Allen, John Carpenter understood that it was the relationship of the two central characters who would make *Starman* a special viewing experience, and so he provided a very supportive, very open atmosphere for the performers:

> Carpenter is surprisingly sensitive. He's very open-minded, very willing to listen to ideas. He uses an interesting combination of skills to direct because he clearly knows what he wants, using storyboards and all, yet he's very open to actors. He wants the actors to play a strong role in making the movie, having them help shape their own characters.[34]

What emerged from *Starman* when it opened on December 14, 1984, was pure movie magic: a beautiful science fiction romance filled with heartfelt emotion, real personalities, natural humor, and even joy. John Carpenter had never made a more "human" film, and again the critics and audiences responded with enthusiasm, making *Starman* a full-fledged hit. More importantly, many critics called *Starman* the best science fiction film of the year — no mean feat in a year crowded with *2010: The Year We Make Contact*, David Lynch's *Dune*, and *Star Trek III: The Search for Spock*. However, many diehard fans of John Carpenter were disappointed that he had veered so far from horror territory and into what some fans term his "Spielberg" phase.

Starman was so successful that it spawned a one-season ABC TV series starring Robert Hays in 1986. Like the film before it, the television series ended up with a substantial cult following that remained enthusiastic long after the series was canceled. Still, the television series was a distortion and distillation of the film's touching love story. With

Carpenter (right) chats with Jeff Bridges and Karen Allen during the making of *Starman* (1984).

Starman and son scouring the country in search of the conveniently missing Jenny Hayden (Erin Gray), the television series was more *The Fugitive* than genre-blending Christ parable. The series lasted for 22 episodes before fading to an afterlife on the Sci-Fi Channel.

From *Starman*, John Carpenter also learned a valuable lesson about himself and his image with audiences. No longer needing to second-guess himself and his perceptions, he went back on the publicity circuit and explained what he had discovered:

> Columbia conducted a market survey of what my name means to an audience. The survey showed that it doesn't mean *horror* movie. The audience thought it means *good* movie, which delighted me. So there was *never* any thought of not doing interviews because I wanted to distance myself

from the film.... Columbia *wants* me to talk — so here I am.[35]

The icing on the cake for John Carpenter after *Starman* was that he was named by *Starlog* magazine as one of the most important people in science fiction. He shared that title with such luminaries as Walt Disney, Stanley Kubrick, Gene Roddenberry, Orson Welles, Robert Wise, Roger Corman, Jim Henson, Irwin Allen, William Cameron Menzies, George Pal, Rod Serling, and Steven Spielberg. Not bad company at all.

Time for an Experiment

Also in 1984, another project with origins in John Carpenter's imagination came to fruition. A screenplay entitled *The Philadelphia Experiment*, originally designed to be directed by Carpenter for Avco-Embassy after *Escape from New York* in 1981, was developed by New World Pictures into a low-budget film. Carpenter had abandoned the project after experiencing trouble in engineering a believable climax after an intense first act build-up. His story concerned a naval experiment in 1943 that went disastrously wrong, and involved that old sci-fi convention, time travel. After *The Final Countdown* (1980) starring Kirk Douglas, Katharine Ross and Martin Sheen trod very much the same territory as his screenplay, Carpenter was no longer interested in directing the story. Still, *The Philadelphia Experiment* caught the eyes of producers Joel B. Michaels and Douglas Curtis, and they assigned Michael Janover to take a shot at the script. The screenplay was then rewritten by William Gray, with the time travel aspects of the tale becoming more prominent.

John Carpenter was given story and executive producer credit and was paid a substantial amount of cash to serve as the film's consultant, a position in which he made comments on the script. Stewart Raffill (*The Ice Pirates* [1983]) directed the $9 million film, which starred Michael Pare (*The Greatest American Hero* [1980–83], *Streets of Fire* [1984], *Village of the Damned* [1995], *Bad Moon* [1996]) and Nancy Allen (*Carrie*, *Dressed to Kill*, *RoboCop*). The film was lensed for roughly 50 days in locations as varied as Charleston, South Carolina; Wendover, Utah; and Southern California.

Although John Carpenter did not direct the film himself, *The Philadelphia Experiment* proved that his name on the credits was as good as money in the bank. *The Philadelphia Experiment* was a hit, and it spawned a sequel nine years later, *The Philadelphia Experiment II*, starring Brad Johnson.

Black Moon Rising: *From the Mind of John Carpenter...*

So profitable was *The Philadelphia Experiment* for New World Pictures and produc-

ers Joel B. Michaels and Douglas Curtis that the studio and producers decided to produce another movie based on one of Carpenter's abandoned screenplays. In this case, they struck on his 1975 screenplay for *Black Moon Rising*, an action teleplay involving a high tech car thief ring. Again, Carpenter received screen credit as executive producer and a "story by" credit for his participation — which amounted to reading the script and giving his comments about it.

Harley Cokliss (*Warlords of the 21st Century* [1981]) was given the nod as director of *Black Moon Rising*, and the picture was provided a budget of $3 million. Tommy Lee Jones, who had starred in another Carpenter script (*Eyes of Laura Mars*) back in 1978, played the protagonist, Quint, and he was joined by villain Robert Vaughn (*Battle Beyond the Stars* [1980], *Superman III* [1983]), and leading lady Linda Hamilton (*The Terminator* [1984], *King Kong Lives* [1986], *Terminator 2* [1991], *Dante's Peak* [1997]). Also aboard was *Starman* co-star Richard Jaeckel. Handling the dangerous special effects on the long night shot for this nonunion job were Cinemotion Pictures and Max Anderson (*The Philadelphia Experiment*, *The Ice Pirates*, *Altered States* [1980]).

A large percentage of *Black Moon Rising*'s action revolved around a specially designed car which could travel faster than 300 miles an hour and ran on hydrogen, so critics were quick to compare the completed film to the Glen Larson *Knight Rider* television series. When it premiered in January of 1985, *Black Moon Rising* was advertised far and wide as being "from the mind of John Carpenter." Despite the fact that the film was well-acted and nicely paced, it did not make much of an impact at the box office. Carpenter was nonplussed by the whole experience because the final product, though sold on *his* name, had very little to do with his original script.

Otherwise, 1985 was a rather unproductive year for John Carpenter in a professional sense. He still wanted to see his western *El Diablo* made, and Dino De Laurentiis almost produced it with star Kurt Russell in the saddle. When that deal fell apart, Carpenter worked for a time with Richard Zanuck and Dave Brown on an adaptation of Eric Van Lustbader's novel *The Ninja*. Carpenter left that project and then shifted to an assignment he had long been excited about: an adaptation of *The Stars, My Destination* by Alfred Bester. After a time, Carpenter left that project as well, unhappy with Lorenzo Semple's screenplay and producer Jack Schwartzman's intention to do a big science fiction movie on the cheap. Carpenter was also offered the opportunity to direct *Tai-Pan*, an adaptation of the novel by James Clavell, but he felt that the work would have entailed too much time outside of the United States. For a time, he also considered doing *Chickenhawk*, a story about American helicopter pilots in the Vietnam War.

For a brief period, John Carpenter was slated to direct a Dan Aykroyd comedy vehicle entitled *Armed and Dangerous*, but Carpenter and Aykroyd each departed the project separately, leaving the film to star Eugene Levy and director Mark Lester. Along with horror veterans Tobe Hooper and Wes Craven, John Carpenter was also invited to direct episodes of the 1985 revival of the Rod Serling television series *The Twilight Zone*, but John Carpenter was not a fan of short stories, and he declined the offer. He did briefly consider, however, a television movie sequel to *The Fog* to be written by Dennis Etchison. This interesting-sounding effort, like so many others, failed to materialize.

Undoubtedly, the best thing that came out of the year was a new addition to the Carpenter clan: John Cody Carpenter, son of John Carpenter and actress Adrienne Barbeau.

Big Trouble *for John Carpenter*

Having tackled outer space (*Dark Star*), suspense (*Halloween*), action (*Escape from New York*), Stephen King (*Christine*) and even romance (*Starman*), John Carpenter turned his attention to another beloved genre in 1986: the kung fu movie! Carpenter had been a fan of martial arts films since he saw *Enter the Dragon* in 1973, and so was very excited when an opportunity arose to make his own, big-budget karate/action/magic/kung-fu adventure. He reviewed a number of Chinese films to prepare himself for the task of directing a kinetic, rollicking high-voltage motion picture:

> These are Chinese films, and you must get into that genre. They are done on a different level than our movies, and they are *stunning*. But you must respect that difference to fully appreciate them. One picture … *The Warrior from Mystic Mountain*, really knocked me out. It's basically the Chinese *Star Wars*. It's *nuts*.[36]

The project that gave Carpenter the opportunity to realize his dream of making a martial arts film was *Big Trouble in Little China*, from a script by Gary Goldman and David Weinstein. In a virtual replay of the events surrounding *Starman*, however, it was not the original Goldman-Weinstein Old West era adventure that Carpenter eventually shot, but instead a contemporary rewrite by scribe W.D. Richter (*The Adventures of Buckaroo Banzai Across the 8th Dimension* [1984]), penned in ten weeks. Richter, a classmate of Carpenter's at U.S.C., wrote so compelling a script that Carpenter turned down the opportunity to direct the similarly themed Eddie Murphy Asian adventure, *The Golden Child*, even though that film, with celebrity Murphy at its center, was a guaranteed blockbuster.

Instead, John Carpenter relied on his own solid repertory star, Kurt Russell, to carry the film. Where Russell had portrayed a scowling, Clint Eastwood style of character named Snake Plissken in *Escape from New York*, he shifted to a sly, swaggering imitation of John Wayne as Jack Burton throughout *Big Trouble in Little China*. This was more perfect a role than either John Carpenter or Kurt Russell may have realized at that time because in many senses Russell had *always* been John Wayne to John Carpenter's Hawks.

Also in the cast were Victor Wong (*Prince of Darkness* [1987], *Tremors* [1989]) and Dennis Dun (*The Year of the Dragon* [1985], *Prince of Darkness* [1987]), both of whom would return in later Carpenter pictures. The immortal villain, Lo-Pan, was played by *Blade Runner*'s James Hong, and the beautiful Gracie Law was played by genre favorite Kim Cattrall (*Star Trek VI: The Undiscovered Country* [1991], *Split Second* [1991]).

Big Trouble in Little China was a big film, like *Starman*, and its budget has been variously reported at $19, 20, 23 and 25 million, with $2 million alone devoted to special effects. After ten weeks of preproduction in which art director John Lloyd designed amazing, labyrinthine sets for the film's subterranean world, production began in October of 1985. The film was shot for 20th Century–Fox over a 15 week period, and it involved huge stunts and fights, the likes of which had not been seen before in American film. One kung fu fight in a back alley involved more than 60 players, and martial arts experts from Hong Kong, including Jim Lau, Kenny Endoso and James Lew, were flown to the set to supervise and comment on the intense action.

With Boss Films, managed by Richard Edlund (*Back to the Future* [1985], *Romancing the Stone* [1984]), handling the effects, Larry J. Franco producing, Carpenter and Howarth composing the musical score, and Dean Cundey back as director of photography, *Big Trouble in Little China* should have been a smash hit and a Carpenter renaissance. But, like *The Thing*, the film was not at all well received when it premiered on July 2, 1986. In fact, the big-budget film bombed, falling to such heavyweight competition as James Cameron's *Aliens* and David Cronenberg's *The Fly*, as well as Tobe Hooper's *Invaders from Mars*, Anthony Perkins' *Psycho III*, Prince's *Under the Cherry Moon*, Disney's *The Great Mouse Detective*, and Jim Henson's

Labyrinth. Adding insult to injury, the critics did not like *Big Trouble in Little China* much either, with some even calling it a rip-off of Steven Spielberg's *Raiders of the Lost Ark*.

John Carpenter was more than disappointed by the failure of his electric kung-fu movie; he was crestfallen. *Big Trouble in Little China*, though not a masterpiece like *The Thing*, was a solid piece of work. The action was terrific, the kung fu fights were awe-inspiring, and the film's steamroller pace obliterated any small inconsistencies. Even better, Kurt Russell and Kim Cattrall brought real charm to their unusual roles, and the film was brimming with tongue-in-cheek humor. Add great special effects to that mix, and *Big Trouble* should have clicked. But it did not, partially because of the lackluster ad campaign, which asked the audience the cryptic question "Who is Jack Burton?" Apparently, finding out the answer was not an important thing for most audiences, and viewers stayed away.

His heart broken after spending almost six years behind the front lines of the Hollywood studio system pouring his soul into genre adventures of great distinction, John Carpenter retreated. Exhausted and burned out, he took a vacation and reconsidered his life and career goals. He had once stated (in *A Biographical Dictionary of Film* by David Thomson) that he felt he would have been happiest in the Hollywood studio system of the '40s and '50s, making big-budget entertainments designed to appeal to a large audience. Now, Carpenter had been at the short end of that very studio system, a victim of marketing problems, executive second-guessing, and other Hollywood politics. He had seen his films, and himself, attacked by critics from all sides, and a revision of his dreams was clearly in order.

Upon introspection, Carpenter realized that the best experiences of his life had been those times in which he had been *outside* the studio system, making small films with complete autonomy. He remembered the fun, and the creative control, of *Assault on Precinct 13* and *Halloween*. Making a bold decision, Carpenter stepped back from Hollywood and returned to the independent arena.

Years later, in the 1990s, Carpenter was able to reflect on his unpleasant experiences inside the Hollywood studio system with a different perspective, and eventually he even found some good amidst all the bad:

> I got to do my romantic comedy with *Starman*. And I got to do my kung-fu movie with *Big Trouble in Little China*. I feel really lucky that, in the context of the horror-fantasy-sci-fi genre, I've gotten to do so many things. But when I really look at it deeply, I *love* those kind of movies.[37]

But in 1987, Carpenter had not yet found that peaceful state of mind or realization. On the contrary, he was worn out, angry, and tired of all the hassle that was required to practice his craft. That is, until a new opportunity sparked his imagination.

Hollywood's Prince of Darkness Signs a New Deal

Stung by his experiences with *The Thing*, *Christine*, *Starman* and *Big Trouble in Little China*, as well as the marketing of his name on *The Philadelphia Experiment* and *Black Moon Rising*, John Carpenter in early 1987 signed a four-film package deal with Alive Films, the small company that had produced *Kiss of the Spider Woman* (1985) starring William Hurt and Raul Julia as well as *The Whales of August* (1986). Alive Film's two executive gurus, Andre Blay and Shep Gordon, wanted John Carpenter to make films for them, and Carpenter appreciated the freedom they were willing to extend to him. As he enthusiastically reported to interviewer Steve Swires:

> They don't even get to read the scripts before approving the deals. I only submit basic concepts to them, in a short paragraph. For *Prince of Darkness* ... it was something like: "The Devil is buried under a Los Angeles church, and graduate science students come to fight him." If they approve the concept, then I deliver them a print. I can't ask for more than that.[38]

Because autonomy was something important to Carpenter (as it was to his hero, Howard Hawks), the Alive Films deal was perfect.

The first movie John Carpenter made under the deal was another homage, like *Assault on Precinct 13*, but this one was dedicated not to Hawks, but to another hero, Nigel Kneale. As a child, Carpenter had been engaged by Kneale's ability in the *Quatermass* film trilogy (*The Creeping Unknown* [1956], *Enemy from Space* [1957], *Five Million Years to Earth* [1968]) to so adeptly mix science fiction, science fact, physics, the supernatural, and of course, horror. Though the same trick had been attempted unsuccessfully with 1982's *Halloween III: Season of the Witch*, Carpenter nonetheless engineered a script under the pseudonym Martin Quatermass that sought to carry on the tradition of the Quatermass films and Kneale's expressive writing. Early on, it was even set in the '50s to cement the association, but that conceit had to be abandoned when Carpenter realized he could spend the film's entire $3 million budget just on renting vintage 1950s era automobiles.[39]

Instead, Carpenter formulated *Prince of Darkness*, a contemporary story about graduate students in physics who encounter an evil life-form, the Anti-God, living under an abandoned church in run-down 1980s Los Angeles. The screenplay featured lengthy discussions about particles (and anti-particles), differential equations, and even tachyon transmissions beamed backwards in time from the future. With all of these details, *Prince of Darkness* emerged as Carpenter's most layered screenplay, and it was a critical step in his transition from visceral horror (*Halloween*) to a more intellectual, chilling horror (*In the Mouth of Madness*).

Prince of Darkness was not just a complex film loaded with science and Quatermass riffs, but also an AIDS allegory. For the devil in this case, the *Prince of Darkness* of the title, was not a humanoid creature with cloven hoof and horned head, but rather a vat of pre-biotic liquid evolving into intelligent life out of chaos. It could transmit itself by "splashing" (ejaculating?) its essence into the faces and mouths of the endangered graduate students. They in turn, spread the "devil disease" through their bodily fluids and emissions. On top of that, *Prince of Darkness* also recalled *Assault on Precinct 13* because it was, at one level anyway, a siege film about people trapped in an abandoned locale by minions of evil.

Far from the universe of big Hollywood budgets and star salaries, John Carpenter went back to relying on his tried-and-true repertory company. Donald Pleasence was back in *Prince of Darkness*, this time playing a Catholic priest confronting the Anti-God. He was thrilled to work with his old friend again, and he enthused about the director to *Fangoria* magazine:

> John Carpenter is the best director I've ever worked with. One of the main reasons is his bravery.... Casting against type is what made *Prince of Darkness* such a lovely bit of business for me. People were ... expecting me to be bad, and I ended up representing all the good in the universe.[40]

Also back from *Big Trouble in Little China* were Victor Wong and Dennis Dun. Rounding out the cast were *Simon & Simon's* Jameson Parker, Lisa Blount, and a new addition to the repertory company, Peter Jason. (Jason would go on to appear in Carpenter's *They Live* [1988], *Village of the Damned* [1995] and *Escape From L.A.*) Also cast in *Prince of Darkness* as a psychotic street person was rock icon Alice Cooper.

After seven weeks of pre-production preparations, *Prince of Darkness* began filming on May 18, 1987. Lensing stretched on for approximately 40 days, and the shoot, from all accounts, was a pleasant and untroubled one. With a Halloween release date planned, Carpenter and Alan Howarth composed the musical score, another pulse-pounding classic, and Steve Mirkovich (*I Know What You Did Last Summer* [1987]) edited the picture. There seemed to be only one potential problem for this smooth-running production: When *Prince of Darkness* was completed, the MPAA nearly slapped it with an X-rating, but distributor Universal backed the picture and the MPAA softened its stance.

When *Prince of Darkness* premiered (with the ad line: "There is Evil. It is Real. He is Awakening"), it faced competition from *Night Flyers*, *Suspect*, and *The Sicilian*, but it was an immediate hit with the horror-knowledgeable. Nevertheless, despite the financial success of the low-budget production, *Prince of Darkness* was fodder for the critics, most of whom took the attitude that Carpenter should have evolved beyond horror at this point in his career. In addition, horror was not taken very seriously as a genre in the mid–'80s because of the proliferation of genre films. Variations on *Hellraiser*, *Nightmare on Elm Street*, *Friday the 13th* and *Child's Play* seemed to be coming out every week, and *Prince of Darkness* was lost in the shuffle.

Today, feelings are very much mixed about *Prince of Darkness*. Some people find it to be a clever, intellectual horror film that asks the questions of existence, whereas others see it as a disturbing turning point, the beginning of John Carpenter's long slide into the valley of mediocrity.

In the continuum of John Carpenter films, *Prince of Darkness* lacks the spare, lean qualities of *Halloween*, the lyrical nature of *The Fog*, the brass balls of *Assault on Precinct*, the oddball humor of *Dark Star*, the sentimentality of *Starman*, and the relentless paranoia of *The Thing*. So perhaps it really is one of the director's lesser films, but that does not at mean it is not a good film in its own right. At the most basic level, it is the film Carpenter wanted to make at that juncture in his career, and it fits in with his career pattern. He had already done variations on favorites Hawks, Hitchcock and Capra, so here he did Kneale. Additionally, the film made some intriguing comments about the place of man in a world dominated by science.

Not long after *Prince of Darkness,* Carpenter once again found himself battling the press, who wanted to pigeonhole him as a horrormeister. He bristled at the suggestion that his image was related only to horror:

> What's my image? Was *Elvis,* the 3-hour TV film, a grisly and gory film?... I'm just trying to do good stories. You should service your story. If your story is about fear, then, certainly, you should draw from real fears. If your story is about myth, you connect the myth to the human condition.[41]

Unfortunately, most critics continued to see John Carpenter as horror's main man, and they lamented the fact that he was not doing more "respectable" films, when in fact the talented director was making exactly the kind of film he loved and wanted to make. At this juncture, Carpenter also revealed that he had turned down two films he had no desire to be involved with: blockbusters *Top Gun* and *Fatal Attraction.* Those films may have been "respectable" to Hollywood, but Carpenter was not interested.

They Live, *Carpenter Thrives*

From *Dark Star* forward, John Carpenter has remained a symbol of subversive film-making. He espoused a hatred of authority in *Dark Star* (where there was no real captain on the ship), in *Halloween* (where the police and medical community were unable to stop the terror of Michael Myers), in *The Fog* (where a town had developed its assets by murdering lepers), in *Escape from New York* (where the hero was a criminal, and society was fascist), and so forth.

In 1988, John Carpenter delivered his most ambitious and well-articulated jab at authority by writing and directing the science fiction satire *They Live* as his second picture in the Alive Films deal. *They Live* suggested that the Reagan Revolution and Yuppie movement of the 1980s were actually the result of an invasion by greedy, skeletal aliens. For Carpenter, the story was designed to be a wake-up call to middle-class America, which he felt had become complacent and avaricious in the capitalist free-for-all of the Reagan presidency. To wit:

> I'm disgusted by what we've become in America. I truly believe there is *brain death* in this country.... *Everything* we see is designed to *sell* us something. My awareness became so acute ... that I couldn't even watch MTV. It's *all* about wanting us to *buy* something. The *only* thing they want to do is take our *money.*[42]

John Carpenter was not alone in his desire to expose the greed and conspicuous consumption of Ronald Reagan's era. Fellow director Wes Craven had also seen the same disturbing signs, and responded with productions such as *Invitation to Hell* (1984), which suggested that Yuppies had sold their souls to the Devil, and *People Under the Stairs* (1991), a modern urban fairy tale about the exploitation of black Americans at the hands of demented white Republicans. So while most of America was relishing in Yuppie fantasies like *The Secret of My Success* and *Wall Street,* and critics were dismissing horror films as too violent and disturbing for the children of our culture, it took two lowly horror movie directors to make socially relevant motion pictures. Those who believed Carpenter should have moved on to more "respectable" material by 1988 should also have been pleased at the awakening social conscience at play in *They Live*—but of course, they did not see it that way.

They Live was John Carpenter's battle cry, and his concentrated effort to expose what he felt was one of the United States' greatest weaknesses: its overwhelming greed and the "winner" mentality.

> I wanted to make some political statements, one of the biggest being that everybody is proud to be an American as long as they can make money at it. For the longest time, I wasn't quite sure how to tell the story. One way was to make it scary, but this element of humor always kept creeping into it.[43]

That element of humor is what made *They Live* entertaining, rather than merely a diatribe about the state of the country.

They Live was based on a short story by Ray Faraday Nelson entitled *8 O'Clock in the Morning*, first published in the 1960s in *The Magazine of Fantasy and Science Fiction*. The story concerned a man who woke up one day and discovered that aliens had infiltrated the human race. Carpenter tackled the adaptation of the story, adding much social commentary, under the pseudonym Frank Armitage (a character in H.P. Lovecraft's *The Dunwich Horror*.) Budgeted at $3 million, like *Prince of Darkness*, the film was shot for eight weeks in downtown L.A. in March and April of 1988. One of the central issues in the film was the ever-growing class of poor Americans, and the plight of the homeless. Carpenter's hero was even named "Nada," meaning "nothing." This was appropriate since Nada was unemployed, and therefore worthless in the eyes of America's middle class.

They Live starred wrestler "Rowdy" Roddy Piper as Nada. Piper was a man who had absorbed 17 years' worth of bruises as a professional wrestler, and even a few bruises as an actor, showing up in lowbrow fare like *Hell Comes to Frogtown* (1988). Carpenter had met Nada at Wrestlemania III, and realized that he was perfect for his new film. It was a good gamble: Piper's performance in *They Live* came across as sincere and believable, and he projected a sort of realistic, mellow charisma that made *They Live* something out of the ordinary. He was supported in his dramatic efforts by Keith David of *The Thing* and the beautiful Meg Foster (*Masters of the Universe* [1987], *Leviathan* [1989]).

Director of photography Gary Kibbe captured the underside of Los Angeles in painstaking detail, and Jim Danforth, a friend from *Dark Star*, contributed a dozen effects cuts to *They Live*, including matte paintings of the alien space gate and miniature stop-motion of an alien surveillance satellite.

Distributed by Universal (again like *Prince of Darkness*), *They Live* premiered shortly before Election Day 1988, and the timing was perfect. Since Carpenter's film was political in nature, it benefited from the political atmosphere. Was George Bush an alien? Was Dan Quayle? As a result of its humor and good timing, *They Live* was a box office hit.

Critics were mixed about *They Live*, however. Some liked its cheeky political touches and humor, but others thought that Carpenter really miscalculated with his action centerpiece: a seven-and-a-half minute brawl between Keith David and Roddy Piper. This bloody brawl went on for so long that it could easily have been described as *Wrestlemania IV*. Carpenter included it not only because of his love of wrestling, but because he hoped to outdo the extended fight sequence in *The Quiet Man*.

For those inclined to see its message, however, *They Live* seemed a great success. It had not only oodles of style (with some sequences lensed in black and white), but some very ironic humor too. When Piper donned the sunglasses that would show the alien-controlled world as it really was, he saw how advertising was converted into alien propaganda. On dollar bills was the legend "This Is Your God." On a billboard for a Caribbean vacation was an alien message "Marry and Reproduce." Even better, John Carpenter staged a sequence in which Siskel & Ebert clones were unmasked as aliens just as they were complaining that the horror movies of George Romero and John Carpenter were much too violent.

Underneath the humor, *They Live* also had a serious message about success, and about how often people have to sell out to achieve monetary and career success. For Carpenter, this was not just a political message, but a personal one as well. He could have directed big budget extravaganzas in Hollywood for the rest of his life, but he did not sell out. *Would not* sell out.

They Live was a reminder to everyone that John Carpenter had not lost his touch. The picture was fast-paced and alive — qualities some felt had been lacking in the slow and rather ponderous *Prince of Darkness*. If *They Live* did not represent a return to classic Carpenter territory, it at least represented an upswing after what many people considered to be a career slump in the mid–'80s. Though it was a financial success, *They Live* did not make as much money as another film John Carpenter had turned down the opportunity to direct, 1988's *Halloween IV: The Return of Michael Myers*.

John Carpenter's other news in 1988 was not so positive. In November of that year, while *They Live* was playing on theater screens around the country, he and wife Adrienne Barbeau divorced after nine years of marriage. Following this break-up, John Carpenter went through what amounted to a three year downtime. His Alive Films *Halloween* spot in 1989 was covered by friend Wes Craven's newest horror venture, *Shocker*, and John Carpenter found himself serving as the author of two television westerns. This was the era of the highly successful *Lonesome Dove* (1989), and every television network was looking for its own western to compete in the Nielsen ratings.

The long delayed *El Diablo* was finally made in 1990. It starred Anthony Edwards of *E.R.*, Louis Gossett Jr. (*Enemy Mine* [1985]), John Glover (*In the Mouth of Madness* [1994]) and *Star Trek: Voyager*'s Robert Beltran as El Diablo himself. Directed by Peter Markle, the television film was shot in Tucson, Arizona, and it aired on July 22, 1990.

The second western was *Blood River*, the project that John Carpenter had written expressly for the first screen teaming of "The Duke," John Wayne, and "The King," Elvis Presley. The television version starred *The Thing*'s Wilford Brimley, Carpenter's ex-wife, Adrienne Barbeau, and Rick Schroeder (*NYPD Blue*). Directed by Mel Damski, *Blood River* aired on CBS on March 17, 1991.

Other projects on Carpenter's plate in the early '90s included a long-hoped-for sequel to *Escape from New York*, titled tentatively *Escape from Los Angeles*; a science fiction adventure for Cher called *Pin Cushion*; a straight vampire flick called *Dracula in Europe*; and even a low-budget film for Larry Cohen called *So Help Me God*. Most interesting of all was the talk that John Carpenter would soon be helming a remake of *Creature from the Black Lagoon* with a script from idol Nigel Kneale. For a brief time, Carpenter also considered doing a sequel to *They Live*, subtitled *Hypnowar*. Again, all of these projects failed to materialize, though *Escape from L.A.* would finally be produced in 1996.

In 1990, John Carpenter remarried, this time to his frequent script supervisor, Sandy King.

Memoirs of an Invisible Film

Confident over the success of his independent pictures *Prince of Darkness* and *They Live*, John Carpenter felt prepared to tackle a major studio project again in April of 1990. The film in question was *Memoirs of an Invisible Man*, an adaptation of the novel by Harry F. Saint. As was the case with *Starman* and *Big Trouble in Little China*, John Carpenter found himself in the middle of a long revision process, shepherding William Goldman's script (originally intended for director Ivan Reitman) into new form courtesy of writers Robert Collector and Dana Wilson. Adding pressure to the situation, *Memoirs of an Invisible Man* was to be a high-profile, expensive film budgeted at $40 million. And star Chevy Chase had an agenda. He was intent on proving that he could be a serious leading

man after a string of daffy slapstick comedies. More directly, Chase had to prove that
his Hollywood star had not lost its luster
after his appearance in Dan Aykroyd's disastrous directorial debut, *Nothing but Trouble* (1991).

As usual, John Carpenter was well aware
of the complicated minefield he needed to
navigate to create a film that would not only
satisfy Carpenter and Chase fans, but also be
a hit. In the quotation below, he voiced some
of his concerns about being in the thick of
Hollywood politics again:

> There's always some pressure when
> you're working for a major studio....
> Chevy wants to show that he can be a
> serious actor, and I'm trying to get the
> most out of him in what is a very com-
> plicated shoot.... Whether or not this
> film is going to do anything different
> for Chevy's or my career is up in the
> air.[44]

It was Chase who had hand-selected the
Harry F. Saint novel for adaptation, and he
was one of the two primary producers on
Memoirs of an Invisible Man. The project
represented Chase's ambitious and sincere
attempt to transcribe a novel he loved into
film, while simultaneously transforming
himself into a serious leading man capable
of some acting range. Unfortunately, Carpenter's view of the film clashed somewhat
with Chase's. He did not see the story as
deadly serious and "dark," but rather as a light
romantic comedy — the exact thing Chase
hoped so desperately to avoid. In a moment
of candid frustration, Chase explained the
problems surrounding *Memoirs of an Invisible Man*:

> Everybody wants this movie to fit into
> some kind of little niche. The studio
> wants it, the press wants it.... With
> John Carpenter directing, I think that
> already suggests this is something that
> people haven't seen me in. There's high
> tension, adventure, romance and a lit-
> tle bit of comedy as well. The closest

thing ... might have been *Deal of the
Century*, but even that doesn't come
close to this film's kind of suspense.[45]

So just as Chase was eager to prove himself solemn, sturdy and serious, John Carpenter was working to opposite ends, hoping to showcase his lighter side. *Memoirs of
an Invisible Man* was his version of *North by
Northwest*, a genre action adventure with
dangerous stunts, romance, and even espion-
age.

Memoirs also boasted a great deal of talent besides Carpenter and Chase, so the differing perceptions of the film could easily be
glossed over during the shoot. Lawrence G.
Paull constructed a fabulous half-invisible
full scale building for an early set-piece, and
George Lucas's ILM outdid itself with the
amazing "invisible" special effects. Among
the jaw-dropping wonders: An invisible man
smoking, throwing up his half-digested food,
and even chewing gum and blowing a bubble. From a visual standpoint the resultant
film, shot at Warner Bros. Studios in Bur-
bank, L.A., and San Francisco, was virtually
flawless. In addition to all these strengths,
Shirley Walker wrote a Hitchcock-esque musical score, and Australian Sam Neill (*Juras-
sic Park* [1993], *In the Mouth of Madness*)
made for a terrific villain reminiscent of
James Mason.

Memoirs of an Invisible Man was originally scheduled to premiere December 13,
1991, the same day as Bruce Willis's action
adventure *The Last Boy Scout* and the franchise entry *Star Trek VI: The Undiscovered
Country*. Although John Carpenter's film had
generated high praise in preview screenings,
Warner Bros. inexplicably held the film back
and dumped it into release the following
February, a season when studios traditionally ditch films they do not expect to hit big.

Not surprisingly, *Memoirs of an Invisible
Man* bombed with audiences and received
mixed notices from the mainstream critical
community. Of all of John Carpenter's films,
it was the most anonymous and innocuous.

There was less of him in *Memoirs of an In-visible Man* than any John Carpenter film before or after it. The film was not *that* bad, however. It had good special effects, Chevy Chase was competent if not inspired, and the film was enjoyable in a middle-of-the-road kind of way. But something did not click. There was not quite enough humor, not quite enough suspense, and not quite enough fun. The final result was just ... average. Of course, in the forum of John Carpenter's career and track-record, "average" equaled "bad" for many of his long-time admirers. Because it is so lacking in his distinctive style, sans even his trademark music, *Memoirs of an Invisible Man* is maybe the most undistinguished entry in Carpenter's film roster, alongside the 1995 remake of *Village of the Damned*.

After *Memoirs of an Invisible Man* failed to generate much enthusiasm, Carpenter dissected the failure of the film:

> The advertising and publicity were promising you a romantic comedy thriller and our star Chevy Chase ... gave interviews saying it was the most serious film he'd ever made and that he needed to explore a very dark side of himself.... Chevy never really under-stood what we were doing. It was a very funny movie ... but I knew we were in trouble when *Memoirs* ... didn't open as big as *They Live*, which was a three million dollar film. [46]

Whatever the reasons for the stillbirth of *Memoirs of an Invisible Man*, Carpenter was saddled with another studio bomb after the failure of another big budget picture, *Big Trouble in Little China*. As he had done before, he responded to failure by retreating and switching gears. This time, he fled to television.

Zipping Up Body Bags

In 1993, Sandy King and Dan Angel pro-duced a horror anthology for Showtime.

Written by Dan Angel and Billy Brown (*The X-Files*: "All Souls") *Body Bags* was also a perfect vehicle for that longtime fan of E.C. Comics, John Carpenter. With Carpenter aboard as executive producer, the special program became known as *John Carpenter Presents Body Bags*. Though Carpenter had traditionally scorned television, even refer-ring to it as "talking furniture," he took on the project when he found that he once again would be able to work autonomously.

The made-for-television movie was in-tended as a back door pilot for an ongoing series like *Tales from the Crypt*. There would be three segments, and Carpenter hired fel-low horror director Tobe Hooper (*The Texas Chainsaw Massacre* [1974], *Eaten Alive* [1976], *Poltergeist* [1982], *Lifeforce* [1985]) to direct the third and final installment of the anthol-ogy, "Eye," while he directed the first two: "The Gas Station" and "Hair."

The genre-intense cast of *Body Bags* in-cluded contemporary horror directors Sam Raimi (*The Evil Dead* [1983], *Darkman* [1990], *Army of Darkness* [1993], *The Quick and the Dead* [1995]), and Wes Craven (*Last House on the Left* [1972], *A Nightmare on Elm Street* [1984], *Scream* [1996]); Craven played a char-acter called "The Pasty-Faced Man." The act-ors populating the tribute to E.C. Comics were also familiar ones: George "Buck" Flower, Tom Arnold (*Freddy's Dead* [1991]), David Naughton (*An American Werewolf in Lon-don* [1981]), David Warner (*Time After Time* [1979], *Time Bandits* [1981], *Waxworks* [1988], *In The Mouth of Madness* [1994], *Titanic* [1997]), Stacy Keach (*Road Games* [1981], *The Class of 1999* [1990], *Escape from L.A.*), Deborah Harry (*Videodrome* [1983]), John Agar (*Revenge of the Creature* [1955], *The Mole People* [1956]), and Mark Hamill (*Star Wars* [1977], *Black Magic Woman* [1990], *Sleepwalkers* [1991], *The Guyver* [1991]) among them. Also present were Sheena Easton, Charles Napier and Twiggy!

Wes Craven and Sam Raimi appeared in "The Gas Station," the first story directed by John Carpenter. It told the tale of gas station night attendant, Alex Datcher, during her first night on the job. As the night progressed, she learned that a killer from nearby Haddonfield (nudge, nudge!) was on the loose. Stalked by the madman, Alex Datcher endured a night of terrifying thrills and scares.

"The Gas Station" is significant in John Carpenter's filmography because it quotes *verbatim* from sequences in *Halloween*. The shots wherein the killer rises from the dead and stalks a surprised, weeping Datcher are *exact* duplicates of the climactic scenes from the 1978 hit. This is significant not because John Carpenter was paying homage to himself, but because he was once again emulating his hero, Howard Hawks. Hawks remade *Rio Bravo* twice, first as *El Dorado* and then as *Rio Lobo*. Both times, he restaged identical sequences in an identical manner. As John Wayne once told writer Leigh Brackett: "It was good once ... it'll be good again." "The Gas Station" shows Carpenter revisiting material from early in his career instead of treading new territory.

The second story in *Body Bags* was more inventive, the very funny "Hair." Playing a man facing middle age and a receding hairline, Stacy Keach experiences horror as he receives a deadly hair transplant. "Hair" moved at a fast clip, and Keach is always a joy to watch, so this was a fun episode. It was followed by "Eye," a story of a deadly eye (instead of hair) transplant.

Throughout all three *Body Bags* stories, John Carpenter appeared as a Crypt Keeper–like host. Covered in ghoulish makeup by Rick Baker, Carpenter tiptoed playfully through a morgue, zipping and unzipping body bags, and delivering *very* bad puns.

Not surprisingly, Carpenter thoroughly enjoyed his experience on low-budget television, finding that it afforded him more freedom than the restrictive, cookie-cutter world of big studio filmmaking:

> The freedom in TV is wonderful. There's something really exhilarating about doing low-budget TV: you have to do it fast, and you have to sometimes be inventive.... It's fun, and I find myself having a good time doing it. The last movie I did was a really grueling experience.[47]

Despite the fun and *Monster Club* atmosphere of *Body Bags*, the pilot did not generate a series. However, the anthology did do quite well when released to videotape in 1994.

In the Movie of Madness

John Carpenter's 1994 film, *In the Mouth of Madness*, is also among the director's most controversial efforts. It is a film despised by many, misunderstood by more, and praised by only a select few. In this case the disdain may be understandable, for in a single viewing which is all the film got from most people — it's hard to perceive what a provocative and unusual work it is. But the film improves on each viewing, and it represents a very different, very intellectual kind of horror film for John Carpenter, one that is understood best after knowing the context of its creation.

In the Mouth of Madness was conceived and written by New Line Executive Michael DeLuca (*Freddy's Dead: The Final Nightmare* [1991]) in late 1987 as an homage to H.P. Lovecraft. Born Howard Phillip Lovecraft, this unusual author wrote various stories from 1917 to 1937 for publications such as *Weird Tales*. Lovecraft is considered a major inspiration for many filmmakers and writers working today, and his work is unusual and extremely frightening, often dealing with strange nether worlds and horrible creatures dwelling just outside human existence and perception. These creatures are always malevolent, and they are described in enigmatic language which escalates the horror of the situation. Lovecraft has been translated to film in adaptations such as *The Dunwich Horror* (1969) and *The Unnamable* (1988), but there is always the same nagging problem:

How does a director portray an unnamable, indescribable horror in clear, concise, *visual* terms? Although each of the above films featured Lovecraftian moments of horror, both also fell short of being full translations, of capturing the essence of Lovecraft's writing.

So DeLuca, inspired jointly by Lovecraft and horror films such as *Equinox* (1971), *Invasion of the Body Snatchers* and *Jacob's Ladder* (1990), showed his script to an interested Carpenter in 1988. Carpenter felt it needed more work and continued with his own projects. Mary Lambert, director of *Pet Sematary* (1989) and *Pet Sematary 2* (1992), was interested in directing *In the Mouth of Madness* for a time, but the project went nowhere.

When Carpenter saw the script again in 1993, DeLuca had improved it dramatically, and Carpenter had several interesting ideas to further develop the Lovecraftian material. One of the primary items of interest in the script was the central conceit, which had a best-selling author writing books that caused unbelievable violence and even insanity in readers. Carpenter saw this as a timely theme, as many conservative politicians were accusing horror film violence of causing people to kill. There was even one notorious case in England where a man who had seen *Halloween* renamed himself Michael Myers and went on a killing spree. As a result, *Halloween* was banned in Great Britain. John Carpenter believed that *In the Mouth of Madness* would allow him to address society's concerns about horror movies and deal frankly with issues on both sides of the Atlantic:

> I wanted to direct the movie because of the relevance it has to what's happening both in America and Britain. This ludicrous argument that television/video violence is the cause of society's ills. When I was growing up it was horror comics that said, "Religion seeks discipline through fear." That's what this current moral crusade is all about. It's called Dominion Theology. Government under God, and you only have

to look at Iran to see where this avenue of thought ends up.[48]

For his part, DeLuca saw other interesting horror tropes in *In the Mouth of Madness*. His goal was to create a film as influential and important to the genre as those that had inspired him to write it in the first place:

> I wanted the film to come off like *Body Snatchers*, with the books being like the pods and turning you into something else, as opposed to saying these people were screwed up beforehand. It's more of a paranoid thriller where you become part of a conspiracy.[49]

With a budget of $10 million — the same budget as *The Thing* in 1982 — Carpenter began production on *In the Mouth of Madness*, casting *Memoirs of an Invisible Man* alumnus Sam Neill as the film's central character, a cynic and misanthrope called John Trent. The talented Australian, who had proven himself a serious leading man in Jane Campion's *The Piano* (1994) as well as *Jurassic Park*, was supported ably by Jurgen Prochnow (*The Seventh Sign* [1988], *The English Patient* [1996]) as the Stephen King–like New England author, Sutter Cane, who orchestrated the return of the Lovecraftian "Old Ones." Present too were favorite genre veterans Charlton Heston (*Planet of the Apes* [1968], *The Omega Man* [1971], *Soylent Green* [1973], *Solar Crisis* [1992]), Bernie Casey (*Gargoyles* [1972], *Never Say Never Again* [1983], David Warner, John Glover, and the beautiful Julie Carmen (*Fright Night Part II* [1989]).

Like Laurie Zimmer in *Assault on Precinct 13* nearly 20 years earlier, Carmen found herself playing a prototypical Howard Hawks female: a centered character with a sharp wit and an innate toughness. Julie Carmen very much enjoyed her collaboration with director John Carpenter, finding that if anything, he was just as enthusiastic about *In the Mouth of Madness* as he had been about any other high-profile film in his 20 year career:

Carpenter is really challenging himself. That's what I like about him. He's the opposite of a hack. Even though he's done similar genre films before, this feels completely new to him and so he's struggling with the cutting edge at the end of the envelope.[50]

With KNB, the firm that handled Wes Craven's *Wes Craven's New Nightmare* (1994), *Vampire in Brooklyn* (1995), *Scream* (1996), and *Wes Craven Presents Wishmaster* (1997), in charge of special effects, and John Carpenter writing another of his patented horror film scores, *In the Mouth of Madness* looked and sounded terrific. Not unexpectedly, it was also packed with Lovecraftian touches such as a character named Mrs. Pickman, a town called Hobb's End, and a story which saw evil entities hoping to cross back into our earthly domain.

In the Mouth of Madness premiered at London's Phantasm 1994 Film Festival in July of 1994, but its American release was held back until January of 1995. Again, as in *Memoirs of an Invisible Man*, the results of this "bomb" release slot were devastating. Audiences ignored the picture, and critics were back to their merciless *The Thing* tenor. Before being pulled from theaters, *In the Mouth of Madness* earned only 8.9 million dollars, earning it 117th slot for the year 1995.[51] There was no doubt about it: The film was a bomb.

The reasons for *In the Mouth of Madness*'s failure are numerous. On first viewing, the film came off like a terrible, confused stew of mismatched elements. But in fact it was simply pitched too high and required total concentration, an attention to detail, and a background in Lovecraftian lore. In other words, *In the Mouth of Madness* required an educated and engaged audience. Like *The Thing*, it was a film ahead of its time, and people looking for just a "good" horror film with a few thrills and chills were put off by the intellectual nature of the tale, not to mention the self-reflexive aspects which domi-

nated the story-within-a-story-within-a-story.

Secondly, Carpenter had been beaten to the punch with *In the Mouth of Madness*. In 1994, *Wes Craven's New Nightmare* handled much of the same territory, self-reflexiveness, defense of horror movies and all. And that film, perhaps Wes Craven's best, felt more cohesive, more linear and more insightful than *In the Mouth of Madness,* also, perhaps, because viewers already had an entree to its world through familiar personalities Robert Englund, John Saxon and Heather Langenkamp. However, the average film-going audience did not like *New Nightmare* either, and they may have been reluctant to see a similarly themed film just months after *New Nightmare*'s release.

Last, but no less important, 1995 was a *terrible* year for horror. The genre had hit hard times. Audiences were tired of the same old tricks, and even though *In the Mouth of Madness* was original and different from most of the other pictures coming out, it also came from John Carpenter, whose track record in the late '80s had not been very good. In 1995, *In the Mouth of Madness* was not the only horror movie to tank at the box office. Sadly, John Carpenter's *Village of the Damned* failed as well, earning even less than *In the Mouth of Madness*. Other failures included Wes Craven's Eddie Murphy picture *Vampire in Brooklyn*, Spike Lee's *Tales from the Hood*, Dean Koontz's *Hideaway*, Clive Barker's *Lord of Illusions, Candyman II: Farewell to the Flesh*, Tobe Hooper's *The Mangler*, and even *Halloween VI: The Curse of Michael Myers*. Although big budget spectacles like *Seven, Species* and *Outbreak* made a great deal of money in 1995, they were high profile studio products pushed aggressively by big advertising budgets and featuring highly bankable stars like Brad Pitt and Dustin Hoffman. *In the Mouth of Madness* and the rest of the pack had fewer front-line draws and less financial support.

Many critics really missed the boat about *In the Mouth of Madness*. It is a film with many layers, and many creepy images (such as a dark-highway bicycle sequence which eloquently speaks the language of nightmares). It is audacious and clever, and it deserved better than the negative reception it received. Michael DeLuca, anticipating the reaction of the masses, apparently knew that *In the Mouth of Madness* was a gamble:

> It's like dropping acid for the first time. It just stretches your whole psyche. Some people will go for the ride, and some people will say, "What was that all about?"[52]

Though the description of *In the Mouth of Madness* as a mind-altering experience is quite accurate, so is the second part of that remark. Too many people were unable to determine what the film was about. Still, things could have been worse; Carpenter could have underestimated his audience instead of overestimating it. If *In the Mouth of Madness* failed, it failed only because its director chose the high road rather than the low road.

Remake of the Damned

At first blush, *Village of the Damned* would have seemed a perfect assignment for John Carpenter. The original film, assembled by director Wolf Rilla in 1960, had scared a generation of filmgoers, and its source material, the novel *The Midwich Cuckoos* by John Wyndham, has been elevated to the status of minor classic. Carpenter, who managed to reinterpret *The Thing* and create a remake that was as good as if not better than Howard Hawks's film, could easily do the same for *Village of the Damned*. Or so the argument went.

Although *Village of the Damned* had almost been remade once before in 1978 by *Invasion of the Body Snatchers* (1978) producer Robert H. Solo and writers Joyce and John Carrington (*Battle for the Planet of the Apes* [1974]), John Carpenter was the first to have a hand at re-directing the classic. Hopes ran high among genre aficionados when they learned the film would be remade. After all, the original film had been about the mores and manners surrounding the unexpected pregnancy of a group of women who were artificially inseminated by extra-terrestrials. Times had changed since 1960, but issues surrounding birth and infancy had proliferated and grown so much more complicated in the '90s. A new *Village of the Damned* for the '90s could deal with surrogate motherhood, the divisive issue of abortion, advances in prenatal care, homosexual couples having children, children's rights, or any number of related topics. The film could have been retitled *It Takes a Village . . . of the Damned*. Clearly, a 1990s version could speak to a new generation just as *Village of the Damned* spoke to the elder one.

Even better, John Carpenter hired a dream "B" movie cast to perform the rewrite of the original Sterling Silliphant script. The three great genre franchises of the 1970s and 1980s were represented with Christopher Reeve (*Superman* [1978]), Mark Hamill (*Star Wars*) and Kirstie Alley (*Star Trek II: The Wrath of Khan* [1982]). Other '80s sensations Linda Koslowski (*Crocodile Dundee* [1986]) and Michael Pare (*The Philadelphia Experiment*) also had substantial roles. Carpenter's repertory squad was represented too, with Peter Jason and George "Buck" Flower present once more. With such talents, a modest but serviceable budget, and modern special effects, *Village of the Damned* should have been a triumph.

Sadly, it was not. What emerged in 1995, scant weeks after *In the Mouth of Madness* was dumped in theaters, was an uninspired remake that seemed dashed together. No new moral issues were explored at even a surface level, and aspects of the film seemed botched. For instance, the film begins shortly before the alien pregnancies are instigated and extends well into the children's lifetime (at least age 7 or 8). Yet throughout the picture, none of the adult actors or actresses age visibly or even change hairstyles and fashions. Worse, the striking image of gray-suited children in white wigs seems silly in the 1990s. The one new touch involved the addition of a "sympathetic" alien child, a character not seen in the original. This character, though interesting, pretty much ruined the "hive mind" impact of the other children. The aliens could not be hated by the audience (like the children in the original film) because it was obvious that they *did* have the capacity to feel human emotions if nurtured properly.

Though Carpenter did stage some terrific effects and action sequences in *Village of the Damned*, the remake of the classic film is only a shadow of the original, and an uninspired piece of work — especially for a director of Carpenter's abilities. His style and his wit are nowhere in evidence in *Village of the Damned*. When the film premiered in January 1995 against *Dolores Claiborne*, *Bad Boys*, *Kiss of Death*, *While You Were Sleeping* and *Tommy Boy*, it received bad notices and disappeared even more quickly than *In the Mouth of Madness*, earning a paltry 8.6 million dollars by the end of the year. It also won the Razzie Award of 1995 for the Worst Remake of the Year.[53]

Time to Escape

Those watching John Carpenter's career in 1996 were very worried. The director who had won the hearts of science fiction critics with *Dark Star* and *Starman*, earned accolades for his stylish *Assault on Precinct 13* and terrifying *Halloween*, inspired cult fandom with *Big Trouble in Little China* and *Starman*, and won grudging respect for his underappreciated but brilliant remake of *The Thing* seemed to be in a slump. Looking back, many were not satisfied with the ponderous nature of *Prince of Darkness*, the wrestling interlude at the center of *They Live*, the mediocrity of *Memoirs of an Invisible Man*, and the per-

ceived low quality of his two 1995 pictures, *In the Mouth of Madness* and *Village of the Damned*.

In 1996, Carpenter returned to the big leagues, but he also played it safe. His project of choice was the long-talked about sequel to his 1981 classic, *Escape from New York*. With Kurt Russell (now 45 years old) and Debra Hill in tow, Carpenter finally prepared *Escape from L.A.* The conceit of the new film, co-written by the *Escape from New York* trio, was that this time America would be the prison, and the actual prison itself, L.A. island, would be a place of freedom. As Debra Hill explained:

> The United States of America has become a sort of right-wing Christian fundamentalist country. What they're doing in order to clean it up and keep it right wing and keep people from exercising free speech, free thought and having any sexual freedom and all that kind of stuff, is they deport anyone they deem to be bad. And Los Angeles, the island, is where they deport them to.[54]

This premise was clearly a return to the politically and socially conscious John Carpenter of *They Live*. Decrying the conservative "Contract with America" that was sweeping the United States ever further to the radical religious right, Carpenter put together not a legitimate action follow-up to *Escape from New York*, but a rollicking satire of 1990s mores and politics. In L.A., Snake Plissken encounters not just old-fashioned despots and villains, but a beautiful, good woman who was banished because she was Muslim (instead of Christian). This character, played by Valeria Golina, reflected Pat Buchanan's 1992 Republican Convention speech, where he incited Christians to win back "their" culture in America. Carpenter's America in *Escape from L.A.* was also a place where political correctness was out of control. Not only was wearing furs illegal, but so was eating red meat.

With a budget of $50 million, Carpenter's biggest yet, *Escape from L.A.* began principal production in late 1995. The shoot went on for a grueling 70 nights. Featured in the film were not only Kurt Russell but Carpenter repertory players Stacy Keach and Peter Jason. Playing the president "for life" of the United States was Cliff Robertson (Academy Award winner for *Charly* [1968]), and appearing as his daughter was the talented young actress A.J. Langer (*The People Under the Stairs* [1991], *My So-Called Life* [1995], *Brooklyn South* [1997]). Noted character actors Steve Buscemi (*Desperado* [1995], *Con Air* [1997]), Bruce Campbell (*The Evil Dead* [1983], *Army of Darkness* [1993]), Pam Grier (*Jackie Brown* [1997]) and Peter Fonda (*Futureworld* [1976], *Ulee's Gold* [1997]) also had extended co-medic cameos.

John Carpenter, Kurt Russell and Debra Hill also cut a mean deal with Paramount Studios to do this sequel to their popular first *Escape*. Russell earned $10 million, Carpenter five, and Hill two. Additionally, the trio was guaranteed 20 percent of the profits.[55]

Escape from L.A. premiered in August of 1996 and received mixed reviews. Roger Ebert called it a better film than the big movie of that summer, *Independence Day*. Other critics were not so kind, especially about the cartoonish CGI special effects that were featured in the film. Diehard Carpenter *Escape* fans were ambivalent about the picture too. It was funny all right, but it was not at all the straight sequel they had expected and desired. Essentially, it was a remake of *Escape from New York*, but with tongue planted firmly in cheek. Of course, the decision to do a remake (which duplicated exactly the story details of the original film) was made because Paramount felt that many people did not remember the original 1981 film, especially young ticket-buyers. Therefore, John Carpenter had to reintroduce Snake and his world to the kiddies while still picking up the older *Escape* crowd with the film's satirical jabs.

In remaking *Escape from New York*, Car-penter again fell into the pattern of his film-land hero Howard Hawks, who repeated incidents from film to film and even cross-pollinated characters (particularly females) from project to project. With his ever-loyal John Wayne in Kurt Russell going through the same paces as he had 15 years earlier, the parallels to Hawks were complete.

Escape from L.A. was also another chapter in Carpenter's subversive film book, representing his utter disregard for the establishment. As he told *Cinescape* about Snake Plissken before the film's release:

> Snake represents my ultimate hatred of authority. You really don't want him to change. It's like saying, "How is Clint Eastwood different in *A Fistful of Dollars* from *The Good, the Bad and the Ugly?"*[56]

On the final scoreboard, *Escape from L.A.* was not seven times more entertaining than *Escape from New York*, even though it cost seven times as much. Indeed, few longtime Carpenter fans would place the sequel to *Escape from New York* in the same class as the original — or even in the same class with *Big Trouble in Little China*, especially because many had waited for so long and harbored such high hopes for the project. Though *Escape from L.A.* was packed with fun social commentary and it had several comedic and action highlights, particularly in a wonderfully ambitious climax, it did not emerge as the career-reviving film that many had hoped for. The film did poorly at the box office after the first weekend and never met Paramount's expectations.

The Stakes Are High: Filming Vampires

In August of 1997, John Carpenter was back doing what he does best: helming a horror film that just might be a western in disguise. In this case, he was in Santa Fe, New

Mexico, working on the big-screen adaptation of John Steakley's 1990 novel *Vampire$*. The book, about the Vatican's vampire-hunting team of soldiers led by Jack Crow, was converted to screenplay form by Dan Jakoby (*Blue Thunder* [1983], *Lifeforce* [1985], *Invaders from Mars* [1986]), Dan Mazur and an uncredited Carpenter. Starring Maximilian Schell (*The Black Hole* [1979], *Deep Impact* [1998]), James Woods (*Videodrome* [1983], *Casino* [1995]), Sheryl Lee (*Twin Peaks* [1990]) and Thomas Ian Griffith, the film version of *Vampire$* was lensed in eight weeks, and it stayed on schedule and within its $19 million budget. The story, about vampire redemption and Catholic hypocrisy, was set in the American Southwest, and its cowboy-like protagonist, an anti-hero in the tradition of Napoleon Wilson, John Nada and Snake Plissken, promised to return Carpenter to the strangely stylized "modern western" genre he spearheaded with *Assault on Precinct 13*. As Sandy King described the picture:

> It's real rough, and has more in common with *The Wild Bunch* than it does with anything else. It's very edge, very violent. These are mercenaries hunting the vampires, not pussyfooters. These are whoring, drinking outcasts from society who take over places and then go kill vampires. This is a Sam Peckinpah vampire film — not just in its level of violence, but also its edginess and roughness.[57]

What this passage makes clear is that *Vampires* was tailor-made for John Carpenter's touch. Filled with suspense, horror and the genre touches he had always hoped to portray on film, *Vampires* promised to be his comeback movie.

The film opened strong in France in the spring of 1998, and was long in coming to the United States. It was scheduled for release first on September 11, and then it was pushed back to an October 30 debut. *Vampires* did, however, face a serious marketing problem. It was not the only Vampire-hunter script

planned for the year 1998. Action star Wesley Snipes was also headlining in the similarly themed *Blade*, which opened August 28. Just as in 1986, when *Golden Child* and *Big Trouble in Little China* went head to head for the "supernatural Chinese ghost story" sweepstakes, Carpenter found himself in 1998 competing with similar material at the box office.

Whether *Vampires* or *Blade* emerged triumphant would be one of the best stories at the box office in 1998. Early indications were troubling. *Blade* had made more than $64 million by October 1, 1998, making it one of the summer's genuine hits. Would people who loved that film go back for more with *Vampires*? Adding further problems, Kurt Russell's science fiction epic *Soldier* was opening on October 23, the week before *Vampires* was to bow in the United States. Would fans choose Russell over Carpenter on October 30?

In 1997, John Carpenter found himself occupied not just with *Vampires*, but with news of a very special project: the twentieth anniversary sequel to *Halloween*, referred to variously as *Halloween: The Revenge of Laurie Strode* and *Halloween H20*. With Jamie Lee Curtis involved in the Miramax production, and *Scream*'s Kevin Williamson writing the original treatment, the film promised to be more than a low-budget continuation of middling fare such as *Halloween V: The Revenge of Michael Myers* and *Halloween VI: The Curse of Michael Myers*. Despite the quality of the people involved, John Carpenter met with Kevin Williamson and told the writer some surprising news, which Williamson reported to an interviewer:

> He wasn't interested at all…. It's silly. He's a wonderful director. John was on some vampire movie and he said, "You know what, I'm not interested in doing the same movie again."[58]

With Carpenter off the project, the director's reins of the eighth *Halloween* fell instead to Steve Miner (*Friday the 13th Part II* [1981], *Dawson's Creek*). Carpenter's refusal to be a part of the sequel is further evidence of his maverick status in Hollywood. Even though public opinion would like to see him reunited with Curtis and the *Halloween* saga, the director continues to make films only for his own reasons.

Halloween H20 was released on August 5, 1998, the middle of a cutthroat summer season, but it almost immediately achieved blockbuster status, grossing more than $40 million in two weeks. Although the picture suffered from the absence of the late Donald Pleasence, it was a good "anniversary edition" of *Halloween*, and it did (it seems) manage to end the killing spree of Michael Myers once and for all. The film was still playing in first run on the weekend of October 1, proving that the summer picture had legs, even if it had fallen out of the top ten.

The Sun Goes Down on Vampires

John Carpenter's Vampires opened on October 30, 1998, the Friday before Halloween. It was heralded in horror circles (*Cinefantastique* and *Fangoria* magazines) as Carpenter's comeback picture, and even as his best film since *Halloween* in 1978. The film was heavily promoted on television and inside theaters. Promos for *Vampires* ran before *Bride of Chucky* (the fourth in the Don Mancini *Child's Play* film series) and during the *Buffy the Vampire Slayer* television series. Despite all this publicity, mainstream critical reaction was quite negative.

Worse, *Vampires* opened into a saturated market. It had to compete not only with *Bride of Chucky*, but *Halloween H20* (which was still playing in theaters almost three months after its release date!), *Urban Legend*, and the pop witchcraft picture *Practical Magic*. In 20 years, a Carpenter film had never opened in a more competitive market. *H20* headlined Jamie Lee Curtis, *Soldier* headlined

Kurt Russell, *Bride of Chucky* genuflected to *Halloween* by displaying a Michael Myers mask in the first scene, and *Urban Legend* was a child of *Scream* (which in turn was a child of *Halloween*). In other words, Carpenter's *Vampires* was not only competing with "horror" pictures and big stars, it was competing with Carpenter's *own* stars, characters and legacy. Additionally, all the talk of a significant "comeback" had upped the ante on expectations for *Vampires*, expectations that would have been hard for any film to live up to.

Despite these considerable obstacles, *Vampires* was the top film of the Halloween weekend. It earned $9.2 million and defeated such heavy competition as *Pleasantville* ($6.6 million), *Antz* ($4.1 million), *Bride of Chucky* ($4 million), *Soldier* ($2.6 million) and *Apt Pupil* ($1.7 million). Incidentally, the opening weekend take of *Vampires* was equal to, if not slightly higher than, the total box office take of *Village of the Damned* and *In the Mouth of Madness* back in 1995.

The bottom line was that *Vampires* opened strong, but faded fast in ensuing weeks. Its final box office tally did not approach *Blade*'s unexpectedly strong midsummer take. Worse, the film was lethargically paced and remarkably lacking in suspense. Though James Woods gave a powerhouse central performance, *Vampires* was not the critical success or Carpenter comeback many had looked for. Like *Village of the Damned* and *Memoirs of an Invisible Man*, it was a deeply flawed film.

The Future

John Carpenter is no stranger to adversity. Had he not been persistent and totally committed to a career in film, *Dark Star* would never have been made at all in the early 1970s. Although the director had his share of box office failures in the '90s, as well as critical disappointments, one thing is certain: He will continue to blend genres and create provocative horror films. The question is, will he enjoy it? The critical reception of *The Thing* shook his confidence badly, and the failures of *In the Mouth of Madness*, *Village of the Damned* and *Escape from L.A.* may have magnified the effect. In 1996, Carpenter made a telling and oft-repeated comment which suggested he felt unloved and unappreciated after a long film career filled with hard work:

> I'll tell you what I am. It depends on what country I'm in. In France, I'm an *auteur*. In England, I'm a horror movie director. In Germany, I'm a filmmaker. In the U.S., I'm a bum.[59]

There is a real sadness in that remark, but John Carpenter, genre director extraordinaire, should remember one thing before he labels himself "a bum." His hero Howard Hawks was unloved and unheralded in his time too. It was not until he was an older man and well past his prime that people (in France, of all places) began to realize the thematic complexity and style of his varied filmography. It was not until the John Carpenters of the world in the early '70s vocally lauded Hawks that his contribution to art of filmmaking was noted and celebrated. John Carpenter is not an old man yet, but already the next generation is seeing the beauty and care with which he has crafted his many motion pictures. Kevin Williamson's screenplay for *Scream* idolized John Carpenter's work in *Halloween*. Quentin Tarantino wore a T-shirt with the legend "Precinct 13" placed prominently on it in his vampire flick *From Dusk Till Dawn* in honor of his favorite film. And *The Thing*, that unfairly maligned masterpiece, has been flattered with imitation on *The X-Files*, *Star Trek: Deep Space Nine*, *Terminator 2* and elsewhere. Carpenter has left his mark on the universe of film, but the world is only now seeing the light behind this maverick dark star.

II

The Films of John Carpenter

Dark Star (1975)

Critical Reception

"An underground classic. *Dark Star* is simultaneously a satire of science fiction conventions, and a black comedy of the absurd. The special effects are well-handled, and the action sequences are utterly enthralling."— Douglas Menville, R. Reginald, *Things to Come: An Illustrated History of the Science Fiction Film*, The New York Times Book Company, 1977, pages 178–80.

"Carpenter produces a sly comedy in the style of Howard Hawks ... whose benign influence suffuses the project. Two sequences ... are amongst the most remarkable and memorable of the modern Science Fiction cinema."— Phil Hardy, *The Film Encyclopedia: Science Fiction*, William Morrow, New York, 1984, page 317.

"A remarkable bit of satirical filming ... *Dark Star* sparkles with wit and originality rare in contemporary filmmaking.... The novelty and humor of the script, coupled with the fine though rough performances of the cast and the modestly spectacular special effects, make a film that is both professional and entertaining."— Douglas Murray, *Space Wars*: "*Dark Star,*" June 1978, pages 24, 63.

"Droll, good-natured existential, or mock existential outer space comedy with style, wit, and a beautifully controlled tone of genial absurdity ... The film's humor depends on the near-lost arts of timing, staging and pacing and seems related to both the Buster Keaton cliffhanging comedy and Kubrick's *2001.*"— Donald C. Willis, *Horror and Science Fiction Films II*, Scarecrow Press, 1982, page 80.

"For my money it is a better and more consistently entertaining movie than Lucas's [*Star Wars*].... Carpenter upturns nearly every space cliché and provides a bubbling spring of fresh ideas."—*Films Illustrated*.

"The film tries to be both a satire and a reasonably straightforward fantasy adventure, and does not really succeed at either. The script is too clumsy to be effective at mocking, and the movie's lunges at direct humor ... are jejune.... *Dark Star* has the clannish, jolly air of a family show even if it needs to have much forgiven in the name of enterprise."— Jay Cocks, *Time*, May 5, 1975.

"An auspicious feature film debut by John Carpenter ... offers a blackly comic vision of man in space overwhelmed by both ennui and technology.... The film offers a refreshingly unheroic look at men challenging the final frontier."— James Gunn, *The New Encyclopedia of Science Fiction*, Viking, 1988.

"Inventive and hilarious ... one of the few films of its kind that has fun with its subject without making fun of it. A kind of black comedy *2001: A Space Odyssey*, it is also good science fiction and never veers into fantasy."— Gene Wright, *The Science Fiction Image*, Facts on File Publications, 1983.

"The best sf film of 1974 ... a major achievement."— John Brosnan, *Future Tense: The Science Fiction Cinema*, St. Martin's Press, 1977, page 229.

Cast and Credits

CAST: Brian Narelle (Doolittle); Cal Kuniholm (Boiler); Dre Pahich (Talby); Dan O'Bannon (Sgt. Pinback).

CREDITS: Jack H. Harris Presents *Dark Star*. *Director of Photography:* Douglas Knapp. *Film Editor:* Dan O'Bannon. *Assistant Director and Associate Producer:* J. Stein Kaplan. *Sound:* Nina Kleinberg. *Additional Photography:* Cliff Fenneman, Dale Beldin. *Camera Assistant:* Nick Castle. *Associate Art Director:* Tom Wallace. *Production Assistant:* Terry Winkless. *Key Grip:* Les Rumsey. *Chief Carpenter:* David Seal. *Production Associate:* Jack Murphy. *Special Effects:* Bob Greenberg, Greg Jein, Harry Walton, Ron Cobb. *Sound Effects:* John Brasher, Nick Spaulding (cutter), Leslie Shatz (re-recording). *Visual Effects Consultant and Optical Effects:* Bill Taylor. *Original Story and Screenplay:* John Carpenter, Dan O'Bannon. *Music:* John Carpenter. *Creative Consultant and Engineering:* Craig Portman. "Benson, Arizona" *Lyrics:* Bill Taylor. *Executive Producer:* Jack H. Harris. *Production Design and Special Effects Supervision:* Dan O'Bannon. *Produced and Directed by:* John Carpenter. Metrocolor. Made in Hollywood, U.S.A. *MPAA Rating:* G. *Running Time:* 68 minutes (director's cut); 83 minutes (initial release.)

Note: Although most reference sources list the release date of *Dark Star* as the year 1974, it was in fact released in January of 1975.

———

"Don't give me any of that intelligent life stuff! Find me something I can blow up!"— Doolittle, to his co-pilots aboard the scoutship *Dark Star*

———

SYNOPSIS: A U.S. base at McMurdo Sound, Antarctica, sends a message to the scoutship *Dark Star*, which is currently 18 parsecs from Earth in the space sector EB-90. The base reports that it is sorry to learn of the accidental death of *Dark Star*'s commander, Powell, and that, unfortunately, the ship is too far out in space for Earth to send any replacement radiation shielding. Instead, the *Dark Star* is ordered to continue its endless mission: destroying unstable planets throughout the galaxy in order to pave the way for future colonization. This mission involves the detonating of thermonuclear smart bombs — bombs which actually communicate with the crew and are even capable of reason.

As the *Dark Star* destroys another planet and jumps to hyperspace, its new commander, the recently promoted Doolittle, orders the crew to set a course for a nearby nebula containing a solar system where there is an 85 percent probability of an unstable planet. Recording his captain's log, Doolittle reports that the ship is out of toilet paper.

After completing log entry 1,943, Doolittle visits the ship's dorsal observation dome to meet with Talby, the bearded officer stationed there. Talby rarely leaves the dome, because he likes to look at the stars. He is very excited about visiting the nebula because the ship might encounter the Phoenix Asteroids, a body of space rocks which circle the universe once every 12 trillion years and glow with all the colors of the universe.

Doolittle is not interested in the asteroids. He longs to be back home in Malibu, surfing the waves at Zuma. He wishes he brought his surfboard along for the trip. Elsewhere on the ship, it is time for Sergeant Pinback to feed the crew's mascot, a bulbous beachball-like alien entity. Pinback does so only reluctantly, and the cunning creature quickly escapes from its cell. It traps Pinback in an elevator shaft and nearly kills him. After breaking into an elevator floorboard and briefly getting stuck there, Pinback tranquilizes the alien. When shot, however, the alien blows up, nothing more than an inflated sack of gas.

Talby soon detects a malfunction somewhere on the *Dark Star*, but Doolittle is obsessed with surfing and takes no notice of his warning. Pinback, Doolittle and Boiler have lunch, and Pinback tells them again how he should not even be aboard the ship. Actually, he is not Pinback at all. Because of an accident, he was wearing Pinback's uniform when *Dark Star* was boarding four years earlier. His real name is Bill Frug, and he is a fuel vat supervisor, not an astronaut.

This fact is especially troubling to Frug because Pinback's underwear is too loose for him, and it hurts.

Meanwhile, Talby rouses himself from the space dome and pinpoints the ship's malfunction in the rear airlock communications laser. He dons a star suit to check out the problem while an angry Pinback pouts because nobody has remembered that it is his birthday.

The *Dark Star* arrives at an unstable planet in the nebula, and the crew arms the bomb that will destroy the world. Unfortunately, the malfunction in the communication laser incapacitates Talby and causes the bomb to go haywire. It is jammed in the bay and will not release, endangering the safety of the ship and crew. Pinback confers with the smart bomb, but it refuses to drop. Additionally, it seems intent on exploding. Unable to stop the countdown to destruction, Doolittle consults with the ship's dead captain, Powell, who is stored in cryogenic suspended animation. Powell is interested mainly in how the Dodgers have been playing, but suggests to Doolittle that he talk to the computerized bomb. Doolittle must teach the bomb phenomenology, and convince it not to explode.

In a star suit, Doolittle travels outside the ship and confers with Bomb 20. He convinces it not to explode by suggesting that it has no concrete evidence that anything else in the universe exists. Since its only experience is sensory data relayed through electronic connections, the bomb realizes it does not know for certain that it received a "real" order to detonate from Pinback. Confused, the bomb agrees to consider the new data, and the detonation is aborted with just seconds to spare.

As Doolittle returns to the interior of the ship, Talby is inadvertently ejected from the airlock and sent spiraling into space. Doolittle goes after him in a daring rescue attempt. As the two men struggle in space, the bomb declares Pinback to be "false" data, intuits that it is alone in the universe, and considers itself a God-like creator. Declaring "let there be light," the bomb detonates, destroying the *Dark Star* and killing Pinback and Boiler.

Talby and Doolittle watch the explosion and realize that they are stranded in space. Talby wanders into the glowing Phoenix Asteroids and joins them, sharing in their eternal, metaphysical glow. Grabbing a piece of his ship's debris, Doolittle surfs toward the atmosphere of a nearby world — before burning up in a flash.

COMMENTARY: John Carpenter's premiere feature, *Dark Star*, has been well-established as a cult classic for almost 25 years now. Considering *Dark Star*'s origin as a student film at U.S.C., this longevity is perhaps surprising. However, it can also be viewed as a direct and logical result of the fact that this low-budget film bears up remarkably well to examination on a number of analytic fronts more than two decades after its debut.

In the days and years in the seventies following its release, for instance, *Dark Star* was heralded mostly as a wicked parody of Stanley Kubrick's classic film *2001: A Space Odyssey* (1968), and it was appreciated almost solely on those grounds, for its echoes and upturning of *2001* plot and productions details. Critics saw the *Dark Star*'s talking bomb as another version of the *Discovery*'s mellifluous-voiced computer, the HAL 9000, and John Carpenter's choice of country music (Bill Taylor's "Benson, Arizona") as a direct contrast to Stanley Kubrick's decision to layer his film with classical pieces like Richard Strauss's *Thus Spake Zarathustra*, Johann Strauss's *The Blue Danube*, Ligeti's *Requiem for Soprano, Mezzo-Soprano, and Two Mixed Choirs and Orchestra* and *Lux Aeterna*, *Gayne Ballet Suite* and Khachaturian's *Atmospheres*.

Someone inclined to document all of the parallels could also note that both films ended with a kind of metaphysical "ultimate" journey: the extended stargate-monolith sequence from the finale of *2001*, and the Phoenix Asteroids interlude of *Dark Star*. Additionally, both projects sought to dramatize the impression that any long-term space flight would be filled with boredom rather than excitement. Where Kubrick recorded astronaut Frank Poole (Gary Lockwood) jogging endlessly around the circular central port of the Jupiter-bound spaceship called *Discovery*, Carpenter and O'Bannon instead recorded the dull life of the *Dark Star* crew at lunch, relaxing in their fraternity-like communal sleeping quarters, staring endlessly into space, taking the ship apart for target practice, and even feeding the ship's pet.

The opening scene of *Dark Star*, wherein McMurdo Base on Earth contacts the crew, is also an immediate reflection of *2001: A Space Odyssey* and the scene in which a news anchor for the BBC-12 program "The World Tonight" interviews Dave Bowman, Frank Poole and HAL about their life aboard ship. In *2001*, the interview discusses a time lag in communication of approximately seven minutes, because the *Discovery* is 80 million miles away. In *Dark Star*, the same concept is taken to absurd levels, though perhaps more realistic in a cosmic sense. The officer who sends the message to the crew notes that there is a ten year time lag between them, because the *Dark Star* is 18 parsecs from Earth. Obviously, a ten year time lag makes any conversation meaningless — just one more meaningless touch in *Dark Star*'s existential world. The recorded messages from home in each film also convey news of Earth's appreciation of the crew. In *2001* "the entire world joins" the interviewer in wishing *Discovery* "a safe and successful journey." In *Dark Star*, the message is played on "prime time" and it gets "good reviews in the trades." In a switch from *2001*, though, *Dark Star*'s sly communiqué quickly follows up such positive news with equally negative news. The Earth Base officer quickly informs the crew that there have been cutbacks in Congress, and that the ship will not be receiving any replacement parts for the damaged radiation shields.

Apart from these story similarities, *Dark Star* echoes *2001* in a visual sense, its first post-communiqué image being that of the huge space vessel *Dark Star* stretching across the screen as it approaches a planet. Of course, *2001* made the same "giant" space-ship shot famous, and *Star Wars* also mimicked it with its opening view of an imperial star destroyer passing, seemingly forever, in front of the camera. The long shot of the *Dark Star* passing through space is important not just as mimicry and visual reference to a cinematic antecedent, but because it reverses the *2001* camera angle of the *Discovery* in space. In Stanley Kubrick's film, the *Discovery* first passes from left to right, film grammar's short-hand for a journey "out" or beyond. Conversely, John Carpenter's film visualizes the *Dark Star* passing from right to left, implying a journey "back" rather than a journey beyond or ahead. As *Dark Star* is a film about man's inability to transcend boredom, individuality and petty self-concern for the betterment and evolution of the species, this shot suggests that the *Dark Star*, though forever journeying, is not really going anywhere important.

On a thematic level, these similarities to *2001* formulate *Dark Star*'s central premise. Where *2001* finds that man's place in the universe is a significant one, *Dark Star* alternately believes it to be wholly insignificant. *2001: A Space Odyssey* places man on a pedestal. He is so important a creation that "God" itself (represented by the awesome black monolith) spurs him to evolve into a tool-using, intelligent creature. Then, generations later, the monolith leads man first to the moon, and then to distant Jupiter. When man arrives at Jupiter in the form of astronaut David Bowman (Keir Dullea) he is catered to and waited on inside a luxurious Victorian sitting room. He is the only living creature visible in a world devoted totally to one, a status that belies his importance to the unseen God. Then, as his ultimate reward, David Bowman evolves into a new life-form, the infant "star child" of *2001*'s final image.

Deliberately undercutting *2001*, *Dark Star* does not exist in a realm where the universe cares about or even appreciates man. Conversely, man is a lost and solitary creation in *Dark Star*. Talby's metaphysical assimilation by the glowing Phoenix Asteroids reflects this status. At the film's denouement, he becomes one of a million glowing lights circling the universe once every 12 trillion years, rather than an alien intelligence's favorite pupil and ward with a position of honor in a heavenly chamber. *Dark Star* thus implies that man is not ready to evolve, as he is in the finale of *2001*.

Additionally, the subtext of Kubrick's *2001: A Space Odyssey* seems to insinuate that man, with his sterile and efficient space technology as well as his God-like creation of an artificial life-form (the very individual and human HAL), is ready to meet his destiny at Jupiter. This would be an impossible ascension for the crew of *Dark Star* because its technology is ramshackle, broken down — and it is eventually what kills most of the crew. Though Talby escapes, his refuge is not a joyous evolution or celebration of intelligence, but rather a union with a mock-spiritual collection of drifting rocks, where it is intimated he will remain forever, unchanged and unevolved.

The country music also deliberately undercuts the "grandness" of John Carpenter's unique space opera. Classical music tends to be grand, lush and occupied with the most lasting and artistic of human emotions and concerns. As the definition of "classic" intimates, such music is of the highest established or recognized standard, and thus artistically perfect to accompany man's highest accomplishments, such as space travel and his long journey from savage to evolved being. As Kenneth Von Gunden and Stuart H. Stock wrote of the music in *2001: A Space Odyssey*:

> The World Riddle [*Thus Spake Zarathustra*] opens with an ascending phrase of three notes, C-G-C, which

represent Nietzche's view of the evolutionary rise of man. The three notes are integral to *2001*'s symbolism. These three notes serve notice that the number three is essential to the film: from the perfect alignment of the three spheres of Earth, moon, and sun at the beginning to the appearance of things in threes.[1]

By contrast, contemporary country music tends to be intensely personal, occupied with the most basic, individual and even frivolous matters; from failed love affairs to remembrances of a special song on the juke box. It is not symbolic, but literal. So, where *2001: A Space Odyssey* utilized classical music to elevate space travel to a grand matter of galactic import, the country music of *Dark Star* further trivializes the efforts of the crew and its mission. The theme song, "Benson, Arizona" by Bill Taylor, evokes not matters of grandeur and cosmic import, but rather a personal remembrance of a specific time and place — importantly, *not* outer space. The lyrics spotlight the human element of space travel, specifically the effects of a long separation between a distant astronaut and his earthbound love. The song represents a personal interpretation of journeys through the void, not a grand one with symbolic impact on human society and even the species itself.

Obviously, any film that can so drastically parallel *2001: A Space Odyssey*'s text and subtext, while at the same time drawing totally different but no less valid conclusions about man's role in space, is worthy of study and even admiration. But as John Carpenter and partner Dan O'Bannon became well-known figures in film and genre circles in the 1980s and *2001: A Space Odyssey* was more or less shoved aside in favor George Lucas's *Star Wars* (1977) as the science-fiction film prototype, *Dark Star* came to be evaluated increasingly less as a startling entertainment which upturned genre tropes. Instead, it seemed relevant as a training ground for two of the decade's most inspired and inspiring filmmakers. By the mid–80s, Carpenter was

the guiding voice behind a string of hits from *Halloween* (1978) to *Starman* (1984), and Dan O'Bannon was well-known for his contributions to films as diverse as *Star Wars*, *Dead and Buried* (1981), Tobe Hooper's *Lifeforce* (1985), *Invaders from Mars* (1986) and even the horror-comedy *Return of the Living Dead* (1985). Thus reviewers were able to put *Dark Star* into a kind of career context. They went back to the student production and saw the roots of Dan O'Bannon's *Alien* (1979) screenplay in the extended beachball alien sequences of *Dark Star*, but with a more comedic creature running amok in the corridors of an advanced spaceship.

Similarly, John Carpenter's knack with timing and pacing, factors critical to the success of *Halloween* in 1978, *The Fog* in 1980 and *Escape from New York* in 1981, was also traced back to his first low-budget feature film. When scholars became aware that Carpenter was a fan of Howard Hawks, the film was reevaluated with that director's filmography as a framework. Not unexpectedly, John Carpenter's decision to parody *2001: A Space Odyssey* in *Dark Star* was also seen in relation to the much-bandied-about auteur theory. Like Stanley Kubrick and only a handful of others (including Howard Hawks), Carpenter was and is inclined to see himself as an auteur. So what better project to establish himself than one with themes and details already handled by that other famous auteur, Stanley Kubrick?

Most recently, however, *Dark Star* has been viewed and studied not for its upturning of genre conventions, or even as the first creative playground of two major film talents, but rather as the initiator of a new generation of films: the slacker movie. In the 1990s, Generation X filmmakers and writers such as Quentin Tarantino (*True Romance* [1993], *Pulp Fiction* [1994], *From Dusk Till Dawn* [1995], *Jackie Brown* [1997]), Kevin Smith (*Clerks* [1994], *Mallrats* [1995], *Chasing Amy* [1997]), Richard Linklater (*Slacker* [1989], *Dazed and Confused* [1993]) and Kevin Williamson (*Scream* [1996], *I Know*

What You Did Last Summer [1997], *Scream 2* [1997]) have perfected the cinema of the "slacker." Their feature films invariably focus on struggling members of Generation X, young adults who for whatever reason seem to lack the traditional morality and values of previous generations. That is not to say that the protagonists in these films lack *any* morality, merely that they seem impaired when it comes to traditional American morality. In *Clerks*, two sarcastic but intelligent young adults have forsaken higher education for the absurdity of life in convenience and video stores. In *Scream*, young adults have been raised by the VCR and television, and so they often treat life like a movie and are numb to the rampant violence in their own lives and society as a whole. In *From Dusk Till Dawn*, the Gecko brothers, though dramatized quite clearly by director Robert Rodriguez as rapists, murderers and kidnappers, are sources of humor and even heroism, again underlining the fact that today's audiences have become callous to brutal acts.

For the most part, the characters in all of these films are quick-witted, but apathetic. When Neve Campbell tells Rose McGowan in *Scream* that the murdered Casey Becker (Drew Barrymore) sits next to her in English class, McGowan replies, heartlessly, "Not anymore." When Ben Affleck admits that he is in love with a lesbian in *Chasing Amy*, he is ruthlessly excoriated by his sarcastic roommate and co-worker.

Besides apathy, the so-called "slacker" films that are so popular today also deal with Generation X's seeming inability to assume the mantle of responsibility, as if the burdens of adulthood are far too heavy to cope with in a world already weighed down by AIDS and other serious problems. Thus a ferocious murderer in *Scream* named Stu (Matthew Lillard) starts to cry like a baby when he is "outed" by society as the slasher. Why? He fears that his parents are going to be "mad" at him. Furthermore, he claims that he only killed because of "peer pressure" and the fact

that he is "far too sensitive." In *Chasing Amy*, the protagonists are comic book artists who share a career drawing an adolescent comic book filled with "dick" and "fart" jokes. They live in a dormitory-like situation, and boast childish preoccupations with video-hockey, sophomoric television (*Degrassi High*) and, of course, the *Star Wars* trilogy.

All in all, these films depict a generation that pretty much refuses to grow up and play by the rules dictated by previous American generations. Well-written, funny, and always insightful, these "slacker" movies document the generational battle raging in America, and the gradual overturning of old rules in favor of new and different rules. Remarkably, John Carpenter and Dan O'Bannon's *Dark Star* foreshadows this shift in modern American attitudes and can accurately be described as the first slacker movie — two decades ahead of its time.

If apathy, lack of responsibility, and selfishness among young adults are considered the three thematic tent poles of the slacker cinema, then *Dark Star* fits the bill almost perfectly. Aboard a supposedly state-of-the-art space craft, the crew is not at all interested in its environs or mission. When Pinback notes that he has discovered a new star, Doolittle responds thoughtlessly, "Who cares?" This blasé response is a far cry from the "responsible" and "concerned" attitudes of *Star Trek* (1966–69), for instance, wherein each new cosmic phenomenon is treated as an occasion for self-enrichment and even celebration. And where the *Enterprise*'s many captain's logs are filled with significant observations about the universe, humanity and philosophy, *Dark Star*'s ship's log deals totally with issues of the crew's physical comfort. To wit: Doolittle reports in the log that ship is out of toilet paper. How would that play with Starfleet Command?

In *Dark Star* there is no responsibility to the species, no responsibility to duty, honor, or one's self-enrichment. In fact, the crew can barely manage to feed the pet, a sentient living creature that Pinback brought aboard because he thought it was cute! Additionally, the crew members are also quite derelict in performing their jobs. When informed of a ship malfunction, Doolittle tells Talby: "Don't worry about it, we'll find out what it is when it goes bad." Of course, when the malfunction does, inevitably, go bad, it ultimately leads to the destruction of the ship and the death of the crew. But these slackers, all underachievers and neurotics to the last, lack the ability to foresee how their present action, or even inaction, can affect their future.

The apathy and selfishness of the *Dark Star* crew is evident in other situations as well. Each astronaut is in one way or another inner-directed, concerned only with his own happiness and material concerns. Talby is totally anti-social, sitting alone all day in the dorsal dome pontificating about the Phoenix Asteroids. Watching the stars and making "groovy" observations, Talby could easily be interpreted as the ship's resident pothead.

Doolittle is equally self-absorbed. He spends his time remembering how happy he was surfing in Malibu. The rest of the crew is much the same: Boiler is obsessed with both his appearance (he is constantly tweaking his mustache) and his own amusement. To keep himself occupied, he plays dangerous games with a knife, and even shoots up parts of the ship's inner mechanisms. The snide and supercilious Pinback is also focused only on his self-image, and his unswerving belief that he is "the only objective person on the ship." He also believes that the others fail to appreciate his "better qualities," when it seems clear that he has *no* good qualities. He treats the others as stupid swine, castigating them regularly in his personal diary, yet he is heartbroken and resentful when they fail to remember his birthday. In other words, Pinback wants what he wants when he wants it, and he cannot understand why the others, whom he has shown no interest in appeasing or appreciating, refuse to cooperate with his wishes. Even the "dead" captain, Powell, is self-interested, motivated only by his curiosity about baseball and the status of the Dodgers.

The crew in *Dark Star* is so inner-directed, in fact, that it is completely oblivious to the destructive nature of the ship's never-ending mission. The crew travels around the galaxy destroying planets! Yet each astronaut seems totally unaware of the power and forces that the crew must bring to bear so regularly. Like the kids of *Scream*, they are numb to the violence and destruction they witness and even cause.

The self-absorption of the *Dark Star* crew is also expressed in the dialogue between crew members. In the lunchroom sequence, nobody listens to one another. As Pinback drones on, repeating a story he has told many times before, Boiler asks Doolittle: "He told us this four years ago, didn't he?" Absorbed in his own world, Doolittle pauses, and then replies nonsensically: "No, I think it was four years ago." And, in one of the ongoing *Dark Star* jokes, nobody pays attention to Talby, even when he has something important and relevant to say ("Talby, don't bother me!").

The impression that the *Dark Star* is populated by overgrown adolescents rather than adults is enhanced by the presence of the former commander, Powell, in cryogenic storage. Powell represents the absentee father of this bizarre family. The others, particularly Doolittle, seek out his advice only when they need him for something, not to provide his still-conscious mind with the comfort of human company. Furthermore, the absence of this patriarchal figure on the control deck has resulted in a slew of anti-social behavior in the ship's "children." Talby has retreated emotionally, and does not leave the dome since Powell died. Pinback is jealous of Doolittle (an older brother, perhaps) for finding favor with Powell and inheriting his dad's job when *he* was the obvious choice to be captain. And Doolittle, representing the first born perhaps, stands forever in Powell's shadow, never able to perform to his father's level of efficiency.

As the more "adult" crewmember, Powell is also ridiculed in the screenplay. Stuck permanently in a refrigerator, he has become senile and useless, unable to help anyone. Still, he nags his surrogate children ("Why don't you have anything nice to tell me?"), is completely out-of-touch with current events (the Dodgers broke up after his death), and is rapidly losing his mental faculties ("I've forgotten so much, so much...").

Since the hierarchy of *Dark Star* resembles a family, with an out-of-touch father and a group of adolescent sons dominating the action, the film could appropriately be called a rites-of-passage motion picture. It is about growing up, or rather, *not* growing up. In an ironic resolution, no one in *Dark Star* but the out-of-touch father survives this particular rite of passage. Talby may find happiness in the Phoenix Asteroids, and Doolittle may enjoy (briefly) his return to surfing, but in the final analysis these characters are unable to overcome their selfishness and apathetic personalities.

Historically, it might be tempting to view *Dark Star* not as the first slacker film, but rather as part of the counter-culture film trend represented by such films as *Easy Rider* (1969). However, there is a significant difference in approach and content in the two distinct film subgenres. Importantly, the rebels of *Easy Rider* exist totally outside of society's laws. Their job, transporting drugs, is illegal in the society they are a part of. The astronauts of *Dark Star* are not so courageous in their defiance. As astronauts, they are the arm of society, the representatives of man in space. Though they complain and whine, they do nothing which establishes them as counter-culture heroes. They are just slackers.

Furthermore, the counter-culture heroes of *Easy Rider* articulate a world view of a sort. They resent the laws of their country, and ignore them. In a sense, they are proponents of freedom (even if it is the freedom to smoke pot), and they express American youth's unwillingness to play the games constructed by their fathers and their father's fathers. The crew of *Dark Star* espouses no world view because each member considers himself to be the most important thing in the world. The crew members adhere to the surface regulations of their society, accepting a career as astronauts, but internally they resent it. Instead of doing and acting, like the trio of *Easy Rider*, the men of the *Dark Star* merely simmer inside, filled with unhappiness and resentment about their predicament.

To enhance audience identification with these most unusual *Dark Star* astronauts, John Carpenter and Dan O'Bannon have provided very appropriate names for the spaced-out slackers. The name Doolittle reminds one, of course, of the title character in the movie *Dr. Doolittle* (1967). In that film, the Doolittle character was a man who could communicate with animals. In *Dark Star*, Doolittle is also a talker, a talker to frozen bodies and smarmy smart computers. Unlike his namesake, however, Doolittle finds himself unable to effectively communicate with anyone. His attempts to teach the smart bomb phenomenology backfire, and they destroy the ship. And he never listens to Talby, who has important information for him. Furthermore, the name Doolittle characterizes the astronaut's lousy work habits. He literally does little — with the result being that everybody aboard the ship dies.

Sgt. Pinback is also an appropriate name, for the character is a literal pinhead, a small-minded, self-important idiot. Even Boiler sports an appropriate moniker as a character who in the finale comes to a physical boil and explodes with violence. After flirting dangerously with knives, tweezers, and a rifle throughout the picture, Boiler finally goes ballistic (he boils over) and nearly kills Pinback in a slugfest outside the control room.

None of this analysis suggests just how truly amusing and fun a film *Dark Star* remains to this day. In one extended sequence, it not only looks forward to 1990s attitudes and futuristic space flight, but gazes back into film history and revives many of the tricks of silent, slapstick comedy. Early in the film, for instance, Sgt. Pinback is sent to "feed the pet." The pet, it turns out, is an alien creature significantly smarter than he is, and it jumps on his back to vex him. Pinback wriggles around like a madman, trying to get the thing off of him, and the scene starts to build steam. The creature is pursued into an elevator shaft, and Pinback, in the tradition of Buster Keaton, finds himself on a cliffhanging ledge of sorts as a descending elevator nearly crushes him.

John Carpenter's direction of this scene reflects his familiarity with film comedy tradition. Once in the shaft, Carpenter shoots the sequence mostly in Charlie Chaplin–like long-shots so that his audience laughs at rather than identifies with the plight of Pinback. The only time Carpenter leaves long shot for close-up is to establish further the comedy of the situation. At one point, the elevator starts to crush Pinback's face, and so the camera catches his grimace as his visage is humorously contorted under the weight of the car. At another point, Carpenter cuts to close-up to catch the mischievous alien beachball tickling Pinback in the ribs, a very funny moment which precedes Pinback's entrapment in the elevator's floor.

The elevator sequence is the longest in the film, and it grows more humorous as Pinback's plight becomes more and more dangerous. He jumps from the tiny ledge and hangs onto the bottom of the elevator car as it travels up and down the shaft again and again like a mechanical yo-yo. Then Pinback strikes on the clever idea of opening a floor grill and crawling inside the car. This portion of the sequence is both funny and suspenseful, as audiences wonder if he will get the damn grill open before he is crushed. It is also funny because as Pinback loosens the grill, it falls down from the base of the elevator and cracks him in the skull. Then, adding insult to injury, Pinback finds himself stuck halfway through the grill — too wide through the middle to pull himself completely inside the car. He has to blow up the floor to escape!

The climax of this humorous sequence comes as an angry Pinback emerges from the smoke-filled elevator immediately after the floor has exploded. Martial-sounding music beats on the soundtrack, and Pinback, shown in menacing low-shot and in tight framing, marches to the drum beat, selects a weapon, and blasts apart the troublesome pet.

Director Wes Craven has often spoken at length about the similarities of horror and comedy, and how both genres depend on timing and suspense to be effective. John Carpenter shows in *Dark Star* that he agrees with that notion. He is as adept at handling comedy set-pieces as he is at creating suspense in *Halloween*. It is an auspicious debut.

Dark Star is a fun movie, and even without close analysis an obvious theme emerges. Pure and simple, *Dark Star* is vehemently anti-technology in its humorous musings. It dramatizes a universe wherein technology has overwhelmed man, to his ultimate detriment. The control room of the ship is the most cramped interior in the history of outer space films. There is no elbow room, and no room to maneuver or even turn around. Furthermore, the seat next to Pinback *explodes* for no reason, killing the captain. Other details also contribute to the notion that technology is harmful to our health. The ship is out of toilet paper because a bulkhead exploded, the telephone in the elevator is out of order, and the talking bomb malfunctions and kills the crew. These encounters with machinery suggest *Dark Star*'s most visible theme: that the more man overthinks his environs, the greater chance something will malfunction and undercut his so-called progress. Through the course of *Dark Star*, the malfunctions are often humorous (as when the elevator computer begins to play *The Barber of Seville* instead of assisting Pinback in his attempt to get inside the car), but there is nothing funny about what happens at the film's climax: Technology destroys the ship.

Dark Star has also been enjoyed for 20 years because of its final ironic conceit, that a human crewman will have to convince a talking and thinking bomb not to explode by teaching it phenomenology. This is indeed a clever sequence, filled with suspense and the funny application of philosophy, but it adds just one more level of absurdity and black comedy to a film already brimming with cleverness. This scene has been reviewed more than any other in connection with *Dark Star*, perhaps because it is an intellectual scene, designed solely to appeal to the "smart" critics — perhaps the only viewers who would be aware exactly what phenomenology is.

Dark Star is a genre pioneer, too, because it is the first science fiction film in the American cinema to devise a visual conceit for faster-than-light travel. As the *Dark Star* leaves orbit of a planet it is about to destroy, all the stars race suddenly towards the camera, like a storm of lightning bolts. Soon after *Dark Star*, this visual notion of "light speed" would become *de rigueur*, a common image repeated in *Star Wars* and *Star Trek: The Mo-tion Picture* among others. Also, *Dark Star* is the first Hollywood motion picture to suggest that astronauts need not be physically superior, by-the-book, All-American military martinets. Instead, the astronauts of John Carpenter's film seemingly have no training or coping skills. They even smoke! The cigarette smoking and the blue collar feel of *Dark Star* would make an even bigger splash in Dan O'Bannon's *Alien* in 1979.

Whether seen as an ironic, anti–*2001: A Space Odyssey*, a training ground for two of the 1980s' most influential genre film talents, or the first movie of the slacker generation, *Dark Star* remains an enjoyable and thought provoking viewing experience at the advent of the twenty-first century, as well as one of John Carpenter's most unusual cinematic efforts. The actors may not be recognizable, but the condition they portray is uniquely human, and strangely, uniquely '90s.

Assault on Precinct 13 (1976)

Critical Reception

"Skillfully paced and edited, *Assault* was rich with Hawksian dialogue and humor, especially in a clever caricature of the classic 'Hawks woman' by Laurie Zimmer." — Jeffrey Wells, *Films in Review:* "New Fright Master John Carpenter," April 1980, page 218.

"A superb, bloody thriller about a siege in an abandoned L.A. cop station ... with one of the most catchy theme tunes in film history." — Dave Golder, *SFX:* "L.A. Story," November 1996, pages 54–56.

"Bravura remake of *Rio Bravo* ... arguably still the best film [John Carpenter] ever made." — Alan Jones, *Starburst:* "John Carpenter — Prince of Darkness," May 1988, page 8.

Cast and Credits

CAST: Austin Stoker (Lieutenant Bishop); Darwin Joston (Napoleon Wilson); Laurie Zimmer (Leigh); Martin West (Lawson); Charles Cyphers (Starker); Nancy Loomis (Julie); Tony Burton (Wells); Peter Brun (Ice Cream Man); Kim Richards (Kathy); John J. Fox (Warden); Henry Brandon (Chaney); Gilman Rankin (Bus Driver); Brent Keast (Radio Announcer); Maynard Smith (Police Commissioner); Cliff Battuello (First Guard);

Horace Johnson (Second Guard). With: Valentine Villareal, Kenny Mayamoto, Jerry Viramontes, Len Whitaker, Kris Young, Randy Moore, Warren Bradley III, Joe Woo, Jr., James Johnson, Alan Koss, Marc Ross, Frank Doubleday, Gilbert De La Pena, Al Nakauchi, William Taylor, Peter Frankland.

CREDITS: The CKK Corporation Presents. *Director of Photography:* Douglas Knapp. *Film Editor:* John T. Chance (aka John Carpenter). *Filmed in:* Panavision and Metrocolor. *Art Director:* Tommy Wallace. *Assistant Cameramen:* William Waldman, Douglas Olivares. *Gaffer:* Jack English. *Best Boys:* William Mareneck, Michael Everett. *Key Grip:* Kurt Young. *Grip/driver:* Trippy Gafford. *Sound Recordist:* William Cooper. *Boom Man:* Alan Cassidy. *Make-up:* Donald Bledsoe. *Special Effects:* Richard Albain, Jr. *Still Photographer:* Rene Small. *Payroll:* John Syrjamaki. *Associate Producer:* Steve Fine. *Script Supervisor/ Assistant Editor:* Debra Hill. *Wardrobe Mistress:* Louise Kyes. *Property Master:* Craig Stearns. *Second Assistant Editor:* Curt Schulkey. *Production Assistant:* Marla Miller, Blake Schaefer, Randy Moore, Jocelyne Stoikovitch, Tom Hanser. *Production Manager:* John Syrjamaki. *Assistant Director:* James Nichols. *Music:* John Carpenter. *Executive Producer:* Joseph Kaufman. *Produced by:* J.S. Kaplan. *Written and Directed by:* John Carpenter. *Sound Effects:* Tommy Wallace. *Re-recordist:* Bill Varney. *Post-Production Supervisor:* James Nichols. *Set Construction:* Get Set, Inc. *Set Painter:* Richard Girod. *Stunt Drivers:* John Roy Rogers. *Titles and Opticals:* MGM. *MPAA Rating:* R. *Running Time:* 90 minutes.

"I was born out of time." — Napoleon Wilson reflects on his life near the much-feared and anticipated "moment of dying."

SYNOPSIS: In urban L.A. in the mid–70s, the juvenile gang problem is out of control. In many areas of Los Angeles, there is open warfare between police forces and armed, organized criminals. On one particularly horrible night, there is a bloody shoot-out in the ghetto of Anderson, and six youths from the gang known as "Street Thunder" are killed by the cops. This bloodbath does not resolve the ongoing crisis, however. Surviving members of "Street Thunder" have stolen a cache of automatic weapons and silencers. The police commissioner warns that if the gang should get organized, no one in the city will be safe.

The next morning, Street Thunder swears vengeance for the death of their six cohorts. Members of the gang ritualistically cut their arms open with knives and fill a bowl with their mixed blood. Meanwhile, in west L.A., black police Lieutenant Bishop receives a new assignment on his first day on the job. He is ordered to proceed to Precinct 9, Division 13, and take over there from Captain Gordon. The precinct house, located in Anderson, is being closed down, and all its equipment and personnel have been transferred to Ellendale. But for one night, Bishop will command his own precinct and a skeleton crew.

Elsewhere, another L.A. cop named Starker prepares to transport a busload of dangerous convicts to death row. Convicts Wells, Cordell and the infamous murderer Napoleon Wilson board the bus, and Starker lays down the law to them. Still, he shows Wilson both courtesy and respect, and Wilson appreciates the unexpected gesture from an officer of the law. En route to Sonora, Cordell unexpectedly becomes deathly ill. As the convict is in need of immediate medical attention, Starker orders the bus off the freeway to the nearest police precinct — which happens to be in Anderson.

Also in Anderson, little Kathy and her father are lost. They have driven to the ghetto to ask her Nanny Margaret to move in with them now that her husband has passed away. Instead of asking directions from the police, however, Kathy's father stops at a phone booth and calls Margaret for directions. Hungry, Kathy spots an ice cream van and excitedly orders a vanilla twist ice cream cone. In seconds, both Kathy and the ice cream vendor are gunned down in cold blood by members of Street Thunder. In a rage, Kathy's father appropriates the ice cream man's pistol and angrily pursues the thugs to a vacant parking lot. In a deadly shoot-out, Kathy's father kills one of the gang, and then runs for his life to the abandoned police station where Bishop has been assigned, and where Starker and the bus of inmates have just shown up.

At the precinct are a desk sergeant named Chaney, a beautiful police officer named Leigh, and a telephone operator, Julie. Though they welcome Bishop, he soon has more trouble than he can handle. Although he protests that the precinct is closed, Bishop allows Starker to incarcerate his dangerous prisoners in the holding cells while awaiting medical attention. Bishop and Leigh also try to get a coherent story from Kathy's father, but he has retreated into a deep state of shock.

Street Thunder strikes. With automatic weapons and silencers, dozens of gang members systematically lay siege to the all-but-abandoned police establishment. Chaney, Starker and the convict Cordell are gunned down in the first fiery siege. Then, representatives from the gang approach the precinct and throw down a chollo—a white banner decorated with their colors—and smash a bowl of blood on the pavement. Leigh and Bishop realize from this ritual that this conflict is "to the death," and that they have been marked for extermination.

A worried Bishop sends Leigh to save Napoleon Wilson and Wells from their locked cells as the determined gang members break inside through the precinct's back door. Through this rescue Lt. Bishop earns Wilson's trust, and an unspoken attraction soon begins between the tough-minded Leigh and the laconic Wilson. As the siege continues, Bishop reveals that he is dedicated to keeping Kathy's dad and all his wards (even Wilson) alive, but it won't easy. With only a few weapons to hold the armed killers at bay, and the phones down, there is little hope of a timely rescue or of an escape. In the next onslaught, the telephone operator Julie is gunned down.

Desperate, Wells attempts to escape through the basement furnace vent. He flees onto the street and hotwires a car, but is murdered by a thug hiding in the backseat before he can find help for his companions trapped in the police station.

Bishop, Leigh and Napoleon Wilson are forced to flee to the precinct basement. As the criminals attack in force, Bishop targets an acetylene tank with his rifle and blasts it to pieces, causing a tremendous explosion. The thugs are routed by the detonation, and the crisis soon ends. Napoleon Wilson is brought back into police custody, but Bishop asks for the honor of escorting him out of the building.

COMMENTARY: John Carpenter's sophomore film, *Assault on Precinct 13*, is a skillful combination of two distinct and noteworthy film antecedents: the Howard Hawks western *Rio Bravo* [1959] starring John Wayne, Dean Martin, Ricky Nelson, Walter Brennan and Angie Dickinson, and George A. Romero's low-budget horror classic, *Night of the Living Dead* [1968] starring Duane Jones, Judith O'Dea and Karl Hardman. As diverse as these two film sources are in style, story and intent, director John Carpenter nonetheless succeeds in blending them to highly dramatic and suspenseful effect. Taking no prisoners, the fast-paced *Assault on Precinct 13* is one lean, mean and exciting motion picture.

Rio Bravo is John Carpenter's favorite film (followed by *Only Angels Have Wings*), so it is no surprise that the filmmaker should devote the bulk of his 1976 independent motion picture to stylishly retelling the tale first put to silver screen by Hawks and writers Jules Furthman and Leigh Brackett in 1959. Based on a short story by B.H. Campbell, *Rio Bravo* explored the story of sheriff John T. Chance (John Wayne). With only a recovering alcholic called Dude (Dean Martin) and an old man named Stumpy (Walter

Brennan) to assist him, Chance had to fend off the forces of Nathan Burdette, a wealthy rancher whose brother, Joe, was incarcerated in Chance's jail for committing murder. In response to his brother's captivity, Nathan Burdette sealed off the frontier town of Rio Bravo, including the Hotel Alamo, so that no forces of the law could get in or out. His hope was that John Chance would surrender his brother, but failing in that unlikely option, Burdette also sent in expensive hired killers to "prod" Chance in that direction. With the additional help of a beautiful and independent woman called Feathers (Angie Dickinson) and a fast-draw kid named Colorado (Ricky Nelson), Chance made his stand at the fringe of town, and successfully faced down the Burdettes. In the end, Feathers and Chance fell in love, Dude conquered his two-year bout with alcoholism, and justice prevailed in Rio Bravo.

At its core, *Rio Bravo* was an adventure about friendship, and about what friends are often called on to do as friends, even if it means trouble. Anchoring the Warner Bros. genre picture were the charismatic icon John Wayne and director Howard Hawks. So successful was the resulting motion picture that Hawks and Wayne remade it together two times, first as *El Dorado* in 1967 and then again as *Rio Lobo* in 1970. Because it was done so often, *Rio Bravo* could quite aptly be termed the Howard Hawks western prototype. Considered in those terms, *Assault on Precinct 13* is John Carpenter's western adventure of the same style and subgenre. When viewed in conjunction with *Rio Bravo*, it is clear that there are many similarities between the two films.

At a literal level, both motion pictures throw a trio of diverse and unlikely heroes into a life or death situation. In *Rio Bravo*, the heroes are (as Joe Burdette describes them) "a sheriff, a barfly, and a cripple." In *Assault*, the heroes are a police lieutenant, a convict, and a woman. In *Rio Bravo*, much of the action stems from the immutable fact that John T. Chance is an honorable man, and that he

will not, for any reason, fail in his sacred trust to dispatch justice. This honorable code will not permit him to turn over murderer Joe Burdette to his brother. This sacred trust results in Chance, Dude and Stumpy becoming prisoners of a sort in their town, unable to leave it or seek outside help, since Burdette has staked out the road beyond.

Assault on Precinct 13 reverses the premise. Lt. Bishop (Austin Stoker) is also an honorable man who will not fail in his sacred trust to dispatch justice. In this case, justice involves protecting an innocent man, Kathy's father, from the violent hordes gathering outside. Bishop's willful protection of Kathy's father results in an all-out siege, with Bishop's team in constant danger inside the police station as mobs of criminals attempt to gain entrance. Whether it be a lawman preserving justice by bringing a criminal to trial or a lawman protecting an innocent man from the hands of bloodthirsty criminals, the situation in the two films is identical.

The conformity between *Rio Bravo* and *Assault on Precinct 13* does not end with the similarity of "noble" heroes and the central conflict. Various incidents from *Rio Bravo* are also reinterpreted in the Carpenter film of 1976. For instance, Dude detects a Burdette thug in the rafters of a saloon because the criminal is wounded and blood is dripping down into a beer mug on the bar. In *Assault on Precinct*, the baffled police force, unable to locate the site of the Anderson disturbance, detects evidence of the crime when the blood of a murdered phone company employee drips down on the roof of their squad car.

In another visual quotation from *Rio Bravo*, Lt. Bishop throws Napoleon Wilson a shotgun at the very instant a group of rampaging criminals are about gain access to the station and open fire on him. This stunt recalls the moment in *Rio Bravo* when Colorado throws Chance his shotgun as a group of Burdette's hit men close in to kill him.

Even the resolution of the two films is identical in concept. In *Rio Bravo*, Chance,

Dude and Stumpy eventually force Nathan Burdette's surrender by utilizing Pat Wheeler's wagon of dynamite. In *Assault on Precinct 13*, Bishop, Wilson and Leigh stop the youth gang cold by igniting an acetylene canister and causing a tremendous explosion. In this case, Carpenter merely found a modern-day equivalent of a wagon filled with dynamite.

Similarities also exist in throwaway details. In *Rio Bravo*, various characters such as Dude and Colorado go around asking others if they have "got a light" for their cigarettes. In *Assault on Precinct 13*, Napoleon Wilson constantly asks of his cohorts: "Got a light?" or "Got a smoke?" Additionally, when Burdette finally marks Chance for death, he orders a Mexican band to perform a specific song, a composition that was played at the Battle of the Alamo. Importantly, the song signifies that there will be "no quarter, no mercy for the losers" of the conflict. This so-called "cut-throat song" also found a modern expression in Carpenter's screenplay, but as a gang affectation called a *chollo*: a white banner and bowl of spilled blood. In this case, much like the cut-throat song in *Rio Bravo*, the chollo signifies to Bishop and the others that the gang outside "is not afraid to die" and that its members would fight and "kill at any cost ... to the death." In each situation, a symbolic act of the villains (whether it be song or banner) effectively puts the heroes on guard that this conflict will be a fight to the finish.

As has often been written, Laurie Zimmer's character (Leigh) in *Assault on Precinct 13* also conforms to the guidelines of the classic Hawksian woman:

> Women are admitted to the male group only after much disquiet, and a long ritual courtship, phased round the offering, lighting and exchange of cigarettes, during which they prove themselves worthy of entry.[2]

In conjunction with this ritual, Leigh is the only character throughout the running time

Austin Stoker, seen here as MacDonald in *Battle for the Planet of the Apes*, was a Hawksian hero in *Assault on Precinct 13* (1976).

of *Assault on Precinct 13* who is able to provide convict Napoleon Wilson not only with a cigarette, but with a light as well. Significantly, her addition to the ranks of heroes also comes only after some, if not much, disquiet. Initially she is rejected by Bishop for implying that he was "taken out" of the ghetto rather than having walked out on his own two feet. On first spotting her, Wilson and Wells also undergo a brief period of discomfort, uncertain where Leigh stands ideologically in relation to them and their status as convicts. Fortunately Leigh proves her worth and loyalty to all the men once the action starts.

Leigh functions as a Hawksian woman in another manner as well:

> She trusts completely her own spontaneous impulses of attraction and repulsion. She has a sense of identity beyond her alliances (with high society), and she is committed only to those personal ties she wishes to acknowledge.[3]

For Leigh, this simply means that despite the fact that society has labeled Napoleon Wilson a murderer, she is attracted to him and able to show (even flaunt) that she feels this way. Thus at the resolution of *Assault on Precinct 13*, Leigh looks to Wilson and meaningfully refuses a stretcher. Having learned toughness and defiance straight from Wilson, she too will walk out of the battlefield on her own two feet. She is comfortable in her identity and choices, and unafraid to broadcast it to the representatives of society (the police) who appear for the clean-up.

Going deeper, Laurie Zimmer's character is Hawksian because of her overall demeanor and personality. She does not ever stoop to panic, she is delicate and tender (with Kathy's dad) when the situation warrants it, and she fully understands the situation outside the precinct house, as well as its ramifications, even explaining to Julie the impact of the downed telephone pole at the end of the street. Most importantly, Zimmer is beautiful, and she broadcasts a character with a sense of humor. After delivering a heartfelt speech to Wells, Leigh realizes that the gun he was pointing at her is empty. "I went through *all* that and his gun wasn't even loaded," she moans, seeing the humor of the situation.

Despite these distinctively Howard Hawks and *Rio Bravo*–type touches, *Assault on Precinct 13* has some notable differences from its source material. For one thing, the villainous antagonists are very different in the two productions. In *Rio Bravo*, Burdette's thugs all have distinguishable faces and names, and they are seen in more than one setting, both in combat and relaxing at the saloon. Furthermore, they are easily controlled when Dude stops and disarms them at the rim of town. In contrast, the gangs who attack the police station in *Assault on Precinct 13* are never depicted in human terms at all. They are simply automatons laying siege to the precinct. When one dies coming through a window, another one merely pops up to take his place. Nor is there any illusion of control: The police are overwhelmed, and they

remain so until the tense climax. Also, there is a very important difference in social classes between the 1959 villains and those on display in 1976. Burdette in *Rio Bravo* represents the top of society: an influential, wealthy man who has the money and the ability to exercise his will. The gangs of *Assault on Precinct 13* represent the bottom of American society, not the top. They are the disenfranchised poor. They are also depicted in "cult" terms, ritualistically bleeding themselves and acting by the rules of a cryptic code of honor.

Not surprisingly, the villains of *Assault on Precinct 13* originate not from the world of Howard Hawks, but a more modern antecedent: the George A. Romero cult classic, *Night of the Living Dead*. In that independent horror film, also a siege picture at heart, a group of diverse people seek refuge in an isolated farmhouse as droves of the carnivorous living dead wander the countryside. As night falls, the hungry zombies became more numerous, mounting deadly attack after attack, forcing the humans to shoot them in the head, burn them, and otherwise destroy them completely. The zombies are faceless goons, an evil force of dangerous numbers. And because they are already dead, they are virtually unstoppable, able to survive multiple attacks.

In *Assault on Precinct 13*, those same unnerving qualities are inherited by the L.A. street thugs. They mindlessly attack the station, one after the other, despite the fact that their numbers are being drastically decimated by enemy gunfire. In essence, the members of Street Thunder are thoughtless robots, programmed by their hatred only to destroy their opponents and gain access to the station. In both *Night of the Living Dead* and *Assault on Precinct 13*, this strange, inhuman behavior is given a surface plausibility and legitimacy through a bizarre scientific explanation. In *Night of the Living Dead*, radiation from a returning Venus Probe causes the plague of the living dead in Pittsburgh. In *Assault on Precinct 13*, Bishop listens to the radio as an announcer reports about heavy sunspot activity. Later, Bishop speculates to the captain of Precinct 13 that the upsurge gang violence may be a result of all that "sunspotting." As in *Night of the Living Dead*, this explanation seems to be a casual afterthought, one of many possible examinations to be mulled over after a viewing of the picture.

Night of the Living Dead and *Assault on Precinct 13* share many other facets of the "struggle for survival" story. In both situations, the primary hero is an African-American. In *Night of the Living Dead*, the hero is the truck driver Ben (Duane Jones), and in *Assault on Precinct 13* it is Lt. Bishop (Austin Stoker). In both films there is an attempt to flee the site of a siege in a nearby vehicle, and in both situations the plan proves fatal to those willing to risk it. Finally, *Night of the Living Dead* was considered revolutionary in 1968 for introducing its heroine, Barbara (Judith O'Dea), and then leaving her comatose in a state of shock for the duration of the picture. In *Assault*, it is Kathy's father who heroically kills a gang member and then retreats into silent shock for the remainder of the film.

Besides the fact that Molotov cocktails are employed in both films too, the primary similarity between *Assault on Precinct 13* and *Night of the Living Dead*, outside the siege scenario, is a heated debate about how to achieve safety. In *Night of the Living Dead*, smart and resourceful Ben wants to remain on the first floor and board up the windows, but the obnoxious (and white) Mr. Cooper (Karl Hardman) wants to hide in the basement. Ben refuses to enter the basement, considering it a one-way ticket to death. Ironically, at the close of the film, he survives the zombie nightmare by hiding in the basement — only to be killed by fellow humans! The same "upstairs-downstairs" debate is voiced in *Assault on Precinct 13*, when Napoleon Wilson (a white man) suggests to a black man (Bishop) that the precinct basement is the best place to hide. Bishop considers the cellar a death-trap, but like Ben before

him ends up surviving by retreating there. The discussion is given less prominence in *Assault on Precinct 13* than in Romero's flick, but it is nonetheless visible and highly reminiscent of *Night of the Living Dead*.

Assault on Precinct 13 is a great film because it audaciously melds the western genre and the Hawks *Rio Bravo* prototype with the graphic violence and gritty reality of modern horror pictures such as *Night of the Living Dead*. The final result is a film of considerable ingenuity and cunning. It may be the offspring of two disparate parents, but its parts fit together very cohesively. Some of this cohesion arises out of the fact that John Carpenter skillfully charts how it is possible, and even plausible, for a group of police officers to become isolated in a modern city. He believably sets up this entrapment step by step. First he introduces the wasted neighborhood of Anderson, an area of condemned and forgotten slums. Next, his plot sets up a transition wherein only a skeleton crew of police officers is left manning a police station in preparation for a relocation. This situation keeps a few people in the dangerous environment until night, when Carpenter sets his deadly siege. In the thick of the darkness, it is impossible to see the city as anything but distant specks of light, so the sequestered nature of the setting feels real.

Things escalate quickly from there. The bad guys are equipped with silencers (so their gunshots are not heard by others), and they cut off the phone lines (making communication outside of the station impossible.) It may seem an unusual scenario to some, but the isolation is painstakingly set up throughout *Assault on Precinct 13*'s logical and very plausible script.

One of the best ways to disarm the questioning minds of film critics is to permit *dramatis personae* to note the irony of the plot before viewers can do likewise. In *Assault on Precinct 13*, Carpenter repeatedly has his characters comment, in disbelief, that "this can't happen, not today!" or even, "We're in the middle of a city ... in a police station ...

someone will drive by eventually!" These pointed remarks serve to make the siege of *Assault on Precinct 13* so frightening and unusual an event that even the characters caught up in it cannot believe how quickly and dangerously it is unfolding. The structure of the script, which quickly piles incident upon jarring incident, also leaves little time for questions of believability.

Assault on Precinct 13 has so many terrific flourishes that it would be a long assignment to note them all in a single review. However, there are further points worth mentioning. The transition from bright daylight into blackest night is dramatized beautifully with a view of a rapidly dimming orange and purple sky. This colorful look at the heavens, which serves as the backdrop of a car chase, is not only lovely, but an element of John Carpenter's deliberately wide open "western" skyline, with the speeding cars representing modern steeds. Since all the primary characters (modern cowboys) are seen individually in driving sequences in cars or buses, "riding into town," as it were, it is not a stretch to consider these vehicles the contemporary equivalent of horses, or even stagecoaches.

Composed by John Carpenter, the music of *Assault on Precinct 13* is also used artfully throughout the film. Delightfully, it even serves as counterpoint in one important scene. As Kathy skips blissfully to the parked ice cream truck, unaware of the approaching gang members, the truck broadcasts the happy and innocent music of ice cream trucks the world over. As the scene grows more tense, the music no longer seems innocent, but harsh and grating. The ice cream man turns the music off, and the scene suddenly turns violent quickly.

Assault on Precinct 13 is also a shocking film in that it undercuts conventional wisdom. Even as it makes reference to *Rio Bravo* and Hollywood's golden past, it is also brutally modern in its depiction of excessive violence. When young Kathy is murdered at point-blank range for no reason, the audi-

ence is taken aback by the act. This kind of thing just *does not* happen to innocent children in the mainstream Hollywood cinema, pre–*Colors* (1986). It is an unexpected and disgusting event, and prescient of the random violence set loose in the free-for-all atmosphere of the 1990s. In *Assault on Precinct 13*, the gang explodes with violence against the ice cream man and a poor little child, and their overwhelming anger seems totally misdirected. In this case, it is rather sad that John Carpenter so expertly predicted the future of American society and cinema.

John Carpenter's direction is lean and effective throughout *Assault on Precinct 13*. His framing during the final sequence is among the best he has ever composed. Following the gas explosion in the precinct basement, Bishop, Leigh and Wilson materialize out of the swirling smoke. The triumvirate is huddled together at the center of the screen in a formation which suggests camaraderie. Framing them, at the extreme right and left edges of the shot, two cops suddenly appear, and everything changes. Society has returned, forcing these three heroes to resume the roles of civilization. To the cops, Bishop is a policeman (and therefore to be respected), Wilson is a dangerous criminal (and therefore to be manhandled) and Leigh is a woman (and therefore to be treated as weak, and offered a stretcher.) In one shot, then, Carpenter expresses the camaraderie of this group, and the rules which make their further association with one another impossible. Following this provocative framing, Bishop protects Wilson and thereby proves he is not only a cop, but a human being as well. Thus the film closes with a heroic two-shot as friends Wilson and Bishop walk out of the basement together, side by side.

Despite the extreme violence of *Assault on Precinct 13*, the film is optimistic in a very strange way. In the cinematic, Howard Hawks–1970s world of *Assault on Precinct 13*, blacks, whites, women, men, cops and convicts work together and even share a common morality. As they all work together to stay alive and protect Kathy's father, an image of hope becomes clear. Race, sex, and even the law are not important to these people when things come down to issues of honor, decency and morality. Inherent in *Assault on Precinct 13* is the belief that yes, we all *can* get along, because as human beings we share a common ground.

This total acceptance of diversity is applied to the villains as well. The thugs of Street Thunder are not of one ethnic group, but of *all* ethnic groups. Though blacks, whites and Hispanics are working together for evil in this case, they seem to exist in a world where there is no prejudice or race hatred. And the bottom line is that they are working together for a common cause, and that again (albeit in a twisted way) that cause is related to honor and a shared (if distinctly alternate) morality. In reality, crime in America is seldom so color-blind or race-blind as it is in *Assault on Precinct 13*. Still, this rainbow coalition of criminals has a bit of a downside as far as reality is concerned. Recalling the goofy, bizarre gangs of *The Warriors* (1979), some of the thugs in Street Thunder are less than menacing in appearance. For instance, the guy who shoots little Kathy is an effeminate blonde in a black muscle shirt. Skinny and small, he hardly seems threatening.

Assault on Precinct 13 is filled with references and notions that are repeated throughout John Carpenter's career. The modern-day siege in Los Angeles is revisited in *Prince of Darkness* (1987). Carpenter's preoccupation with street people is also carried over into both that film and his follow-up, *They Live* (1988). Also, *Assault on Precinct 13*'s opening shoot-out, with cops raining bullets down a narrow alleyway trench at escaping criminals, would be restaged during *They Live* with alien-controlled police massacring the Los Angeles resistance cell.

The number "6" crops up repeatedly in John Carpenter productions. In *Assault on Precinct 13*, six youths are killed, and in *The Fog*, the lepers significantly must claim six lives for the six co-conspirators in Antonio Bay. In *Halloween* and *Assault on Precinct 13*, there are references to the sixth grade. Kathy's father says to Kathy that her teacher, Mrs. Steward, has never taken any big steps out of the sixth grade. In *Halloween*, Laurie shares with Tommy Doyle a variation of that line: that his friend Lonnie will never make it out of the sixth grade.

Besides these touches, *Assault on Precinct 13* depicts a perennial Carpenter theme: the faceless brand of evil (*Halloween*, *The Fog*, *The Thing*). It also dramatizes a criminal who is in fact a hero (*Escape from New York*). Beyond these common brushstrokes, the screenplay of *Assault on Precinct 13* features characters named after Howard Hawks characters and associates, just as the sheriff of Haddonfield is named Leigh Brackett in *Halloween*. And finally, Carpenter uses an alias on this film (John T. Chance), as he would later do on the credits of *Prince of Darkness* (Martin Quatermass) and *They Live* (Frank Armitage).

Halloween (1978)

Critical Reception

"The most frightening flick in years ... a superb exercise in the art of suspense ... Nasty, voyeuristic, relentless, it aims at nothing but to scare the hell out of you."— David Ansen, *Newsweek:* "Trick or Treat," December 4, 1978, page 116.

"The screenplay ... is simple but it is not simple-minded. It is admirably functional and to the point. It also keeps us off guard and is sometimes even funny.... Mr. Carpenter obtains a lot of chills by using a subjective camera."—Vincent Canby, *The New York Times:* "Lessons in Scaring," January 21, 1979.

"Not only the scariest horror film since *Psycho* (1960), but also the most imaginatively directed ... foremost a fascinating exercise in style. Carpenter truly understands how to make a good horror film according to the rules of the genre, blending together the dark, spooky atmosphere essential to Val Lewton; the humor and suspense that go hand in hand in Hitchcock; the cheap-but-fun-tricks and shocks found in William Castle; and the graphic violence that is a staple of the post–*Night of the Living Dead* (1968) American horror film."—Danny Peary, *Cult Films*, Delacorte Press, 1981, page 123.

"*Halloween* is a genuine *tour de force.*... Carpenter is able to build a tempo that keeps audiences leaping out of their seats.... Carpenter begins with a few Val Lewton touches ... and escalates from there to full scale carnage.... Carpenter also creates a sense of paranoia through his imaginative use of light and shadow."—Darrell Moore, *The Best, Worst and Most Unusual: Horror Films*, Beekman House, 1983, page 121.

"A terrifying and creepy film ... Carpenter is uncannily skilled at the use of foreground in his compositions.... And it's interesting how he paints his victims.... The performances are ... absorbing.... The movie's a slice of life that is carefully painted (in drab daylights and impenetrable nighttimes) before its human monster enters the scene."—Roger Ebert, *Roger Ebert's Home Movie Companion*, Andrew and McMeel, 1993, page 273.

"The first 10 minutes are a blatant rip-off of the shower scene in *Psycho* and the entire movie is studded with fancy camera angles and obtrusive tracking dolly shots. All this trickery ... cannot disguise the basic inanity of the enterprise. *Halloween* is, simply, a high school horror film.... The direction, by someone named John Carpenter, who also wrote the script ... and music, is pedestrian."—Robert Asahina, *The New Leader:* "Halloween Film Fantasies," December 18, 1978, pgs. 17–18.

Cast and Credits

CAST: Donald Pleasence (Dr. Sam Loomis); Jamie Lee Curtis (Laurie Strode); Nancy Loomis (Annie); P. J. Soles (Lynda); Charles Cyphers (Sheriff Brackett); Kyle Richards (Lindsey); Brian Andrews (Tommy Doyle); John Michael Graham (Bob); Nancy Stephens (Marion); Arthur Malet (Graveyard Keeper); Mickey Yablans (Richie); Brent LePage (Lonnie); Robert Phalen (Dr. Wynn); Tony Moran (Michael age 23); Will Sandin (Michael age 6); Sandy Johnson (Judith Myers); David Kyle (Boyfriend); Peter Griffith (Laurie's father); Nick Castle (The Shape).

CREDITS: A Compass International Pictures Release. Moustapha Akkad Presents a Debra Hill Production. *Screenplay:* John Carpenter and Debra Hill. *Director of Photography:* Dean Cundey. *Film Editors:* Tommy Wallace, Charles Bornstein. *Music:* John Carpenter. *Associate Producer:* Kool Lusby. *Production Manager:* Don Behrns. *Production Designer:* Tommy Wallace. *Executive Producer:* Irwin Yablans. *Produced by:* Debra Hill. *Directed by:* John Carpenter. *Camera Operator:* Ray Stella. *Assistant Cameraman:* Fred Victor. *Second Assistant Cameraman:* Krishna Rao. *Set Decorator/Property Master:* Craig Stearns. *Assistant Art Director:* Randy Moore. *Set Painter:* Richard Girod. *Script Supervisor:* Louise Jaffe. *Assistant Director:*

Rick Wallace. *Second Assistant Director:* Jack DeWolf. *Sound Mixer:* Tommy Causey. *Boom Man:* Joe Brennan. *Make-up:* Erica Ulland. *Wardrobe:* Beth Rodgers. *Stills:* Kim Gottlieb. *Gaffer:* Mark Walthour. *Best Boy:* Josh Miller. *Stunts:* Jim Windburn. *Electrician:* Reed Freeman. *Key Grip:* Dylan Shepard. *Best Boy:* Steve Mathis. *Grip:* Walt Hill. *Production Assistants:* Barry Bernardi, Paul Fox. *Panaglide:* Ray Stella. *Supervising Sound Editor:* William Stevenson, MPSE. *Re-Recording:* Samuel Goldwyn Studios. *Music Recording:* Sound Arts. *Orchestration:* Dan Wyman. *Music Recordist and Mixer:* Peter Bergren. *Music Coordinator:* Bob Walters. *Music Performed by:* The Bowling Green Philharmonic Orchestra. "Don't Fear the Reaper" by Blue Oyster Cult, courtesy of C.B.S. Records. *The Thing* courtesy of R.K.O. General. *Forbidden Planet* courtesy of MGM. Filmed in *Panavision.* Metrocolor. *Titles and Opticals:* MGM. *MPAA Rating:* R. *Running Time:* 91 minutes.

"I met him 15 years ago. I was told there was nothing left. No reason, no conscience, no understanding … and even the most rudimentary sense of life and death, of good or evil, right or wrong. I met this six year old child with this blank, pale, *emotionless* face, and the blackest eyes … the Devil's eyes. I spent eight years trying to reach him, and then another seven trying to keep him locked up because I realized that what was living behind that boy's eyes was purely and simply evil." — Dr. Loomis explains his history with escaped mental patient Michael Myers.

SYNOPSIS: On Halloween night in 1963, six year old Michael Myers spies on his older sister, Judith, as she fools around with her boyfriend. After the teenagers have made love, Michael dons a clown mask and kills Judith with a long butcher knife. After the deed is done, he walks outside his house, still grasping the knife and wearing his Halloween clown costume. His parents come home and find him alone on the street, staring vacantly into space with the bloody weapon.

The scene shifts to 1978, when Dr. Sam Loomis and a nurse for the state, Marion, drive to Smith's Grove Sanitarium on a rainy night. Their job: to pick up an adult Michael Myers, who has not spoken for 15 years, and bring him before a judge for a hearing. When Loomis and Marion arrive at the hospital gates, patients are wandering around in the night in their white gowns. As Loomis phones for help, the escaped Michael Myers attacks Marion, steals the car, and drives away into the night.

In Haddonfield on Halloween morning, studious teenager Laurie Strode brings the keys to the abandoned Myers house for her father, a real estate agent. Little Tommy Doyle warns that the Myers house is an evil place, but Laurie drops off the keys anyway, unaware that Michael Myers is watching her from inside the house. He has come home, after 15 years. Curious, Myers follows Laurie to school and watches as Tommy Doyle is bullied by sixth graders. During English class, Laurie gazes out the window and sees the Smith's Grove vehicle parked outside. After a few moments it is gone, but Laurie is curious about it.

Meanwhile, Dr. Loomis picks up Michael's trail. He finds his discarded hospital clothing and a crashed truck from Phelps Garage. Although Loomis does not know it, the escaped mental patient is now garbed in blue mechanic's overalls, armed with a stolen butcher knife, and wearing a pale white Halloween mask. Loomis phones the authorities in Haddonfield and warns them that they may have a serious problem.

Laurie and her two friends, the sarcastic Annie and the ditzy Lynda, walk home from school and discuss their Halloween plans. Lynda and her boyfriend Bob are planning to rendezvous at the Wallace house, where Annie is babysitting little Lindsey Wallace. Three houses down, Laurie will be babysitting Tommy Doyle. On the walk home, Laurie thinks she sees a masked man nearby, first in the bushes, and later by a laundry line in Mr. Riddle's backyard.

Unaware that Michael Myers has targeted her as well, Annie picks Laurie up for the evening festivities. They smoke pot and go about their babysitting rituals. As night falls, Myers spies on the girls as they babysit alone in individual homes. On the television, six straight hours of horror movies play out.

Dr. Loomis arrives in Haddonfield and rushes to the cemetery. There, he discovers that Judith Myers's grave stone has been stolen. Now he knows for certain that Michael Myers is in Haddonfield. Later, Loomis meets with Sheriff Leigh Brackett, Annie's father, and warns him about Myers. Loomis and Brackett visit the abandoned, dilapidated Myers house and find a slaughtered, half-eaten dog in a dark corner — further proof of Myers's arrival. Loomis recounts to Bracket how he has known Myers for 15 years, and how he considers the boy an inhuman, emotionless monster.

Michael Myers closes in on Annie at the Wallace house. When she spills popcorn on her clothes and walks out to the laundry shed, Michael stays close. Tommy Doyle sees Michael outside in the night and panics, believing he has seen the Bogeyman. Laurie calms him down, unaware that Tommy has seen a real-life predator. Meanwhile, Michael Myers kills the Wallaces' dog.

Annie gets back into the house and hears from her boyfriend Paul, who wants to come over. Annie takes Lindsey to Tommy Doyle's house to stay with Laurie. On her way to pick up Paul, Annie is strangled and then stabbed by Myers in her car.

Lynda and Bob show up at the vacant Wallace house and wonder briefly where Annie is. They go upstairs and make love. Afterwards, Bob is murdered in the kitchen by Michael Myers. Wearing Bob's glasses and a bed sheet over his body, Myers approaches Lynda. He strangles her while she is talking on the phone with Laurie.

Laurie doesn't know what has happened to Lynda, but she is concerned by the abrupt end to their conversation. She puts Lindsey and Tommy to bed and walks alone to the Wallace house. It is dark and quiet inside, but once upstairs Laurie finds a shrine to Judith Myers: Annie lies sprawled on a bed, the stolen grave marker behind her. The corpses of Lynda and Bob have also been put on display, and Myers soon strikes again, stabbing wildly at Laurie. After falling down the stairs, Laurie escapes the Wallace house and seeks safety. Tommy lets her back into the Doyle house, but Michael finds a way in as well. Forced to defend herself, Laurie stabs the psychotic killer in the neck with a knitting needle. Believing him dead, she runs upstairs and informs Tommy and Lindsey — but Michael is still alive. Laurie locks the children in a bedroom and then hides in a closet. Michael attacks her again, and Laurie stabs him in the eye with a wire hanger. When Myers drops his knife, Laurie stabs him in the gut with it.

Believing again that the nightmare is over, Laurie sends Lindsey and Tommy down to the Mackenzies to call the police, but Michael sits up, and rushes for her. He starts to strangle her, and Laurie pulls his mask off, revealing a handsome young man. Dr. Loomis shows up at just the right moment, and he shoots Myers at point-blank range.

Still alive, Myers backs towards a second story ledge, and Loomis fires again and again until Michael falls backwards from the ledge. When Loomis looks down into the yard below, however, Myers has disappeared. A terrified Laurie realizes that Myers really *is* the Bogeyman. A shaken Loomis affirms her belief. And somewhere in the night, Myers watches…

COMMENTARY: Perhaps the most difficult task facing the intrepid film critic is the adequate expression of reasons why a good movie merits praise. Although details such as acting, directing, cinematography, screenplay and *mise-en-scène* all play an important part in a film's success and a subsequent "positive" review, each item is merely a component,

"What's the matter, Bob? Can't I get your ghost?" A shrouded Michael Myers stalks Lynda in *Halloween* (1978).

a piece of a larger and often mystifying puzzle. An extraordinary film is much more than the sum of its ingredients, often existing as much as a mixture of magic and chemistry as of qualitative critical strengths and easily definable points of interest.

John Carpenter's *Halloween* is just such a film. From acting and cinematography to music and screenplay, its constituent elements are superbly handled. And yet, the overall atmosphere of the film is spellbinding far beyond the high quality of these individual factors. Simply expressed, *Halloween* is a 90-minute nightmare of the highest order, a horror film that transcends its genre and transports the viewer into a world filled with terror and suspense. It is one of the most frightening films ever made, and it remains equally frightening after multiple viewings.

To be so effective a journey into terror,

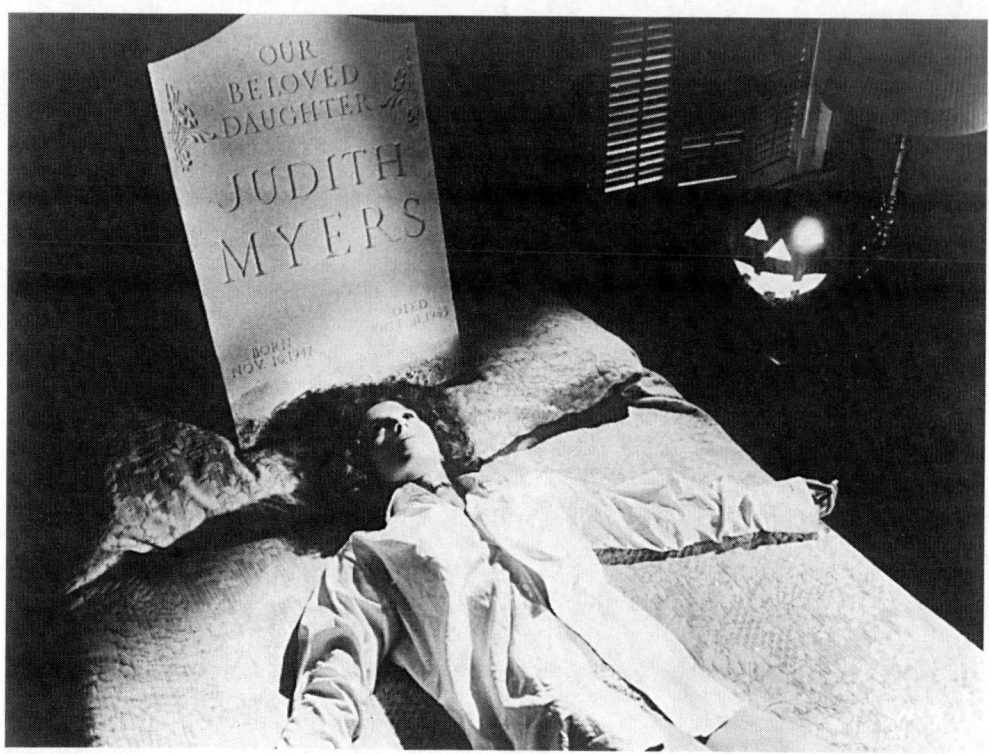

Michael Myers has created a deadly treat in the Lindsay house: a dead Annie (Nancy Loomis) in *Halloween* (1978).

Halloween makes expert use not just of film techniques, but of the universal elements of fear which still plague humanity even in the well-lit modern world. Its strength as a horror picture relies on its wholesale plundering of our deepest, darkest, and most instinctual reactions to frightening situations. Thus *Halloween's* playground is mankind's shared heritage: our primitive beginning as creatures of the cave who once huddled in darkness and feared everything in the world that we could not understand. A rainy night, a crash of thunder, a lightning storm, shadows emerging in darkness, and even an evil force that will not die; these are all elements which grab viewers in the most unevolved places of their psyches.

To effectively bring these primitive fears to life, *Halloween* does what few films have had the intelligence and wherewithal to do: It deconstructs our technological, contemporary world. In *Halloween*, humans exist as

they did in the caves of our prehistory. Science, medicine and psychology, the technological and sociological tools man utilizes today to rationalize and explain scary things such as rain, thunder and lightning, are useless in the film. Dr. Loomis is a failure as a psychologist, unable to heal Michael Myers, let alone understand him, even after 15 years. His role in *Halloween* is not that of a doctor. He is a knight or a hunter instead, a man who has set out to slay a dragon. And Michael Myers? Myers cannot be explained rationally in terms of psychology. He does not suffer from a specific, diagnosable or treatable disorder, and Dr. Loomis describes the monster unscientifically, just as one of our ancestors at the dawn of time might have: Myers is purely and simply evil.

This is an important distinction in any analysis of *Halloween*, because "evil" is very much dead as a concept in modern-day America. "Evil" as such does not exist anymore.

The Columbine teens who in 1999 committed the brutal murders of schoolmates in Colorado are not described as "evil" by the media or psychology experts. They are described instead as a "product of their environment," or as "disturbed." Motives are attributed, and reasons for the behavior are documented. Experts rifle through the DSM-IV to find some reason, some clue as to why a child could commit murder. Likewise, the killers who sit on death row across the country are not "purely and simply evil" either. They are instead a result of genetic predispositions to alcoholism, drug addiction, child abuse, crime. Those who commit deeds of violence are not denounced as "devilish" entities, but rather as explainable, understandable creatures who are even pitiable in their own way. *Halloween's* Michael Myers is a determinedly different animal.

He cannot be explained. He is shot six times at point-blank range, and he survives. He kills and kills again, but no one knows why. He can catch up with you at a brisk walk, even while you *run* away from him, fleeing for your life. If you think of closing a window to protect yourself, he has already gotten inside through that very window and is waiting to catch you as you approach the portal. He watches you and waits, biding his time, forever patient. He is the perfect embodiment of primitive evil: the bogeyman whom man cannot escape, no matter what, no matter how much man grows or thinks he learns. This is a terrifying concept to us as rational, thinking creatures, because as a society we are not accustomed to dealing with the irrational, or worse, the inexplicable.

At least the shark in *Jaws* (1975) kills because of its biological nature, because of what it is. It has a stomach to feed, and it eats to survive. Though man may be afraid of a great white shark, at least on some level he can understand what drives the shark. By contrast, Michael Myers is the walking, stalking embodiment of mankind's fear that we do not control or understand the world. That

is what makes him a terrifying figure. He is a killing machine, but exactly what pleasure or need is fulfilled by the act of killing is left unclear to the viewer.

The victims of Michael Myers in *Halloween* do not expect to die at the hands of such a monster because they live in what should be a safe society. There is medicine, science, law, education; there is the security blanket of parental protection. In *Halloween*, none of those protections function adequately. Parents are universally absent, the law is completely ineffective, and science has released (but not created) the monster which stalks the streets. Thus teenagers Laurie, Annie, Lynda and Bob have no protection at all from Michael Myers. In fact, they are even worse off than the cavemen of antiquity. At least those early representatives of the species *knew* to be afraid, knew to fear the forces they could not understand. The characters in *Halloween* are unprepared and unable to conceive of a reality that includes so irrational a monster.

In fact, the inability to cope with Michael makes his deadly mission to Haddonfield all the more successful. Partly because of the "Halloween" celebration, which allows a monster to walk around in daylight unnoticed, and partly because of a determined stubbornness *not* to see that which is unpleasant or unacceptable, the characters in *Halloween* for the most part have only a borderline awareness of this very noticeable ghoul. None of the adults take notice of him, though he drives past Dr. Loomis and Sheriff Brackett at one point, and steals a gravestone unnoticed at another. Even the teens are unable to perceive him, as he drives by them, stands ahead of them on a wide open street, and peers at them through windows. Myers is invisible to society because society does not permit for the possibility of such a creature's existence. As J.P. Telotte noted in his analysis of *Halloween*:

> What Carpenter seems intent on demonstrating is how consistently our perceptions and our understandings of

the world around us fall short.... We are conditioned by our experience and culture to see less ... to dismiss from our image contents those visions for which we might not be able to account.... It is only natural that the children ... see more than do their adolescent babysitters, who in turn have a slightly more encompassing view than do their adult counterparts.[4]

If one accepts this notion, then it becomes clear that Tommy Doyle is really *Halloween*'s most insightful character. Earlier than anyone else, he understands who and what Michael Myers really is: the Bogeyman. Of course, no one listens to his warnings, until finally Laurie is confronted with the evil first-hand. Her last line of dialogue ("It was the bogeyman, wasn't it?") is a vindication not just of Tommy personally, but of the perceptive eyes of childhood. Only the youngest of the species, for whom the monsters in caves still live as monsters in closets and under beds, can see that the world really does include inexplicable terrors.

Halloween is so effective thematically because it takes an irrational horror and then places it firmly in what seems to be a very realistic world, populated by realistic people. The night rituals of Halloween (trick-or-treating, jack-o-lanterns, bobbing for apples, costume parties, babysitting, horror movie marathons) are easy to recognize as familiar symbols, and the main characters (except for Dr. Loomis) always talk about their lives, rather than about the plot. Projecting an easy grace in front of the camera, Jamie Lee Curtis plays a character who seems true to viewers in both heart and spirit. She worries about boys, takes school seriously, likes to have a little fun — but at the same time is concerned that she will get caught for smoking pot. She has a sense of humor, and a vulnerability that makes her charming and easy to like. She is Everyteen, a good kid on the verge of growing up, and the screenplay is smart enough to make her fully aware of Michael only near the climax. This development insures that

Laurie comes across as a person first, and a victim second.

Annie's sarcasm ("It's hard growing up with a cynical father"; "I hate a guy with a car and no sense of humor") and Lynda's dumb blond demeanor and innocent charm ("Books? Who needs books?") also play as uncomfortably real. There is no forced theatrical dialogue to call attention to the fact that these people are in a movie. And, except for the numerous killings, *Halloween* could almost be described as a teenage slice of life movie. Later *Halloween* pictures are not so real simply because the characters all begin the picture with an awareness of who and what Michael Myers really is. By contrast, in the first picture he is the wild card thrown into a routine, believable world. When the ordinary and extraordinary meet in the film, the horror is amplified because no one knows or expects the irrational monstrosity lurking outside their doors. There is no meeting of unusual and usual circumstances in the sequels, and each begins in an extraordinary world, replete with a celebrity bogeyman.

To make his collision of nightmare and real worlds more effective, John Carpenter pulls out all the stops in *Halloween*. Like a general deploying his troops, he rallies his cinematic resources to create a film that is unexpectedly suspenseful. In the early sequences, Carpenter introduces Laurie and her friends. He does so in long tracking shots through the neighborhood. His choice not only lends a feeling of movement to the picture, it sets up the spatial dynamics that will become important as the horror escalates. The relationship of the homes, the front yards, the streets, the sidewalks all form part of his geography of horror, and the early scenes occurring in and around suburban Haddonfield in day and early evening arm viewers with a very necessary mental map. Of all the *Halloween* films, the first is the only one in which the town of Haddonfield seems like a real town, and it is because Carpenter explores it so fully before beginning Myers's reign of terror. The director introduces you to the terrain, and the routine of the terrain, and then spices it with horror. He establishes people and places first, before plunging them into a night of terrors.

Other fine stylistic elements abound. As Loomis and Marion drive to pick up Myers at the Smith's Grove Sanitarium, it is raining heavily in the dark night, and the rain throws moving shadows across Pleasence's face. On the soundtrack, the metronome-like repetition of the windshield wipers puts one on edge instantly. The overall impression of the scene, with the blob-like shadows and the beating of the wipers, is one of dread, anticipation and fear. There is the tacit acknowledgment that man can be overcome by the elements of nature (rain) and is protected only by his own artifice (the windshield wipers). It is a creepy moment which leads immediately to another creepy moment: the car's headlights soon register a ramshackle group of white-gowned prisoners walking the sanitarium's grounds. There is a feeling of chaos in this sequence reminiscent of *Night of the Living Dead*, as the tormented souls wander mindlessly about, illuminated in the bright white glare. There is something very wrong about their freedom, about the fact that the unstable have crossed the threshold from captivity to freedom without society taking notice.

In contrast to the inmates, who are illuminated in the stark white of the car's front lights, Michael Myers is first seen as an adult in the rich red hue of the tail lights. Red, of course, remains the color of the devil, blood, and symbolically, evil. He is not a deer caught in a white headlight, like the lost souls wandering the sanitarium's grounds; he is the devil in a red dress.

Another nice touch comes when Laurie pulls off Michael Myers's mask near the conclusion of the film, and a strange timeless moment follows. Loomis, who has just run up the stairs with his pistol in hand, hesitates before shooting. A shocked Michael also hesitates. In a film filled wall-to-wall with action, there is a moment of total stillness and inaction. Only when Michael pulls the mask on again and is once more "The Shape" does Loomis pull the trigger and shoot him. The implication of this scenario is that Myers's anonymity, his status as "the Bogeyman," is enhanced by his costume. He *hides* in the costume. Devoid of the mask, he is human again, and Dr. Loomis cannot bring himself to kill a fellow human. In that split second when Myers is without his armor, Loomis acknowledges both his and Michael's humanity.

Finally, Carpenter leaves perhaps his best touch for last. After Michael's body has disappeared from the yard below the Wallace ledge, *Halloween* takes a decidedly nasty turn. Instead of simply ending with evil defeated, the film turns to a well-edited and timed montage which shows, in reverse order, all the places where Michael Myers has hidden during the course of the film. The montage starts in the Doyle house, goes backwards through the Wallace house, and finally ends at the abandoned "haunted house" of the film, the Myers place where all the terror began in 1963. All through the montage, the sound of heavy breathing is audible on the soundtrack, signifying Myers' continued existence nearby. Though some people think this trick borders on directorial cruelty, the montage establishes the film's overall theme: that evil can be alive anywhere. Thanks to this stylish montage of the film's setting, it is with this final, chilling thought that one leaves the theater.

Halloween is so very scary because it takes advantage of a factor other slasher pictures ignore. Michael is not just a dumb killer who appears, stalks his victim and kills. On the contrary, he is frightening because most of the time he does not kill. Instead, he is the ultimate voyeur, hiding outside windows, watching lovers from an unseen corner, and so forth. He is patient, and he bides his time. This fact makes *Halloween* suspenseful. The film does not just charge forward with a death every five minutes. Instead, it introduces three very likable teenage girls and sets a murderer down nearby to watch them. When will he act? Whom will he kill? Whom will he spare? What triggers him? Will anyone notice him out there by the hanging flower pot or the laundry room window? John Carpenter restrains the film's rapid pace just enough that these questions can be asked and escalating terror will result. A violent death is scary, but much scarier is the constant wondering when the next violent death will occur.

As author David Hogan wrote in his analysis of *Halloween* in *Dark Romance*: "The randomness of Michael's violence ... is the intelligence that sets *Halloween* apart from other less thoughtful examples of the subgenre."[5] That is indeed true. In *Halloween VI: The Curse of Michael Myers*, for instance, almost no time is spent on stalking. Michael appears out of nowhere, and he kills suddenly. Consequently, there is no suspense because viewers are not aware of his presence before the "shock" set-piece. Directors of future *Halloween* pictures should remember that it is the knowledge of Myers's presence, watching and waiting in the shadows, that makes these films scary.

Within the context of its genre, *Halloween* is also continually interesting. It is the instigator of a rash of "stalker" films, and it has become so popular, so well known, that it is constantly referred to both visually and in the dialogue of later productions. In Wes Craven's *Scream*, for instance, scenes from *Halloween* are played during the movie. At other junctures, there are eerie parallels. Casey Becker's father tells his wife to go "down the streets to the Mackenzies' house," recalling Laurie Strode's similar advice to children Tommy and Lindsey. (Oddly, this reference is reversed in *Halloween H20* when Laurie Strode instructs her teenage son to go down the street to the *Beckers'* house). And Blue Oyster Cult's hit "Don't Fear the Reaper" is also played in both *Scream* and *Halloween*. But beyond pop-culture references, *Halloween* also espouses a distinct philosophy of life that is at odds with other horror films

such as *A Nightmare on Elm Street*. In fact, John Carpenter's *Halloween* and Wes Craven's *A Nightmare on Elm Street* share what appears to be a very similar scene, and yet in each film the scene plays out a different ideology.

In *Halloween*, Laurie sits restlessly in English class while the (offscreen) teacher drones on at length about "fate" and "destiny." In the midst of the lecture, Laurie is distracted when she spots Michael Myers's car parked on the street just beyond the window. Carpenter's implication is that Laurie has, in fact, just glimpsed her fate. As the teacher explains on the soundtrack, "You can't escape fate," and so Laurie cannot escape her impending connection with the escaped serial killer.

A Nightmare on Elm Street also finds its heroine Nancy Thompson (Heather Langenkamp) in English class while another dull teacher discusses literature. This time, the subject is the resourcefulness of the melancholy prince *Hamlet*. The teacher notes that Hamlet stamps out the lies of his mother, something which Nancy will do in *Elm Street* as well, and that the prince probes and digs to find the truth, again as Nancy will do before the climax of Craven's picture. The *Elm Street* philosophy suggests that only by digging beneath the surface, by looking explicitly for the truth, can one overcome the lies of one's parents and survive.

Halloween's discussion of fate and predestination effectively transforms Laurie into a "trapped" character. No matter what, she cannot escape her fate: victimization by Michael Myers. Even the sequel to *Halloween* enhances this perception. *A Nightmare on Elm Street*'s literature discussion reflects Wes Craven's view that a resourceful person *can* control fate by digging for the truth. Nancy is thus an active force in her life, rather than a passive object victimized by a cruel destiny. Both philosophies are fascinating ones, and very different. Carpenter takes a more existential and nihilistic approach (we are all victims of chance and destiny), whereas

Craven believes that a person can affect the future for the better. As Carpenter made more films, this would be the philosophy he adopted as well, and *Starman*, *Prince of Darkness*, and *They Live* reveal how individuals can shape fate.

Not unexpectedly for a film of its quality, *Halloween* remains John Carpenter's most analyzed and dissected motion picture. What is surprising, perhaps, is the vast number of differing conclusions that have been drawn from the film and presented by critics. Some analysts even persist in seeing the film as a despicable, albeit stylish, exercise in horror because of Carpenter's adoption of the point-of-view, subjective camera. The long-held argument insists that this technique puts the audience in the position of "being" Michael Myers, *Halloween*'s mass-murderer. Some critics consider this a bad thing, claiming that it causes one to identify with violence and even become numb to it.

What this theory fails to take into account is that the subjective camera is explicitly involved in only one death scene, the film's opening sequence in which the young Michael spies on his sister, Judith, and eventually stabs her. The other deaths in the film are not lensed in this style. Furthermore, the one death that is subjective is staged in less explicit terms than those later in the film. Michael's plunging butcher knife (seen through the peepholes of a clown mask) is never seen to touch or penetrate human flash. What is seen instead is simply a large knife going back and forth in mid-air, grasped by a human hand. Thus John Carpenter is not inviting us to experience the "thrill" of murder "with our own murderous eyes, listening to the beat of our heart and the breathing of our lungs,"[6] because we do not see the moment of impact or its catastrophic results. It is not palpable to us and we, as the audience, do not feel responsible.

Furthermore, the subjective camera approach and subsequent murder in the preamble to *Halloween* are not designed to incite feelings of violence in viewers, but rather to

set up the scene's final surprise, the bizarre twist. The revelation that the callous "murderer" is a child, the victim's little brother in fact, is the sequence's exclamation, its moment of primal shock. John Carpenter makes this unexpected horror vividly clear when his camera pulls slowly up and away from young Michael on the street. As the camera assumes a high angle, it also distances itself both physically and metaphorically from the repellent image it records, as if ashamed. Tellingly, Michael and the other inhabitants of the frame remain frozen as the camera takes this stance, as if the horror of the moment has frozen time itself. Michael killing his sister is like Oedipus killing his father in the Greek tragedy: an opportunity for an exploration of societal mores. Seen in that light, *Halloween* invites viewers to be terrified and surprised by the murder it depicts, but not necessarily enthralled. Carpenter's modus operandi here, as often in his career, is also homage: the P.O.V. subjective camera opening of *Halloween* was inspired by similar sequences in Orson Welles's *Touch of Evil* (1958).

Other critics believe that Carpenter is exploring modern sexual mores in *Halloween*. These scholars tend to see the murder weapons (knives, knitting needles) as phallic symbols, and the murders as punishment for sexual misconduct. Annie and Lynda are promiscuous, and they die at Myers's hands. Laurie is a virgin, and she survives. Therefore, *Halloween* is (according to these critics) a puritan "cautionary" story about what happens to bad girls. John Carpenter himself came out against this theory, feeling it was a misinterpretation of the film's content and theme:

> The critics completely missed the boat there, I think…. The one girl who is the most sexually uptight just keeps stabbing this guy with a long knife. She's the most sexually frustrated. She's the one that's killed him. Not because she's a virgin, but because all that repressed sexual energy starts coming out. She uses all those phallic symbols

on the guy ... she doesn't have a boyfriend ... and she finds someone —
him.[7]

This explanation, though unusual, certainly explains some bizarre aspects of the
film. In one sequence, Laurie sings "Just the
Two of Us," a song about wishing to be alone
with a lover. As she sings, Michael Myers
springs into the foreground, as if on cue. She
is singing, subconsciously at least, to him.
This unusual relationship is continued in
Halloween II. The theme song of that film is
"Mr. Sandman," in which a female vocalist
implores Mr. Sandman to bring her a "dream,"
the perfect man. That too, is the theme song
of Laurie Strode. She wishes for the perfect
man, and Michael Myers appears. This becomes all the weirder when she realizes that
her perfect man also happens to be her
brother.

John Carpenter is not the only one to suggest that Laurie Strode's hidden sexual im-
pulses are thematically important to *Halloween*'s success. Vera Dika saw further
evidence of this Freudian relationship in the
text of the picture:

> Carpenter openly represents Michael as
> Laurie's "id." This reading is supported
> by the inclusion of footage from *For-
> bidden Planet* (1956).... The earlier film
> had portrayed a situation in which
> the unconscious desires, or the id, of
> the main character became manifest
> and threatened to destroy him and
> his world. Similarly, Laurie is almost
> destroyed by the strength of her
> repressed unconscious impulses. Her
> battle with Michael is a substitute for a
> sexual act.[8]

Though all of this subtext is interesting,
and it is refreshing that its proponents have
at least turned to specific moments from the
Halloween text to support their theories, a
more natural and honest response to *Halloween* and the character of Laurie Strode involves merely a close identification with her

as a sympathetic character. If one is to take
Dika's and Carpenter's arguments to their
logical conclusion, Laurie is guilty of the
murders because she has "wished" Michael
Myers into her life through her repressed
sexuality. This is fine, of course, and a legitimate possible reading of the film, but it is
important to recall that Jamie Lee Curtis
plays a completely sympathetic character. The
existence of her opponent, Michael Myers,
predates her own blossoming into sexual
awareness. Myers was a murderer at six, two
years before Laurie was even born. She is not
accountable, in any realistic or conventional
sense, for his killing spree, unless one takes
a totally deconstructionist view of the film.
Furthermore, to suggest that Laurie is guilty
(and thus "bad") is faintly misogynistic since
Laurie is not only a positive female character,
but a role model for a generation of women
(and men). She is a resourceful and heroic
character in *Halloween*. She fights the Bogeyman and wins through her resourcefulness
and determination. Through the extended
battle, Laurie remembers her responsibilities
(the safety of the children) and shows good
judgment. Interpreting her as responsible for
the Haddonfield massacre takes the pure evil
of Myers off the hook, and casts blame at the
feet of a very likable character, a nice person
and a film icon.

Halloween remains memorable not so
much because of what can be read into it,
but because of what actually unfolds on the
screen. *Halloween* is elegant in its simplicity
and its lean storytelling. Anything can be
read into the film, really, because that gruesome white mask of Michael Myers reflects
different things to different viewers. That
blank, pale face is a repository for all of our
deepest fears, and it can mean anything we
think it means. Michael may simply be an
escaped mental patient, a developmentally
arrested child playing deadly pranks (as has
been suggested by *Cult Movies* author Danny
Peary), or even a symbol of pure evil: the
Bogeyman. What remains important about
Halloween is not what it represents, but that

its execution as a film merits so many different interpretations. It is the most analyzed horror film since *Psycho*, and for good reason. It speaks the language of nightmares, and forever evokes the chill of fear.

The Fog (1980)

Critical Reception

"Like the best horror movies, *The Fog* is held together by a visual motif of perversion, a visually poetic idea. Opaque and amorphous ... the fog is both an expanding medium of death and a shroud.... The most horrifying episodes are often uncannily beautiful, and the movie is beautiful in moments of peace, too. Carpenter knows how to give his landscapes the hard-edged look of hallucination.... A low budget triumph, a genuinely poetic horror film." — David Denby, *New York*, February 18, 1980.

"An elegant, scary thriller of the supernatural that's far more impressive and satisfying than ... *Halloween*." — Kevin Thomas, *The Los Angeles Times*, February 2, 1980.

"As stunningly effective as anything John Carpenter has done to date ... an uneasy venture down a blind alley." — Tom Milne, *Monthly Film Bulletin*, November 1980.

"*The Fog* is pathetically vacant in between the shock sequences.... The actors are simply filler material. The onslaught of the supernatural fog is amusing ... but its explanation is labored and the ghosts which it harbored are ... nondescript. (Like the *other* characters.)" — Donald C. Willis, *Horror and Science Fiction Films II*, Scarecrow Press, 1982.

"Having given us a substantial start on a spooky, old-fashioned ghost story, Mr. Carpenter appears to forget what kind of movie he wants to make. *The Fog* ... is neither a rewarding ghost story nor is it science fiction, though it borrows freely from both genres.... There are too many story-lines which necessitate so much cross-cutting that no one sequence can ever build to a decent climax.... The material is thin." — Vincent Canby, *The New York Times*: "*Fog* Comes in at 3 Theaters," February 29 1980.

Cast and Credits

CAST: Adrienne Barbeau (Stevie Wayne); Jamie Lee Curtis (Elizabeth Solley); Janet Leigh (Kathy Williams); John Houseman (Mr. Machen); Tom Atkins (Nick Castle); James Canning (Dick Baxter); Charles Cyphers (Dan O'Bannon); Nancy Loomis (Sandy Fadel); Ty Mitchell (Andy); Hal Holbrook (Father Malone); John Goff (Al Williams); George "Buck" Flower (Tommy Wallace); Regina Waldon (Mrs. Kobritz); Jim Haynie (Dockmaster); Darrow Igus (Mel); John Vic (Sheriff Sims); Jay Jacobs (Mayor); Fred Franklyn (Ashcroft); James Windburn (Stunt Driver); Ric Moreno, Lee Sacks, Tommy Wallace (Ghosts); Bill Taylor (Bartender); Rob Bottin (Blake); Charles Nicklin (Blake's Voice); Darwin Joston (Dr. Phibes); Laurie Arent, Lindsey Arent, Shan Jacoby, Christopher Cundey (Children); John Strobel (Grocery Clerk).

CREDITS: Avco Embassy & E.D.I. Present a Debra Hill Production. *Director of Photography:* Dean Cundey. *Production Design:* Tommy Lee Wallace. *Costume Design:* Bill Whitten, Steven Loomis, Workroom 27. *Production Manager:* Dan Berhrns. *First Assistant Director:* Larry J. Franco. *Editor:* Tommy Lee Wallace, Charles Bornstein. *Music:* John Carpenter. *Electronic Realization:* Dan Wyman. *Written by:* John Carpenter, Debra Hill. *Executive Producer:* Charles B. Block. *Produced by:* Debra Hill. *Director:* John Carpenter. *Associate Producers:* Barry Bernardi, Pegi Brotman. *Art Director:* Charles R. Moore. *Production Accountant:* Don Borchers. *Second Assistant Director:* James Van Wyck. *Script Supervisor:* Jeanne Rosenberg. *Camera Operator/Second Unit Camera:* Raymond Stella. *First Assistant Camera:* Steve St. John. *Second Assistant Camera:* Krishna Rao. *Gaffer:* Mark Walthour. *Key Grip:* Ben Haller. *Best Boy:* Dylan Shepherd. *Best Boy Electric:* Steve Mathis. *Electrician:* Steve Fierberg, Scott Butfield. *Grip:* Tim Doughten, Dave Michels. *Wardrobe Master:* Richard Bloore. *Make-up:* Dante Palmiere, Ed Ternes, Erica Ulland. *Special Make-up:* Rob Bottin. *Hair Stylist:* Tina Cassady. *Props:* Kathleen Hughes. *Production Assistants:* Steve McMillian, Mary Francis Flynn, Randy Zook, Alexandra Hawler. *Assistant Editor:* Joe Woo, Jr. *Sound Mixer:* Craig Felburg. *Boom Operator:* Joe Brennan. *Re-recording Mixers:* Roy West, Bob Minkler, Dick Tyler. *Post Production Sound:* Samuel Goldwyn Studio. *Electronic Orchestration:* Dan Wyman. *Music Coordinator:* Bob Walter. *Music Editor:* Jim Cypherd. *Music Recording Studio:* Sound arts. *Music Performed by:* The Bowling-Green Warren County Chamber Orchestra. *Supervising Sound Editors:* Greg Barbanell, Ron Horwitz, Mag City, Hollywood. *Special Sound Effects:* Mag City, Frank Serafine. *Sound Design:* William Stevenson M.P.S.E., Stevensound, Inc. *Special Effects:* Richard Albain, Jr., A & A Special Effects. *Blake Effects:* Rob Bottin, Dean Cundey. *Publicity:* Maslansky-Koenigsberg. *Unit Publicity:* Katy Sweet, Ed Pine. *Special Photographic Effects:* James F. Liles, A.S.C. *Title Design:* Burke Mattsson. *Titles & Opticals:* MGM. Filmed in Panavision, Metrocolor. *Special Thanks to:* Pt. Reyes Station, CA; Inverness, CA. An Avco-Embassy Release. *MPAA Rating:* R. *Running Time:* 89 minutes.

"Is all that we see or seem
But a dream within a dream?"
— Edgar Allan Poe

SYNOPSIS: At 11:55 P.M. on April 20, 1980, old Mr. Machen tells a group of school children one last ghost story around a bright campfire. He recounts the events of April 21, 1880 — events that will soon be one hundred years old.

A clipper ship called the *Elizabeth Dane* drew towards land near Antonio Bay. A ghostly fog rolled in at Spivey Point, and the ship lost its bearings. Then the crew saw a fire burning through the swirling, thick mist. Believing it to be a lighthouse, the ship steered towards the illumination, only to discover it was a campfire burning on the shore, a decoy. The *Elizabeth Dane* smashed into the rocks, and the men of the ship died an icy, cold death. The unearthly fog lifted and receded back across the ocean, never to be seen again. But it is told that when the ghostly fog returns to Antonio Bay, the men of the *Elizabeth Dane* will rise up from their watery graves and seek out the campfire that led them to their dark death at the bottom of the sea.

While Mr. Machen recounts his story, the witching hour begins. From midnight to 1:00 A.M., strange happenings plague Antonio Bay. Alone in the church, Father Malone is shocked when a piece of wall falls apart without warning and exposes the diary of his grandfather from 1880. Elsewhere, a gas station comes to life of its own accord, televisions turn themselves on, and furniture even moves about of its own volition.

Driving on the outskirts of town, Nick

Castle picks up a beautiful young hitchhiker, Elizabeth Solley, and they are both stunned as all the glass in his truck simultaneously shatters. Startled but safe, they drive on to his place and make love there. Soon they are interrupted by a ghostly apparition at the door, but at the exact stroke of 1:00, the night visitor disappears suddenly.

Also during the witching hour, Stevie Wayne, the DJ at WCAB, reports a fog at sea. Moving against the wind, the glowing fog envelopes the sea trawler called the *Sea Grass*. Aboard the craft, the drunken crewmen are shocked to spot a clipper ship, the *Elizabeth Dane*, cruising silently through the fogbank. Half-seen figures board the *Sea Grass* and brutally murder the crew with hooks and swords.

The next morning, Stevie Wayne's son, Andy, goes exploring on the shore near his house. He eyes a sparkling gold coin on the rocks and attempts to retrieve it. As he moves to pick it up, the coin is replaced by a piece of driftwood with the word "DANE" carved into it. Andy takes it home and shows it to his mother, who is trying to get some much-needed sleep after her night shift at the radio station.

By the bay, Nick Castle is worried because his friends aboard the *Sea Grass* have not come home. He charters a ship with Elizabeth and heads out to open ocean to find it.

In Antonio Bay, Mrs. Williams plans the town's 100th anniversary celebration with her assistant, Sandy. The big event is set for that night, but Mrs. Williams is preoccupied because her husband, Al, is aboard the missing *Sea Grass*. Still, she wants to visit the old church to see Father Malone and determine if he is ready to give the benediction following the candlelight procession.

Sandy and Mrs. Williams find Malone in the church alone, obsessed with his grandfather's diary. Malone has learned how his grandfather and five co-conspirators swindled a man called Blake, the rich leader of a leper colony, out of his fortune in gold. The conspirators wanted his gold, but they did not want his sick community to settle nearby the fledgling Antonio Bay, so they built a campfire on shore as his ship approached. Aided by an unearthly fog, the six conspirators watched as Blake's ship, the *Elizabeth Dane*, broke up at sea. The murderers recovered Blake's gold and built the town Antonio Bay with Blake's wealth. Malone is horrified because the 100th anniversary celebration of the town will actually be honoring murderers.

At sea, Nick and Elizabeth find the *Sea Grass*. The ship is a wreck, and all the gauges are smashed. In the hold, they find a corpse with the eyes gouged out. They bring the body back to shore for an autopsy. Meanwhile, Stevie Wayne returns to work at the lighthouse radio station. She is startled when water suddenly drips incessantly out of Andy's find, the driftwood marked "DANE." The water falls onto a tape recorder playing WCAB promos, and an inhuman voice suddenly speaks in ghostly tones, warning that six must die. The legend on the driftwood transforms into the same frightening warning, "6 MUST DIE," before suddenly igniting in flames. Stevie calls home and urgently warns Andy to stay away from the beach.

Antonio Bay's pathologist, Dr. Phibes, reports to Nick and Elizabeth that the corpse from the *Sea Grass* drowned. This explanation does not make sense, however, since the body was found in the ship's hold, not in the water. Phibes also insists that the body was underwater for days, not hours. While Nick and Phibes discuss these contradictions, the corpse staggers to life and shambles towards Elizabeth. It soon falls dead, but it scrawls the number "3" on the floor with a scalpel.

The 100th anniversary of Antonio Bay commences that night. The speeches begin, and Mrs. Williams continues to worry about her husband, whose body has still not been found. Nick contacts Stevie at the radio station after she makes a comment on the air about ships getting lost in the fog. She informs him about the driftwood and its weird ultimatum. Elizabeth and Nick drive for the station to see Stevie's strange treasure, but the fog soon rolls in. It reaches Antonio Bay's weather station first, and its vengeful spirits come out to murder Dan O'Bannon, the town's meteorologist. Then the fog drifts toward Stevie Wayne's beach house, where Mrs. Kobritz is babysitting young Andy. The ghosts murder Kobritz, but Nick and Elizabeth arrive just in time to save Andy from the horrible, leprosy-ridden monsters that dwell within the fog. From her perch in the lighthouse, Stevie reports on the fog rolling through Antonio Bay. Mrs. Williams, Sandy, Andy, Elizabeth and Nick flee for the church, where Father Malone is waiting. Stevie then watches in fear as the fog surrounds her radio station. She fends off the vengeful spirits, climbing to the pointed roof of the lighthouse in desperation.

Inside the church, Father Malone realizes that reparations must be made to Blake and his men. The dead lepers are killing six modern residents, making them pay the price for the actions of the six historical conspirators who caused their deaths. Only one life remains to be taken.

Malone reads the remainder of the diary and learns that his grandfather saved some of Blake's gold and had it molded into the shape of a cross. Malone finds the solid gold crucifix hidden in the walls of the church, and he presents it to the spirit of Blake. The fog dissipates rapidly and the nightmare ends, leaving a shaken Stevie Wayne to warn the ships at sea of the fog's evil nature.

Alone in the church, Malone wonders why Blake did not murder him as the sixth conspirator. The fog returns briefly to the church, and Blake seeks final vengeance.

COMMENTARY: Although many critics were disappointed to see John Carpenter return to the horror milieu so soon after directing *Halloween*, his 1980 venture *The Fog* is light years distant from the first Michael Myers saga in both style and substance. Where *Halloween* sought to provoke terror by contrasting the routine of teenage life in middle America with the unexpected pres-

ence of a monster who was no less than the Bogeyman, *The Fog* offers a different, perhaps more intellectual, brand of chills. Where *Halloween* startles viewers with its elegant simplicity and its devotion to frightening viewers by any and all means possible, *The Fog* relies instead on what might be termed a "literary" approach to horror. Although the film is rife with visual shocks and jolts, *The Fog* generates most of its texture of fear through the simple, and often lost, art of oral storytelling.

The Fog is a ghost story itself, and thus the film is obsessed with the verbal nature of storytelling, of frightening tales repeated from one generation to the next. To emphasize this ghost-story passing of the torch, John Carpenter opens *The Fog* with an artful preamble: Actor John Houseman recites a ghost story to frightened children around a blazing campfire.

The first shot of *The Fog* is of a ticking pocket-watch as it dangles in the frame. Not only does this close-up immediately establish the time as a ghostly one (midnight) but the prominence of the clock in the frame is also a reminder of passing time, of the generational differences between the storyteller and listeners around the fire. Indeed, as the story begins, Houseman's words convey an obsession with time. The quotation below represents the beginning of Houseman's story, and all references to time have been italicized so as to accent them:

> 11:55. Almost *midnight*. Enough *time* for one more story. One more story before *12:00*, just to keep us warm. In *five minutes*, it will be the *21st of April*. *One hundred years ago* on the *21st of April*, out in the waters around Spivey Point, a small clipper ship drew towards land…

This opening passage is a portion of a folk story told to the fishermen of Antonio Bay by their "fathers and grandfathers," a notation which again expresses the passage of time and a generational sharing of communal stories. Yet all the references to time, including the ticking clock and the repetitive opening dialogue, serve another purpose in *The Fog* as well: They set the stage for the horror to come. How does one successfully tell a scary story at midnight, around a burning fire? By setting the stage, of course; by pinpointing a specific time and a place and making it feel "real" and tangible to the listeners. Mr. Machen's story begins by reminding the listeners that a fateful anniversary is approaching. In just five minutes, it will be a hundred years since this ghost story began. This brings an immediacy and therefore a heightened sense of menace to the listeners. Suddenly, they are as much a part of this ghost story as the *Elizabeth Dane*, because they are hearing it at midnight, exactly a century after the ship crashed. Mr. Machen heightens this awareness further by pointing out that the ghosts of the *Elizabeth Dane* will rise from their graves to seek out the campfire that resulted in their deaths. Of course, the children listening to the story are sitting around a campfire, and therefore, again, they are connected to the terror explicitly. The ghosts could arrive for them at any minute, or so the serious-looking children believe.

As Houseman proceeds in forceful, eloquent tones to enumerate the details of a 100 year old *Elizabeth Dane* disaster, Carpenter zooms in rapidly on the actor's face as he moves from setting the stage (telling the time) to elaborating on the details of the ship. "Suddenly..." Houseman says, and the camera rushes in on his illuminated face, surrounded by darkness, as if it is hanging on his every breath. Importantly, the horror Houseman forges in this sequence is primarily one of words, and this is quite an uncommon trick in modern films. A more routine approach might have seen a director actually depict the events of a hundred years earlier, and then flash forward to 1980. Instead, John Carpenter takes a more subtle approach to the material, and allows the venue of the ghost story to provide the necessary exposition.

Of course, *The Fog* is a film, not radio, so the artful, almost poetic stream of words formulating the ghost story is beautifully enhanced by Carpenter's aural and visual imagery. *The Fog* begins quietly, with only the ticking of a clock audible on the soundtrack as a panning shot focuses on the faces of scared children. The lack of music, the monotonous ticking, and the frightened faces immediately establish a mood of anticipation, of dread. The eerie light of the fire, Houseman's old visage in blunt close-up, and the ensuing reaction shots of the children as they recognize that they are near a campfire (and therefore in danger) add much to the effectiveness of the sequence. But first and foremost are those words written by John Carpenter and Debra Hill. Everything comes back to those frightening, mood-creating words as *The Fog*'s Mr. Machen takes his audience (and thereby *The Fog*'s audience) to the world of April 21, 1880.

In the best tradition of Edgar Allan Poe, the ghost story ends tragically, and with a warning that the "evil" is not yet dead. To buttress this final assertion, Carpenter's camera pans up and up, away from Mr. Machen's solemn face, until it is facing a dark blue shore with rolling waves crashing against the lonely landscape. Carpenter makes the connection obvious but artful: First from Mr. Machen's mouth, and then to a view of the sea where the tragedy occurred, terror will begin.

The Fog's obsession with orally transmitted ghost stories does not end with the stylish opening sequence. Later in the film, Father Malone (Hal Holbrook) tells another version of the same tale, this time to Sandy (Nancy Loomis) and Mrs. Williams (Janet Leigh). Again the horror of the situation is wrought with a story, with a tale of the sudden, violent and *planned* deaths of the *Elizabeth Dane* crew. In this case, the audience is already familiar with the general story, but this repetition is a necessity. For these stories to be remembered and carried by future generations, they must be repeated. So the repetition not only ensures the survival of the story; for *The Fog* it also uncovers further evidence of wrongs done by specific people, the six co-conspirators. As Blake's vengeance is tied to the acts of this dirty half-dozen, these specifics provide further exposition.

A third ghost story comes from Nick Castle (Tom Atkins) who shares with Elizabeth Solley (Jamie Lee Curtis) an encounter his father — another member of the older generation — once had aboard another mysterious ghost ship at sea. This last story is a bow to another ghost story necessity: It must be universal. In this case, the encounter with a ghost ship and a disappearing Spanish coin minted in 1867 reminds viewers that the *Elizabeth Dane* is not the only ship in the ocean. Nick's story attempts to extend the horror of *The Fog* by suggesting that ships disappear at sea all the time under mysterious circumstances, that the ocean is a realm of fear and the unknown, and that we should be afraid of it.

The final ghost story is perhaps *The Fog's* most important. In it, Stevie Wayne (Adrienne Barbeau) brings together all the important aspects of the earlier stories:

> I don't know what happened to Antonio Bay tonight. Something came out of the fog and tried to destroy us.... If this has been anything but a nightmare, and if we don't find ourselves safe in our beds, it could come again. To the ships at sea who can hear my voice: Look across the water into the darkness. Look for the fog...

This tale not only recounts a new ending to the story (the ghosts came back from the dead for vengeance), it highlights the importance of the Edgar Allan Poe quote that precedes the film and ties *The Fog* to the world of dreams and nightmares. Even better, this ghost story is told by a newcomer to the town, Stevie Wayne. She is now a "true" member of Antonio Bay, having suffered for its crimes, and so she is entitled to broadcast the story, as she does from the radio station. Lastly, her final warning, "Look for the fog," is a parallel to the "Keep watching the skies!" tag of

The Thing (1951). In that film, Howard Hawks hoped to leave audiences chilled by sending them away with a dire warning: Outer space is a realm of terror, and we must remain ever vigilant. Likewise, *The Fog* culminates with a warning that the sea is a realm of terror and mystery, and that we must always be conscious of the evil at its murky bottom. Whether the arena of danger be outer space or the deep blue sea, the effect is the same: Audiences will leave the darkened theater thinking about what they have seen, wondering about the dangers all around man's world.

Few horror films can legitimately be termed poetic, but *The Fog* certainly qualifies. Aside from the artful use of ghost stories to generate terror, the film is enriched by beautiful imagery throughout, even in the most horrible of moments. *The Fog* is filled with picturesque landscapes and vistas. From the rolling blue ocean, to the peaks around the isolated lighthouse, the film is shot in the most beautiful locations imaginable. But what is truly unique is how unusually handsome the "scare" sequences are in *The Fog*. For instance, the *Sea Grass* interior is shot entirely in red light, with reflections from the sea dancing on the actors' faces. It is a view from Hell's gate perhaps, but it is unusually lush and beautiful. It is not realistic, certainly, but it seems appropriate since the denizens of the craft will soon find themselves in touch with hellish forces. And, when the ghosts attack Father Malone's church at the climax of the film, their ragged hands burst forward through lovely stained glass windows. The moment is filled with horror and fear, but it is staged with an artist's eye for detail and composition. The ragged, grasping hands again represent Hell's attempt to break through a sanctuary, this time a godly one (as evidenced by the stained glass).

Most beautiful of all, however, is the threat of the fog itself. It glows, it moves, it thins, it thickens, and it remains eerily luminescent throughout the film. In one spectacular shot, probably run in reverse, a thick fog whips up suddenly and forms only inches in front of Nick's pick-up truck. As it sweeps through the idyllic Antonio Bay, one cannot help being reminded of *The Blob*. The fog is a village-devouring entity, sweeping across Everytown U.S.A. filled with insatiable vengeance. Yet the fog is ever so much more lovely than the blob — and much more interesting. The fog is a great villain because it can hide things, it can envelop things, it can move fast or slow, creep under doors, or roll across entire landscapes. It is versatile, lovely, and perfectly deployed in *The Fog*.

As is typical for John Carpenter, as much time is spent on sound in *The Fog* as on the images. At the beginning of the picture, Carpenter depicts a poltergeist attack on Antonio Bay. Telephones ring, television sets whir, gas station bells ring nonstop, and the church bells herald the arrival of midnight. These sequences express the growing power of the *Elizabeth Dane* spirits. At first, they can manifest themselves only in small ways, by honking horns, ringing phones and turning on headlights. As the picture develops, so does Blake's ability to control his environment. At the end of the film, Blake's threat has gone from mostly an audible one (disturbing the town at midnight) to a visceral one wherein the fog can sever telephone lines and sweep through populated areas, bringing murder with it.

For all of its lyricism and beauty, *The Fog* also works on a thematic front. Like the world of Haddonfield in *Halloween*, Antonio Bay in *The Fog* is a place where science, medicine and technology cannot save man from the evil within himself. Telephones are controlled by the enemy, polices forces are unable to cope with the terror, and pathologists cannot explain the situation; the authorities are unable to cope with the irrational. Yet the situation is real: Ghosts do exist. Also akin to *Halloween*, it is a child, young Andy, who is among the first to discover the horror, bringing home a piece of driftwood that eventually sends a dire warning to his mother.

The Fog is also very much in keeping with Carpenter's negative opinion of America's capitalist history. In essence, the story is about the underside of the American dream. The town Antonio Bay was built on the blood of Blake's men, and on his stolen fortune. For a hundred years, Antonio Bay thrived because its developers had cast themselves as "winners" and the lepers as "losers." Worse than that, their descendants celebrate the conspirators for winning, even holding an extravagant celebration in their honor. The current inhabitants of Antonio Bay are also rather selfish, describing the tragic wreck of the *Elizabeth Dane* euphemistically as "the catalyst that brought wonderful people together" in the town. Ironically, Mrs. Williams even refers to the co-conspirators as heroes, despite her knowledge that they are murderers. In her speech, she declares, "We must keep their kind of spirit alive!" Of course, Blake has his vengeance, visiting the sins of the fathers upon the children. For that reason, the ghosts of *The Fog*, though frightening, are also "right" in their own way. They have a clear-cut motive for killing, though they target the wrong people.

The Fog is John Carpenter's most complicated film up to this point in his filmography, and he handles all the complexity ably. His direction of the actors is outstanding, with Adrienne Barbeau proving herself to be quite a talent. She is the film's voice. She conveys data, provides exposition, combats the monster alone, and delivers the final chills in her climactic ghost story. Hers is not an easy role for all those reasons, plus the fact that she acts in virtual isolation throughout the film, interacting with others only by telephone.

Jamie Lee Curtis also creates a very different kind of heroine in *The Fog*. She is sexually aggressive, funny, and totally outgoing. The shy teenager of *Halloween* is gone, replaced by a confident woman in a confident performance. In one amusing moment, the audience finds opportunity to laugh with Jamie Lee Curtis as her character quips,

"Things happen to me." Considering the events of *Halloween* and *The Fog*, she is absolutely correct!

Any aficionado of horror films will also appreciate *The Fog* because it delivers the goods. It comes through with the jolts that cause people to leap out of their seats or turn over their popcorn. In *The Fog*, Carpenter wrings maximum suspense out of a sequence in which Andy is in jeopardy and Nick has to rescue him from a fog-filled house on the ocean. As the scene builds, they flee for their truck, but of course it will not start. The sequence builds to a fever pitch as the fog rolls in and the ghosts become visible, only inches from the headlights of the vehicle. For nail-biting suspense, nobody does it better than John Carpenter. Another "scare" scene worthy of mention revolves around the evil piece of driftwood which conveys an unexpectedly scary message to Stevie Wayne. Water drips from the wood onto a tape recorder, and an evil voice begins speaking. In that sloweddown, enhanced human voice, Blake's hatred is beautifully conveyed. This scene may not cause a jump, but it will result in goosebumps.

At the same time that *The Fog* shows Carpenter dealing with new material and more complicated themes, it also fits squarely into his previous filmwork. Blake's final attack at the church is a mini-siege reminiscent of *Assault on Precinct 13*. Darwin Joston reappears as a pathologist named Dr. Phibes, after Vincent Price's character in *The Abominable Dr. Phibes* (1971) and *Dr. Phibes Rises Again* (1972). And characters such as Nick Castle, Dan O'Bannon and Mrs. Kobritz are all named after personal friends. At one point in the film, Adrienne Barbeau announces that she is going to play a song from "The Coupe DeVilles," which happens to be a musical group comprised of John Carpenter, Tommy Lee Wallace, and (the real) Nick Castle. Lastly, in a reference to *The Birds*, Tom Atkins's character makes reference to a town nearby called Bodega Bay.

With a great screenplay that displays Carpenter and Hill's versatility in writing, another pulse-pounding soundtrack, interesting characters, and a poetic quality, *The Fog* is one of John Carpenter's best films. Though it exists in that "dream" period between 1978 and 1981, when every film Carpenter directed was a hit, *The Fog* is not especially well-regarded today, and that is a shame. It is a very different film from *Halloween*, and it reveals a very poetic side of the genre director. Later in his career, he would give literary horror a stab again in *Prince of Darkness* (1987) and *In the Mouth of Madness* (1994) but neither of those films is as unequivocally poetic, literate and cohesive as *The Fog*.

Escape from New York (1981)

Critical Reception

"Brutal, very fine-looking suspense melodrama by John Carpenter.... It's a toughly told, very tall tale, one of the best escape (and escapist) movies of the season."— Vincent Canby, *The New York Times*, July 10, 1981.

"A fast-paced funky action flick. It's a mixture of high velocity filmmaking and low grade sensibility. Characterization is nil. Dialogue is banal. But there are compensations.... The visuals are provocative. Production design is arguably the film's strongest attraction. And the pace is taut and relentless."— Joseph Gelmis, *Newsday*, July 10, 1981.

"A ferocious parody of popular notions about Manhattan today ... John Carpenter is offering this summer's movie-goers a rare opportunity: to escape from the air-conditioned torpor of ordinary entertainment into the hothouse humidity of their own paranoia. It's a trip worth taking."— Richard Corliss, *Time*, July 13, 1981.

"What Carpenter has projected with his usual effectiveness is a vision of hell on Earth. His view is utterly cynical, but his cynicism is one of exploitation rather than protest.... A film of sleekly impressive surfaces ... can be compelling ... but many will not be able to go along with the corrosive, pessimistic view of humanity that Carpenter projects with such force."— Kevin Thomas, *The Los Angeles Times*, July 10, 1981.

"All the elements of an exciting action picture are here—but Carpenter apparently can't figure out how to use them. His sense of invention and pacing flags after a terrific beginning sequence of Snake piloting his glider into a silent nighttime landing on a Manhattan rooftop. From then on, it gets dull. There's never any real feel of menace generated.... Talented veterans Harry Dean Stanton, Season Hubley, Adrienne Barbeau and Ernest Borgnine try valiantly to keep things afloat, but the dialogue is uninspired."— Douglas Menville and R. Reginald, *Futurevisions: The New Golden Age of the Science Fiction Film*, Newcastle Publishing Company, 1985, page 113.

Cast and Credits

CAST: Kurt Russell (Snake Plissken); Lee Van Cleef (Bob Hauk); Ernest Borgnine (Cabbie); Donald Pleasence (President); Isaac Hayes (The Duke); Season Hubley (Girl in Chock Full O'Nuts); Harry Dean Stanton (Brain); Adrienne Barbeau (Maggie); Tom Atkins (Rehme); Charles Cyphers (Secretary of State); Joe Unger (Taylor); Frank Doubleday (Romero); John Strobel (Cronenberg); John Cothran, Jr. (Gypsy #1); Garrett Bergfield (Gypsy #2); Richard Consentino (Gypsy Guard); Robert John Metcalf (Gypsy #3); Joel Bennett (Gypsy #4); Vic Bullock (First Indian); Clem Fox (Second Indian); Tobar Mayo (Third Indian); Nancy Stephens (Stewardess); Steven Gagan (Secret Service #1); Steven Ford (Secret Service #2); Michael Taylor (Secret Service #3); Lonnie Wun (Red Bandan Gypsy); Dale House (Helicopter Pilot #1); David R. Patrick (Helicopter Pilot #2); Bob Minor (Duty Sergeant); Wally Taylor (Controller); James O'Hagen (Computer Operator); James Emery (Trooper); Tom Lillard (Police Sgt.); Borah Silver (Theater Manager); Tony Papenfuss (Theater Assistant); John Diehl (Punk); Carmen Filpi (Bum); Buck Flower (Drunk); Clay Wright (Helicopter Pilot #3); Al Cerullo (Helicopter #4); Ox Baker (Slag); Lowmoan Spectacular, Ronald E. House, Alan Spearman, Joseph A. Perrotti, Roger Bumpass, Ron Vernan (Dancers).

CREDITS: Avco-Embassy Pictures International Film Investors Goldcrest Films International Present a Debra Hill Production. *Director of Photography:* Dean Cundey. *Production Designer:* Joe Alves. *Film Editor:* Todd Ramsay. *Music:* John Carpenter. *In Association with:* Alan Howarth. *Associate Producer:* Barry Bernardi. *Written by:* John Carpenter, Nick Castle. *Produced by:* Larry Franco. *Produced by:* Debra Hill. *Directed by:* John Carpenter. *Stunts:* Dick Warlock, Bob Minor, Bill Hart, Jesse Wayne, Loren Janes, George Sawaya, Gloria Fioramoni, Sandy Gimpel, Mike McGaughy, Jim Winburn, Ted White, John Moio, Tony Brubaker, Jack Verbois, Fred Lerner, Bill Lane, Harvey Barry, Huff Brady, Mags Kavanaugh, Jack Tyree, Kent Hays, George Wilbur, Mike Johnson, Eddie Hice, Roydon Clark. *Production Manager:* Alan Levine. *First Assistant Director:* Larry Franco. *Second Assistant Director:* Jeffrey

Chernov. *Casting Assistant to Producers:* Pegi Brotman. *Production Office Coordinator:* Chip Fowler. *Script Supervisor:* Louise Jaffe. *Camera Operator:* Ray Stella. *First Assistant Camera:* Clyde Bryan. *Second Assistant Camera:* Doug Olivarus, Steve Tate. *Second Unit Director of Photography:* Jim Lucas. *Second Unit Camera Operator:* Doug Knapp, Frank Ruttencutter. *Second Unit Assistant Camera:* George Mooradian, Jack Grant. *Assistant Art Director:* Chris Horner. *Set Decorator:* CLOUDIA. *Lead Man:* Don Sutton. *Swing Gang:* Lee Drygas. *Property Master:* Mike May. *Assistant Property Master:* Gene Booth. *Assistant Film Editor:* Randy D. Thornton. *Apprentice Editor:* Barbara Ann Gandalfo. *Assistant to Film Editor:* Dean Beville. *Graphic Designer:* Arthur Gelb. *Location Manager:* Barry Bernardi. *Sound Mixer:* Tommy Causey. *Boom Operators:* Joe Brennan, Carl Fischer. *Gaffer:* Mark Walthour. *Rigging Gaffer:* Drain Marshall. *Best Boy Electric:* Tom Marshall. *Electricians:* Terry Marshall, Scott Buttfield. *Flicker Box Technician:* Steve Mathis. *Second Grip:* Seymour Owens. *Dolly Grip:* Tommy Sands. *Grip:* Leo Behar. *Make-up Artist Supervisor:* Ken Chase. *Make-up Artist:* Ben Douglas. *Hair-stylist:* Frankie Bergman. *Costume Designer:* Steven Loomis. *Men's Costumer:* Mel Sawicki. *Women's Costumer:* Katrina Bronson. *Stills:* Kim Gottleib, Jim Coe. *Unit Publicist:* Kelli Garris. *Stunt Coordinator:* Dick Warlock. *Special Effects Supervisor:* Roy Arbogast. *Special Effects:* Pat Patterson, Eddie Zurkin, Gary Zink. *Weapons Advisor:* Syd Stembridge. *Craft Service:* Lowe Chircho. *Nurse:* Maurice Costello. *Transportation Coordinator:* Eddie Lee Voelker. *Transportation Captain:* Tom Thomas. *Production Assistant:* Geoff Ryan. *Office Production Assistant:* Sarah Preece. *Accountant:* Jack Buckley. *Construction Foreman:* Mary Salsberg. *Propmaker Foreman:* Art Moel, Andrew Earl Overholtzer. *Propmaker:* Joe Fama. *Paint Supervisor:* Ward Welton. *Painter:* Ed Zingel. *Avco Nominee:* Dan Borchers. *Assistant Location Manager:* Frank Capra, III. *Creative Mobile Technician:* John Brumby. *Drivers:* Mike Connolly, Mario Simon, Steve Boyd, Dick Lee, Rod Berg, Chuck Mauer, Eddie Worth, Joe Benet, Wayne Roberts, Wayne Williams, Robby Benton. *Meals:* Bert Jetter, Juan Betancourt. *Assistant to the Assistants:* Matt Franco. *Publicity:* Pickwick/Maslansky, Koeningsberg. *Location Casting:* Ron Littrell, Terry Murphy. *Extra Casting (St. Louis):* Talent Plus, Inc. *Extra Casting (L.A.):* Susiels Casting. *Special Visual Effects:* New World Venice. *Producer-Liaison:* Mary Ann Fisher. *Project Supervisor:* R.J. Kizer. *Director of Photography (FX):* James Cameron, George Dodge, Dennis Skotak, Austin McKinney. *Elicon Camera Operator:* Brian Chin. *Engineer:* Tom Campbell. *Matte Artwork:* Jim Cameron, Jena Holman, Rob Skotak. *Rotoscope:* Steve Elliot, Dan Smith. *Lab Liaison:* Anthony Randel. *Gaffer:* Gary Wagner. *Camera Assistant:* Steve Caldwell, Randy Frakes. *Associate Producer:* Aaron Lipstadt. *Production Manager:* Charles Skouras, III. *Production Accountant:* Sara Nelson. *Production Secretary:* Robin Thomas. *Graphics Displays:* John Wash/Motion Graphics. *Sound Editors:* David Yewdall, Warren Hamilton. *Special Synthesizer Sound:* Alan Howarth. *Stereo Recordist:* John Mosley. *Recorded at:* Goldwyn Studio Facility. *Re-Recording Mixer:* Bill Varney c.a.s, George Landaker c.a.s, Steve Maslow c.a.s. *Original Music Performed by:* John Carpenter, Alan Howarth. "Bandstand Boogie" music by Charles Albertine, courtesy of Cherio Corporation. "Everyone's Going to New York" music and lyrics by Nick Castle. "Engulfed Cathedral" by Claude Debussy. *Filmed in:* Panavision. *Color:* Metrocolor. *Titles/Opticals:* Pacific Title. *Special Thanks to:* City of St. Louis, City of New York, National Guard of Missouri, U.S. Army Reserve, Mr. Walter Abell, Lt. Colonel Dennis Foley, the Orient Express, P.T.S., Centerville. A City Film. An Avco Embassy Release. *MPAA Rating:* R. *Running Time:* 99 minutes.

"Call me Snake." — A glowering Snake Plissken

"Welcome to the future!" Snake Plissken (Russell) is deported to the penal island of Manhattan in *Escape from New York* (1981).

SYNOPSIS: In the year 1988, the crime rate in America rises 400 percent. The once great city of New York becomes the nation's only maximum security prison. It is sealed off, and the connecting bridges and waterways are mined to prevent escape. There are no guards inside the prison, but a heavily armed police force patrols the perimeter wall of the city, maintaining order. Once a convict goes into New York, he does not come out.

In 1997, ex–war hero and criminal Snake Plissken is apprehended by the United States Police Force and shuttled by bus to the debarkation point on Liberty Island for the New York Maximum Security Penitentiary. Hauk and Rehme, two high-ranking officials in the Penal Department, ignore Plissken's arrival because Air Traffic Control has detected a small jet in distress in close-by airspace. Air Force One has been hijacked by the terrorist forces of the National Liberation Front of America. The plane heads into

New York City and crashes in a fireball, but the president of the United States escapes the conflagration in an egg-shaped life pod. Captured by the convicts inside the prison, the president must be rescued.

Hauk believes that Plissken is the perfect man to mount a rescue, and he offers the criminal a full pardon for robbing the Federal Reserve Depository if he goes inside the prison and retrieves the chief executive. Snake reluctantly accepts the offer, but his mission is even more complex than Hauk has indicated. Snake must bring the president out within 24 hours, in time for the politician to present an audiocassette concerning recent scientific advances in nuclear fusion to the Russians and the Chinese at the Hartford Summit. The future of the human race is at stake, and if the president does not present that tape, he is valueless to the country.

To assure that Snake does not decide to make a run for it once free, Hauk injects two tiny explosive capsules into the arteries in

Snake's neck. If Snake is not back in 24 hours, the capsules will detonate and kill him. The capsules will be neutralized with X-rays if and only if Plissken has freed the president.

As Snake's life clock ticks away, he flies a glider called the *Gullfire* into New York City. He lands the craft on the roof of the World Trade Center and then proceeds to the crash site. Using the Vital Data Monitor, which displays the president's life signs, Snake proceeds to the Olde Manhattan Theater. Inside, convicts are putting on a Broadway-style musical. Snake meets Cabbie, an eccentric taxi driver who has been driving his cab in Manhattan for 30 years. Cabbie warns Snake not to go down to the basement, but Snake goes anyway. There he finds a drunken bum wearing the president's condition indicator. Clearly, Snake will have to locate the chief executive without the aid of technology. Angry, Snake goes back outside and sits down. Soon, Crazies start to gather on the street, and Snake is forced to hide in Chock Full o' Nuts. He meets a beautiful woman there, but the Crazies attack and pull her down through the floor. Snake escapes the Crazies when Cabbie gives him a ride in his taxi.

Cabbie reveals to Snake that the president is being held captive by the Duke of New York, a warlord who dominates the city-wide prison. Plissken wants to see Duke, but instead Cabbie takes him to the New York Public Library to meet Duke's scientific advisor, Brain. Brain and his "squeeze," Maggie, welcome Snake. Plissken recognizes Brain as Harold Hellman, a former associate who four years earlier ran out on Snake and Fresno Bob in Kansas City. When Snake threatens to kill Harold, Brain and Maggie agree to help free the president with Snake.

As the group departs the library, Duke's caravan approaches. The Duke has crossed town because Brain has charted the location of the mines that have been placed on the 69th Street Bridge. Duke requires the map because he plans to walk all of the city's prisoners across the bridge in exchange for the safe return of the president.

Afraid of crossing the Duke, Cabbie leaves Snake and the others behind. Maggie, Brain and Snake steal one of the Duke's vehicles and race for the train yards where the president is being held. To get there, Snake must traverse Broadway, where carnivorous, murderous Crazies have erected a roadblock. Snake drives through the roadblock, but is captured by the Duke after momentarily freeing the president. During the rescue attempt, Snake is wounded in the leg by a crossbow's arrow.

When Snake awakens, it is daylight and he has been stripped of all his high-tech equipment. The Duke has been target shooting at the president, and in the process he finds the important cassette tape for the Hartford Summit. While Maggie and Brain attempt to rescue the president, Snake is forced to fight an ox-like giant in the Duke's boxing ring. Snake emerges victorious, recovers, and activates his stolen tracer so Hauk knows he is alive.

Snake flees the premises and learns that Maggie and Brain have rescued the president and are attempting to flee the city in Snake's glider. Snake arrives as two gangs fight over the glider and it plummets from the roof of the World Trade Center. Now he needs another escape route. In Cabbie's taxi, Maggie, Snake, Brain, Cabbie and the president flee for the 69th Street Bridge while Duke pursues in his car.

The cab hits a mine on the bridge and Cabbie is killed when his beloved car is split in two. The others make a dash for the far end of the bridge and safety, but Brain hits a mine and is killed. A devastated Maggie remains behind to kill the Duke, but Duke runs her down and continues to chase the escapees.

Hauk's forces lift the president off the bridge and over the prison wall while the Duke and Snake grapple on the bridge. The president kills the Duke with a machine gun, and Snake is transported over the wall. The capsules in his neck are defused, and the mission is over with just two seconds to spare.

But before turning over the important cassette tape to the authorities, Snake asks the president how he feels that so many people died to save his life. The president's response is political gobbledygook, so Snake gives the president Cabbie's own audio tape, "Bandstand Boogie," and then destroys the all-important nuclear fusion tape.

COMMENTARY: While Steven Spielberg was looking back to the cliffhanger traditions of the 1930s for his 1981 Indiana Jones feature, *Raiders of the Lost Ark*, director John Carpenter instead imagined the future of sci-fi cinema by visualizing the unique dystopian adventure film, *Escape from New York*. Although Carpenter has always been quick to acknowledge that *Escape from New York* has its roots in the mythic American western films of the 1950s, *Escape from New York* undeniably exists in the science-fiction milieu as well. It is a film with a startling "what if?" premise, and an adventure that asks questions, like *Halloween* before it, about human nature and the American dream. These questions are asked in one of cinema's most memorable, and grim, dark futures. Although George Miller's 1981 opus *The Road Warrior* also featured a bleak world with a charismatic anti-hero of few words, Carpenter's vision preceded such notable "dark city" movies such as *Blade Runner* (1982), *The Crow* (1994) and the appropriately named *Dark City* (1998).

The future world that John Carpenter predicts in *Escape from New York* is a bleak and nihilistic one. The crime rate has quadrupled, America is a conservative fascist state run by the police, and the nation's (and the world's) only hope for survival rests with a hardened criminal named Snake Plissken who, in typical Howard Hawks fashion, tends to ask, "Got a smoke?" of his friends and enemies alike. Much of *Escape from New York*'s sense of innovation evolves from its audacious central concept: that New York City of the future has been converted into a maximum security prison. This scenario not only allows Carpenter and co-writer Nick Castle to stock the motion picture with a bevy of New York jokes, including a mock–Broadway production entitled "Everyone's Coming to New York," but gives them an opportunity to brilliantly explore the premise that New York City could believably be sealed off from the rest of America. It may sound silly or even far-fetched, but the island of Manhattan makes a perfect, and rather believable, jail in this film. Special effects contribute to the reality of the scenario, as Carpenter's camera tracks the high walls of Liberty Island or prowls the mined moat between free territory and prison land.

Much as in *Dark Star*, which expressed the inner emptiness of its *dramatis personae* through the lonely, dehumanizing and rather bizarre set design of the titular ship, *Escape from New York*'s set design mirrors the inner space of its central characters. This is a cold, dark, lonely world filled with barriers, walls, and dangers. Every place Snake visits in the film is a prison in one sense or another, and the film is actually a series of prison escapes as Snake must evade the Crazies, escape from the World Trade Center, escape a mined bridge, and finally, as the title suggests, escape from New York altogether. This series of action pieces lends *Escape from New York* a commendable pace and keeps it entertaining throughout its running time.

The characters are memorable as well, since they too represent walls that Snake must scale if he is to survive. Brain is a duplicitous enemy who once betrayed Snake, so his wall is one of trustworthiness. Cabbie is a coward, again only semi-trustworthy, and even the beautiful Maggie has walls around her heart, seemingly unable to feel anything for anyone — until the conclusion when her love for Brain finds its voice in a final, courageous shoot-out. These characters all make interesting chess pieces for Snake to manipulate, and it is the presence of so many ulterior agendas that gives *Escape from New York* a sense of relentlessness. Loyalties switch, friendship gives way to expediency and everyone is out for himself.

The main players of *Escape from New York* (1981). *From left to right:* Brain (Harry Dean Stanton), Maggie (Adrienne Barbeau), Snake Plissken (Kurt Russell) and the president of the United States (Donald Pleasence).

Snake Plissken himself is one of John Carpenter's most interesting protagonists. His hatred of authority stems from the fact that he once represented authority; he was a much decorated ace pilot in the U.S. Air Force during a war over Russia. At some point prior to his incarceration on Liberty Island, Snake apparently came to feel that he had been "used" by the military in their war against the Soviet Union. Still, it is fairly obvious that somewhere inside Snake Plissken beats the heart of a patriot, or perhaps more appropriately, an idealist. He undertakes the mission to save the president, and he tests the president's ideals afterwards, giving the chief executive the opportunity to show kindness, decency, remorse or gratitude. When the president fails to convincingly show any of these essential human characteristics, Snake condemns the president, and the country, to humiliation and possible defeat. In other words, somewhere under Snake's gruff, anti-hero exterior there is a man who believes in the core values that America once represented: freedom, humanity, sacrifice, love, honor, and so forth. If he could see those values, *his* values, in the face of America's role model, a president described by Carpenter and Pleasence as a "right wing ideologue," he might again be a patriot. Snake asks the president how he feels about the sacrifice made by Maggie, Cabbie, Brain and Snake himself, and the president replies in rote, unthinking fashion that "this nation appreciates their sacrifice." Thus Snake's ideals are not restored. Snake sees only greed, corruption and selfishness, and so he makes the judgment that the president and his cause deserve only his contempt. The president is seen as being no better than the Duke: Both are leaders concerned more with themselves than those they lead.

In a way, Snake Plissken is a mirror image of director John Carpenter, another man who *wants* to believe in America, but is cursed by a clarity of vision. He sees America's obsession with money and neglect of the poor in *They Live*. He sees the failings of science and religion in *Prince of Darkness*. He sees the hypocrisy and danger of the conservative religious right in *Escape from L.A.* He is open-minded in a sense, just as Snake is, and he will give people a chance, but he is almost always disappointed to discover that an authority he once believed in has failed to live up to its own high standards. John Carpenter believes in the "city on the hill," in the grand precepts of democracy and freedom, imagined by the architects of this country. But he also feels that today's leaders are not living up to that ideal. *Escape from New York* is thus more than an adventure film; it is an exploration of one man's cynicism about our country's future.

For those looking to establish patterns in John Carpenter's films — a necessity if one is to make the argument that he is an auteur repeating the same stories and the same themes over and over again —*Escape from New York* is a gold mine. Like Napoleon Wilson before him, Snake Plissken arrives at the scene of the action on a prison bus, in shackles. Like Wilson in *Assault on Precinct 13*, Snake clearly establishes that he, himself, is "an asshole." And, of course, there are the Hawksian touches (the overlapping dialogue, the woman in Chock Full O'Nuts who asks for a smoke). More generally, *Escape from New York* recycles several western genre traditions. It is an odyssey film (like *The Searchers*) with a lone gunfighter in search of his prey. Furthermore, a gang is called "The Redskins," and the villain of the film is "the Duke," referring, of course, to John Wayne. In the horror milieu, Carpenter also pays homage to some of his favorite directors. One character is named

Romero after George Romero, director of *Night of the Living Dead*, and another is called Cronenberg after David Cronenberg.

More than *Halloween, The Fog, Assault on Precinct 13* or even *Dark Star*, it is hard to state precisely why *Escape from New York* is a great film. This picture's greatness comes from many diverse sources. Its premise is fascinating, and perfectly executed. Its hero is memorable not just because of Kurt Russell's star-making performance, but because of Snake Plissken's decidedly anti-heroic bent. The film is also exciting and fast paced, and the future it predicts is compelling.

Perhaps the factor that most elevates *Escape from New York* beyond the norm is that undercurrent of hostility towards authority which runs through it. There is an awareness in *Escape from New York* that America's direction toward conservative values in the Reagan era would not be a positive thing for the country. There is also acknowledgment that overreaching defense spending, harsher criminal law, and an enlarged police force could effectively turn all of the United States into a prison. Therefore *Escape from New York* is powerful because it acknowledges that though Snake might have escaped from one prison, he is dwelling inside another. When he leaves Liberty Island at the film's climax, he is not finding freedom or liberty at all. He has earned his survival, but what kind of "survival" will it be? In leaving that question unanswered, *Escape from New York* asks its audience to consider fascism, the future of our country, and what "freedom" really means to all individuals in the United States. How many action films can foster so important a debate, while still remaining cloaked in the shield of "entertainment?"

A sequel to *Escape from New York* followed in 1996. *Escape from L.A.* was also directed by John Carpenter.

The Thing (1982)

Critical Reception

"There's a big difference between ... effects and suspense, and in sacrificing everything at the altar of gore, Carpenter sabotages the drama. *The Thing* is so single-mindedly determined to keep you awake that it almost puts you to sleep. Lancaster's script is so low on characterization that even a first-rate cast of character actors ... is unable to work up any team spirit. It's the New Esthetic — atrocity for atrocity's sake and it ill becomes a neoclassical action director like Carpenter."— David Ansen, *Newsweek:* "Frozen Slime," June 28, 1982.

"A slick thriller with expertly handled monster scenes that are as scary as they are sickening ... a complete throwback to the most paranoid attitudes of the past, as if the popularity and influence of *Close Encounters of the Third Kind* never existed."— David Sterrit, *Christian Science Monitor*, June 24, 1982.

"The title of the remake was *John Carpenter's The Thing*, so it is the director who must take most of the blame for the grisly, misconceived movie.... As a noxious special-effects showcase, *John Carpenter's The Thing* was exceptional. As a movie it was nearly a total bust."— Richard Meyers, *S-F 2: The Great Science Fiction Films from Rollerball to Return of the Jedi*, Citadel Press, 1983, pages 241–242.

"Unfortunately, Carpenter's compelling story is buried beneath an avalanche of special effects. These effects are so extreme ... that they prevent many people from focusing on the story. *The Thing* takes a strong story and lets it meander around the many, many shocks. The mix is not masterful, but the dedicated viewer will give it a chance."— Darrell Moore, *The Best Worst and Most Unusual: Horror Films*, Beekman House, 1983, page 77.

"A surprising failure ... in contrast to the wit and invention of *Dark Star* (1974), *The Thing* has no discernible style.... The narrative seems little more than an excuse for various set-pieces of special effects.... The result is Carpenter's most unsatisfying film to date."— Phil Hardy, *The Film Encyclopedia: Science Fiction*, William Morrow, New York, 1984, page 378.

"Bereft, despairing, and nihilistic ... the most disturbing aspect of *The Thing* is its terrible absence of love. The film is so frigid and devoid of feeling that death no longer has any meaning.... Technically the film is superb. It has terrific sound effects, a pounding edgy score by Ennio Morricone and frostbitten cinematography by Dean Cundey. But what we are finally left with is the film's abiding paranoia and its gruesome empty effects."— Linda Gross, *The Los Angeles Times*, June 25, 1982.

"*John Carpenter's The Thing* smells, and smells pretty bad. It bears plenty of Carpenter's trademarks as a director. It has no pace, sloppy continuity, zero humor, bland characters.... It's my contention that John Carpenter was never meant to direct science fiction horror movies. Here's some things he'd be better suited to direct: Traffic accidents, train wrecks and public floggings...."— Alan Spencer, *Starlog* #64, November 1982, page 69.

"Abounding in primal fears, *The Thing* constantly surprises. *The Thing* does benefit from the strong presence of Russell.... Dean Cundey's cinematography is hauntingly atmospheric, making the base's dimly lit maze of rooms ... claustrophobically real.... A tour de force for twenty-four year old Rob Bottin, creator and designer of special make-up effects ... when viewed at a distance from the E.T. syndrome, *The Thing* should enjoy critical respectability as a riveting exercise in horror." — Pat H. Broeske, *Magill's Cinema Annual 1983*, pages 347–348.

Cast and Credits

CAST: Kurt Russell (MacReady); A. Wilford Brimley (Blair); T.K. Carter (Nauls); David Clennon (Palmer); Keith David (Childs); Richard Dysart (Dr. Copper); Charles Hallahan (Norris); Peter Maloney (Jennings); Richard Masur (Clark); Donald Moffatt (Garry); Joel Polis (Fuchs); Thomas Waites (Windows); Robert Weisser (Norwegian); Larry Franco (Norwegian Passenger with Rifle); Nate Irwin (Helicopter Pilot); William Zeman (Pilot).

CREDITS: A Universal Picture. A Turman-Foster Company Co-Production. *Music:* Ennio Morricone. *Editor:* Todd Ramsay. *Special Make-up Effects Created and Designed by:* Rob Bottin. *Production Designer:* John L. Lloyd. *Director of Photography:* Dean Cundey. *Associate Producer:* Larry Franco. *Co-Producer:* Stuart Cohen. *Produced by:* David Foster, Lawrence Turman. *Screenplay:* Bill Lancaster. *Directed by:* John Carpenter. *Stunts:* Anthony Cecere, Kent Hays, Larry Holt, Melvin Jones, Eric Mansker, Denver Mattson, Clint Rowe, Ken Strain, Rock Walker, Jerry Wills. *Executive Producer:* Wilbur Stark. *Based on the story "Who Goes There?" by:* John W. Campbell, Jr. *Art Director:* Henry Larrecq. *Production Manager:* Robert Latham Brown. *First Assistant Director:* Larry Franco. *Second Assistant Director:* Jeffrey Chernov. *Special Visual Effects:* Albert Whitlock. *Casting:* Anita Dann. *Set Decorator:* John Dwyer. *Special Effects:* Roy Arbogast. *Camera Operator:* Raymond Stella. *First Assistant Cameraman:* Clyde Bryan. *Second Assistant Cameraman:* Steve Tate. *Assistant Film Editors:* Jan Wesley, Kim Ray. *Production Sound:* Thomas Causey. *Supervising Sound Editors:* David Lew Yewdall, Colin Mouat. *Sound Re-Recording:* Bill Varney c.a.s, Steve Maslow c.a.s., Greg Landaker c.a.s. *Sound Editor:* Kendrick B. Sweet.

Loop Dialogue Editor: Jack Gosden. *Sound Effects Editor:* Warren Hamilton, Jr. *Assistant Sound Editor:* Ernesto Mas. *Sound Effects Assistant:* John Post, Duane Hansel. *Foley Supervisor:* John K. Adams. *Matte Photography:* Bill Taylor. *Technical Advisor (Juneau):* Dr. Maynard M. Miller. *Music Editor:* Cliff Kohlweck. *Computer Graphics:* Motion Graphics. *DGA Trainee:* Bruce Humphrey. *Synthesizer Sound:* Craig Harris. *Make-up:* Kenneth Chase. *Costume Supervisors:* Ronald T. Caplan, Gilbert Loc. *Script Supervisor:* Candy Marcellino. *Stunt Coordinator:* Dick Warlock. *Animal Trainer:* Rob Weatherwax. *Norwegian Dog owned and trained by:* Cliff Rowe. *Assistant Trainer:* James Colovin. *Property Master:* John Zemansky. *Transportation Captains:* Dan Anglin, Bob Cornell. *Key Grip:* Robert T. Woodward. *Gaffers:* Mark Walthour, Thomas Marshall. *Boom Man:* Joe Brennan. *Recordist:* David Katz. *End Titles and Optical Effects:* Universal Title. *Publicity Coordinator:* Peter Silbermann. *Special Publicity:* Pickwick/Maslansky/Koeningsberg, Inc. *Propmaker Foreman:* Bob Noholes. *Leadman:* Bart Susman. *Swing Gang:* Richard A. Gonzales, Joseph R. Savko, Milton Wilson. *Special Effects Foreman:* Hal Bigger. *Special Effects Assistant:* William D. Lee, Hans Metz, John Stirber. *Electric Best Boy:* Charles E. Nippell. *Lamp Operators:* Jon Antunovich, Terry Marshall, Jr. *Best Boy Grip:* Laszlo Horvath. *Dolly Grip:* Kris Krosskove. *Grip:* Ray Kinzer. *Assistant Property Master:* Michael R. Gannon. *Craft Services:* Rocky Corsini. *Painter:* James Callan. *Assistant to Stuart Cohen:* Linda von. *Assistant to John Carpenter:* Ellen Benjamin.

Special Make-up Effects Unit: *Line Producer:* Erik Jensen. *Mechanical Animation Coordinator:* Dave Kelsey. *Special Make-up Effects Coordinator:* Ken Diaz. *Production Illustrators:* Michael Ploog, Mentor Huebney,

Gary Meyer. *Special Technicians:* Gunnar Ferdinansen, Margaret Beserra. *Crew:* Lance Anderson, Dale R. Brady, Rob Burman, David Robert Cellitti, Don Chandler, Bob M. Cole, Jan Cook, James Cummins, Robert Davison, Frank Foster, Danny Gill, Archie L. Gillet, Tom Gillet, John Goodwin, Jim Kagel, Jeff Kennemore, Derek O'Reilly, Art Pimentel, Vincent Prentice, William Snyder, Michiko Tawaga, Brian G. Wade, Billy Whitten, Bob E. Worthington. *Special Thanks to:* Stan Winston. *Production Accountant:* Karen Miller. *Production Assistant:* Ron MacInnes. *Production Secretary:* Debra Collier. *Special Wigs:* Vivienne Wallen, Josephine Turner. *Craft Services:* Yervan Babisan, Rocky Corsini. *Driver:* George Lawson.

Animation Effects Sequence: *Dimensional Animation Effects Created by:* Randall William Cook. *Crew:* James Aupperle, James Belohovek, Ernest D. Farino, Carl Surges.

Main Title Sequence: *Visual Effects Designed by:* Visual Concept Engineering, Peter Kuran. *Miniature Supervisor:* Susan K. Turner. *Animators:* Katherine Keane, Keith Tucker. *Opticals:* RGB optical, James Hagedorn, George Lockwood.

Stewart, British Columbia Crew: *Set Decorator:* Graeme Murray. *Unit Production Manager:* Fitch Cady. *Second Assistant Director:* Michael Steele. *Production Secretary:* Karen Kalton. *Costume Supervisor:* Trish Keating. *Make-up:* Phyllis Newman. *Technical Advisor:* Robin Mounsy. *Camera Operator:* Cyrus Block. *First Assistant Camera:* Paul R. Prince. *Second Assistant Camera:* David Geddes, Douglas Pruss. *Script Supervisor:* Christine Wilson. *Prop Master:* Frank Parker. *Special Effects:* Leroy Routly, Michael A. Clifford. *Gaffer:* Dave Anderson. *Key Grip:* John Dillard Brinson. *Transportation Captain:* Alois Stranan. *Auditor:* Robert Kroechel. *Assistant Auditor:* Susan King. *Stills:* Chris Helcermanas-Benge. *Best Boy Grip:* James L. Hurford. *Dolly Grip:* David Gordon. *Electric Best Boy:* Len Wolf. *Lamp Operator:* Michael Orefice. *Generator Operator:* Barret J. Reid. *Craft Services:* Spencer Hyde. *Cooks:* Shelby Hetherington, Tana Tocher. *Helicopter Pilots:* Nate Irwin, Lawrence Perry, Ken Strain.

Special Thanks to: British Columbia Film Commission Office-Ministry of Tourism; The People of Stewart, British Columbia, Tongass National Forest, Jeaneau. "Don't Explain" Performed by Billie Holiday, Courtesy of MCA Records. "One Chain Don't Make No Prison" Performed by The Four Tops, Courtesy of MCA Records. *Filmed in:* Panavision. *Color:* Technicolor. *MPAA Rating:* R. *Running Time:* 109 minutes.

"Maybe every part of him was a whole. Every little piece was an individual animal, with a built-in desire to protect its own life.... When a man bleeds, it's just tissue, but blood from one of you things won't obey when it's attacked. It'll try to survive."—A tense MacReady explains the blood test he is about to administer.

SYNOPSIS: In the distant past, an alien spacecraft crashlands in icy Antarctica. Aboard it is something horrible: a terrible alien entity determined to survive...

In the winter of 1982, a Norwegian helicopter vigilantly pursues a frightened dog as it runs across barren Antarctica seeking shelter. The helicopter soon flies over American National Science Institute Station 4, all the while shooting at the dog and dropping grenades. The men of the base, including Childs, Palmer, Bennings and ace chopper pilot R.J. MacReady, watch as the helicopter lands nearby. The helicopter is unexpectedly destroyed when one of the Norwegians accidentally drops a bomb in the snow. The surviving Norwegian continues to shoot at the dog, brandishing his rifle with an insane paranoia. Instead of hitting the dog, however, the Norwegian shoots Bennings in the leg! Garry, the American Base Commander, returns fire with his revolver, and he kills the mad Norwegian.

The Americans are confused by their strange encounter with the Norwegians, wondering if Norway has declared war on America. The animal-keeper of the group, Clark, grows fond of the new dog in the company's midst and allows it to roam the hallways and rec-rooms of the base freely. Doctor Copper is concerned for the other members of the Nor-wegian base, and wants to visit their head-quarters to see if they were also victimized by the crazy pilots.

MacReady flies Copper to the base, and they find it in shambles. Parts of the destroyed building are still on fire and everything in-side is ruined. MacReady discovers a large ice block in a rear corridor. Something appar-ently quite large was once frozen inside, but now it is missing. Copper retrieves videotape shot by the Norwegian expedition in hopes that it will give the Americans some clue as to what happened to the foreign scientists.

Outside the camp, MacReady and Copper find the half-burned remains of some kind of mutated creature, something part-human and part-animal. They bring it back so Blair can perform an autopsy. Meanwhile, the radio man, Windows, worries because he cannot reach McMurdo Base to communicate the situation. Bad weather conditions across the continent are preventing any communica-tion whatsoever.

That night, Bennings is bitten by the new dog, and Clark escorts the animal to the ken-nel. There, in darkness, the dog starts to change. It transforms into a hideous alien life-form. It shoots out dozens of slimy tentacles, attempting to assimilate all of the other hus-kies in the kennel. MacReady hears the ruckus and sounds the alarm. Everyone gath-ers around the kennel and sees the shocking metamorphosis. MacReady orders Childs to bring the flame thrower, and Childs burns the alien as a portion of it escapes through the kennel roof.

Later, Blair performs an autopsy on the strange creature and learns that it is an entity capable of imitating other life-forms. Had the transformation continued unimpeded, all the dogs would have been replaced by exact duplicates. Blair becomes concerned when he learns that the affected dog was

loose in camp all day, because in that span the "thing" could have gotten to one or more of the people on the base and replaced *them* with alien duplicates.

The worried scientists review the Norwe-gian video footage and see the foreign team dig up a huge *something*, a flying saucer, from the ice. MacReady and Norris fly their heli-copter due east to that site and see the ruined spacecraft lodged in a mammoth crater. Near the wrecked saucer a cubical block of ice has been cut out of the landscape. Was this where the escaped alien rested for 100,000 years before the Norwegians thawed it?

After MacReady and Norris return to camp, the group debates the situation. Is it possible that an extra-terrestrial is hiding in their midst? Concerned, Blair runs a com-puter simulation showing the assimilation process of the entity. Grimly, the computer predicts that at least one American team-member is already infected. Even worse, if the intruder reaches civilization, the entire world will be assimilated in 27,000 hours.

While Bennings and Windows transport the burned alien remains to storage, Fuchs meets with MacReady and offers urgent news. Blair has locked himself up in his room, ob-sessed with the alien and its insidious nature. He believes it could be a million life-forms from a million different worlds, and that now the entire future of humanity is in grave dan-ger.

Before the issue can be addressed, Win-dows spots Bennings being absorbed by the still-living thing. MacReady and the others track the imitation down in the snow. A per-fect replica but for unfinished, alien hands, the new Bennings nearly escapes. MacReady and the others burn up the duplicate and all remaining alien tissue, but Blair is missing.

As it turns out, Blair has gone crazy. He has destroyed all the instrumentation in the helicopter and disabled the radio equipment so as to prevent the total infection of civili-zation. He is captured, sedated, and locked alone in a toolshed for his own good. Con-cerned, Blair orders MacReady to watch

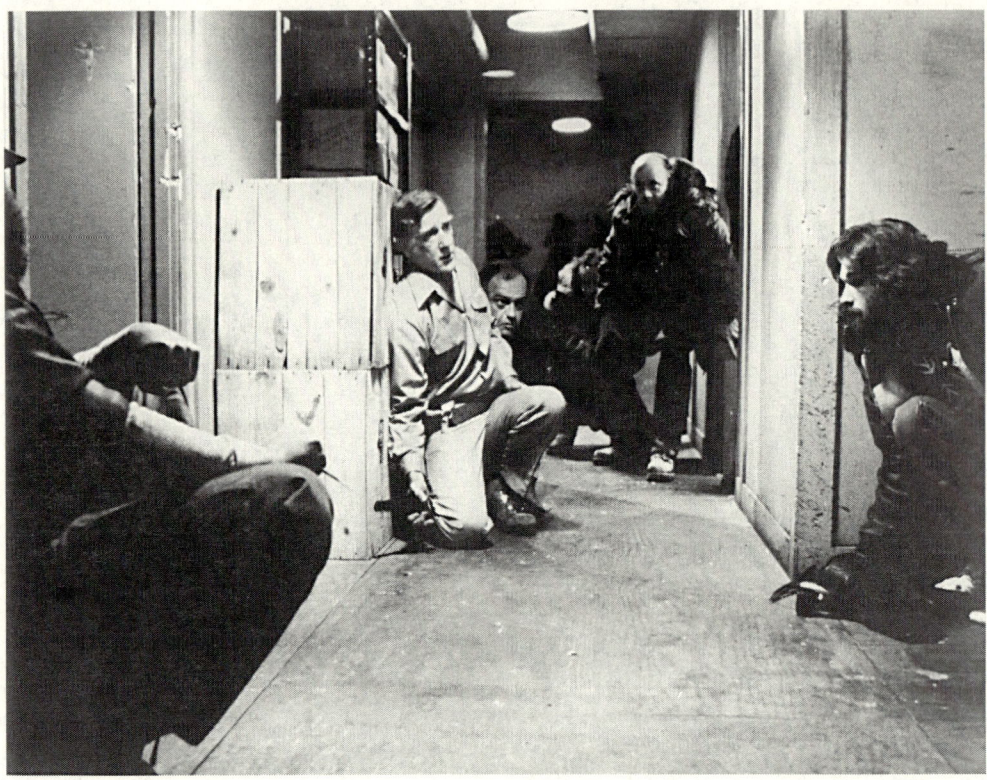

Under siege: The cast of John Carpenter's *The Thing* (1982) hunkers down for a long, cold winter.

Clark, because the animal keeper was alone with the infected dog for such a long time.

With a storm fast approaching, the group decides that it must determine who is the contaminating alien. Doc Copper suggests a blood serum test to determine the identities of the scientists, but the whole blood stores are soon sabotaged so his test cannot be conducted. This act of sabotage sparks a round of accusations, with Garry and Copper the two likeliest suspects since only they had access to the blood refrigerator. Garry relinquishes command to MacReady when Norris says he is not up to the challenge. Garry, Cooper and Clark, the likeliest suspects, are then tied up and sedated.

A storm hits the camp hard for 48 hours and the crew grows tired, unable to trust each other. Soon Fuchs disappears, and false evidence points to MacReady as the alien culprit. Nauls cuts MacReady loose on an expedition outside, and warns the others that

MacReady is the thing. Still alive, MacReady breaks into the camp and holds his accusers at bay with a stick of dynamite. In the commotion, Norris suffers a debilitating heart attack.

When Copper attempts to save his life, Norris's chest explodes and becomes a gaping, hungry mouth. Razor sharp teeth chew off Copper's arms and kill the doctor while the remaining Americans watch in shock. MacReady incinerates the Norris imitation but the thing wants to survive. Norris's head stretches off his dying body, sprouts six spiderish legs, and skitters away unnoticed. Just in time, MacReady torches it too.

While MacReady prepares a new blood test, Clark attempts to kill him, still believing him to be a thing. MacReady is forced to shoot Clark, but the blood test reveals that the dog-keeper was human. It also reveals that Nauls and Windows are human as well. However, when MacReady sticks a hot copper needle into Palmer's jar of blood, it springs to life and tries to escape ... to survive. Palmer erupts into a horrible monstrosity and kills Windows, ripping the radio operator's body to shreds. MacReady burns Palmer and Windows and saves the remaining humans. Gary and Childs soon check out as normal, and MacReady realizes they have to test Blair as well. While Garry, MacReady and Nauls head outside to do just that, Childs remains in the camp.

In the toolshed, MacReady and the others find Blair missing. But beneath the house is a cavern and a small alien escape craft he has constructed from the destroyed helicopter. Blair is infected and seeking a way to fly from the danger here. The Americans blow up the escape craft with a grenade, and decide that they cannot let the alien survive any longer, lest it reach civilization. Instead, they use dynamite to level the camp.

Blair is indeed the thing, and he strikes back, killing Garry and Nauls in the underground generator room. Alone, MacReady throws a stick of dynamite at the creature, now a disgusting combination of dinosaur, dog and human. The creature is blown to smithereens at last, but MacReady faces a new uncertainty when Childs shows up, unharmed. Uncertain if Childs is human or alien, MacReady sits across from his "friend" in the burned remnants of the camp, and the two share a drink.

COMMENTARY: *The Thing* represents John Carpenter's best, and most underrated, directorial effort. It also happens to be the best science fiction/horror film of 1982, an incredibly competitive year, and perhaps even the best genre motion picture of the 1980s. *The Thing* expertly states its two central themes (the frailty of human flesh, and the dehumanization of man and his increasing paranoia in the modern age) at the same time that it features amazing "shape-shifting" mechanical effects courtesy of *wunderkind* Rob Bottin. Importantly, these show-stopping special effects have not been outdone in more than 15 years, even in the era of CGI

wonders like *Terminator 2* (1991) and *Starship Troopers* (1997).

Although it was attacked during its theatrical release for being excessively gory and graphic, there is a method to John Carpenter's madness in *The Thing*. Perhaps above all else, his remake of the Howard Hawks film shows a recognition and fear of that most deadly of invisible invaders: disease. Whether it be an early variation of AIDS (then called the "gay plague") that Carpenter was responding to, or merely, in more general terms, cancer, hepatitis, or even aging, his 1982 horror film boasts an acute awareness of how desperately vulnerable human flesh is to external attack, perversion, and even subversion. The frailty of the flesh is the issue at the core of *The Thing*, and so director Carpenter continually shows his audience (often in nauseating close-up) how the flesh can be distorted, ruined, destroyed, or even repaired. To wit: Almost immediately in the film, the viewer sees a close-up of the dead Norwegian attacker. His eye is a shattered mess, destroyed by a bullet from Garry's gun. In the same portion of the film, there is also a close-up of Bennings getting his gun wound stitched up by Dr. Copper. His perforated flesh pulls and *stretches* as the stitches run through it like thread through cloth. Both of these images establish immediately, even before the insidious *modus operandi* of the otherworldly intruder is introduced, that humankind is vulnerable to an attack on or reshaping of the skin ... our very contact with the world around us.

Though these close-ups were often dismissed by critics as being present in the final cut of *The Thing* solely for "shock" effect, nothing could be further from the truth. The shape of human flesh is the shape of human life, and John Carpenter builds a sense of discomfort in his audience by revealing (in detail) how vulnerable flesh really is to all manners and methods of attack (from gunshots to alien invaders).

The motif of stretched or reshaped humanity is at the heart of *The Thing*, and so Carpenter continues to reveal, in horrific form, how man is continually victimized by "diseases," or in the case of *The Thing*, extra-terrestrials. As the tension builds, Dr. Copper and MacReady discover a dead Norwegian at the ruined foreign encampment. The corpse's flesh has been permanently "separated" at his neck, and solidified frozen blood, like an icicle, is hanging from slit wrists. This is another hint of the horror still to come: Flesh can appear different at different times. Here it is solid, frozen in an unnatural pattern that is inimical to human life. Once again, mankind is shown to be vulnerable, but this time it is a vulnerability to the environment (the cold) that surrounds him. Carpenter faces these grotesqueries head-on, and much of the film's believability originates from his choice to take a clinical approach to these early scenes of violence and death.

There are two autopsy scenes in *The Thing*, each one handled in a clinical, cool manner as the doctors (Blair and Copper) do their ghoulish business professionally and calmly. They remove organs and analyze each one scientifically, again revealing to viewers how little it really takes to pull a man apart, piece by piece. Innards are seen as important in this scene, for it is a man's innards that will differentiate him from "the Thing" in the hours to come. These scenes were also misinterpreted as "gratuitous" in 1982, but blunt-faced autopsies of this variety are done almost every week on *The X-Files* in the 1990s. They are part and parcel of the scientific/horror genre. *The Thing* reminds us that we human beings are but vulnerable packages inside vulnerable sheathing.

As the titular creature of *The Thing* is introduced in the film, John Carpenter takes his "frailty of the flesh" approach to extremes never seen before (or since) in film — extremes that generate genuine terror. After preparing audiences for the horror to come with multiple shots of stitches, wounds, and even half-burned remains wherein human skin is stretched and contorted in an expression of anguish, Carpenter then breaks the bonds of flesh completely by showing how humanity can be infected and re-shaped by a malevolent force. Eyeballs pop open in leathery skin. Yawning mouths transform into blossoming flower-like maws on the end of ever-growing appendages. Norris's severed head uses a lizard-like tongue to pull itself across the floor, and then spider legs come crunching out of his cranium to help the Thing skitter away. At one point, the infected Blair puts his hand *through* Garry's face, stretching Garry's mouth and face all out of proportion. In the most disgusting moments of *The Thing*, Norris's neck elongates, stretching and popping and ejaculating green liquids everywhere. These moments, all shocking and fear-inducing, deconstruct the sanctity of the flesh. Just as disease destroys man, this otherworldly invader does likewise, and Carpenter's long and steady slow build (from gruesome close-ups to all-out full-body carnage) expresses this theme visually.

Much of the terror from *The Thing* originates from Carpenter's thesis that the flesh can be perverted in innumerable ways; that the flesh can hide something horrid underneath the surface. Thus Rob Bottin's special effects demonstrate how seemingly disparate life-forms can be juxtaposed into one entity. The soft, beautiful fur of a husky pup suddenly gives way to slimy, cartilaginous insect legs, and the impact of the metamorphosis is startling. Death and decay, horror and pain, can exist just beneath the surface of normality. *The Thing* warns man to beware of disease, to beware of the invisible invader who can turn us into ugly, sick things filled with death. "Man is the warmest place to hide" is *The Thing*'s ad line, and it is totally appropriate to the content of the film. Horror comes not in haunted houses, not from outside, like the "stalker" (a la *Halloween*) but in the very cells and organs that encompass our "wholeness." The Thing is a frightening screen monster because just one cell of it can survive to infect a human being. It is unstoppable, and for a time it is undetectable.

Carpenter's metaphor for disease reaches its height in a scene straight from the short story "Who Goes There?" by John W. Campbell (as Don Stuart). The only way to determine who has been infected by the Thing is with a "blood test." What could be more appropriate in contemporary America? It is the blood test that detects hepatitis and AIDS, after all; the blood test that determines what is *really* going inside the human body. *The Thing* takes advantage of that fact, and offers its most suspenseful set-piece as MacReady tests the blood of his compatriots. Eduard Guerrero saw the blood test sequence, and indeed the entire scenario of *The Thing*, as a direct reference to the mysterious AIDS epidemic that was unfolding in America as *The Thing* was created:

> Once the person is absorbed by the Thing, it dissembles flawlessly while spreading and taking over the bodies of other victims. In this sense, the monster's mode of operation clearly parallels the AIDS virus' geometric spread.... The great fear that drives much of the film's action is that of not being able to detect those who have been penetrated and replicated by the thing.[9]

Guerrero went even further in his analysis. He believed that *The Thing* was actually a metaphor for the homosexual lifestyle, noting that the all-male cast of characters lived in a self-indulgent (pot smoking, alcohol using) same-sex liberal life-style. Thus they were open to "infection." While this interpretation may be pushing the matter a bit, it is clear that the film's monster can be seen as a metaphor for disease, if not AIDS specifically. Carpenter dramatizes this metaphor by depicting the attack of an aggressive infecting force, an extra-terrestrial who can corrupt and compromise the flesh more rapidly and catastrophically than any known disease might.

John Carpenter's second thematic strand in *The Thing* involves another issue that was gaining notoriety in the early '80s, specifically that a person can *appear* normal, while just under the surface be quite the opposite. Although suburbia was thriving all across America in 1982, there was a growing awareness dawning among many middle-class Americans that they did not really know their neighbors at all. After all, the advent of fast and inexpensive air transportation coupled with the very American tendency to put down roots far away from one's original home assured that people within one suburban development might be morally and ethically separate from the ideals of their neighbors. The resulting uncertainty about what goes on "next door" created an era in which people could not necessarily be sure of their neighbors. Call it an undercurrent of paranoia, or even a lack of trust, but it is also the playing field of John Carpenter's *The Thing*. Bill Lancaster has fashioned a screenplay in which trust, paranoia, and secrets beneath "normal" appearances are all of paramount importance.

Trust, specifically, is a concept the film constantly pinpoints. "I don't know who to *trust*," Blair declares. "*Trust*'s a tough thing to come by these days ... why don't you *trust* in the Lord?" MacReady replies. Finally, "Nobody *trusts* anybody anymore," MacReady moans once the Thing has infiltrated the camp. Division among the ranks has been caused by the fact one of the "neighbors" is not what he appears to be. Blair is unable to trust his neighbors, as it were, and he resorts to violence. By doing so, he is acting as if he is *not* himself, which generates suspicion on the part of Fuchs and others. Simple, honest motives are taken as deceitful ones. Suspicion builds upon suspicion until each man is an island and thus a potential victim for the Thing. The inability to trust people just makes the situation worse in *The Thing*, and that is why, in the final analysis, it is hard for mankind to muster a defense against the monster who wants to destroy it. If brother cannot trust brother, how can humanity thrive?

A different kind of "thing," from a different kind of Hollywood. James Arness as the "intellectual carrot," the star of Howard Hawks's *The Thing* (1951).

Besides documenting the breakdown and perversion of human flesh, *The Thing* showcases a pretty clear malfunctioning of the human condition. Everybody becomes so afraid of being "contaminated" by a neighbor that friendship, understanding, love, and trust all die. The titular creature of *The Thing* thus breaks both the skin and the heart of man. This high level of paranoia and fear is documented powerfully by Carpenter's camera. As MacReady faces his companions and discusses how the creature is hiding behind normality, the camera faces a group of men in goggles, snow masks, and hoods. They are all bundled, hidden as it were, from each other, from the audience, and from the camera. They are all hiding behind snow gear, just as the Thing is hiding behind the face of humanity. In a crowd like this, it is impossible to know who to trust, or who is smiling an evil smile beneath a wool scarf.

Just as Howard Hawks's *The Thing* reflected its time (the 1950s), so does John Carpenter's version reflect the era it was made in. In the earlier motion picture, a group of hearty men led by Captain Pat Hendry (Kenneth Tobey) showed camaraderie as they joined together to face an external menace. Riding high off of the victories of World War II, these men believed that ingenuity, teamwork, patriotism, core American values and good old fashioned American know-how could defeat even the extraterrestrial menace (James Arness) that threatened them. The men were all of one unified (patriotic) mind, but for the foolish scientist (read: Communist) played by Robert Cornthwaite who wanted to show unnecessary sympathy to the invader.

John Carpenter made his *The Thing* in a very different world. The "me" decade (the 1970s) had just ended, and the unfortunate era of the yuppie was beginning in America. It was no longer important to be part of a community, to have camaraderie, or to believe in ideals such as patriotism. The new goal was to make as much money as possible, as quickly as possible, and to live only to accumulate more wealth for one's self. Coworkers were no longer team members, they were *competitors* instead. They might show a friendly face on the surface, but underneath, their goal was to get ahead of you, and they would stab you in the back if it meant stock options and a bigger office. And, each one of them might have AIDS ... so by all means do not drink out of their coffee cup, or have sex with them! Thus, in the words of Thomas Doherty, *The Thing* depicts a societal trend, specifically an

> interpersonal implosion. Radically destructive of the ethos of the original, the second film features a collection of autonomous, angry, unpleasant and self-interested individuals, as chilly as the stark Antarctican landscape they inhabit. That men could live in close quarters, in total isolation, depending on each other for survival and succor — and not develop a fraternal bond defies ... dramatic logic.[10]

Indeed, the nature of the Americans at the Antarctican camp in *The Thing* does defy dramatic logic. Instead, it reflects a different ethos: a didactic one. The "heroes" of *The Thing*, and their environment, represent a microcosm for 1980s America. Often mislabeled as simply a "horror movie" director, John Carpenter has actually built an artistic, reflexive world in *The Thing*. It is a world where an invisible but terminal disease can destroy without warning, and nobody trusts their neighbor for fear that they are "infected" with the plague. The film has social relevance at the same time that it breaks social convention by dramatizing, in the most visceral terms imaginable, extreme violence and destruction.

The Thing can be appreciated on another level as well. At the same time that it underscores the change in American core values from the 1950s to the 1980s, it also undercuts audience expectations by providing, under the guise of mass entertainment, a nihilistic view about mankind's ability to cope with disease, the invisible intruder to which the Thing is likened to throughout the picture. Science, military action, medicine, and force all fail to stop the alien invader. The resourceful hero, MacReady, is forced at the conclusion of the film, to exist in a world of détente. The alien may still be alive, but he is no condition to fight it. He is facing the possibility of living in a world where man will have to share dominance with the disease. There is no easy victory, no miracle cure ... just the beginning of what could be a new social order. Shelter (in the form of the base) is destroyed, and a long winter is coming. Man and the disease will *both* have to face the elements — the only common ground these adversaries share. Although MacReady has sacrificed his future to stop the threat of disease, he has not quashed it. As long as there is one human being alive to transmit it, the disease can grow strong again.

In this ambiguous climax Bill Lancaster and John Carpenter managed to foreshadow the AIDS story again. In 1999, the world is no closer to a cure for AIDS than it was in 1982. On the contrary, AZT and other "treatments" exist, but they simply keep AIDS paralyzed, under some form of control. In *The Thing*, that is exactly the solution MacReady must settle for as the end credits roll. He has blown up the Thing, but he knows that even one cell of his nemesis can grow and destroy as easily as the powerful entity he just wiped out. *The Thing* warns that in the war with disease, the best mankind can hope for is an uneasy truce, an uncertain control over the invisible but highly flexible invader.

Another interpretation is this: MacReady, protagonist and everyman in *The Thing*, ends the picture contaminated by disease himself. It is he, not Childs, who is the beast, but in the ultimate anonymity of the assimilation process, even the audience does not realize it. If this is the case, then *The Thing* is surely the beginning of the end for humanity because we cannot even recognize the intruder in our midst.

Because *The Thing* offers no easy answers to difficult questions, it confounds audience expectations. In horror movies there are two stock endings. In the first, the hero is victorious and the evil is vanquished (*Alien, Jaws, Scream.*) In the second ending, evil lives to fight another day (*Halloween, A Nightmare on Elm Street.*) *The Thing* is different because it does not fit squarely with either solution. Audiences do not know if the "thing" is alive, or if it is dead, and so they leave the theater with a sense of uncertainty and insecurity. As Jonathan Lake Crane wrote:

> The 1982 remake of *The Thing* is a perfect example of a film designed to disturb … audience members who still

want to watch decent men triumph over evil in exciting but utterly predictable showdowns. *The Thing* is exquisitely constructed to deny every attempt, from the pathetic to the brilliant, on the part of its supposed protagonists, to master their world. Every moment that would have assured success in earlier eras is marked by total failure…. Logic, or more broadly, knowledge, refuses to operate the way it used to.[11]

All of these thematic touches, from the "frailty of the flesh" to the paranoia and uncertainty of the climax, would mean little were *The Thing* not a beautifully realized film from a visual perspective. Fortunately, Carpenter and Cundey have made a picture that is always compelling. Of all of Carpenter's films, *The Thing* is the one which best establishes a feeling of place, and in particular, of isolation. The film opens with an aerial view of an ice-field. There are jagged mountains and harsh whites everywhere, and the overall image is of frozen wasteland. The chill of Antarctica is palpable. The jagged mountains also reveal that the location is forcibly separated from what lies beyond. The people who inhabit the story are not only isolated from one another because of their fear of infection, but because of *geography*. There is nowhere to go, no place to escape to. This setting also plays into the disease motif of the picture. It is only because the alien landed in a remote, isolated setting that it is fought to a standstill. Imagine what would happen if there was a "thing" outbreak in New York City: where a single infected person has easy access to ships, trains, airplanes, and millions of people.

After establishing the frozen locale of *The Thing*, Carpenter (with the assistance of Lancaster's literate screenplay and Cundey's claustrophobic framing) establishes the routine of boredom which dominates the lives of those dwelling inside the American camp. MacReady plays chess with his computer and drinks liquor till he is drunk; Blair and Copper play endless games of Ping-Pong; Childs

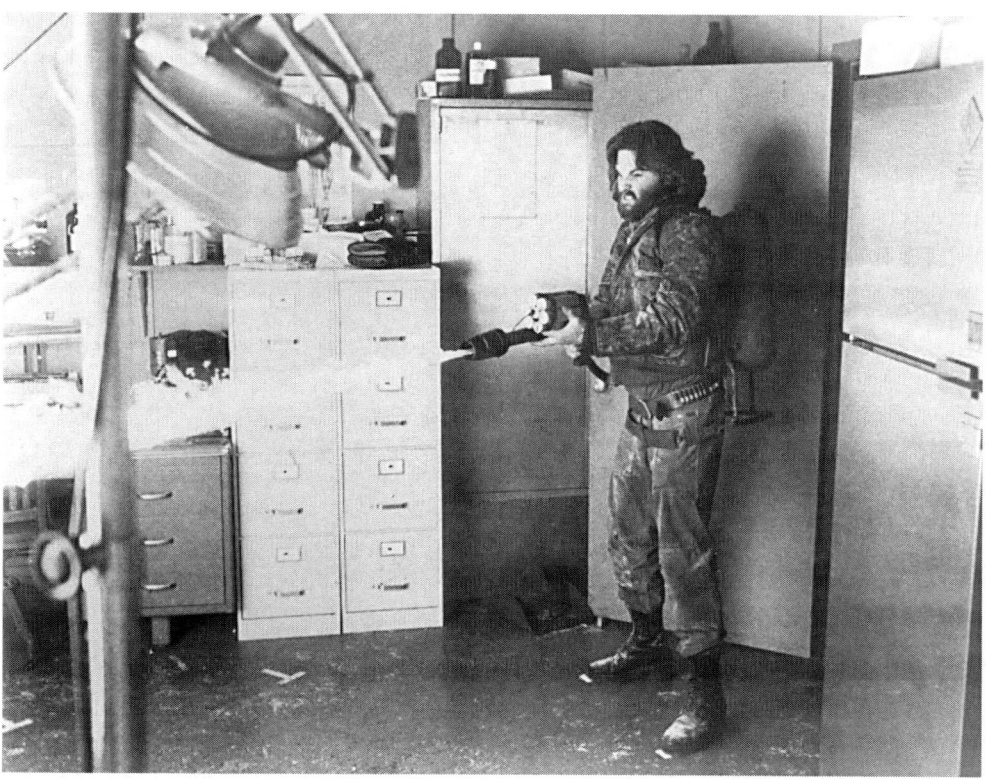

MacReady (Kurt Russell) wastes no time incinerating the enemy in *The Thing* (1982).

and Palmer watch videotaped game shows (*Let's Make a Deal*) and smoke pot. Overall, it is a purposeless, aimless existence. More than that, these scenes establish the documentary, realistic filmmaking style of *The Thing*. In none of these sequences is the audience rewarded with important character background or information, or dialogue that will relate to the central plot. On the contrary, these scenes look like images from a documentary about Antarctica. We see people's faces, watch them do their thing, but there is no false drama, no edifice of art to suggest that this is a work of fiction. The characters of the film are thus established as real people, rather than as pawns in a greater narrative piece. This is important because a sense of realism is necessary if the filmgoer is to accept what comes next: the appearance of a shape-shifting extra-terrestrial. Were the early scenes of *The Thing* not thoroughly convincing and evocative of real life, the next

step to a less believable plane would not be accepted. One of the reasons *The Thing* is so frightening relates to this realistic approach. The audience is roped in by the rote, repetitive natural existence of these men. It seems so true to life and untheatrical ... and then *boom!* Horror lands!

In establishing "place," John Carpenter again relies on a technique he had used successfully in earlier pictures: the subjective, point of view camera. In *The Thing*, his camera prowls the camp at night, when it is quiet and seemingly empty. The camera glides smoothly through the kitchen, labs, the recroom, and a long hallway — until the infected dog unexpectedly appears. As in the montage at the end of *Halloween*, Carpenter is charting the terrain of the battlefield here. He is making us comfortable with the "space" of the base.

Because he is a Hawks fan, Carpenter also peppers *The Thing* with visual references to the 1951 picture. In the first instance, Norris, MacReady and the others watch footage of the Norwegian team planting thermite charges around a flying saucer buried in the ice. The framing, the *mise-en-scène*, of this sequence is identical to that in the Hawks picture (referenced once before in the Dr. Demento horror film festival in *Halloween*). The second reference occurs when MacReady torches Childs after the infamous blood test. Childs runs through a wall, on fire, and falls down in the snow outside the shelter. Again, this sequence is a total restaging of the sequence in the original *Thing* wherein the Thing attacked the Americans and was subsequently set afire.

If *The Thing* fails in any regard as a totally compelling film-going experience, it is in its depiction of the technology of the shape-shifting alien, which seems wrong. It is dramatized (both in the flying saucer and make-shift craft constructed by the infected Blair) as a totally mechanical technology. Considering the alien's abilities to change forms, and its capability to changes sizes and shapes, a more organic, original design seems called for. After *The Thing*, films such as *Lifeforce* (1985) and *Invaders from Mars* (1986) would experiment with the look of organic technology, and a similar approach seems called for here.

Despite this small flaw, *The Thing* remains a thoroughly engaging and horrifying film. It is John Carpenter's scariest picture, by a long shot, not only for what it shows, but for what it suggests about man's physical and emotional weaknesses.

Christine (1983)

Critical Reception

"It's to the credit of John Carpenter, who directs *Christine*, that he sees the comic side of King's metaphor. The story of a killer car in love is not all that scary on the screen, so he doesn't try to bowl the audience over with gore.... *Christine* is a tight, modest job ... silly but not unwitty ... *Christine* has just enough comic energy to carry this fable to its crash-bam conclusion."— David Ansen, *Newsweek:* "Hell on Wheels," December 19, 1983.

"The first part of the movie is a good slick pairing of director John Carpenter with a Stephen King story, though it has many holes.... The high school sequences are nicely credible, especially the budding sexual feelings; and the camaraderie between the youngsters is well-done.... But then *Christine* deteriorates into an inevitable scenario, with no suspense whatsoever."— Pat Anderson, *Films in Review*, February 1984.

"Director Carpenter and screenwriter Bill Phillips have compacted and customized Stephen King's screaming jalopy of a novel until it moves with sleek '50s lines and a sassy tailfin flap at the end.... Carpenter's best since *Halloween* is at heart a deadpan satire of the American man's love affair with his car. This *Christine* is one lean mean funny machine."— Richard Corliss, *Time*, December 19, 1983.

"It's stylishly done all the way, thanks to Carpenter, who's working from a Bill Phillips adaptation. The automotive effects ... are phenomenally eerie, courtesy of Roy Arbogast, but the film's crisp suspenseful atmosphere is ultimately sabotaged by too much teenage angst and a bland climax.... The soundtrack really wins the race."— David McDonnell, *Starlog* # 88: "The Fantasy Films."

Cast and Credits

CAST: Keith Gordon (Arnie); John Stockwell (Dennis); Alexandra Paul (Leigh); Robert Prosky (Darnell); Harry Dean Stanton (Junkins); Christine Belford (Regina Cunningham); Roberts Blossom (LeBay); William Ostrander (Buddy); David Spielberg (Mr. Casey); Malcolm Danare (Moochie); Steven Tash (Rich); Stuart Charno (Vandeberg); Kelly Preston (Roseann); Mark Poppel (Chuck); Michael Cunningham (Robert Darnell); Richard Collier (Pepper Boyd); Bruce French (Mr. Smith); Douglas Warhit (Bemis); Keri Montgomery (Ellie); Jan Burrell (Librarian).

CREDITS: Columbia Pictures Presents from Polar Films, a Richard Kobritz Production. *Casting:* Karen Rea. *Associate Producer:* Barry Bernardi. *Music:* John Carpenter. *In Association with:* Alan Howarth. *Co-Producer:* Larry Franco. *Executive Producer:* Kirby McCauley, Mark Tarlov. *Edited by:* Marion Rothman. *Production Designer:* Daniel Lomino. *Director of Photography:* Donald M. Morgan, a.s.c. *Based upon the novel by:* Stephen King. *Screenplay:* Bill Phillips. *Producer:* Richard Kobritz. *Directed by:* John Carpenter. *Production Manager:* Robert Doudell. *First Assistant Director:* Larry Franco. *Second Assistant Director:* Jack Philbrick. *Special Effects Supervisor:* Roy Arbogast. *Transportation and "Christine" Coordination:* Eddie Lee Voelker. *Set Decorator:* C L O U D I A. *Production Illustrator:* George Jenson. *Leadman:* Daril Alder. *Set dressers:* J.D. Smith, Richard Chirco. *Sound Mixer:* Thomas Causey. *Boom Operators:* Joseph Brennan, Frank Garfield. *Camera Operator:* Chris Schwiebert. *First Assistant Camera:* Anthony J. Rivetti. *Second Assistant Camera:* Marc Marguilies. *Panaglide Operator:* Joseph Valentine. *Still Photography:* Kim Gottlieb-Walker.

Publicity Coordinator: Peter J. Silbermann. *Property Master:* Kent H. Johnson. *Assistant Prop Master:* Louis S. Fleming. *Script Supervisor:* Kisuna Jacobsen. *D.G.A. Trainee:* Connie Garcia-Singer. *Costume Supervisor:* Darryl Levine. *Women's Costumer:* Dawn Jackson. *Make-up Supervisor:* Bob Dawn. *Hair-stylist:* Frankie Bergman. *Assistant Film Editor:* Virginia Katz. *Casting Assistant:* Annette Benson. *Extra Casting:* EXTRACAST, Peter and Janice Spitzer. *Location Manager* Karlene Gallagay. *Assistant to Mr. Kobritz:* Shirley Bonner. *Assistant to Mr. Carpenter:* Ellen Benjamin. *Production Coordinator:* Bridget Murphy. *Production Secretary:* Carol Rosenthal. *Production Accountant:* Larry Hand. *Assistant Production Accountant:* Bethany Brown. *Office Assistant:* Mary McKiernan. *Special Effect Foreman:* Bill Lee. *Special Effects:* David L. Simmons, E. Hui, Kevin Quibell, Richard Wood, Michael Reedy. *Modelmakers:* Jeff House, Richard Ruiz. *Construction Coordinator:* Walt Hadfield. *Paint-Foreman:* John Tyrell. *Painter:* Anthony J. Leonard, Jr. *Gaffers:* Gary H. Holt, Iou Tobin. *Electrical Best Boys:* Thomas K. Baron, Alex Skvorzov. *Set Electricians:* Ralph Barone, Michael Amorelli, Ed Tobin, Michael Laws, James Crawford, Richard Hartley, Jr. *Key Grip:* Cal Sterry. *Second Grip:* Clay Wilson. *Dolly Grip:* Gary Parker. *Grips:* Richard Dow, David Canestro. *Craft Services:* Midge Ogle. *First Aid:* Maurice Costello. *Transportation Captain:* Ed Arter. *Transportation Co-Captain:* Eo Braden. *Drivers:* Gordon W. Wiles, George Alden. *Driver Mechanic:* Gary Burch. *Custom Body Work:* Rubin Saens. *Supervising Sound Editor:* David Yewdall. *Dialogue Editors:* Ken Sweet, Michael Gutierrez. *Sound Editors:* David Stone, Duane Hartsell, John Post. *ADR Supervisor:* Devon Heffley. *Foley:* John Adams, Steve Rice. *Music Editor:* William Calbruth. *Opticals:* Modern Film Effects.

Re-Recording Mixers: Robert J. Litt c.a.s., Elliott Tyson c.a.s, Steve Maslow c.a.s. *Music Coordinator:* Michael Ochs. *Music Clearance:* David Marsh. *Music:* "Bad to the Bone" performed by The Destroyers; "Best of Burden" performed by The Rolling Stones; "Bony Marrone" performed by Larry Williams; "Come on Let's Go" performed by Ritchie Valens; "Keep a Knockin'" performed by Little Richard; "Rock 'n' Roll Is Here to Stay" performed by Danny and the Juniors. *Stunts Coordinator:* Terry Leonard. *Stunts:* Buff Brady, Ted Duncan, Donna Evans, Robert Lee Harris, Mike H. McGuachy, Conrad E. Palmisano, Ben R. Scott, Dean Smith, Jim Wilksey, David D. Darling, Todd Elliott, Clifford Happy, Norman Howell, John Meier, Kerry Rossall, John Clay-Scott, Dick Warlock, Walter Wyatt. *Filmed in:* Panavision. *Color:* Metrocolor. *MPAA Rating:* R. *Running Time:* 110 minutes.

———————

"Let me tell you a little something about love, Dennis. It has a voracious appetite. It eats everything: friendship, family. It kills me how much it eats. But I'll tell you something else, you feed it right and it's a beautiful thing. That's what we have…. No shitter ever came between me and Christine." — a deranged Arnie explains love to his best friend.

———————

SYNOPSIS: In Detroit during the late '50s, a 1958 Fury is born bad on the assembly line. Its hood crushes one worker's hands, requiring a trip to the hospital. Then the vengeful car murders another worker when he puts his cigar out on its fresh upholstery.

Many years later, in September of 1978, Dennis Guilder picks up his nerdy friend Arnie Cunninghman and drives him to their first day of senior year. They arrive at Rockbridge High School and soon spot a new student, the beautiful Leigh Cabot. Later in the day, Arnie is surrounded by bullies in shop class. Dennis intervenes on behalf of his friend, and a fight erupts. Buddy Rafferton

pulls a switchblade, and his friend Moochie urges him further. Buddy spears Arnie's lunch, spilling white yogurt on the floor. Then Buddy crushes Arnie's glasses. Mr. Casey interrupts the fight and Dennis and Arnie inform the teacher that Buddy is armed. An angry Buddy gets probation and swears to get even with Arnie.

On the way home from school, Arnie spots a beat-up 1950s automobile rotting in a front yard close to his neighborhood. The car's current owner is a strange old man named George LeBay. He reveals that the 1958 Fury, named Christine, belonged to his brother, Roland LeBay. For Arnie, it is love at first sight, and he quickly purchases Christine for 300 dollars. Dennis thinks the car is a piece of junk, and Arnie's overbearing mother is furious with him for buying a car without consulting her. She refuses to let him keep the wreck in their yard, so Arnie berths it at Darnell's garage. Darnell is a cantankerous old man who gives Arnie the rules of the garage and warns that he will be watching the teenager.

In early October, Arnie is still working hard to restore Christine to cherry condition. Darnell begins to adjust his attitude towards Arnie, and he offers him a part-time job transporting parts and making "deliveries" of an unspecified nature to shady clients. At school, Dennis asks Leigh out dancing, but she turns him down. She already has a date — with Arnie!

That night, Dennis visits Arnie to find that his friend has changed rather dramatically. Arnie has stopped wearing glasses, combed his hair, and he is even wearing better clothes. Dennis has no time to ask Arnie about the strange changes because Arnie must run an errand for Darnell. Instead, Dennis talks to Arnie's mother, who informs Dennis that Christine's last owner died in the car of carbon monoxide poisoning.

The next day, Dennis visits LeBay, who informs him that Arnie has the same look in his eyes as his brother once did. LeBay also shares the grisly fact that his brother's wife

A close-up portrait in automative terror: The deadly car is born. From *Christine* (1983).

and daughter also died in the car. Concerned, Dennis sneaks into Darnell's to check out the vehicle. As he attempts to tamper with Christine's door handle, the Fury's radio comes on and starts playing the song "Keep a Knockin'." Frightened, Dennis leaves Darnell's.

At the big game that weekend, quarterback Dennis is distracted during a crucial pass when he sees Leigh and Arnie necking beside a fully restored Christine. Dennis is injured just short of a touchdown, and he ends up in the hospital. Arnie visits him there, and Dennis learns he was nearly paralyzed from the waist down in the football accident.

Later, Leigh and Arnie go out to the drive-in in Christine and make out there, but Leigh is reluctant to have sex in the car. She hates it because Arnie spends more time with Christine than with her. When a windshield wiper breaks, Arnie leaves the car to fix it and Christine attacks Leigh. The radio activates, and Leigh starts to choke. When Arnie cannot get back inside the car, Leigh is rescued by another patron at the drive-in. Leigh

returns home angry and tells Arnie to get rid of Christine. Because he refuses, Leigh and Arnie break up.

Late that night, Buddy Rafferton, Moochie and the gang break into Darnell's Garage and trash Christine completely, even defecating on the dashboard. Arnie discovers the damage the next day and is furious about it. Arnie's parents suggest he buy a new car, but Arnie is in love with Christine. He decides to rebuild her instead. After he offers Christine tender words, the car begins to rebuild itself before his very eyes. An angry Christine then sets out after Buddy and his gang, murdering them one at a time in grisly fashion. A police detective soon shows up at the high school and questions Arnie about Christine and the car's damage.

Christine soon strikes again, killing Darnell. As the police close in on Arnie, Leigh and Dennis meet to discuss the situation. They are both afraid for Arnie's life. He has changed so dramatically since buying Christine. He is no longer Arnie Cunningham, but a living reflection of Roland LeBay's gruesome and hateful personality. Dennis talks to Arnie about the situation on New Year's Eve, but Arnie is out of control and totally obsessed with his car. The next day, Dennis scrapes a challenge on Christine's hood with a screwdriver: "Darnell's Tonight."

Leigh and Dennis make final preparations to combat Christine. They hotwire a bulldozer and hope that it will be able to stand up to Christine's supernatural powers. Christine arrives and the battle royal begins. In the end, Dennis and Leigh are victorious, but the cost is high. Arnie Cunningham is killed behind the wheel of his beloved automobile.

COMMENTARY: John Carpenter often refers to *Christine* as his least favorite film project, and perhaps that is not a surprise. Not only was he recovering from *The Thing*'s box office and critical drubbing at the time he directed the film, but he was also facing several other obstacles. The first, of course, was *Christine*'s famous author, Stephen King. King is a prolific author, and no doubt the King of horror fiction, but his often-splendid novels have resulted in terrible films on far too many occasions. His work is not easy to adapt in the first place, and many talented directors have been unsuccessful in translating his scary prose into suspenseful or scary motion pictures.

The short list of problems associated with Stephen King adaptations would look like this: First of all, audiences familiar with King's writing carry expectations into the theater —*high* expectations that cannot be met since film is a different art form from novel writing, and novels must be condensed if the film is fit within a two hour (usually ninety minute) time frame. Second, most film directors who have taken a shot at Stephen King books on celluloid are themselves artists of an unusually high caliber. Directors such as Brian DePalma (*Carrie*), Stanley Kubrick (*The Shining*), David Cronenberg (*The Dead Zone*), George Romero (*The Dark Half*), Mary Lambert (*Pet Sematary*), Tobe Hooper ('*Salem's Lot, The Mangler*) and John Carpenter inevitably bring their own ethos, their own sense of style and technique, to a filming of any Stephen King story. Thus Stephen King's vision is changed, some might say distorted, to accommodate the men or women calling the shots. The result is that the images on screen represent hybrid thinking. *Christine* is King-Carpenter. *The Shining* is King-Kubrick. *The Dead Zone* is King-Cronenberg. For people who just want pure, unadulterated King, this accommodation is unacceptable.

Lastly, and perhaps most importantly, Stephen King stories are exceedingly difficult to translate visually. He often writes about moods and terror, but these feelings collapse into corny hokum when the source of terror is actually seen and thus *known*, and quantified, by the audience. *Silver Bullet* (1985) might make for terrifying reading as the novella *Cycle of the Werewolf*, but as a film it lacks scares because the lead werewolf is just a man in a phony, rubbery costume. The limitless imagination is thus supplanted by concrete production considerations such as special effects, costuming, and makeup — and the inevitable result is that the film lacks the same scariness of the book.

There have been exceptions, of course. For instance, *Cujo* (1983) turned out particularly well because it was simply *Jaws* (1975) with a rabid dog instead of a great white shark (call it *Paws*). *Misery* (1990) was also quite good, because of its claustrophobic setting and the fine performances of James Caan and Kathy Bates. The book was a two-person play, and the movie was able to visualize that limited world successfully, without resorting to zippered monsters or cheesy optical effects. John Carpenter's *Christine*, while not a failure by any means, is certainly not one of the best King adaptations, even though its script is, for the most part, rather faithful to the source material.

Why does *Christine* fail to inspire the same level of dread and terror as *Misery* or *Cujo*? Quite simply, Carpenter is working with a concept that is not scary, or even particularly inventive. Cars are not really a frightening nemesis, and *Christine* never recovers from that obvious fact. A dog, a shark, or a human serial killer can all seem truly frightening because each of them has an intellect, or at least instinct. An animal, like the rabid St. Bernard in *Cujo*, has personality, something distinctly unique about it (relentlessness, compassion, humor, rage, whatever), but a car, no matter what the trappings, is just an inanimate thing. It has no personality; it has no instinct; it is merely a device that requires human manipulation, and for that reason *Christine* never really comes to life as a horror show. Logically and dramatically, a car as antagonist is problematic plain and simple. If being chased by Christine, why not simply run somewhere where she cannot get you, like inside a house, on the second floor, in crowds, off the road? *Christine*'s "chase and kill" sequences are silly because the victim is always seen running right down the middle of a road, with the car in hot pursuit. It is obvious that any person, no matter how fast, cannot outrun a car on open road, so these scenes only point to the inherent ridiculousness of the situation, and the stupidity of the characters under siege. In one inventive passage, Moochie does hide in a narrow alley, where he believes himself impervious to Christine's touch. In a clever move, the car squeezes into the alley and crushes him. If all the scenes had been as unexpected as that one, the film might have worked a little better.

Other films such as *The Car* (1977), *Killdozer* (1974) and Stephen King's own *Maximum Overdrive* (1986) have all attempted to make "evil" cars a frightening thing, but none have worked much better than *Christine* does. Perhaps the best "vehicular attack" film is Steven Spielberg's *Duel* (1971), which brought the Man vs. Machine story back to basics in more ways than one. As Fritz Weaver's motorist was stalked by an insane, unseen driver in a truck, the story of *Duel* took on a paranoid and mythic bent. Weaver was isolated and alone out there in the endless desert, and his nemesis was unstoppable and

merciless. There literally was no place to escape to in that flat, otherworldly landscape, and the relentless nature of the vehicular opponent made the film a *tour de force* of suspense. Was it all a desert-induced hallucination? An egregious example of road rage? There was no reason for the truck to attack in *Duel*, no motive for the battle, and so viewers were able to project their own motives onto the mysterious villain. In *Christine* the motive is "jealousy"; in *Overdrive* and *Killdozer* an extraterrestrial intervention is the cause of the attacks. And the setting in each situation, suburbia, fails to provoke horror or dread. So while a car is an inherently unfrightening nemesis since it is just a thing, *Christine* tries to imbue it with a recognizable motivation, jealousy, that is not only impossible in a machine, but uninspired. Once the viewer realizes that jealousy is the issue at hand, and that Christine will exact revenge against all those who mess with Arnie, the film has no surprises left. It's like *Death Wish* with the car as Charles Bronson. Of course, this is a story flaw that can be traced back to Stephen King's work. Carpenter just inherited the problem.

Even though the horror rarely works in *Christine*, Carpenter does his stylish best to orchestrate the numerous violent set-pieces of the film. At one point, Christine catches fire and is seen racing through the black night like a bat out of Hell. It is an awesome sight, the stuff of a surreal nightmare, and it definitely evokes a shiver if not a scream as the car burns brightly in the forest of the night. In another memorable moment, the car appears out of nowhere, silent and unmoving. Its blaring radio signals its arrival on the scene, and again there is a palpable chill in the air, if not the electricity of real suspense. These moments, coupled with some good, human performances from leads Keith Gordon, John Stockwell and Alexandra Paul, make *Christine* eminently watchable. Though the jolt of *The Thing* or *Halloween* is missing, a mellow mood of humor and humanity is infused through the mayhem of *Christine*.

Don't ever get a 1958 Fury angry: Moochie (Malcolm Danare) runs from *Christine* (1983).

Perhaps aware that the "horror" aspects of his titular villain are particularly lame in *Christine*, John Carpenter truly does an exceptional job of wittily and intelligently handling the non-horror material in the screenplay. For instance, unlike the *Friday the 13th* or later *Nightmare on Elm Street* pictures, *Christine* really seems to exist in the closed off environment of high school, the world of the dominant, athletic male teenager. Besides capturing the high school lingo perfectly, with mentions of "beating off" and "getting laid," the film knowingly takes on the perspective of a disenfranchised teenager. Thus the film's characters become paranoid at times, convinced that dark forces (adults?) are working against them. The word *probation*, a high school term like *suspension*, keeps coming up in the screenplay, reminding us all that high school is the microcosm for the world. Arnie's mother is a controlling shrew; his father is meek and useless. The teenagers want what they want, and parents are seen as

obstacles to that happiness ("Part of being a parent is trying to kill your kid"; "They just don't want me to grow up"). What matters in Arnie's world are cars, girls, and football games. In fact, *Christine* might be seen, overall, as a metaphor for puberty. Arnie is at first awkward, clumsy and nerdy. As he reaches adulthood, his appearance and reputation improve, but he also becomes cold and distant, as if he has been assimilated into the uncaring world of adulthood. His car is not the only thing that has possessed him; his stature as "grown-up" has done the same. As Dennis declares near the climax, "I don't think Arnie is Arnie anymore." In rebelling against his parents, he is changed into a lifeless old creature akin to his parents.

Perhaps the most enjoyable aspect of *Christine* is John Carpenter's light, witty touch on the soundtrack. He uses music humorously, and so each 1950s be-bop song from Christine's radio comments ironically on the situation dramatized. When Christine is being assembled in 1958, she kills a worker in the factory to the tune "Bad to the Bone" by the Destroyers. When Christine flattens fat old Mr. Darnell between her seat cushions and the dashboard, the radio blares "Bony Marrone" by Larry Williams — a song about a skinny girl. When Dennis tries unsuccessfully to break into the hell car, the sound track responds with "Keep a Knockin'" by Little Richard. To dramatize Arnie's love for Christine, Carpenter selects "We Belong Together." And finally, when there is the threat that Christine might return from the grave, Carpenter chooses "Rock 'n' Roll Is Here to Stay" by Danny and the Juniors. The song establishes that Christine, like rock 'n' roll music, will never die. Taken together, these songs prove that an artist alert to the possibilities of irony and comedy is at work on *Christine*. The premise of an evil car may be pure B-movie, but Carpenter gives the less-than-satisfactory material his all through his choice of music, his thematic metaphor, and his direction of the performances.

Christine is by no means a bad film. On the contrary, it demonstrates talent, wit, and humor. But in the final analysis, a horror movie should *scare* people, and *Christine*

never quite pulls that off. Perhaps part of the reason for this failure lies more with King's template than Carpenter's direction. Stephen King is exceptionally good at writing truly despicable characters. On the page, they seem believable and horrible, but on screen, they appear cartoonish. *Christine* demonstrates this sad fact of translation. The bullies who torment Arnie are not just vile and reprehensible, they are caricatures. Buddy is a thug, flat out. Moochie is a fat, disgusting slob. They both come across as walking, talking comic books, and thus when Christine kills them there is an unwanted and perhaps unmerited sense of justice. If this were an E.C. Comic like *Vault of Horror*, Christine would be the tool through which morality was restored and the scales of justice equalized. These scenes, with the car avenging Arnie's humiliation, tend to play against the inherent drama of the film, which wants desperately to establish that Christine is the villain of the piece. On the contrary, the vehicle Christine is every teenager's dream for much of the film: a loyal, avenging angel who will dispatch those who tyrannize the weak. It is an object of power, an object of fantasy, rather than a vehicle for real horror.

Starman (1984)

Critical Reception

"A delightful film, encompassing both the warmth and charm of *E.T.* and the wonder of *Close Encounters....* Sometimes sentimental, sometimes moving, *Starman* was the best science-fiction film of 1984."— Douglas Menville and R. Reginald, *Futurevisions: The New Golden Age of the Science Fiction Film*, Newcastle, 1985, page 161.

"A likable, unheralded surprise directed by John Carpenter ... it's an exciting sci-fi adventure and a sexy love story, and it succeeds happily on both levels. Director Carpenter ... proves himself adept at handling not only the action sequences but the gentle side of human nature as well ... a real charmer."— Rex Reed, *The New York Post:* December 14, 1984.

"Carpenter displays a fairly stiff and obvious approach toward romance, and the occasional satiric touch that redeemed some of his more leaden efforts has abandoned him here.... If the love story between Bridges and Miss Allen were written with even the slightest poignancy, or if the humorous possibilities ... had been envisioned, this wouldn't have been such a phlegmatic voyage to nowhere."—John Nangle, *Films in Review*, March 1985.

"Carpenter takes his technology no more seriously than his romance, but he condescends to neither. He has come a long way since *Halloween*, and in *Starman* he displays considerable subtlety, irony and taste. Carpenter uses his special effects sparingly and plays them well against intimate details. And he can't resist comic twists on classic turns."—Andrew Kopkind, *The Nation:* "The Cartoon Epic," January 26, 1985.

"This is a quiet, modest motion picture. There are few special effects or displays of directorial virtuosity.... Bridges is amazingly deft at communicating various versions of naïveté, clumsiness, and curiosity.... In the discovery of the Starman's profound link with humanity, the audience rediscovers its own."—Carl E. Rollyson, Jr., *Magill's Cinema Annual 1985*, Salem Press, pages 448–449.

Cast and Credits

CAST: Jeff Bridges (Starman); Karen Allen (Jennie Hayden); Charles Martin Smith (Mark Shermin); Richard Jaeckel (George Fox); Robert Phalen (Major Bell); Tony Edwards (Sgt. Lemon); John Walter Davis (Brad Heinmuller); Ted White (Deer Hunter); Dirk Blocker (Cop #1); M.C. Gainey (Cop #2); Sean Faro (Hot Rodder); Buck Flower (Cook); Russ Benning (Scientist); Ralph Cosham (Marine Lieutenant); David Wells (Fox's Assistant); Anthony Grumbach (N.S.A. Officer); Jim Deeth (S-61 Pilot); Alex Daniels (Gas Station Attendant); Carol Rosenthal (Gas Customer); Mickey Jones (Trucker); Lu Leonard (Roadhouse Waitress); Charlie Hughes (Bus Driver); Byron Walls (Police Sergeant); Betty Bunch (Truckstop Waitress); Victor McLemore (Roadblock Lieutenant); Steven Brennan (Roadblock Sergeant); Pat Lee (Bracero Wife); Judith Kim (Girl Barber); Ronald Colby (Cafe Waiter); Robert Stein (State Trooper); Kenny Call (Donnie Bob); Jeff Ramsey (Hunter #1); Jimmy Gatlin (Hunter #2); David Daniell (Letterman); Randy Tuiton (Second Letterman).

CREDITS: Columbia Pictures Presents A Michael Douglas–Larry J. Franco Production. *Music:* Jack Nitzsche. *Casting:* Jennifer Shull. *Co-Producer:* Barry Bernardi. *Editor:* Marion Rothman. *Production Designer:* Daniel Lomino. *Director of Photography:* Donald M. Morgan, a.s.c. *Executive Producer:* Michael Douglas. *Written by:* Bruce A. Evans, Raynold Gideon. *Produced by:* Larry J. Franco. *Directed by:* John Carpenter. *Stunt Coordinator:* Terry Leonard. *Stunts:* Marguerite Happy, Bob Jauregui, Ben Scott, John Scott, Kerry Russell, Bill Land. *Aerial Coordinator:* Jim Deeth. *Pilots:* Steve Sirk, Harry Hauss, Scott Maher, Larry Kirsch, Robin Rogers, Bill Evans, Duane Williams, Kevin LaRosa. *Production Manager:* To Joyner. *First Assistant Director:* Larry Franco. *Second Assistant Director:* Jeffrey Chernov. *Visual Consultant:* Joe Alves. *Camera Operator:* Chris Schweibert. *First Assistant Camera:* Tony Rivetti. *Second Assistant Camera:* Mark Marguelies. *Panaglide Operator:* Joe Valentine. *Camera Operator (Tennessee):* George Kohut. *Camera Assistant (Tennessee):* George Mooradian. *Script Supervisor:* Sandy King. *Set Decorator:* Robert Benton. *Set Designer:* William Joseph Burrell, Jr. *Ad-Pub Coordinator:* Peter J. Silbermann.

Sound Mixer: Tommy Causey. *Re-Recording Mixers:* Bill Varney c.a.s, Steve Maslow c.a.s, Kevin O'Connell c.a.s. *Assistant Editors:* Virginia Katz, Craig Ridenour. *Supervising Music Editor:* Curt Sobel. *Supervising Sound Editor:* Tom McCarthy, Jr. *Sound Editors:* Don S. Walden, Michael Redbourn. *ADR Editor:* Jay Engle. *Music Arranged and Performed on Syndrive Digital Music System by:* Brian Banks, Anthony Marnell. *Boom Operators:* Joe Brennan, Hank Garfield. *Men's Costumer:* Andy Hylton. *Women's Costumer:* Robin Michel Bush. *Make-up Artist:* Peter Attobelli. *Hair Stylist:* Marina Pedraza. *Production Coordinator:* Anna Zappia. *Leadman:* Bill Gay. *Property Master:* Larry Byrd. *Assistant Property Master:* Ken Zimmerman. *Gaffer:* Hugo Cortina. *Best Boy:* Mike Amerelli. *Key Grip:* Cal Sterry. *Second Grip:* Clay Wilson. *Dolly Grip:* Richard Dow. *Construction Coordinator:* Walt Hadfield. *Location Manager:* Paul Pay. *Location Manager (Tennessee):* Patricia Ledford. *Standby Painter:* Bob Lawless. *Catering:* Michaelsons and The Arrangement. *Still Photographer:* Sidney Baldwin. *Still Photographer (Tennessee):* Dean Williams. *Assistants to Mr. Carpenter and Mr. Franco:* Bridget Murphy, Theresa Curtin. *Assistant to Mr. Bernardi:* Carol Rosenthal. *Transportation Coordinator:* Eddie Lee Voelker. *Transportation Captain:* Dave Turner. *D.G.A. Trainee:* Nilo Otero. *Production Accountant:* Mike Hill. *Production Illustrator:* Tom Cranham. *Researcher:* Carl Mazzacone. *Location Assistant:* Doug Raine. *Additional Casting:* Pennie Du Pont. *Location Casting:* Doster, Kengley and Rhodes. *Extra Casting (Arizona and Tennessee):* Stacey Rhodes. *Extra Casting (Los Angeles):* Richmar. *Extra Casting (Nevada):* Goldman and Associates. *Special Effects Coordinator:* Roy Arbogast. *Special Effects:* Bill Lee, Kevin Quibell, Dick Wood, David Simmons. *Location Projection:* J. Dolan Projection Units. *Negative Cutters:* Brian Ralph. *Starman Transformations:* Dick Smith, Stan Winston and Rick Baker.

Second Unit: Director: Joe Alves. *First Assistant Director:* Jeffrey Chernov. *Location Manager:* Ken Lavet. *Director of Photography:* Steve Poster. *Camera Assistant:* Peter Kuttner.

Special Laser Effects: Laser Mania Inc., Laser Images Inc., Laserium. *Computer Graphics:* Video Image. *Helicopters:* Jetcopters Inc. *Starman Transformation Crews: Dick Smith Crew:* Douglas Drexler, George Engel, Norman Bryn. *Stan Winston Unit:* Jack Bricker, Elias Burman, Jr. and Crew. *Rick Baker Unit:* Tom Hester, Allen Coulter, Tim Lawrence. *In Co-production with:* Industrial Light and Magic, a division of Lucasfilm, Ltd. *Supervisor of Visual Special Effects:* Bruce Nicholson. *Special Visual Effects:* Industrial Light and Magic, a division of Lucasfilm, Ltd. *Director of Visual Effects:* Michael McAlister. *Supervising Model maker:* Ease Owyeung. *Matte Painting Supervisor:* Michael Pangrazio. *Animation Supervisor:* Charlie Mullen. *Chief Visual Effects Editor:* Michael Gleason. *Production Coordinator:* Patricia Blau. *General Manager, ILM:* Warren Franklin. *Visual Effects Camera:* Pat Sweeney, Scott Farrar. *Assistant Camera:* Toby Heindel, Peter Daulton, Bob Hill, Joe Fulmer. *Optical Camera Operators:* Ralph Gordon, Al Jones, Tom Rosseter. *Matte Artists:* Caroline Green, Chris Evans, Frank Ordax. *Matte Camera Supervisor:* Craig Barron. *Assistant Matte Camera:* Wade Childress. *Model makers:* Barbara Affonso, Jeff Mann, Larry Tann, Chuck Wiley. *Head Effects Animator:* Bruce Walter. *Assistant Animator:* Barbara Brennan. *Visual Effects Editor:* Michael Moore. *Stage Technicians:* Dick Dova, Lance Brackett. *Miniature Pyrotechnics:* Moehnke, Stolz and Finley, Jr. *Still Photography:* Kery Nordquist. *Equipment Engineering Supervisor:* Michael McKenzie. *Associate Producers:* Bruce A. Evans, Raynold Gideon. "I Can't Get No Satisfaction" written by Mick Jagger and Keith Richard, published by Abko Music and performed by the Rolling Stones. "Theme from New York, New York" written by John Kander and Fred Ebb, courtesy of Reprise Records, performed by Frank Sinatra. "All I Have to Do Is Dream" written by Boudeleaux Bryant, published by

House of Bryant Publications. "What Would Your Memories Do" written by Harry Cochran and Dean Dillon, courtesy of Compleat Records, performed by Verne Gosdin. *Special Thanks to:* University of North Carolina, Northrop Corporation, Tennessee Film, Tape and Music Commission, Arizona Governor's Office, Nevada Motion Picture Division, Iowa Film Commission, Colorado Motion Picture and Television Advisory Commission. *Color:* MGM. *Titles:* Pacific Titles. *MPAA Rating:* PG. *Running time:* 115 minutes.

"There is only one language. One law. One people. There is no war, no hunger. The strong do not victimize the helpless. We are very civilized, but we have lost something. You are all so much alive, so different. I will miss the cooks and the dancing and the singing and the eating…"—Starman contrasts his otherworldly culture with humanity.

SYNOPSIS: Launched in 1977, the space-going vehicle Voyager 2 is intercepted in outer space by a spherical alien vessel. Unseen aliens bring the craft inside and watch numerous video broadcasts of Earth greetings. The aliens then decide to send a kind of greeting of their own, and a small alien scout craft is sent to visit Earth.

In Madison, Wisconsin, a despondent Jenny Hayden sits alone in her mountain cottage, watching home movies of herself and her recently deceased husband, Scott, for the hundredth time. Drunk and saddened, she falls asleep and tries to forget the pain that has dominated her life of late. Meanwhile, the alien scout ship descends into Earth's atmosphere and is shot down by American jets. It crashlands in Wisconsin, very near Jenny's home. The government mobilizes its forces to recover the alien ship, and two men, George Fox and Mark Shermin, join up to investigate the incident.

A blue sphere emerges from the crashed vessel, and it floats across a beautiful lake to Jenny Hayden's cottage. The blue sphere enters her house and proceeds to examine her home movies. Utilizing a strand of her husband's hair to alter its own DNA, the alien then recreates a human appearance. Jenny awakens to see her living room aglow with blue light, and a naked human baby developing quickly into adulthood. It soon becomes an exact replica of her husband, Scott! Jenny faints when the alien in her midst abruptly begins to recite greetings to her in various human tongues.

While she is unconscious, the transformed alien creature further views the home movies and acquaints himself with the universe of human expressions, movement and sounds. He also sees Scott's easy familiarity with guns, and Jenny's sensitive nature and kindness to animals. Using several small energy spheres, Starman then sends a message of distress to his faraway home. He will meet a rescue ship at the "Third Day Landing" location in Arizona. When Hayden awakens, she is frightened, and attempts to flee her home. Starman forces her to accompany him on his journey, and they begin a long drive cross-country in the dead of night.

Elsewhere, Mark Shermin is helicoptered to the alien crash site in Wisconsin. He soon grows curious because this "meteor," as the government is calling Starman's craft, changed course before it plummeted to the Earth. Also, it appears to be hollow. The alien spaceship is recovered, and taken to a government lab in Madison. Shermin asks the helicopter pilot to monitor the radio for any out-of-the-ordinary stories that might represent a close encounter with an alien life form.

On their journey to the alien rendezvous, Jenny attempts to escape from her captor. She screams to a passing trucker that she has been kidnapped, but Starman causes the trucker to run away in fear when he utilizes another of his alien spheres to turn the human's tire iron (a makeshift weapon) white-hot. Later, when Starman and Jenny stop at a gas station, Jenny scrawls a message indicating she has been kidnapped and pins it to the bathroom mirror. Starman finds it and takes it down. Later, he asks what it means to be kidnapped.

Starman and Hayden stop at an all-night diner after a long day of driving. There, Starman learns the pleasures of eating while Jenny again tries to escape her connection with him. When Starman spots a dead deer on the hood of a hunter's truck, he brings the animal back to life. Jenny is amazed by this resurrection, and she decides to stay with the alien when she realizes he is alone and defenseless against the men and women of Earth.

After escaping from a bunch of angry rednecks, Jenny and Starman hit the road once more. After a brief (platonic) stay in a motel, they run a police roadblock. Jenny is injured in an explosion of several vehicles and Starman carries her miraculously to safety. He breathes life back into her dead body and then leaves her behind, fearing that his journey is too dangerous to share.

Jenny awakens alone the next morning. After contacting Mark Shermin and reporting her whereabouts, she has a change of heart and decides to rejoin her alien friend. She catches up with him at a roadblock, and together the duo hops a train that is cutting through a beautiful desert landscape. At night, Starman and Jenny make love, and Starman gives Hayden the miracle of a child, even though she knows she is sterile.

While Jenny and Starman develop a deep love, the government, under Fox's direction, continues its pursuit of the alien. Fox tracks Hayden and Starman to Las Vegas, where Starman uses his powers to win traveling money in a casino. George Fox plans to acquire Starman for study at all costs, and he prepares an emergency autopsy room should the alien be shot down. Mark Shermin is troubled by this merciless attitude, but he is overruled as George Fox orders attack helicopters to stop Starman before he and Jenny reach their destination, a giant crater in Arizona.

Starman and Jenny are briefly apprehended by the authorities, but Shermin frees them so they can make the rendezvous which will save the alien's life. At the bottom of a giant crater, Jenny and Hayden share a tender farewell as an alien ship descends from the heavens.

COMMENTARY: In John Carpenter's 1995 remake of *Village of the Damned*, one of the devilish extra-terrestrial children (Lindsey Haun) reminds her schoolteacher father (Christopher Reeve) that the "eyes are the window to the soul." *Starman* is an earlier Carpenter production which remembers that truism very well. Indeed, *Starman* is all about the eyes of a benevolent alien, and how he "sees" humanity with those caring, "newborn" eyes. To the surprise and delight of many Carpenter critics, who felt that the director could only create worlds of death, destruction and depression, what the alien sees all around him in *Starman* is a planet of endless possibilities. That the world can be construed as a positive place at all is perhaps a revelation in a John Carpenter film, and if not downright optimistic, *Starman* remains Carpenter's most hopeful film. That fact alone makes *Starman* stand apart in Carpenter's film pantheon.

Although *Starman* concludes in a sad scene, the film's ending is nothing less than hopeful and uplifting compared to the resolution of most Carpenter-helmed motion pictures. Consider this: Jenny and Starman are forced apart, but they have found a wonderful thing, emotional connection. Even though they will never see each other again, they have found love and happiness, even if for only a brief period. Carpenter's lighting technique in this sequence captures their oneness beautifully and has thematic value. The two lovers stand together under a beam of rich blue light, while all around them, the world has turned to a fiery red hue. This lighting, which pinpoints Jenny and Starman's togetherness, also points out what exists outside the blue serenity of human connection: a red light suggestive of hell. Jenny and Starman can survive this hell because they have made a connection. Though they will be

Jenny Hayden (Karen Allen) and Starman (Jeff Bridges) share a last moment of companionship before the alien ascends heavenward in *Starman* (1984).

separated, she will have a child to remember him by, and he will be able to take his knowledge of warm, individual humanity back to a universe of cold civilization and conformity.

Now contrast *Starman*'s hopeful conclusion to that of *Halloween*, in which a frightening montage informs the viewer that Michael Myers, representing evil, is still on the loose; *Dark Star*, in which the ship and crew are killed in an explosion; *The Thing*, in which the alien might remain alive, might even be hiding inside the protagonist; *Christine*, in which the deadly car is slowly and surely coming back to life; *Escape from New York*, in which Snake Plissken intentionally rips up the cassette tape that could save the world; *They Live*, in which John Nada dies for the cause; or *In the Mouth of Madness*, in which John Trent finally succumbs to the insanity that has taken over the world. In light of

these disturbing climaxes, *Starman* indeed represents John Carpenter on an up day.

The notion of the extra-terrestrial other as perfect visitor and social commentator on human affairs is certainly not a new concept in the galaxy of science fiction film and television. Before *Starman* arrived in multiplexes in 1984, the idea had already been seen in Robert Wise's *The Day the Earth Stood Still* (1951), in which visitor Klaatu (Michael Rennie) discovered the joys of humanity at the same time he warned against nuclear annihilation, as well as Steven Spielberg's filmic essay about the wonder of childhood, *E.T.* (1982). On television, Leonard Nimoy's Mr. Spock on *Star Trek* performed much the same task as Klaatu, Starman or E.T., but he tended to comment ironically on the human condition. Starman sees mostly with wonder and awe.

The alien is a good dramatic tool for a filmmaker or television producer because this unique character permits the people behind the scenes to comment on society from an important perspective, a seemingly objective stance. In *Starman*, for instance, Starman discovers love, sensation, sadness and happiness at the same time that he realizes that the human greetings which brought him were not necessarily as open-ended as was suggested. As an outsider not invested in America, or even Earth, Starman can say important things about our culture without sounding like a hate-spewing, criticizing revolutionary. Instead, he sounds truthful and sweet, and his comments are taken as credible insight rather than as biting criticism.

At the same time, fish out of water–style humor can be exploited in *E.T.*, *Star Trek*, *Starman* and the like as the alien outsider misperceives human customs or rituals. In *E.T.*, the little alien mistook a trick-or-treater dressed as Yoda for a countryman. In *Star Trek IV*, Spock took to cussing to fit in with the populace of 1986 San Francisco. Likewise, in *Starman*, the alien misperceives the nature of the yellow traffic light, which by his thinking means "go very fast." He also unexpectedly sings (badly) and even misinterprets human hand signals when he gives a passerby the finger instead of a thumbs-up.

Through the joint commentary and humor, science fiction films and television series allow their audiences to see how truly foolish, and truly special, the human species can be. If one were to enunciate the philosophy of John Carpenter and *Starman*, it would closely resemble a remark made by *Star Trek* creator Gene Roddenberry in the mid–1970s:

> You human biped thing called Man, you strange creature, still in a sort of violent childhood of your evolution, you're awkward and often illogical, you're weak, vain, but damn it, you're also gorgeous.[12]

It is a bit strange that the eternal optimist Roddenberry and the eternal realist Carpenter should find any common ground, especially since John Carpenter has declared time and time again that he is not a fan of *Star Trek*, but the above quote from Roddenberry perfectly captures *Starman*'s flavor. At one point, Starman (Bridges) almost re-frames that remark perfectly:

> You are a strange species ... intelligent but savage ... you are at your best when things are worst.

The screenplay thus captures both the up and down of humanity. On one side, it is obsessed with the savagery of the human species. As Mark Shermin frames the question to George Fox in the latter half of the motion picture: "Who is the missionary, and who is the cannibal?" That question informs much of the film's central debate, and Starman finally punctuates it when he notes that man, despite all his faults and savagery, is wonderfully individual and alive—qualities that might be lacking in a totally "civilized" species. This debate, so well established in *Starman*, also impacted the ongoing universe of *Star Trek*. When *The Next Generation* premiered in 1987, the debut story concerned an alien outsider who put the crew of the *Enterprise* on trial for being "savage," just as *Starman* had suggested years earlier. To some extent, the Data character was also a reprise of the *Starman* alien since he was an innocent commentator on human behavior, rather than an ironic one as Mr. Spock had been in the original series.

Despite its similarities to preceding and succeeding generations of *Star Trek*, *Starman* remains an interesting and unique motion picture. Some critics have called it the "flip side" of *The Thing*, and that is certainly a valid observation. Where *The Thing* was a story in which an alien creature fostered only hatred, vulnerability and paranoia in the human race, *Starman* shows an alien visitor bringing hope and even redemption (for Shermin and for Jenny).

Still, seeing *Starman* as a sort of anti–*The*

Thing is not particularly illuminating. One picture is simply about a benevolent alien, the other about a malevolent one. What is more telling, perhaps, is *Starman's* variation on the world defined in Steven Spielberg's *E.T.* Since both *E.T.* and *Starman* represent the attempts of a film auteur to dramatize the impact of a peaceful alien arrival on Earth, it is illuminating to see how Carpenter and Spielberg are different in their approaches.

In *E.T.*, Spielberg builds sympathy for the stranded alien by shooting at night-time, and by masking the forces of the government as shadowy hunters who stalk their prey. They are silhouetted by light from behind, and they brandish flashlights, which dance crazily in the darkness to suggest a kind of frantic, frenzied hunt. In these early sequences, Spielberg makes his audience identify with the alien by suggesting that the minions of faceless humans will kill E.T. if he is caught. There can be no truce or peace with these nameless, faceless adults, for they are merely servants of an evil government out to destroy what they cannot understand. This is a child's view of authority as one large, menacing "thing." As youngsters might fear policemen, so does E.T. fear the agents of the American government.

The remainder of the film then involves E.T.'s integration into the world of young Elliott, a ten year old boy who treats the alien like a favorite pet. Though there are many possible readings of *E.T.*, it is essentially a Peter Pan story in which a little boy keeps an alien in his closet, like an imaginary friend, and then refuses to grow up. In this magical, childish world, bicycles can fly, best friends never die, and audiences everywhere remember a time when they were so young and innocent that they could believe in an E.T. who was best friend, surrogate parent, plaything and pet. Spielberg has created a world in which a belief in E.T. is symbolic of youth and innocence. E.T. is Tinkerbell, no more, no less.

Starman is not a film that asks viewers to find the child inside, or to remember a time

of innocence and wonder. On the contrary, Carpenter's film says that the greatest thing in the universe is the bond that can connect two adult creatures, human or otherwise. For *Starman*, humanity's greatest gift is love, that bond which two adults can carry through any experience together. And make no mistake, it is not just romantic love, either. Mark Shermin is a pivotal character in *Starman* because he too is positively affected by the alien, and makes a conscious decision to save him despite the consequences to his career. Above all else, *Starman* shows that mankind can be decent. This was a thesis that would soon come into question in Carpenter films such as *They Live* (1988), *In the Mouth of Madness* (1994) and *Escape from L.A.* (1996). In those pictures, man is a manipulator and user who Carpenter thinks the planet might be better off without. But in *Starman*, the message is different and far more hopeful. As if to stress that humanity was of primary importance in *Starman*, Carpenter opts for a noticeably less flashy *mise-en-scène*, as if he refused to let camera placement or movement overshadow the acting of professionals like Jeff Bridges and Karen Allen. Instead, Carpenter shoots mostly in two-shots and close-ups, except for those scenes requiring scope (such as the alien landing.) This preoccupation with faces and eyes gives the picture an intimate feel perfectly in keeping with the relationship aspects of the screenplay.

Though much has been written about Jeff Bridges's excellent performance in *Starman*, comparatively little has been said about Karen Allen's. This is a travesty, because it is the haunting image of Allen, facing the camera alone but empowered, which ends the film. In just one shot, Allen is able to suggest great sadness and hope, all at the same time. Her owl-like, inquisitive eyes are the heart of *Starman*, and Carpenter goes back to them time and time again to reconnect the viewer with the human aspect of this story.

Jenny Hayden is a remarkable character who, like Shermin, is redeemed through her encounters with an alien life-form. When the viewer first sees Hayden, she is torturing herself by reliving the past. She exists in a world of home movies, honeymoon pictures and photo albums. She is a lonely woman who lives in the images of the past and of her dead husband, Scott. Then, lo and behold, she is confronted by the ultimate image — a replica of Scott. But surprisingly, that replica, that image of the past, forces her to seriously contemplate the future, something that before the alien's arrival, she could not bear to face. Allen is a wonder in this role, and though she was not nominated for an Academy Award, she deserves much credit for bringing the central relationship of *Starman* to life.

Starman is filled with interesting genre characteristics beyond its love relationship and alien invader. It is also a road picture, like *It Happened One Night* (1934), *Something Wild* (1985), or *Thelma & Louise* (1991). As a director who remembers Hollywood's past, Carpenter must have found this aspect of the story particularly appealing. Thus the world of *Starman* exists not just in science fiction locales like craters and autopsy labs, but in all-night diners, long dark highways, gas stations, and of course, the automobile.

John Carpenter's 1984 film is also, rather surprisingly, a Christ allegory. *Starman* is a being of extraordinary powers and love who has the power to heal the sick, resurrect the dead, and perform miracles (like walking through fire.) Even more pointedly, he has only three days after his seeming death in the spaceship crash to return to a certain location and ascend heavenward. If one also takes into account Starman's report that his people have been on Earth before, the parallel becomes even more obvious. This "God is an astronaut" concept, reminiscent of Von Daniken, was the thematic center of 1978's *Battlestar Galactica* TV series, as well as Carpenter's 1987 film, *Prince of Darkness*.

Starman is something of an anomaly in the John Carpenter film roster. It is an upbeat film in which love can be found, even if eventually it is lost. Some people accused Carpenter of going "Spielberg" with this film, but in many ways *Starman* is a more layered and adult version of the alien contact story than either *E.T.* or the classic *The Day the Earth Stood Still*. Because it paints such an epic story against such an intimate and personal background, it remains one of John Carpenter's most emotionally open and heartbreaking films. It is proof positive that Carpenter can make viewers *feel* as skillfully as he makes them jump.

Big Trouble in Little China (1986)

Critical Reception

"Excellence in the service of balderdash ... Carpenter isn't a Spielberg. He doesn't have either Spielberg's genius for spectacular kitsch or his overwhelming desire to please. Usually, Carpenter's dark side makes his movies work; it's also the source of most of his humor." — Michael Wilmington, *The Los Angeles Times*, July 2, 1986.

"It is plenty savvy in deploying plot devices from a dozen hoary genres while playing up the absurdities in the familiar Deadpan Facetious style. Director Carpenter propels things faster, and way smoother, than a speeding '40s serial.... It offers dollops of entertainment, but it is so stocked with canny references to other pictures that it suggests a master's thesis that moves."— Richard Corliss, *Time:* "Everything New Is Old Again," July 14, 1986.

"Carpenter has allowed technology to dominate his story. Since so many of his big set-pieces look so awesomely expensive and complicated, and since the effects are undeniably mind-boggling, there's a temptation to praise him…. But special effects don't mean much unless we care about the characters."— Roger Ebert, *The Chicago Sun-Times*, July 2, 1986.

"Director John Carpenter's movie is peppered with cliché after cliché that, instead of being sent up, just lie there like lumps. Kung-fu action sequences seem to be thrown in to keep the audience awake…. The film has a workable campiness at times, and the special effects … are terrific. But they aren't enough reasons to see this movie."— Tom Cunneff, *People Weekly*, July 28, 1986.

Cast and Credits

CAST: Kurt Russell (Jack Burton); Kim Cattrall (Gracie Law); Dennis Dun (Wang Chi); James Hong (Lo Pan); Victor Wong (Egg Shen); Kate Burton (Margo); Donald Li (Eddie Lee); Carter Wong (Thunder); Peter Kwong (Rain); James Pax (Lightning); Suzee Pai (Miao Yin); Chao Lichi (Uncle Chu); Jeff Imada (Needles); Rummel Mor (Joe Lucky); Craig Ng (One Ear); June Kim (White Tiger); Noel Toy (Mrs. O'Toole); Jade Go (Chine Girl in White Tiger); Jerry Hardin (Pinstripe Lawyer); James Lew (Chang Sing #1); James Lau (#2); Ken Endoso (#3); Stuart Quan (#4); Gary Toy (#5); George Cheung (#6); Jimmy Jue (Wounded Chang Sing); Noble Craig (Sewer Monster); Danny Kwan (Chinese Guard); Min Luong (Tara); Al Leong, Gerald Okamura, Willie Wong, Eric Lee, Yukio G. Collins, Bill M. Ryusaki, Brian Imada, Nathan Jung, Daniel Inasonto, Vernon Rieta (Wing Kong Hatchet Men); Daniel Wong, Daniel Eric Lee (Wing Kong Security Guards); Lia Chang, Diana Tanaka, Donna L. Noguschi, Shimko Isobe (Female Wing Kong Security).

CREDITS: A Taft/Barish/Monash Production. *Music:* John Carpenter. *In Association with:* Alan Howarth. *Executive Producers:* Paul Monash, Keith Barish. *Associate Producers:* Jim Lau, James Lew. *Casting:* Joanna Merlin. *Costume Designer:* April Ferry.

Visual Effects Produced by: Richard Edlund. *Edited by:* Mark Warner, Steve Mirkovitch, Edward A. Warschilka. *Production Designer:* John L. Lloyd. *Director of Photography:* Dean Cundey. *Written by:* Gary Goldman, David Z. Weinstein. *Adaptation:* W. D. Richter. *Produced by:* Larry J. Franco. *Director:* John Carpenter.

Stunts: Richard Warlock, Jeff Imada, Robert Cummings, Tom Bergman, Conan Lee, Kelly Akai, Simon Boisseree, David Cadiente, Debbie A. Davison, Ellarye, Ken Fritz, Kent Hays, Denise Kellogg, James Nickerson, Beth Nufer, Steve Santo, Leland Sun, Joe A. Tornatore, Jr., Eddie Wong, Joseph K. Wong, Jack S. West, Dennis R. Scott, Phil Chong, Mike Washlake, Gary McLarty, T. K. Anthony, Janet Brady, Chuck Clark, Eddie Donno, George Endoso, Mark Giardino, Bob Itaya, Ginger K. Miyazaki, Sherri Nickerson, Bill Suito, Hayward Soo-Hoo, Tamiko, Dean Wein, Harry Wong.

Unit Production Manager: James Herbert. *First Assistant Director:* Larry Franco. *Second Assistant Director:* Matt Earl Beesley. *Art Director:* Les Gobruegge. *Set Decorator:* George R. "Bob" Nelson. *Camera Operators:* Ray Stella, Gary Kibbe. *First Assistant Camera:* Clyde Bryan, Steve Tate. *Second Assistant Camera:* Larry Davis. *Script Supervisor:* Sandy King. *Sound Mixer:* Thomas Causey. *Boom Operators:* Joe Brennan, Darcey Vebber. *Gaffer:* Mark Walthour. *Key Grip:* Thomas

Marshall, George LaFountaine. *Best Boy:* John Donnelly. *Company Grip:* Charles "Tex" Williams. *Make-up Supervisor:* Ken Chase. *Hairstylist:* Susan Kalinowski. *Men's Costumer:* Paul Lopez. *Women's Costumer:* Michele Neely. *Set Costumer:* Oda Groeschel. *Property Master:* Kent Johnson. *Assistant Property Master:* Richard Cowitt, David Evans. *Special Effects Coordinator:* Joseph Unsinn. *Special Effects Assistant:* Stanley Amborn. *Special Effects Foreman:* James Fredbury. *Assistant to Mr. Franco and Mr. Carpenter:* Theresa Curtin. *Assistant to Mr. Monash:* Kim Kasey-Costello. *Secretary to Producer:* Christine Baer. *Stunt Coordinator:* Kenny Endoso. *Martial Arts Choreographer:* James Lew. *Martial Arts Consultant:* James Lau. *Production Coordinator:* Mary Sutton Hallmann. *Production Assistants:* Artist Robinson, Linda Brachman. *Production Secretary:* Sandra Holden. *First Assistant Editor:* Steven E. Ramirez. *Assistant Editors:* J.W. Kompare, Nancy Froelich. *Apprentice Editors:* David Jansen. *Marketing Supervisor:* Peter J. Silbermann. *Marketing Coordinator:* Daniel Kwan. *Still Photographer:* John Shannon. *Unit Publicist:* Alan Ebner. *Production Accountant:* Harry Kohoyda. *Assistant Auditor:* Gary Weddington. *Transportation Coordinator:* Eddie Lee Voelker. *Transportation Captain:* Steve Duncan. *Set Designers:* Craig Edgar, Steve Schwartz. *Production Illustrator:* David Jonas, Edward Verreaux. *Location Manager, Los Angeles:* Steve Shkolnik. *Location Manager, San Francisco:* John Bush. *Casting Associate:* Pamela Rack. *Extra Casting:* Central Casting. *Construction Coordinator:* John Lattanzio, Robert Scaife. *Construction Foreman:* Ken Scaife, Richard Morgan, Jim Davis, John Villarino. *Lead Man:* Larry McGuire, Donald Craft. *Sound Effect Supervisor:* William Hartman. *Special Sound Effects Supervisor:* Anthony R. Milch. *Sound Effects Editors:* David Ice, Eric Lindeman, Lenny Jennings, Peter Hubbard, Hal Sanders. *Special Sound Effects Editors:* Martin Dreffke, David A. Fechtor, Monika Dorfman-Lightstone, David Williams, Laja Holland. *Supervising ADR Editor:* Hank Salerno. *ADR Editors:* Glad Pickering, Bill Voigtlander, Steve Rice. *Assistant ADR Editor:* David Poole. *Foley Artists:* Gary "Wrecker" Hecker, Alicia Stevenson. *Foley Mixer:* Dean Drabin. *Sound Synthesizer:* Gary Macheel. *Music Editor:* Scott Grusin. *Re-Recording Mixers:* Don Bassman, Richard Overton, Kevin F. Clary. *Recordist:* Robert Renga. *Contact Lenses:* Dr. Morton Greenspoon.

Second Unit: *Second Unit Director:* Tommy Lee Wallace. *Director of Photography:* Steve Poster. *Underwater Director of Photography:* Jack Cooperman, Barry Herron.

Visual Effects Crew: Boss Films Corporation. *Visual Effects Art Director:* George Jensen. *Creatures Created by:* Steve Johnson. *Matte Department Supervisor:* Neil Krepela. *Production Coordinator:* Lynda Lemon. *Production Supervisor:* George E. Mather. *Visual Effects Editor:* Dennis Michelson. *Effects Editorial Consultant:* Ronald Moore. *Special Effects Foreman:* Thaine Morris. *Director of Photography:* Bill Neil. *Production Advisor:* James Nelson. *Optical Supervisor:* Craig Nelson. *Special Projects Supervisor:* Gary Waller. *Chief Engineer:* Charles Whiteman. *Optical Camera Operators:* Charles Cowles, Alan Harding. *Optical Coordinator:* Mary Mason. *Optical Line-up:* Mary Walter, Ed Jones, Brad Kuehn. *Lab Technicians:* Patrick Repola. *Technical Animation Supervisor:* Annick Therrien. *Technical Animators:* Rebecca Petrull-Heskes, Samuel Recinos. *Animators:* Glen Chaika, Jeff Howard, Mauro Maressa, Peggy Regan. *Assistant Animators:* Renee Holt, Debora Ann Gaydos, Eusebio Torres. *Production Illustrator:* Brent Boates. *Assistant to Richard Edlund:* Claire Wilson. *Production Administrator:* Mindy Rothstein. *Assistant Production Coordinator:* Dana Miller Schornstein. *Assistant to Ronald Moore:* Alan Cappuccilli. *Camera Operator:* Matt Beck. *First Assistant Photographer:* Peter Berman. *Still Photographer:* Virgil Mirano. *Film Loader:* Stefanie Wiseman. *Special Effects Technician:* Randy Cabral, Daniel Hutten. *Grip:* Patrick Van Auken. *Gaffer:* Robert Eyslee. *Creature

Shop Coordinator: Dave Kelsey. *First Technicians:* Screaming Mad George, Eric Fielder. *Chief Effects Model Maker:* Richard Ruiz. *Creature Crew:* Dale Brady, Kevin Brennan, Theresa Burkett, Roberto Carlos, Craig Caton, Ken Diaz, Alex Felix, Ed Felix, Eddie Garcia, Jim Kagel, Makio Kida, Ron MacInnes, Dave Matherly, Lesa Nielson, Roberto Olivas, Wayne Strong, Mark Silson. *Design Engineer:* Mark West. *Electronics:* Jeffrey Jefress, Robin Leydon, Robert Wilcox. *Software Programmer:* Paul Van Camp. *Precision Cinetechnicians:* Ken Dudderan, Mark Matthews. *Production Accountant:* Paulette Fine. *Production Assistant:* Jon Schreiber, Sue Alpert.

Special Thanks to: Freightliner Corporation. "Big Trouble in Little China" written by John Carpenter, performed by The Coup De Villes. *Filmed in:* Panavision. *Color:* DeLuxe. *Color Timer:* Bob Hagans. *Titles Designed by:* Dan Curry. *Titles:* Cinema Research Corporation. *Opticals:* Pacific Titles. *MPAA Rating:* PG. *Running Time:* 99 minutes.

"It's all in the reflexes..." — Jack Burton describes his many talents.

SYNOPSIS: Egg-Shen, tour bus driver in San Francisco's Chinatown and Chinese magician extraordinaire, recounts an incredible story to a suspicious lawyer. The tale involves macho truck driver Jack Burton and the strange and mystical world of Chinese black magic.

It all begins one innocuous morning when Jack Burton, philosopher and *bon vivant* at large, wins a big bet with his friend Wang Chi. Wang agrees to pay his debt to Jack, but first he asks Burton to accompany him on an important errand. He must pick up his betrothed, Miao Yin, at the airport. Yin is leaving China for good to marry Wang Chi, whose family owns a restaurant in Chinatown. At the airport, however, the beautiful, green-eyed Miao Yin is captured by a gang of thugs: the Lords of Death. Jack and Wang

race back to Chinatown to rescue Miao Yin, but Jack drives his truck right into a back-alley that is more war zone than roadway. Fighting it out on the streets there are two rival Asian gangs. The Three Storms, supernatural minions of the cursed spirit called Lo-Pan, materialize suddenly and interrupt the fierce combat. Frightened, Jack plunges his truck deeper into the alley and runs down the malevolent sorcerer, Lo-Pan himself. Lo-Pan survives the incident unscathed and his evil eyes glow with hellish fire. Jack and Wang Chi are forced to abandon Jack's truck and run for safety from the strange supernatural forces at work in Chinatown. Miao-Yin is still missing.

At the restaurant of Wang Chi's uncle Chu, Jack attempts to ferret out the reality of what he witnessed in the alley. With the help of a sassy but beautiful American lawyer, Gracie Law, Wang's easygoing friend Eddie, and a naive reporter named Margo, Jack and Wang soon launch another campaign to rescue Miao Yin. This time, they must save her from the White Tiger, a house of prostitution. Jack infiltrates the house of ill-repute by pretending to be a john. He locates Miao-Yin inside, but she is spirited away suddenly by the Three Storms. Jack watches in awe and horror as the Storms leave the White Tiger riding on bolts of lightning, and generating a ball of green fire a block wide.

Word on the street suggests that Miao Yin has been taken to the headquarters of David Lo-Pan, the Chinese sorcerer and wealthy industrialist. Launching a third rescue attempt, Jack and Wang infiltrate Lo-Pan's establishment and discover that it is a dark underworld ruled by the ancient tyrant. Lo-Pan himself is a raving maniac, a ghost who has been denied the solidity of flesh for a thousand years. He has captured Miao Yin because he must sacrifice a green-eyed girl to his deity if he is to regain his existence as a flesh-and-blood human being. Soon, Jack, Wang, Eddie, Gracie and Margo have all been captured by Lo-Pan. While incarcerated, Wang tells Jack about Lo-Pan, and how he was

From left to right: Gracie Law (Kim Cattrall), Jack Burton (Kurt Russell) and Miao-Yin (Suzee Pai) in *Big Trouble in Little China* (1986).

defeated by the first sovereign emperor of China in 272 B.C. Lo-Pan was then cursed to this existence as a fleshless thing, a dweller in the spirit city beneath the Earth.

Jack and Wang manage to escape with Eddie. After rescuing Margo and a dozen other imprisoned women, they return to Uncle Chu's Chinese restaurant, aware that they have still failed to save Miao Yin. If they do not free Miao Yin and Gracie Law, another green-eyed girl, from Lo-Pan, they will be his brides and his sacrifices — and the very tools Lo-Pan needs to reach out and rule the world from beyond the grave.

Fortunately, things start to look up when Egg-Shen, the tour bus driver, joins the fight. Leading a squad of highly trained fighters, Egg-Shen escorts Jack and Wang back underground to interrupt Lo-Pan's elaborate wedding ceremony. In an incredible battle royal, the forces of good and evil, white and black magic, clash violently. Gracie Law and Miao Yin are saved after Lo-Pan has become flesh-and-blood again. With the Three Storms on the attack and Lo-Pan eager to assert his dominance over the world, it is up to Jack to save the day. Using his cat-like reflexes and a small knife, Jack does just that, bringing down Lo-Pan and his subterranean world.

After a party celebrating the release of Miao Yin and Gracie Law, Jack accepts payment from Wang for his services. With his truck back in his custody, Jack heads out across the lonely highway. While telling his amazing story over the CB radio, Jack fails to notice that one of Lo-Pan's minions, a hairy ape creature, is clinging to the back of his truck.

COMMENTARY: "It's all in the reflexes" is Jack Burton's stock post-action sequence remark, and it might as well be a description of John Carpenter's 1986 tribute to the Chinese martial arts genre, *Big Trouble in Little China.* For this is a movie that jumps along from set-piece to set-piece with a swift pace and stylish, over-the-top gymnastics. John Carpenter's other films, even the elegantly simple *Halloween*, tend to be a bit more intellectual in nature, but this entry in his film pantheon looks to have been made on the back of his infallible filmmaking instincts and muscles, consisting of one delightfully humorous and action-packed scene after another. The first major action scene in the Chinatown alley is a *tour de force*, some kind of bizarre high-water mark in the annals of

film fights. This particular sequence consists of more than 50 martial experts doing their unique thing, as Carpenter follows the action with intensity. After the cross-alley gunplay ceases and the close quarter combat begins (following what Wang calls a "Chinese stand-off"), all hell breaks loose. In approximately 100 seconds of film time, there are 83 separate editing cuts alone, making a cut almost every second. These cuts come so rapidly and smoothly that they are almost invisible to the eye, consequently generating a fevered sense of pace and motion. What Carpenter has done here is create a smooth flowing dance of death out of dozens of individual components. The editing, the fighting, the camera placement, and the musical composition underlying the action are all staggeringly effective. It may not be an intellectual thrill to watch a bevy of soldiers duke it out, but it is rewarding to watch an artist at the top of his form. Even in the service of a fight sequence, Carpenter proves that he knows exactly what to shoot and how to reach a desired effect. As a film technician, he is almost unmatched.

Thematically, *Big Trouble in Little China* is, perhaps, not quite as empty as some critics have suggested. First and foremost it is an entertainment (as are all Carpenter films). It is an action picture, no doubt about it. It is a pulp adventure with a brave, but dense, warrior and a sidekick who is infinitely superior in both mind and physical skill. And yet, at the same time, Carpenter manages to stick in a few comments worth mentioning. Although Jack is blundering and arrogant and loud mouthed, he is also brave, persistent and loyal. Although he is incapable of believing in Chinese black magic and such, he is completely capable of accomplishing a mission and doing what is practical. By making his hero so stereotypically "American" (right down to Kurt Russell's ferociously on-target John Wayne imitation), John Carpenter seems to be dramatizing an east versus west dynamic. American brawn joins with Asian faith, and the result is, optimistically, a great victory. Jack Burton is an American

"It's all in the reflexes." Jack Burton (Kurt Russell) prepares for action while sidekick Wang (Dennis Dun) and Lo-Pan's would-be brides (Kim Cattrall, left, and Suzee Pai, right) look on.

in the sense that most of the world views Americans: big and strong, traditional, arrogant, and perhaps a little too grounded in "classical" western reality. Contrast that view with the Asians in *Big Trouble in Little China*. They are more complex, believing in their ancient mystical customs and understanding that the current world does not support these beliefs.

The *Big Trouble in Little China* screenplay makes another distinction between east and west: the Americans are defined basically as what they do and where they're from. First and foremost, Jack is a truck driver and an American ("May the wings of liberty never lose a feather," he says, toasting the good ole U.S. of A.) Like Jack, Gracie is what she appears to be on the surface: a lawyer and almost a parody of that American Hollywood film cliché, the lady crusader. "I'm always pokin' my nose where it doesn't belong," she even says at one point, effectively defining herself as a character. Importantly, the strength of these American characters comes from their

mouths. Both Jack and Gracie have an exaggerated sense of their own skill and importance. (At one point Jack blusters into a scenario and says, "Don't worry, I'm here.") The American characters in this film see themselves as the leaders, the saviors, but, ironically, they have no real skills to lead or save anyone.

The eastern characters are, by contrast, not what they appear to be on the surface. They are defined in a different way. Egg-Shen is a little old man, a bus driver by profession, but in reality he is a sorcerer extraordinaire and a force of good as powerful as his opponent, Lo-Pan. Similarly, Wang Chi looks average. He is a man of medium height, with medium build. He has typical American concerns about getting married, and so forth. Yet Wang is also, like Egg-Shen, a superb fighter, a warrior of almost superhuman abilities. Where American power is mostly in the talking, the Chinese gain their power in *the doing*. Deeds, not words, might be Egg-Shen or Wang's motto. They do not talk about skill, they demonstrate skill.

If *Big Trouble in Little China* is viewed as a collision of a western and eastern values, it takes on a new level of meaning. And the picture remains optimistic because Carpenter never says, "Americans are bad" or "The Chinese are good." What he seems to state is that east and west can be great allies. It is the American, for instance, in a typical moment of bravado, who takes out the menace to the world, Lo-Pan. Jack has been proven ineffective with virtually every kind of weaponry imaginable before the climax of the film. He raises his gun before the big fight, fires it into the air, and ceiling tile lands on his head and knocks him out. At another point, he goes to draw his knife from his boot, and it flies out of his hand and subsequently out of the frame. So, when Jack finally stands up to face Lo-Pan, knife in hand, the audience thinks they are going to see another bungle. Instead, Jack nails Lo-Pan in the head with his knife, killing him instantly. That's the thing about us Americans: we may be a little slow, but we're dependable, and we'll be there when push comes to shove.

All of this culture clash subtext in *Big Trouble in Little China* is played out against a screenplay filled with wacky, almost campy humor, spectacular sets, and action sequences that have to be seen to be believed. The picture is a perfect entertainment. So why was it destroyed by critics and ignored by filmgoers?

There are a few explanations, and they have more to do with timing and marketing than with the quality of this Carpenter picture. When *Big Trouble in Little China* came out in 1986, it followed hot on the trail of several other "underground" pictures. *Indiana Jones and the Temple of Doom* (1984), *C.H.U.D.* (1984), *A View to a Kill* (1985), *The Goonies* (1985) and *Enemy Mine* (1985) were just a few of the subterranean film adventures that had made a mark in America. Each film, in varying ways, told the same story: Beneath the "real" world up top, there was either an evil world (*A View to a Kill, Enemy Mine*), a magical one (*The Temple of Doom*)

or even an anachronistic "out of time" one (*The Goonies*). In the same summer of *Big Trouble in Little China*, there was also Tobe Hooper's film *Invaders from Mars*, also about an alien world beneath the normal one. It is entirely possible that *Big Trouble in Little China* was avoided because people felt they had seen it already.

Secondly, the film's tone borders on camp. Kurt Russell's Jack Burton is a droll protagonist, the kind of guy that some people are not sure how to take. It is important to remember that in the mid-eighties film heroes were of the *Rambo* (1985), *Cobra* (1987), and Maverick (*Top Gun* [1985]) mold: strong and silent, deadly serious. They were, essentially, musclemen killers who would spit out atrocious one-liners after killing an opponent. *Big Trouble in Little China* pokes fun at that cliché by showcasing a hero who thinks he's Rambo or John Wayne but is surely not. Although Kurt Russell preferred the competent Snake Plissken to the incompetent Jack Burton, he delivers a sly, humorous and consistent performance nonetheless. *Big Trouble in Little China* proves just how versatile an actor this performer is.

So why did the critics hate *Big Trouble in Little China*? The answer to that question would be pure guesswork, as critical consensus tends to be quite random at times. Perhaps some critics were still eager to shoot down John Carpenter after *The Thing*. Perhaps others felt it was simply frivolous to spend a huge amount of money on a martial-arts action film with no obvious social value. (Of course, those would have been the same critics who lambasted *Star Wars*, another high-budgeted film that was intended as fun.)

Whatever the reason, *Big Trouble in Little China* has never come out of the shadow of its critical and box office failure even though it is an accomplished entertainment.

A testimony to its power, however, is the fact that is has a gigantic cult following in America. People who like their action *fun*, spectacular, and expertly composed are drawn to this silly, happy film, and for many good reasons.

For John Carpenter watchers, *Big Trouble in Little China* introduces three new members of the Carpenter repertory company: Dennis Dun (who would be back in *Prince of Darkness*), Victor Wong (*Prince of Darkness*) and Donald Li (who reappeared in *Memoirs of an Invisible Man.*) *Big Trouble in Little China* was also John Carpenter's last teaming with Kurt Russell for a decade, until *Escape from L.A.* in 1996.

Prince of Darkness (1987)

Critical Reception

"The buck stops at *Prince of Darkness*, which is badly paced, badly acted, and minus the occasional flourishes which have made his [Carpenter] past mechanical efforts seem much better than they actually were.... What *Prince of Darkness* loses in practically every key department — thumbnail sketch characterizations, a fey lead actor ... unfocused script, leaden narrative thrust, amateurish special effects ... it gains by Carpenter injecting some vague atmosphere through the pulsing sound-track." — Alan Jones, *Starburst* #10, July 1988, pages 30–31.

"With *Prince of Darkness*, the siege of *Assault on Precinct 13* is vividly reconstructed: the derelict fortress, the comfortless corridors, the silent army in the night outside, the collapse of logic and security. Updated to the AIDS era by the ejaculatory manner from which the 'disease' of evil spreads ... Carpenter's obsessive theme of confrontation also finds a new area of exploration in the concept of anti-matter.... And the ultimate power struggle ... is conveyed not in the writing but, as one requires of a real filmmaker, in the visuals: the contemplative shots of isolated losers wandering the gloom or reaching with fascinated perplexity for their own mirrored reflections." — Philip Strick, *Monthly Film Bulletin*, May 1985.

"A surprisingly cheesy horror film to come from Mr. Carpenter, a director whose work is usually far more efficient and inventive.... You may well suspect things are not going to go well when the movie spends its first 15 minutes intercutting between the opening credits and scenes introducing the characters." — Vincent Canby, *The New York Times*: "*Prince of Darkness* by John Carpenter," October 23, 1987.

"Carpenter co-wrote the soundtrack and it reflects this film perfectly: standard ominous intonations which nevertheless grab you and take command of your heartbeat. There is plenty of subdued tension.... Too bad the ensuing philosophical science and mythic story leads only to a night of zombie murders, grotesque make-up and good guys vs. bad guys action." — Allen Malmquist, *Cinefantastique* Volume 13, #2, March 1988, page 117.

"Carpenter's worst film ... inept and barely coherent. The ambitious but confused script evokes Godel and Schrodinger in the first few minutes, explains precognition as tachyon messages from the future, solemnly broods on indeterminacy and the spiritual inferences to be drawn from quantum mechanics."—John Clute and Peter Nicholls, *The Encyclopedia of Science Fiction*, page 962.

"To give the movie its due, it's been directed, at least on the visual level, with unusual elegance: filled with graceful, gliding tracking shots, and icily precise Hitchcockian setups of the bleak decor and scary effects. Wong and Pleasence are both fine ... and, even if the shocks throughout seem as patterned as an aerobics class, the movie's climactic kicker is electrifying."—Michael Wilmington, *The Los Angeles Times*, October 23, 1987.

"I could plainly see the secondrateness of this horror flick—its plot inconsistencies, its klutzy dialogue and its rote performances. But despite my conscious contempt ... my body behaved as if it were frightened ... and I left the screening room feeling jittery."—Joseph Gelmis, *Newsday*, October 23, 1987.

Cast and Credits

CAST: Donald Pleasence (Priest); Jameson Parker (Brian); Victor Wong (Birack); Lisa Blount (Catherine); Dennis Dun (Walter); Susan Blanchard (Kelly); Anne Howard (Susan); Ann Yen (Lisa); Ken Wright (Lomax); Dirk Blocker (Mullins); Jesse Lawrence Ferguson (Calder); Peter Jason (Dr. Leahy); Robert Grasmere (Wyndham); Thom Bray (Etchinson); Joanna Merlin (Bug Lady); Alice Cooper (Street Schizo); Betty Ramey (Nun); Jesse Ferguson (Dark Figure).

CREDITS: Universal, an MCA Company. Alive Films Presents a Larry Franco Production. *Make-up:* Frank Carrisosa. *Production Sound Mixer:* Thomas Causey. *Production Executive:* Stratton Leopold. *Production Associate:* Kent H. Johnson. *Script Supervisor:* Sandy King. *Music:* John Carpenter. *In Association with:* Alan Howarth. *Unit Production Manager:* Stratton Leopold. *First Assistant Director:* Larry Franco. *Second Assistant Director:* Bruce Alan Solow. *Edited by:* Steve Mirkovich. *Production Designer:* Daniel Lomino. *Director of Photography:* Gary B. Kibbe. *Executive Producers:* Shep Gordon, Andre Blay. *Written by:* Martin Quatermass (aka John Carpenter). *Produced by:* Larry J. Franco. *Directed by:* John Carpenter. *Stunt Coordinator:* Jeff Imada. *Stunts:* Christine Baur, Ellarye, Bob Herron, Simone Boisseree, Justin DeRosa, Debbie Evans, Randy Hall, Wayne King, Mario Robert. *Assistant to Producer:* Sandra Holden. *Production Coordinator:* Marian Shambo. *Camera Operator:* Jud Kehl. *First Assistant Camera:* Joseph Thibo. *Second Assistant Camera:* Fred Hamm. *Second Camera/Panaglide Operator:* Christopher Squires. *Second Camera First Assistant:* Case Hotchkiss. *Gaffer:* Kenneth Spencer. *Best Boy Electric:* Robert McCarthy. *Electricians:* Kevin Arnold, Charles Smock. *Key Grip:* Charles Saldana. *Best Boy Grip:* Ron Peebles. *Dolly Grip:* Kirk Bales. *Grip:* Dan Falkengren. *Boom Operator:* Joe Brennan. *Set Decorator:* Nick Gentz. *Lead Man:* Rick Caprarelli. *Swing:* Jack Forwalter. *Property Master:* Kent H. Johnson. *Assistant Prop Masters:* Richard Kerns, Audrey Johnson. *Costume Supervisor:* Deandra Scarano. *Costumer:* Mark Peterson. *Hair Stylist:* Janis Clark. *First Assistant Editor:* Timothy Alverson. *Assistant Editor:* Fred M. Wardell. *Apprentice Editor:* Lee Grubin. *Re-recording Mixers:* Terry Porter, c.a.s., Mel Metcalfe, David J. Hudson. *Recordist:* David Gertz. *Sound Editing:* Dimension Sound. *Supervising Sound Editor:* Michael Hilkene, Val Kuklowsky. *Sound Editors:* Jeremy Gordon, Frank Howard, Eric Lindeman. *Assistant Sound Editors:* Charles Davis, John O. Wilde. *Apprentice Sound Editor:* Fran Kaplan.

Special Sound Effects created by: Dane Davis, John Oaul Fasal. *Foley Artist:* Jerry Trent, Joan Rowe. *ADR Mixer:* Doc Kane. *ADR Recordist:* Laura Hekking. *Foley Mixer:* Greg Curda. *Foley Recordist:* Bruce Bell. *Negative Cutter:* Dode Wexant. *Casting:* Linda Francis. *Casting Assistant:* Melanie Massey. *Extra Casting:* Bess Gilber — Cinex Casting. *Production Accountant:* Joy Ewing. *Location Manager:* Ken Lavet. *Production Associate:* Doug Raine. *Still Photographer:* John Hamilton. *Unit Publicist:* Kimberly Cox. *Computer Effects Coordinator:* Robert Grasmere. *Special Effects Coordinator:* Kevin Quibell. *Construction Coordinator:* Larry Verne. *Construction Foreman:* Michael Wright. *Laborer Foreman* Jeffrey Truby. *Pain Foreman:* Ward Walton. *Property Shop Consultant:* Craig Talmy. *Standby Painters:* Claudia Gilligan, Anthony Tomes. *Bug Wranglers:* Steven Kutcher, Gary Gero. *Matte Painting:* Effects Associates Inc., Jim Danforth. *First Aid:* Maurice Costello. *Craft Service:* Richard Chavez. *Transportation Captain:* Eddie Lee Voelker. *Transportation Captains:* Mario Simon, James Vargas. *Drivers:* Jim Huffey, Marty Huffey, Steve Brooks, John Pratt, Dennis Yank, Randy Cantor, Bob Muehlig, Gordon Wiles, II. *Catering:* Unique Catering, Scandia Village Catering. *Technical Advisor:* Joseph R. Gonzales. *Photographic Doubling:* Rezza Badakshan, Michelle Costello, Phronsie Franco. *Stage Facilities:* Valencia Independent Studios. *Computer supplied by:* Tandon. *Computer Technical Consultant:* Michael Nelson. *Computer Programming:* Mike Berro. *Video Engineer:* Ian Wayne. *Canister Constructed by:* Show-Glass Props and Molds. *Operator/Supervisor:* Steve Patiro. *Shop Foreman:* Randy Killen. *Effects Crewman:* Burt Davidson. *Cranes and Dollies:* Chapment. Pre-recorded footage supplied by CNN. "Heavenly Puss" by Scott Bradley, courtesy of SBL Robbins Catalog. "Prince of Darkness" performed by Alice Cooper, courtesy of MCA Records. Filmed in Panavision. *Color:* Deluxe. *Titles and Opticals:* Pacific Title. Recorded in Ultra Stereo. A Universal/ Northern Distribution Partners Release.

MPAA Rating: R. *Running Time:* 102 minutes.

"The Brotherhood of Sleep ... anyone in close proximity has the same dream, the one you had just now.... The guardian priests had the dream for years ... a premonition. The dream evolves, unfolds.... We shall start to have it every time we go to sleep, as if it's pushing everything else out, making room for itself." — The priest describes the dream "warning" from the future.

SYNOPSIS: When the elderly Father Carlton, a priest in the religious sect known as the Brotherhood of Sleep, passes away with a small box resting on his chest, another Catholic priest investigates the situation. This British priest reads Carlton's diary, and finds an oversize key inside that mysterious box. He soon learns that the key opens up the basement door in a rundown Los Angeles Church called St. Godard's. Descending into the basement of the establishment, the priest finds a strange ancient canister atop an altar. Inside is a volatile, swirling fluid. Not only is this fluid alive, but the priest senses that it is evil.

Hoping to understand the nature of this unusual beast, the priest enlists the aid of Professor Birack, a physics professor at the Doppler Institute of Physics. Upon learning of the mystery, Birack recruits his best physics graduate students to help. As extra credit to boost their classroom averages, the grad students set up shop in St. Godard's and begin to analyze the canister found in the basement. Beside the altar is a Latin text detailing the canister's mystical origins.

While the investigation begins, two of Birack's students, Catherine Danforth and Brian Marsh, begin a romantic affair. They both tread carefully at first, realizing there is a real danger that they might fall in love.

The other students move in their advanced equipment as derelict street people watch curiously from a nearby alley. The pale, gaunt street people stagger out of the dark streets and proceed to surround the building. They are controlled by an awakening force. In the sky above, light from a supernova millions of years old reaches Earth for the first time.

Inside St. Godard's, the research group soon includes Professor Paul Leahy, a sarcastic physics student named Walter, a radiologist with glasses named Susan, a tall African American microbiologist named Calder, a beautiful blond named Kelly, and a specialist in translating ancient texts, Lisa. The priest and Birack gather their troops and take them downstairs to view the strange container first-hand. In their own ways, each individual feels the evil emanating from the strange fluid. Meanwhile, more street people circle the church, and hordes of insects start to cling to all the windows. In the presence of the contained fluid, Kelly's arm is bruised when she knocks into a piece of equipment.

As the students learn more, they become frightened by both the text and the presence of the mysterious fluid. The text, written 2,000 years ago, contains differential equations — which had not at that time been invented by human beings! The translation of the text, a palimpsest, also establishes that Satan, the Prince of Darkness himself, was sealed up in that container. Worse, X-ray analysis by Susan indicated that the container can only be opened from *the inside.* Additionally, the canister is established as being more than seven million years old.

When one of the graduate students leaves the church, the street people descend on him like a swarm and murder him. Inside, Brian Marsh worries that the fluid inside the container is a life-form. It is self-organizing out of chaos; it is in the progress of *becoming.* Lisa continues to translate the text, which suggests that Satan and Jesus were extra-terrestrials. And Satan, like water from the flood, was cast down on Earth in this container.

In the basement, Susan the radiologist approaches the canister and it blasts a toxic liquid into her mouth. The liquid changes and fills her, transforming her into a minion of evil. Upstairs, more chilling information comes out of the translation: The container was buried in the Middle East by the Father of Satan, a God-Being who once walked the Earth but was somehow banished to the "dark side." Jesus, an alien creature from a humanoid race, came to warn us. After Jesus was executed for his wild ideas, the Catholic Church and the Brotherhood of Sleep hid the container for 2,000 years, until man was capable of explaining its evil scientifically.

Soon, Brian detects that the thing in the basement is capable of directing energy, but he is unsure what its purpose is. He tells Catherine that it is reaching out, influencing, changing things, and moving objects through the power of thought. Birack then theorizes that Christianity as a religion is essentially correct, that there is a universal mind controlling everything, a God. But if there is a God, there must also be an anti–God, a force for universal evil. Worse than that, Birack fears that mankind dwells in the universe of the anti–God, and that God exists in the other world, the mirror image beyond our cognition.

As the group continues to argue about what they have discovered in the basement of a rotting church, Susan spreads the infection of evil to others, including Lisa and Calder. Another student, Wyndham, attempts to leave the church but is executed by a swarm of cockroaches and a street person wielding scissors. As the team sleeps inside, each member of the group experiences the same dream: A dark presence steps out of the church. A voice reports that it is transmitting this image as unconscious thought from the year 1999. The message warns that this is *not* a dream. The priest tells Birack that the Brotherhood of Sleep had this dream every night for forty years.

At 3:30 in the morning, Susan and the transformed translator, Lisa, bring the container of fluid to the sleeping Kelly, whose bruised arm now bears the mark of evil. They

The two faces of good in *Prince of Darkness* (1987). On the left is the priest (Donald Pleasence), representing religion, and on the right is Brian (Jameson Parker), representing science.

pour the liquid into her sleeping form, and Kelly becomes the host of evil. In the lab, the others hold a meeting to discuss the strange dream. Is it a message being sent from the future via tachyon particles? Is the dream a series of video clues, even a video signal, from other humans, which has been sent back in time? Brian and Catherine suspect it is a remote camera view of a future that can still be changed. Before this idea can be discussed more thoroughly, an all-out attack begins. Wyndham, infected with evil and now comprised of a million scurrying cockroaches, warns the students to pray for death. Fighting the evil now within him, an infected Calder also attacks. Before long, the students find themselves barricaded in the church, unable to escape.

Elsewhere, Walter discovers that Kelly's body chemistry is adapting to the evil within. He seeks shelter in a closet when Susan and Lisa attack him. He then watches as Kelly's flesh begins to fall off and change shape.

Before long, Leahy is also infected by the rampaging evil. The group of survivors are surrounded by evil, and as dawn arrives outside, Brian, Catherine, and Birack lock themselves in a secure room. They attempt to dig through a wall and free Walter from his closet prison. In another room, the priest hides alone beside a giant mirror. He watches from his vigil as a saddened, infected Calder gazes into the mirror, presumably looking at his anti-self ... a self still good and pure.

When Kelly's transformation is complete, the creature inhabiting her body attempts to bring her Father, the anti–God, back from the "other side." Kelly spots the large mirror and reaches inside it to pull the evil into our world. As the students continue to fight the minions of the Devil, Catherine spots Kelly. As Brian, Birack and the other survivors are busy fighting the Devil's soldiers, Catherine realizes that she must act before the anti–God emerges from the mirror. Bravely, Catherine tackles Kelly and pushes both Satan and the anti–God back to the other side of the mirror. Unfortunately, Catherine also goes through the mirror to the dimension of evil. Realizing that he too must act, the priest shatters the mirror with a pickax, trapping both evil and Catherine on the other side for all eternity.

The siege ended, human life continues. The servants of evil die without the host organism. Later, Brian dreams again of the message from the future, but this time he sees his beloved Catherine, now trapped forever with evil, emerging from the entrance of St. Godard's.

COMMENTARY: Although *Prince of Darkness* received (mostly) poisonous notices from critics when it was released in October of 1987, it remains one of John Carpenter's most interesting and thematically rich films to date. It is a film that seeks to establish a hierarchy in the universe in some rather unique ways. Utilizing the notion that for every particle of matter there is an opposite particle of anti-matter, his script intuits the existence of something truly frightening: an anti–God, a universal mind dedicated to evil. The flip side, of course, is that if there is an anti–God, there must also be a God (or at least a God particle), but that logical deduction has often been neglected in reviews of this particular film, reviews which would rather see *Prince of Darkness* and John Carpenter's career in the context of total nihilism and cynicism rather than one where there is often (at least) guarded hope that things will turn out okay. In his excellent essay about the films of Carpenter, entitled "John Carpenter: Cinema of Isolation," John Thonen noted that *Prince of Darkness* was a pessimistic film that was "utterly" nihilistic and "damn" proud of it. Specifically, Thonen saw the team of students in an unsympathetic light:

> These are selfish, lifeless, soulless people. There is a hint of a developing relationship between Catherine and Brian, but it's obvious it will go nowhere. Even Catherine's act of self-sacrifice, a brief promise of victory in

death, proves to be futile.... Everyone is alone. All actions are pointless.[13]

There is much to disagree with in that passage, although it is certainly a valid (and stimulating) interpretation of *Prince of Darkness*. Of paramount importance is this question: Are all the characters "selfish, lifeless, soulless people"? The best way to answer that assertion is to look at the text of the film itself.

In their desire to see good prevail over evil, Professor Birack, the priest, Brian, and Catherine certainly seem far from soulless. Perhaps they are disconnected from one another emotionally, but the desire to defeat evil and to survive (and thereby save the future of humanity) seems to indicate that these folks at least have a sense of obligation and loyalty to the species. If they had no souls, there would be nothing to lose in a world dominated by Satan and the all-powerful anti–God, so why fight it? Furthermore, if the characters are lifeless, soulless people, what is one to make of Calder, a character who is possessed by evil and yet positively shattered by that evil "ownership"? After being seduced by evil (Susan kisses him and passes the evil down his throat), Calder is seen in tears as he ascends a staircase and sings "Amazing Grace." He weeps as he sings; he weeps because he has a soul and it is being countermanded by the forces of evil now bubbling within him.

Furthermore, the people in *Prince of Darkness* repeatedly try to connect with one another. When Brian and Catherine share their first dialogue (sitting together on a bench on a picturesque campus), Brian sees that Catherine has misunderstood his intent and his comments ("I'm a confirmed sexist, and proud of it"). Were he a soulless, heartless person to whom human connection did not matter, he would not ask to begin the conversation over again. Catherine is also a positive figure: She forgives Brian his "miscue" and does permit him to start the conversation again. Both of these people desperately desire a connection, an intimacy with

In two separate photographs, the researchers of *Prince of Darkness* gaze into evil's unfathomable face, aware that danger and destruction await. *Top, left to right:* Victor Wong, Peter Jason, Donald Pleasence, Dennis Dun, Lisa Blount, Jameson Parker, Jessie Lawrence Ferguson. *Bottom:* Victor Wong and Anne Howard.

another human being, and they are open to that connection, even though personal communication is difficult and sometimes impossible.

In fact, *Prince of Darkness* is a distinctly hopeful film because as humanity stands on the abyss of evil, Catherine and Brian do find that connection with one another. Catherine asserts to Brian that love, not science or religion, is all that matters in the universe. Like *Starman*, *Prince of Darkness* suggests that in a world where evil often resides, the connection of human intimacy, of love, will be our only salvation. Make no mistake, Catherine and Brian are both searchers in this film: people who have had failed relationships and who are questing for love. Catherine stops Brian from telling her that he loves early in the film because she is desperately afraid that the words "I love you" will not mean to him what they mean to her. Catherine and Brian are not soulless, selfish people, they are vulnerable people in search of the only thing that makes life worth living: love.

Lastly, how is it possible to argue that Catherine's self-sacrifice is futile? When she chooses to face certain death rather than the possibility of a life which will include love with Brian, she consciously chooses to give up that love (thereby preserving the object of it: Brian). And she is successful! She casts the Devil and the anti–God back to the dark side and preserves not only Brian's life, but the future of humanity. This is not a brief victory; this is the eternal victory of man over pure evil. Life will go on because Catherine was brave enough to give up her life and her future of love with Brian. Catherine is a hero, and to undermine her beautiful and grand final act in the film is to invalidate the theme of *Prince of Darkness*: that love is selfless and indomitable.

After Catherine's self-sacrifice, Brian is haunted by his loss, haunted by her final act, haunted by her bravery (he sees her in his dreams). Is this the behavior of a soulless, selfish, lifeless man? Instead of being about how bad humanity is, and how disconnected

from one another we all are, *Prince of Darkness* actually reveals that within each human is the spark of something divine: the ability to overcome fear, hatred, and loneliness and to fight for good, fight for love.

John Carpenter has long been a fan of the writings of Nigel Kneale and the Hammer Studios *Quatermass* film trilogy (*The Creeping Unknown* [1956], *Enemy from Space* [1957], *Five Million Years to Earth* [1968]). His *Prince of Darkness* screenplay — written under the pseudonym Martin Quatermass — seeks to walk the same line as those films: It re-defines religion (some might say myth) through the instruments of modern science.

Consider *Five Million Years to Earth*, which concerns a discovery unearthed in London. An alien spacecraft is found beneath a subway station at Hobb's End. Aboard the craft are the corpses of aliens who arrived on Earth five million years earlier, and who apparently served as the basis for human legends about demons and devils. Additionally, a forcefield or energy matrix from the spaceship which utilized human psionic abilities was responsible for the myth of demonic possession. A British rocket scientist, Bernard Quatermass, makes these discoveries and ends the threat to London by analyzing, through science, how to defeat the seemingly dormant alien evil.

In *Prince of Darkness*, the situation is analogous: Evil is found in an unlikely locale (this time the basement of a church.) The evil is extra-terrestrial in origin and is the foundation of Christian legend about Satan. Demonic possession comes about through the spread of this evil (a fluid involuntarily ingested by human beings), and science brings mankind an understanding of the evil so that it can be destroyed. In *Prince of Darkness*, computer translations of ancient texts and equations define the religious concept of evil in believable/quantifiable terms. As Bryan Dietrich wrote in his essay "*Prince of Darkness/ Prince of Light*":

> *Prince of Darkness* presents us ... with a
> direct metaphor for the paradigm shift

taking place in the real world of science…. The role of the Church is passed on to the only institution it sees capable of honestly defining meaning in the universe in this day and age, to the sciences.[14]

This metaphor is reinforced by Carpenter's visuals. As the priest views St. Godard, the camera gives us an establishing shot of the church from beyond an iron gate. Between the vertical slats of this gate, a cross can be seen jutting up from the church's roof. Yet above the church is another gate slat, this one horizontal. In other words, the cross (representing religion) is boxed from above and on both sides. It is trapped, confined by its inability to diagnose evil as a tangible thing.

In its attempts to define science as the rightful heir to religious belief, *Prince of Darkness* is definitely an homage to the works of Nigel Kneale and to the specifics of the *Quatermass* film saga. Yet *Prince of Darkness* takes the *Quatermass* thesis a bit further because, ultimately, it is not science or technology that saves the day in this Carpenter film. Science diagnoses the problem (through computers, through radiology, through carbon-dating, through differential equations) but the actual problem itself (the ascension of evil) is resolved by the noble act of one measly human being: Catherine Danforth. In this sense, Carpenter is again being rather optimistic here. *Prince of Darkness* preaches that science, though helpful, is no substitute for a soul. Humans use technology as a tool, but it is still up to the humans — emotional miscues, intimacy disconnections, and personality flaws aside — to wield that technology responsibly and with an eye toward right and wrong.

One of the reasons that *Prince of Darkness* is such an eerily effective film resides in Carpenter's decision to place human beings at the bottom of a cosmic hierarchy. Throughout the film, there are close-ups of the heavens. The film begins with a close-up shot of

a full moon. That shot is later repeated, as are views of the strange light emanating from the far-off supernova. By including these shots, Carpenter is suggesting that humanity is small on a cosmic scale. Carpenter also equates human beings with insects throughout the film (both life-forms are susceptible to Satanic control, living in a much larger universe than they can possibly suspect), again suggesting that mankind does not understand his place in creation. Carpenter's screenplay also suggests man's status as perpetual petitioner at the altar of God. We are defined, by the screenplay, as creatures who live in a world of unfathomable mechanics. As Birack states near the film's opening, "Our logic collapses on the subatomic level into ghosts and shadows." In other words, even what we think we understand (the human-defined concept of logic) is not what it seems. It is (like religion) an attempt to explain something that terrifies us. This point is again brought to the fore by Birack:

> We've sought to impose order on the universe…. While order does exist … it is not at all what we had in mind.

This remark begs the question: If there is an order in the universe (one we did *not* have in mind) what is it? Who imposed it? Why can we not understand it? When Carpenter (through Birack) raises these questions, he is again attempting to define some kind of hierarchy in the universe. But he suggests that even science, as advanced as it is, cannot fathom it. This is the perfect set-up for a horror movie, for what is more frightening than the idea that we exist in a universe without logic, without comprehensible order, without even a rule or guidebook? *Prince of Darkness* draws much of its power from this thesis of uncertainty.

Prince of Darkness is also interesting in other ways. The plague of evil which overcomes the graduate students in St. Godard's is an allegory for the AIDS virus, a topic that was receiving intense public scrutiny in the year 1987. People were so afraid of contracting AIDS that even the traditionally hedonistic James Bond films were eschewing rampant promiscuity in favor of restrained monogamy (*The Living Daylights* [1987]). Appropriately, in *Prince of Darkness*, the evil is passed through bodily fluids, like AIDS. Susan contaminates Calder by kissing him and forcing the evil substance down his throat. Likewise, she "converts" the translator Lisa in a sexually charged sequence. As Lisa reclines on her bed face-up, Susan mounts her, climbing into a dominant position, straddling her. She then ejaculates the devil fluid into Lisa's protesting, open mouth. This AIDS allegory is not particularly subtle, but it infuses *Prince of Darkness* with another layer of meaning and relevance within its historical context. In 1987, people were afraid to sit on toilet seats in public bathrooms for fear of contracting AIDS. They were afraid of their sexual partners because death could quite literally be transferred through the act of love. *Prince of Darkness* captures that fear by allowing its particular brand of evil and death to be transferred through ejaculations of a fluid.

Indeed, a reviewer could even go further with this analogy. Throughout the film, the character of Walter (Dennis Dun) is defined repeatedly in homosexual terms. When he sees the Satanic bruise on Kelly's arm, he notes that at age 12 he broke out too—from "homosexual panic." At another point, he offhandedly comments that he is missing a date with a beautiful trial attorney, and Brian responds, "What's his name?" And lastly, where is poor Walter trapped during the finale of *Prince of Darkness*? In a closet, of course. When he digs his way out, pursued by the women who want to share their bodily fluids with him, he is literally coming out of the closet, racing from a heterosexual experience. Since in 1987 many people (wrongly) blamed homosexuals for the AIDS epidemic, it is perhaps relevant, if not entirely fair or appropriate, that one of the people endangered in *Prince of Darkness* should be seen in the veiled context of homosexuality. Indeed, homosexuality is an issue bubbling beneath the surface of *Prince of Darkness*. It is not difficult to notice that most of the "evil" contact in *Prince of Darkness* is of the same-sex variety. Susan infects Lisa; Susan and Lisa infect Kelly; Leahy and Calder both go after Brian. The one instance when a woman does infect a man (Susan to Calder) represents another sexual taboo: interracial coupling. By contrast, when Brian and Catherine make love early in the film, there is no evil involved in that sequence. Because it is an "appropriate" heterosexual coupling, there is no dangerous transfer of the evil fluid at that juncture.

Instead, the evil comes to Brian only much later: Once Catherine has passed over into the dimension of evil (and therefore been exposed to the infection). Brian dreams of her, and he awakens with a start to find a rotting corpse in bed beside him. It is a dream, but the image lingers. Brian is sweaty and shaken, afraid perhaps, that his partner was not so clean after all. As he touches the mirror and looks into his own image, there is a convergence of themes. He is not only wondering if Catherine is watching him from the other side; he is looking into his own face, sweaty and pale, and wondering if, by chance, the evil has been passed on to him. As he touches the mirror he is not only touching the woman whom he loves, he is touching the possibility that he too has been infected in some way. Nowhere in American film has the fear of AIDS been so succinctly stated in visual terms.

Abandoning subtext for the moment, *Prince of Darkness* is also, in some ways, a remake of *Assault on Precinct 13*. The siege scenario is restaged (but in a church instead of a police station), and again the possibility is raised that strange light from the heavens is impacting human behavior on Earth. In *Assault on Precinct 13*, Bishop informs his superior that strange sunspot activity might be responsible for the sudden and gruesome outbreaks of violence in L.A. In *Prince of*

Darkness, the light of a supernova (light that originated in the pre–Cambrian age) is substituted as the catalyst which awakens the evil djinn in the jar. Both films also rework the Hawksian template of *The Thing* (1951) in which a group of people with diverse agendas (science, religion, the military) either cooperate or fail to cooperate to meet a deadly threat in an isolated setting.

Prince of Darkness lacks the simplicity and fun of *Assault on Precinct*, however. It is a much more serious film, and though it is populated by Satan and zombies, it is perhaps among the most important American films of the '80s because it captures the fears of the times (through its AIDS metaphor) at the same time that it pointedly asks some rather big questions about human nature,

our existence, and even the universe at large. It is also one of Carpenter's scariest films because it generates terror not merely through *mise-en-scène*, a superb soundtrack and violent happenings, but through a screenplay which highlights how much humans take for granted. In *Prince of Darkness*, John Carpenter ruthlessly creates a world where logic is of no use, evil exists, and man's only salvation is love. Critics insist that *Prince of Darkness* is slow-paced, tacky and even dumb, but with its predilection for scientific explanations and its masterful and gradual build-up of a cerebral terror, Carpenter proves that, at least in this case, he brought a lot more to the creation of a movie than the reviewers did in analyzing it. *Prince of Darkness* is an underrated jewel.

They Live (1988)

Critical Reception

"*They Live* is a junkheap, but it's scrappy and inventive, and it casts a spell.... The movie has an eerie drone. As in *Halloween*, the very dullness of Carpenter's wide-screen style can be entrancing; his throbbing, repetitious music ... can plug into your heartbeat like the bass line on a video game.... *They Live* is a delirious anthem for paranoid, left-wing street loons, the kind who once in a while make more sense than our leading columnists.... I frankly thought [Carpenter had] lost whatever juice he had.... But he's back where he started now, making cheapies clean and fast, and the return has revitalized him."—David Edelstein, *The New York Post*, November 4, 1988.

"Credibility isn't the problem with John Carpenter's *They Live* ... but execution is. Mr. Carpenter has directed the film with B-movie bluntness, but with none of the requisite snap. And his screenplay (written under the pseudonym Frank Armitage) makes the principals sound even more tongue-tied than they have to.... The best part ... is the opening, when the story still holds some surprises and the promise that it may catch fire.... Since Mr. Carpenter seems to be trying to make a real point here, the flatness of *They Live* is doubly disappointing."—Janet Maslin, *The New York Times:* "A Pair of Sunglasses Reveals a World of Evil," November 4, 1988.

"It's a consummate, oddly exciting vision of Orwellian thought control filtered through old movies and the pages of *Fortune* magazine.... Ever the skilled technician, Carpenter remains a master at welding Panavision, music, and editing into a streamlined piece of product.... The uncharacteristically bluesy ... score plays well against the paranoid, nocturnal sharply cut visuals. But as always, technique out-distances content.... The flaccid lines and careless delivery make us doubt Carpenter the screenwriter."— Charles D. Leayman, *Cinefantastique:* "As Always with Carpenter, Technique Far Outdistances Content," May 1989.

"The movie daffily mixes up the paranoia of the Red Scare monster movies of the '50s, with a different kind of nightmare: the radical's belief that everything is tightly controlled by a small, malicious ruling elite. Everything — the flat lighting, the crazily protracted action scenes, the monolithic beat and vamp of the score — reinforces a mood of murderous persecution mania.... Carpenter and his team seem to be having lots of fun. *They Live*, one of his best films, has the paranoid buildup of *The Thing* or *Halloween* and the lazy malicious anti–Establishment humor of *Dark Star*."— Michael Wilmington, *The Los Angeles Times*, November 4, 1988.

"A satire of the Reagan years: raunchy, low-budget, inventive and goofy."— John Clute, *SF: The Illustrated Encyclopedia*, Dorling Kindersley, 1995.

"[Carpenter's] best film for years ... is a model of taut B-Movie narrative skills.... An excellent formula film, *They Live* is almost something more ambitious as well."— Peter Nicholls, *The Encyclopedia of Science Fiction*, page 1218.

Cast and Credits

CAST: Roddy Piper (John Nada); Keith David (Frank); Meg Foster (Holly Thompson); George "Buck" Flower (Drifter); Peter Jason (Gilbert); Raymond St. Jacques (Street Preacher); Jason Robards, III (Family Man); John Lawrence (Bearded Man); Susan Barnes (Brown Haired Woman); Sy Richardson (Black Revolutionary); Wendy Brainard (Family Man's Daughter); Lucille Meredith (Female Interviewer); Susan Blanchard (Ingenue); Norman Alden (Foreman); Dana Bratton (Black Junkie); John P. Goff (Well-Dressed Customer); Norm Wilson (Vendor); Thelma Lee (Rich Lady); Stratton Leopold (Depressed Human); Rezza Shan (Arab Clerk); Norman Howell (Blond Haired Cop); Larry Franco (Neighbor); Tom Searle (Biker); Robert Grasmere (Scruffy Blonde Man); Vince Inneo (Passageway Guard); Bob Hudson (Passageway Guard #2); Jon Paul Jones (Manager); Dennis Michael (Male News Anchor); Nancy Gee (Female News Anchor); Claudia Stanlee (Young Female Executive); Christine Baur (Woman on Phone); Eileen Wesson (Pregnant Secretary); Gregory Barnett (Security Guard #1); Jim Nickerson (Security Guard #2); Cibby Danyla (Naked Lady); Jeff Imada (Male Ghoul); Michelle Costello (Female Ghoul).

CREDITS: Alive Films Presents a Larry Franco Production. *Music:* John Carpenter and Alan Howarth. *Associate Producer:* Sandy King. *Executive Producers:* Shep Gordon, Andre Blay. *Edited by:* Gib Jaffe, Frank E. Jimenez. *Art Directors:* William J. Durrell, Jr., Daniel Lomino. *Director of Photography:* Gary B. Kibbe. *Based upon the short story:* "Eight O'Clock in the Morning" by Ray Nelson. *Screenplay:* Frank Armitage (aka John Carpenter); *Produced by:* Larry Franco. *Director:* John Carpenter. *Unit Production Managers:* Stratton Leopold, Alan Levine. *First Assistant Director:* Larry Franco. *Second Assistant Director:* Artist Robinson. *Camera Operator:* Jud Kehl. *First Assistant Camera:* Jeffrey Norvet. *Second Assistant Camera:*

Larry Davis. *Second Camera/Panaglide Operator:* Raymond V. Stella. *Second Camera/First Assistant:* Clyde E. Bryan. *Script Supervisor:* Sandy King. *Gaffer:* Kenneth Spencer. *Best Boy Electrician:* John Kennedy. *Electricians:* Robert DePerna, Kevin Arnold, Sanford Barr, Richard Smock. *Key Grip:* Ronald Cardarelli. *Best Boy Grip:* John Palka. *Dolly Grip:* David Wachtman. *Grips:* Anthony DiMase, Robin Roberts. *Sound Mixer:* Ron Judkins. *Boom Operator:* Robert Jackson. *Set Decorator:* Marvin March. *Lead Man:* Jack Eberhart. *Swing Gang:* Gregory Renta. *Property Master:* Victor Petrotta, Jr. *Assistant Prop Master:* Richard Kerns, John Sweeney. *Costume Supervisor:* Robin Bush. *Costumers:* Robert Bush, John Young. *Make-up:* Frank Carrisosa. *Hairstylist:* Elle Elliott. *Special Effects Coordinator:* Roy Arbogast. *Special Effects Assistants:* William Lee, David Butstein, Michael Arbogast. *Assistant Film Editor:* Margaret Godspeed, Fred M. Wardell. *Stunt Coordinator:* Jeff Imada. *Stunts:* Rick Avery, Christine Baur, Simone Boisseree, John Borland, Brad Boyee, John Branagan, Anthony Brubaker, Kurt Bryant, David Burton, David Cadiente, Jimmy Casion, John J. Casion, Phil Chong, Gary Comis, Gilbert Combs, Bob K. Cummings, Gary Charles Davis, Tim Davison, Shane Dixon, Richard Duran, Euralyne Epper, Carl Epper, John Epstein, Debbie Evans, Diamond Fransworth, George Fisher, John Gilbride, Andy Gill, Alan Graff, Randy Hall, Steve Hart, Eddie Hice, Freddie Hice, Norman Howell, Brian Imada, John Michael Johnson, Matt D. Johnston, Chris Kent, Henry King, Joel Kramer, Daniel Eric Lee, Al Leong, James Lew, Billy D. Lucas, Eric Mansker, Matt McColm, John C. Meier, Bennie E. Moore, Jr., Donna L. Noguchi, Charles Picerni, Jr., Branscombe Richmond, Danny Rogers, Ronny Rondel, Jr., Thomas Rosales, Jr., Timothy Roslan, Debbie Lynn Ross, Mike Runyard, Ben Scott, John Clay-Scott, Walter Scott, Jan Michael Shultz, Russell Solberg, Ceci Vendrell, Michael M. Vendrell, Ric Waugh, Danny Wesels, Cheryl Wheeler-Dixon, Scott Wilder, Diane Wilson, Merritt

Youhnka. *Helicopter Pilots:* James Deeth, Bille Don Evans. *Re-recording mixers:* Robert J. Litt, Sergio Reyes, Elliot Tyson. *Recordists:* Tim Web, Walter A. Gest. *Supervising Sound Editors:* Jeffrey L. Sandler, Gordon Ecker Productions. *Sound Editors:* J. H. Arrufat, Larry Carow, Samuel Crutcher, Hector C. Gika, John Leveque, Don Warner. *Foley Supervisor:* Richard E. Yawn. *Foley Editors:* Shawn Sykora, Mike Hoskinson, Bob O'Brien. *Assistant Sound Editor:* Mark Boisseau. *Supervising ADR Editor:* Beck Sullivan-Coblentz. *ADR Editor:* Solange Schwalbe Boisseau. *Sound Effects Research:* Frank A. Fuller, Jr. *Sound Effects Recordist:* Gary Blufer. *Sound Effects Coordinators:* Laurie Ecker, John Michael Fanaris. *Synthesized Sound Effects:* Alan Howarth. *Foley Artists:* Gregg Barbanell, Gary Hecker. *ADR Mixer:* Gary Rogers. *ADR Recordist:* Tom O'Connell. *Foley Mixer:* Timothy Hoggatt. *Foley Recordist:* Roberta Alstadter. *Extras Casting:* Sally Perle & Associates. *Voice Casting:* Barbara Harris. *Assistant to Mr. Franco:* Sandra Holden. *Assistant to Mr. Carpenter:* Karin Costa. *Production Accountant:* Joy Ewing. *Production Coordinator:* Marian Shambo. *Location Manager:* Ken Lavet. *DGA Trainee:* Scott Senechal. *Production Associate:* Mathew Dunne. *Art Department Assistant:* Sean Howarth. *Still Photographers:* Sidney Baldwin, Bruce Birmelin. *Stand-Ins:* Gregory Barrish, T. Z. Garrison. *Construction Foreman:* Michael Wright. *Propmaker:* Frank Leasure. *Labor Foreman:* Kenneth Truby. *Paint Foreman:* Richard Girod. *Standby Painter:* Ernie Millanponce. *First Aid:* Maurice Costello. *Craft Services:* Richard Chavez. *Transportation Coordinator:* Kenny Searle. *Transportation Captain:* Tim Roslan. *Drivers:* George Bess, Fred Brookfield, Jim Brown, Bob Cromwell, Jim Langhorne, Steve Latna, Leo Loa, John Marendi, Frank Mielcarek, Denny McLaughlin, Mike Reposa. *Color Timer:* Phil Downes. *Negative Cutter:* Gary Burritt. *Commercials Produced By:* Larry Sulkis, Denali Productions. *Special Photographic Effects:* Effects Associates/Jim Danforth. *Video Playback:* Inter Video. *Process*

Compositing: The Hansard Group. *Caterers:* Marco's Catering, Angelo Trujillo. *Music Recorded at:* Electric Melody Studio, Goldwyn Sound Facility. *Dolby Stereo Consultant:* Douglas Greenfield. *Filmed in:* Panavision. *Color:* DeLuxe. *Titles and Opticals:* Pacific Title. *Special Thanks to:* Control Data Corporation and ETA Systems, Inc.; The Goodyear Airship *Columbia*; Greater St. Peter's Ame Church, Atlanta, Georgia. *MPAA Rating:* R. *Running Time:* 95 minutes.

"Maybe they've always been with us ... those things out there. Maybe they love it: seeing us hate each other; watching us kill each other off; feeding on our own cold fucking hearts." — Frank pontificates on the nature of the aliens.

"It's business ... that's all it is.... What's wrong with having it good for a change.... What's the threat? We all sell out every day, you might as well be on the winning team!" — The logic of collaboration.

SYNOPSIS: An out-of-work loner, John Nada, arrives in Los Angeles in search of work. He labored for ten years in a factory in Denver before losing his job when a series of banks folded in one day. At the L.A. employment office, he finds nothing available for someone of his skills — not even sympathy. As he walks the street, John Nada listens as a blind street preacher raves about "the Truth." The preacher wonders why Americans worship greed and wealth. Even more curiously, the preacher seems convinced that an unseen oppressor is responsible for the new American society of apathy and prejudice.

After spending a night on the street, John Nada seeks work at a construction site. After a long day of back-breaking labor, he befriends a burly African American man, Frank, who tells him of Justiceville: a homeless encampment with hot food, showers, and plenty of hospitality. Nada follows Frank to Justiceville and finds a real community thriving there. He enjoys a hot meal prepared by the good people of the town. Even though these people have no home and few belongings, they share everything with their fellow man, and work together to build a better future.

That night, a hacker breaks in on a local television signal and warns the populace, including the folks of Justiceville, that they are being kept asleep by an unseen oppressor. The poor underclass is growing, and the oppressors have created a repressive society through the annihilation of conscience and consciousness. Nada watches the transmission with interest and notes that the blind street preacher he noticed before is mouthing the words of the speech, although he is not even near a television! Suspicious, Nada pursues the preacher to a close-by church. Nada suspects the hacker's signal is originating from the church, and the next morning he investigates it. To his surprise, he finds a fully functioning laboratory inside, as well as crates filled with designer sunglasses.

Nada listens in hiding as several resistance members, including people from Justiceville, talk about putting the "shipment out on the street" and exposing the oppressors. A police helicopter soon circles overhead, and Nada realizes the jig is up. That night, the L.A.P.D. attacks the church and bulldozes Justiceville to the ground, sending its people fleeing to the streets. Cops with flares, helmets and bullet-proof shields shoot tear gas through the Justiceville community and round up the so-called "criminals" who lived there illegally. Frank, Nada and a few others flee the siege. Nada sees the resistance leaders, including the street preacher, being brutally beaten by the gestapo-like police force.

The next morning, Nada searches the aftermath of Justiceville. He goes to the church once more, and he finds the sunglasses. He puts on a pair and is stunned by what he sees. The world is in black and white.

Advertisements on billboards carry giant, formerly hidden messages like "OBEY" and "MARRY AND REPRODUCE." When Nada looks at a dollar bill through the sunglasses, he sees that it is encoded with a message: "THIS IS YOUR GOD." Even worse, there are aliens—gray, skeletal monstrosities—mingling among the humans throughout Los Angeles. These are the oppressors: money-hungry yuppies from outer space!

Infuriated by what he has learned, Nada launches a counter-attack. After a vicious encounter with two alien police officers, Nada arms himself with a shotgun and attacks a bank. There, he shoots down every alien he can draw a bead on. Unfortunately, the aliens have advanced communications devices embedded in their fancy watches. These devices also serve as transport devices, and at least one alien "beams" away to safety before Nada can shoot him.

Outside the bank, Nada sees himself being monitored by a hovering surveillance satellite. He destroys it, and then flees to a parking garage, where he kidnaps a beautiful human woman, Holly Thompson, and forces her to drive him to safety. She takes him to her house and Nada tells her about the alien threat. Nada learns that Holly is the assistant program director at Channel 54, a television station in the city. Since she is involved with the world of television, Nada believes she might be able to help him understand the alien mode of transmission. Holly proves to be uncooperative and at her first opportunity she smashes a wine bottle over Nada's head. Reeling from the blow, he falls out a screen door and down a long, winding hill. Holly immediately calls the police and then notices that Nada has left behind his sunglasses.

The next day, Nada returns to the construction site and attempts to recruit Frank to the cause. Frank gives him a week's salary, but refuses to otherwise help Nada. Nada returns to a back alley where he stashed a box of the special sunglasses and he demands Frank try them on. When Frank refuses, the two men get into a knock-down drag-out fight that leaves them both bruised and exhausted. Finally, Frank puts on the sunglasses, and his eyes are suddenly opened to the real world. The two men then seek shelter at a fleabag hotel. After a time, they decide to search for the people who made the glasses, but a Justiceville resident and resistance leader, Gilbert, finds them first. He tells them of a secret resistance meeting that night.

At the meeting, Frank, Nada and the others are given special contact lenses to replace the sunglasses. From Gilbert, Nada and Frank learn the truth. The aliens are broadcasting a signal through the television that keeps humans "sedated" and unaware. The Earth's atmosphere is being acclimatized to the alien needs as well. Gilbert reveals that the aliens are "free enterprisers" and that the Earth is *their* third world. Later, Frank runs into Holly, who has donned the sunglasses he left behind and come to realize the truth about an alien invasion. While Nada talks with Holly, the resistance members discuss their plan to overcome the threat to humanity. The resistance must find the source of the alien signal and destroy it.

Suddenly, the police, who believe that the resistance consists of commies trying to bring down the government, attack the resistance. In a brutal shoot-out, all but a few members of the resistance are murdered. Frank and Nada escape in the chaos and use a stolen alien transportation device to beam away. They arrive, to their surprise, in an alien complex far beneath the city. The two men then find themselves at a banquet honoring the rich from Earth and from outer space. They listen as an alien leader talks about the success of his "ongoing quest for multi-dimensional expansion."

Before long, Frank and Nada meet a bum from Justiceville who has "sold out" to the aliens. He takes them through the installation, unaware that they are actually insurrectionists. He shows them a fantastic launch station, an interstellar subway of sorts, to Andromeda as well as other planets. Then, he leads them to a massive control room where the alien master signal originates. Nada recognizes the logo: It is Channel 54, the station where Holly Thompson works!

Nada and Frank make for the roof, where the alien satellite dish is located. They find Holly en route and she joins their flight to freedom. As the alien forces close in, Holly reveals her true colors: She kills Frank and holds Nada captive at gunpoint. She too has sold out. Nada kills Holly with a hidden firearm and then blows apart the alien satellite dish. As the dish explodes, a police helicopter circles by and a sharpshooter kills Nada.

Around the world, the aliens are revealed on television, in bars, and in all walks of life.

COMMENTARY: A "message" film by its very name suggests something that is good for you, even if it does not taste good. John Carpenter's 1988 feature, *They Live*, is unequivocally a message film, but it is unusually and surprisingly tasty: an easily digestible entertainment which nonetheless raises some serious and thought-provoking questions about life in 1980s America, what Carpenter sees as the effect of MTV, yuppieism, and the fallout of the so-called "Reagan Revolution." That is quite a heady brew for a 95-minute action picture, which, on the surface, deals with one of the genre's oldest tropes: the alien invasion. Still, by grafting on so much social commentary to his story, Carpenter offers a science fiction adventure with as much heart and mind as spectacle and action. Though in the final analysis the film falters badly — particularly in an overlong street-fight which represents the fascination the director then felt for professional wrestling — *They Live* remains an inventive, wildly funny film with shocks, suspense, and even subtext.

In his screenplay for *They Live* (as Frank Armitage), John Carpenter sees poverty, homelessness, unemployment, racial prejudice and violence as the result of two things: the Reagan era of voodoo economics in which the wealth never really trickled down beyond the most financially successful "upper" echelon of American society; and the emergence of television as an avenue through which to sell, sell, sell. The eminence of MTV and its quick-cut imagery only insured that a product could be sold more quickly, more effectively, and with more glitz. So while people became poorer because of economic reality, they also wanted more because of the constant stream of messages being fed to them by the boob tube. Appropriately then, *They Live* is a depiction of the post–Reagan malaise, an America suffering serious consequences for the prosperity of the few: a shrinking middle class, increased homelessness, a resurgence of racial prejudice, and so forth. To dramatize this world, Carpenter opens *They Live* with a shot of graffiti, an art form of America's underclass. Tracking left from the wall of graffiti, his camera detects a loner, John Nada (Nada, of course, meaning "nothing"), as he walks into the opulence and majesty of the Los Angeles metropolis. The camera then stays on Nada (Roddy Piper), and the mood is perfect for Carpenter's message. Piper is not traditionally good looking or heroic in appearance. On the contrary, he was cast for his look. This is a man who has taken his knocks (quite literally, on the wrestling mat). This casting works, and as Piper walks L.A. accompanied by the bluesy strains of John Carpenter's score, a tone of melancholy and bad times is established. We are now in the world of a drifter, of a homeless man. This mood is further enhanced as Nada seeks work and is shooed away by an officious bureaucrat as if he is an insect to be swatted away. Again, a pointed message is being driven home here: Society wants men like Nada to be silent and invisible, to leave the rest of us "productive members of society" alone because he is a reminder that not all Americans are created equal, that many people with solid work records and good family values were not carried away by the artificial prosperity generated in the Reagan 80s. This self-assured opening sequence, all set against a granite-gray sky, is one of *They Live*'s best. It sets the texture of the film perfectly, before the narrative about aliens even kicks in.

The thesis of yuppieism — "Me first, me second, and me third" — is also questioned in *They Live*. Where corporate America and the "free enterprise" aliens seek to gain wealth by separating men from their consciences, the homeless and jobless in *They Live* are dramatized in a different emotional hue. Justiceville is determinedly what Los Angeles is not: a community. Children (of different races) play together in peace, a mother reads to her child, people cook for one another and share responsibilities. Thus Justiceville, as its name suggests, is a place of liberty and equality "where everybody knows your name." It is a utopia, an oasis of decency in a world dominated by selfishness and greed. And, in typical Carpenter fashion, it is short-lived. Justiceville and all it represents is a threat to the aliens (who thrive when people think only of their own needs and not the needs of the community) and thus is mercilessly torn down. Justice(ville) is exterminated like a roach infestation in Carpenter's vision of '80s America. According to the elite, whether it be yuppies or aliens, it is better that Justiceville should be a parking lot for BMWs than a place where economic "losers" pollute the view of the city.

They Live establishes a mood of melancholy almost immediately, successfully introduces the viewer to a "real community" in Justiceville, and then does one other thing in its opening passages. It establishes the pervasiveness of television in American culture. There are televisions everywhere in this film, even in the utopia of Justiceville. Carpenter displays on these sets some of the most vapid programs and commercials imaginable so as to demonstrate how television sells America an image and then asks its people to emulate it. "All I need is to be famous," one actress on the tube croaks, measuring her life success by the television culture spawned by the wealthy. If she only has a talk show, or becomes a celebrity, she will have found heaven. This insight seems particularly rel-

evant in the new millennium. What Carpenter was clearly envisioning in 1988 was a world in which Americans are consumed and enslaved by the television, at the expense of such historical pillars as culture, decency and justice.

In the most inspired use of television, Carpenter at one point shows a program in which a bald eagle flies gracefully over the United States, a symbol of liberty, opportunity and patriotism. He then contrasts that image with grim reality. Over Justiceville, black helicopters circle like vultures. Oppression has replaced opportunity. Helicopters have superseded bald eagles.

Much of *They Live* serves as an indictment of capitalism. Frank, a good man who has been unable to see his wife and kids back in Detroit for six months because he cannot find work at home, enunciates a new Golden Rule: "He who has the gold, rules." He also states in succinct terms the essential unfairness of capitalism as rule of law: "Do what you can to get ahead, but I'm going to do my best to blow you away." How can anybody prosper in a world of such intense competition? What about helping your fellow man? Where does that fit into the world of "free enterprise" and "incentives" and "competition?" Frank also suggests an inflammatory course of action if another factory is closed and more workers are mercilessly laid off: violence. Frank advocates taking a hammer to the executives' fancy foreign cars. This advocacy of violence in response to the unfairness of capitalism is the voice of Carpenter, a revolutionary. To temper that side, however, Carpenter's beliefs are also revealed through Nada's response:

> I believe in America. I follow the rules. Everyone's got their own hard times these days.

That more even-handed view, however, is ultimately overturned as *They Live* moves towards its inevitable climax. Carpenter's film suggests that there is no longer an America to believe in, merely state-sanctioned greed and an alien upper class (possibly representing yuppies, Republicans, or even the Japanese) which feeds off the labor of the poor. Carpenter, like Nada, wants desperately to believe in his country, but the values that once shone brightly in American life have become meaningless catch-phrases or sound-bytes for politicians (aliens, per *They Live*) who want to get richer and richer and open new markets so that even more wealth can be available.

When Nada wakes up from the Reagan dream of prosperity for all and realizes the cost, he rebels. He becomes, essentially, an anti-government radical bent on destroying the establishment. Nada may be nothing by the alien way of thinking, but in one sense he is a patriot because he rebels against the alien message. He will not conform; will not consume; will not submit; will not stay asleep while community becomes extinct. He *will* question authority, a favorite Carpenter tenet, and even as he dies, his final act is one of defiance: He gives the police the finger. Nada is thus the perfect Carpenter protagonist. He is disenfranchised, pissed off, and fighting for a good, if unpopular, cause. In death he ultimately wins by revealing the aliens to the world.

This is another Carpenter theme: the belief that one man can change the world and that sacrifice is noble. Indeed, sacrifice was a word not heard much during the Reagan era. It was unpopular, and nobody wanted sacrifice when there was no inflation and interest rates were low. Carpenter's films in the '80s worked against the trend of the times because they so often embraced sacrifice as a positive force for change. MacReady and the others in *The Thing* destroyed their base (and their only chance of survival) so that humanity would not die at the hands of a malevolent extra-terrestrial. Catherine Danforth gave up her life to keep the devil at bay in *Prince of Darkness*. In the '90s, this idea of sacrifice would again appeal to Carpenter. In *Village of the Damned*, Dr. Chaffee would

give up his life to stop the alien children from destroying the human race.

Besides attacking yuppie values, Carpenter takes some shots at other forces in modern America in *They Live*. There are alien presidential candidates and even alien film critics: Gene Siskel and Roger Ebert types are revealed as aliens even as they complain that George Romero and John Carpenter have gone too far in depicting violence on film. In another relevant moment, Carpenter references the horrible late–'80s Ted Turner trend of colorizing old films. To Carpenter, the real world is black and white and the aliens have "colorized us!" Carpenter also takes deadly aim at the L.A.P.D. in *They Live*, and in one sequence brutally prescient of the Rodney King beatings, he dramatizes cops clubbing an unarmed man to the point of death.

If *They Live* falters anywhere, it is certainly in the overlong fight sequence in a Los Angeles alley. Nada and Frank deliver devastating blows, one after the other, that would kill any man. Yet the fight goes on interminably, with only bloody noses and bleeding lips as the result. This strange fight comes from Carpenter's love of professional wrestling, and the battle indeed comes across like a WWF event. The characters lift and throw each other, but they are not on a cushioned mat — they are on hard asphalt streets! This fact throws believability out the window in a way that aliens, conspiracies and gunfight never could. Indeed, this fight sequence seems to confirm the alien point of view that human beings are stupid animals.

The obvious truth about this fight scene is that there is no real dramatically motivated reason for Frank and Nada to fight one another. Yet, to give the devil his due, this fight is pure Carpenter: brilliantly staged, shot and edited. And it again demonstrates Carpenter's total individuality as a filmmaker. He included this fight because *he* enjoyed it — audience and dramatic needs be damned! A viewer might prefer the more elegant style of fighting demonstrated in *Big*

Trouble in Little China, but at the time of *They Live*, Carpenter wanted to explore the use of professional wrestling in film — and *They Live*, like all Carpenter's films, clearly is a product of its director's personal vision.

They Live is also interesting from the auteur perspective. Seen in the context of Carpenter's career, this film offers another anti-hero (like Napoleon Wilson in *Assault on Precinct 13*, Snake Plissken in *Escape from New York*, and MacReady in *The Thing*). Stylistically, the film also reframes a critical action scene from *Assault on Precinct 13*. The opening images of that 1976 motion picture included a fight in which police officers, from the high ground atop a back alley, blasted a street gang running through the alley surrounded by high brick walls. *They Live* recycles that image of urban warfare with the alien police taking the high ground and shooting down at the "criminals" (resistance fighters). In the case of *They Live*, the dynamics have changed (cops are now bad and criminals are good) but the staging remains identical.

Meg Foster's Holly Thompson is also the latest in a long line of Carpenter's Hawksian women. Like Leigh in *Assault on Precinct 13* or Adrienne Barbeau in *Escape from New York*, she is capable of giving as good as she gets. Unlike previous Hawks women in Carpenter films, however, Foster's Holly is also a turncoat, a betrayer who foreshadows Linda Styles in *In the Mouth of Madness*.

Making his second appearance in the John Carpenter acting company is Peter Jason, Professor Leahy in *Prince of Darkness*. He would return regularly in Carpenter's films, appearing in *Body Bags*, *In the Mouth of Madness*, *Village of the Damned*, and *Escape from L.A.*, playing good guys and bad guys with equal skill.

Memoirs of an Invisible Man (1992)

Critical Reception

"The good news is that John Carpenter ... is no hack filmmaker, and Chevy Chase, the most mannered of the first class of *Saturday Night Live* grads, has picked this implausible story to create his most plausible character.... Halloway's confusion and earnest reaction to his predicament saves *Memoirs*, as much as possible, from being just another silly exercise in special effects."— Jack Matthews, *Newsday*, February 28, 1992.

"The plot is lazy and conventional.... This material is intriguing enough that I wish there had been more to it. Comedy consists of the application of logic to the absurd, and there are many more opportunities here than the screenplay takes advantage of.... John Carpenter seems convinced we care about the resolution of the plot involving spies and government secrecy. We couldn't care less.... Every character and every line of dialogue in these scenes is demoralized by the countless times they've been recycled."— Roger Ebert, *Roger Ebert's Home Movie Companion*, Andrews and McMeel, 1993, page 406.

"Director John Carpenter ... plays it fast and funny in this chase picture. And he rings in just about every possible sight (or non-sight) gag about invisibility, aided by excellent special effects."— Martin Burden, *The New York Post*, February 28, 1992.

"There's every indication that director John Carpenter was trying for more than another rinky-dink Chevy Chase comedy. Except for the effects, though, *Memoirs of an Invisible Man* comes disappointingly close to being just that.... The plot is boring.... Still, if you've ever wondered what it looks like when the invisible man chews bubble gum..."— Owen Gleiberman, *Entertainment Weekly* #108, "Vanishing Act," March 6, 1992, page 41.

"Carpenter, best known for *Halloween* and *The Thing*, works up a few ghostly effects, like the shot of Nick silhouetted by pouring rain, but for the most part his models are grimmer and more mundane—*Double Indemnity*, the TV series *The Fugitive*, early Hitchcock, and so on. The special effects are often nifty, but where's the wit? *Memoirs of an Invisible Man* doesn't earn its seriousness. It fades into invisibility while you're watching it."— Peter Rainer, *The Los Angeles Times*, February 28, 1992.

"Slick, if slightly wayward, comic melodrama.... For the most part ... everything is blithely orchestrated by thrillmaster John Carpenter.... Though not completely sure of his footing here ... Carpenter manages to conspire nimbly enough with Chase's fabled blundering to produce some funny moments."— Mark Goodwin, *People Weekly*, March 9, 1992.

Cast and Credits

CAST: Chevy Chase (Nick Halloway); Darryl Hannah (Alice Monroe); Sam Neill (David Jenkins); Michael McKean (George Talbot); Stephen Tobolowski (Warren Singleton); Jim Norton (Dr. Bernard Wachs); Rosalind Chao (Cathy DiTolla); Pat Skipper (Morrissey); Paul Perri (Gomez); Richard EpCar (Tyler); Steven Bar (Clellan); Gregory Paul-Martin (Richard); Patricia Heaton (Ellen); Barry Kirel (Drunk Businessman); Donald Li (Cab Driver); Jay Gerber (Roger Whitman); Shay Duffin (Patrick the bartender); Edmund L. Shaff (Edward Schneiderman); Sam Anderson (Chairman of the House Committee); Elaine Corrall (News Anchor); Ellen Albertini Davi (Mrs. Coulsen); Jonathan Wigan (Delivery Boy); I. M. Hobson (Maitre d'); Rip Haight/John Carpenter (Helicopter Pilot); Chip Heiller (Man who hails taxi); Aaron Lustig (Technician).

CREDITS: Warner Bros. Presents, in Association with Le Studio Canal, Regency Enterprises and Alcor Films, A Cornelius Production. *Casting:* Sharon Howard-Field. *Music:* Shirley Walker. *Visual Effects Supervisor:* Bruce Nicholson. *Costumes Designed by:* Joe I. Tompkins. *Edited by:* Marion Rothman. *Production Designed by:* Lawrence G. Paull. *Director of Photography:* William A. Fraker, A.S.C. *Executive Producer:* Arnon Milchan. *Based on the book by:* H. F. Saint. *Screenplay:* Robert Collector, Dana Olsen, William Goldman. *Producers:* Bruce Badner, Dan Kolsurd. *Directed by:* John Carpenter. *Unit Production Manager:* Arthur Seidel. *First Assistant Director:* William M. Elvin. *Second Assistant Director:* Alan Edminster. *Art Director:* Bruce Crone. *Set Decorator:* Rick Simpson. *Set Designers:* Elizabeth Lapp, Lauren Polizzi, Gerald Sigmon. *Script Supervisor:* Larry K. Johnson. *2nd Second Assistant Director:* Otis Brown, Arlene Fukai, Kurt C. Hodenfield. *Illustrator:* Marty Kline. *Art Department:* Stephanie Schwartzman. *Camera Operator:* David Diano. *First Assistant Camera:* Lex Rawlins. *Second Assistant Camera:* Tim Roe. *B Camera Operator:* Richard Turner. *B Camera Assistant:* Ted Chu. *Still Photographer:* Ron Phillips. *Production Mixer:* Jim Alexander. *Re-recording Mixer:* Robert J. Litt, Greg P. Russell, Elliott Tyson. *Property Master:* Edward Aiona. *Assistant Property Master:*

Michael Sexton, Steven Blakney. *Animal Trainer:* Paul Calabria. *Special Effects Coordinator:* Ken Pepiot. *Special Effects Foreman:* Albert Delgado. *Special Effects:* Larz Anderson, A. J. Thrasher, Dan Sudick, Wayne Rose, Ginta Repecka. *Costume Supervisor:* Roberto M. Carneiro, Kathy Moderine. *Men's Costumer:* Steve Ellsworth. *Women's Costumer:* Adrianna Bernard, Annie Polland. *Make-Up Artists:* Rick Sharp, Lee Harmon. *Hair-Stylists:* John Isaacs, Cheri Ruff. *Chief Lighting technican:* Jerry Boatright. *Assistant Lighting Technician:* Don Yamasaki, Alen Rodriguez. *Rigging Gaffer:* Mike Van Woert. *Key Grip:* Marlin E. Hall. *Second Grips:* John Lubin, Howard Hagadorn. *Dolly Grip:* Nick Papanickolas. *Assistant Film Editors:* Saul Saladow, Reine-Claire. *Music Editor:* Thomas Milano. *Supervising Sound Editor:* John Leveque, Gordon Ecker. *Sound Editors:* Michael E. Yawn, Kim Secrist, Hector Gika, Bob Bradshaw, Anthony Milch, Rocky Moriana, John Kwiatrowski, Glenn Hoskinson, Bruce Fortune, Don Warner. *Assistant Sound Editor:* Steven Gerrior. *Supervising ADR Editor:* Becky Sullivan. *ADR Editor:* Holly Huckins. *Assistant ADR Editor:* Lee Lemont. *Sound Effects Recordists:* Gary Bluter, John Davis. *Foley Supervisor:* Scott D. Jackson. *Foley Artists:* John Roesch, Katy Rowe. *Foley Editors:* Shawn Sykora, Leslie Gaulin, Steve Schwaibe. *Production Coordinator:* Karen Shaw. *Production Accountant:* Susan Montgomery. *Assistant Accountant:* Jeff Kloss, Jay Roberts. *Assistant Production Secretary:* Joan Wellman. *Assistant to Mr. Carpenter:* Loraine Coutin. *Assistant to Mr. Chase:* Angela Kaye. *Assistant to Ms. Hannah:* Lana Opp Morgan. *Office Assistants:* Julie Shaw, John Labib. *Production Runners:* Seth Miller, Scott Rosencrans. *Casting Associate:* Susan Peck. *Location Manager (San Francisco):* John Lehane. *Location Manager (Los Angeles):* Lisa Blok Linson. *Assistant Location Manager:* Dan Gorman. *Stunt Coordinator:* Jeff Imada. *Lead Man:* Mike Higelmire. *Swing Gang:* John Scott, Gary Kudroff, Luigi Muganero, William Wright. *Construction Coordinator:* Bryan Belair. *Construction Foreman:* Doug Rosenberger, Steven Fuller, Ted Haims, Dan Pemberton, Tom Lifsey. *Construction Coordinator (San Francisco):* L. J. Van Perre. *Construction Foreman (San Francisco):* Alan J. Meyer. *Transport Coordinator:* Keith Dillian. *Transportation Captain:* Randy Luna. *Helicopter Pilot:* Jim Deeth. *First Aid:* James Bakeman. *Craft Services:* Steve M. Miliotti. *Stand-by Painter:* Barbara Murphy. *Unit Publicist:* Anne Reilly. *Caterer:* Pazzo Services. *Negative Cutter:* Donah Bassett and Associates. *Color Timer:* Ray Martin. *Titles and Opticals:* Pacific Title. *Special Visual Effects:* Industrial Light and Magic. *Visual Effects Producer:* Ned Gorman. *Digital Effects Supervisor:* Stuart Robertson. *Key Visual Effects Camera Operator:* Marty Rosenberg. *Optical Photography Supervisor:* Bruce Vecchitto. *Visual Effects Art Director:* Mark Moor. *Computer Graphic Supervisor:* Doug Smythe. *Model-shop Project Supervisor:* Ted Krzanowski. *Matte Painting Artist:* Chris Evans. *Chief Visual Effects Editor:* Bill Kimberlin. *Animation Supervisor:* Wes Ford Takahashi. *Visual Effects Camera Operator:* Ray Gilberti. *Visual Effects and Plate Coordinator:* Camille Cellucci. *Chief stage Technician:* Michael Olague. *Rotoscope Supervisor:* Ellen Mueller. *Camera Assistant:* Michael Santy, Carl Miller, Ken Koblenzer. *Digital Effects Artists:* Barbara Brennan, Gregory Gorsiski, Jim Hagedorn, Laurel Klick, Greg Maloney, Thomas J. Smith. *Computer Graphic Animators:* Stephen Rosenbaum, Scott E. Anderson. *Optical Camera Operator:* Keith Johnson, James Lim, Kenneth Smith. *Effects Camera Photographer:* Steve Reding. *Visual Effects Editor:* Tim Eaton, Ron Fode. *Optical Line-up:* Jennifer Lee, Thomas Rossetter, Kristen Trattner. *Rotoscope Art:* Sandy Houston, Terry Molatore. *Effects Animators:* Jay Cotton, Chris Green. *Stage Technicians:* Bob Finley, Jr., Dan Michalske, Craig Mohagen, Chuck Ray. *Action Prop Performers:* Rob Cooper, Mark Siegel. *Stop Motion Animators:* Harry Walton. *Chief Model Makers:* Steve Gawley, Chris Goche, Chris Reed. *Conceptual Design:* Benton Jew. *Digital Scanning:* Joshua Pines, James M.

Goodman, Jill Brooks. *Engineering Services:* Mike Mackenzie, Shannon Cassidy. *Visual Effects Assistant:* Vicki Engel, Sandra Almond Williams. *Visual Effects Production Liaison:* Dennis Michelson. *Matscenes:* Effects Associates, Inc. *Matte Supervisor:* Jim Danforth. *Miniature Construction:* The Garden of Allah. *Thermal Imaging Hardware:* Willow Peripherals. *Computer Effects Supervisor:* Steve Grumette. *Computer Graphics:* Doug Zeffer, Brett Bentley. *Stunts:* Simone Boisseree, Alin Olinee, Brad Bovee, Cris Thomas-Palomino, Troy Brown, Chuck Picerni, Jr. Kurt Bryant, Louis J. Ramirez, IV, Kerrie Cullen, Chad Randall, Jeff Dasraw, John Robotham, Shane Dixon, Dan Rogers, Jim Hatty, Thomas Rosales, Jr., Jimmy Jue, Bill Saito, Henry Kingi, Jeff Smolek, Garry McLarty, Cheryl Wheeler-Dixon, Dick Ziker. *MPAA Rating:* PG-13. *Running Time:* 99 minutes.

"He has the perfect profile. He was invisible before he was invisible."— Agent David Jenkins plots to bring Nick Halloway in from the cold.

SYNOPSIS: Pursued by secret government agents, an invisible Nick Halloway sets up a video camera in an electronics storefront and tells his story on tape. Slowly, he explains how everything started one Tuesday in March…

A visible Nick Halloway goes to his club in San Francisco and meets up with a beautiful friend-of-a-friend, Alice Monroe, a documentary filmmaker who is recently back from Brazil. They hit it off immediately and have a romantic encounter in the ladies' room. Nick realizes he is in love, but Alice is not so sure. They arrange to meet for lunch on Friday, and Nick proceeds to drink himself into a stupor.

The next morning, a hung-over Nick arrives at the Magnascopic building for a dull business meeting. Sick with a headache, he lies down in an out-of-the-way office. As he sleeps, something goes terribly wrong in a control room nearby. An experiment has gone awry because of a spilled cup of coffee. Molecules fluctuate and alarms blare. The building is evacuated, but a sleeping Nick is left behind unnoticed. Parts of the building then become invisible, and when Nick awakens, he is invisible too.

Assigned to investigate the case is a slippery black operations agent code-named Scorpion, also known as David Jenkins. He realizes immediately that an invisible man could be a valuable secret agent for American national security interests both domestic and overseas. He rushes to Magnascopic to capture Halloway, who has panicked and knocked himself unconscious by running into an invisible wall. As Nick is carted to the ambulance, he overhears members of Jenkins's team talking about experiments that will be conducted on him. He refuses to trust Jenkins, who claims that Nick is in a state of molecular flux, like the building itself. Nick escapes, and Jenkins attempts to apprehend him as the entire Magnascopic building vanishes.

Chased across San Francisco, Nick hides in his dining club. He then decides to pursue Dr. Wachs, the one man at Magnascopic who may be able to help him. He intercepts Wachs in a public park and shows him that he is invisible. An upset Dr. Wachs explains that his research had nothing whatsoever to do with invisibility; it was a freakish, random accident that cannot be recreated without years of preparation and millions of dollars. Jenkins's men attack Nick, who flees the park and rips off his clothes, becoming progressively more invisible. Meanwhile, Dr. Wachs is apprehended and murdered by Jenkins.

Halloway then decides to turn the tables on his pursuers, and he goes to their offices to listen in on their plans. He listens to their surveillance reports and remains in Jenkins's office far into the night. Jenkins detects him when Nick yawns, and the spy proceeds to offer Nick a job. He wants him to be a secret agent, an American operative who can commit assassination without chance of capture.

Nick escapes from Jenkins and leaves San Francisco. He travels to his friend George's house in Marin County. There, he has groceries delivered (on George's account) and decides on a strategy: He will become the invisible tycoon, playing the stock market and amassing a fortune. This plan goes awry, however, when George and his wife arrive at the beach house, along with Alice Monroe and an obnoxious playboy named Richard. The new arrivals find evidence of an intruder: a fully stocked refrigerator and a recently used fireplace. Nick soon reveals himself to Alice when she is alone. Meanwhile, Jenkins is put under pressure by his superior to find the invisible man.

When George and his friends leave the beach house, Alice remains with Nick and applies cosmetics to his invisible face so he can be seen. They go out to a restaurant on a date, and Alice suggests seeking help from Washington. When Jenkins arrives, in force with helicopters and dozens of operatives, Alice and Nick flee to the train station. A downpour begins and Nick becomes a glowing silhouette in the rain. The couple goes to a motel to make love, and the next morning they board a train bound for Mexico. However, the train is intercepted by Jenkins. Alice is captured and Nick attempts to escape, but he is shot with a tranquilizer dart. Falling unconscious, he jumps from the speeding train into a river far below a bridge.

After recovering, he makes his videotape and sends it to Jenkins. He promises to surrender himself if Alice is released. If Alice is not released, Nick will release the videotape to the authorities.

The switch is made, and Alice is released, but the invisible Nick has double-crossed Jenkins. Nick and Alice nearly make good their escape, but Jenkins is dogged in his pursuit, even though this operation has been officially terminated by his superior in the government. Nick and Jenkins have a final confrontation on a San Francisco rooftop, and only the invisible man survives. Nick and Alice leave America for Switzerland,

where Nick spends his days skiing. Meanwhile, Alice prepares for the imminent birth of their child.

COMMENTARY: John Carpenter's 1992 stab at Alfred Hitchcock–style intrigue and action (à la *North by Northwest*) opens quite promisingly. There is a dramatic pan across the San Francisco skyline (not unlike the view from atop a city in the opening of *Psycho* [1960]), and Shirley Walker's bombastic overture suggests a grand, epic adventure in the style of many cinematic adventures past. Then, Carpenter's camera watches as a highly organized, well-equipped spy ring tightens its net around a mysterious, unseen (and unseeable) subject. The combination of music, location and action raise viewer interest, and add a level of suspense to the proceedings. Throw into this mix a strong voice-over narration courtesy of the ever-laconic Chevy Chase ("In a way it was all Alice's fault; maybe if I hadn't met her that night...") and a mannered yet thoroughly effective performance from Australian Sam Neill which can only be described as worthy of James Mason, and *Memoirs of an Invisible Man* indeed sports the ingredients necessary to be a successful film venture. In its opening moments, *Memoirs* seems like another one of John Carpenter's trademark genre-blenders: one part H.G. Wells, one part Alfred Hitchcock, and one part Chevy Chase comedy. From a man who has melded western and urban adventure (*Assault on Precinct 13*), the road movie and science fiction film (*Starman*), and the alien invasion with political satire (*They Live*) this move does not feel like a betrayal or misstep.

Unfortunately, by the time *Memoirs of an Invisible Man* has reached the 30 minute mark, all early hopes of a John Carpenter masterpiece have been shot down by a confused screenplay that never manages to find the right tone. That established, the film remains a brilliant showcase of invisible-style special effects. To wit: A piece of gum seems to chew itself; a large building's molecular composition is compromised and

**Chevy Chase as everyman Nick Halloway, a latter-day invisible man in *Memoirs of an Invisible Man*
(1992).**

significant parts of the structure become invisible while others remain visible; rain falls
on the invisible man, creating an eerie but
somehow beautiful silhouette; the invisible
man sheds his clothes a piece at a time in an
exciting chase through a park. All of these
moments are captured beautifully by Car-

penter and the special effects team at ILM,
but they fail to enliven a story which at times
seems uncertain about exactly what it in-
tends to highlight thematically.

Part of the problem is surely Chevy Chase
himself. Strangely, it is not the problem one
might suspect when this performer comes to

mind. Chase is renowned for appearing in wacky films that indulge his penchant to go crazy. Think of the Chase repertoire: There's the overstimulated, psychotic air traffic controller of *Modern Problems* (1980), the deranged, overbearing suburbanite of *National Lampoon's Vacation* (1987), the many varying faces of *Fletch* (1990), the devil-may-care yuppie of *Nothing but Trouble* (1992). In each of those adventures, Chase *is* the film: a larger-than-life presence who dominates over virtually everything else. His mugging, his delivery, his reactions are what make his comedies work. Yet in *Memoirs of an Invisible Man*, Chase has seemingly sublimated both his desire and his uncanny ability to take charge of a scene and send it one wacky direction or another. Instead, he is excessively low key in this picture, and he plays every scene (regardless of its requirements) with such conviction and seriousness that he actually kills the comedic aspects of the film. Yet, importantly, the film is supposed to be funny, at least at a some critical points. Chase's performance is thus at odds with the story's karma: He is too serious, too heavy in mind and spirit to carry a film that should, above all else, be fun. This must be the most angst-ridden invisible man in history. Not even for a moment does Nick Halloway seem to get off on the idea that he can be a voyeur, an observer, a trickster. To him, invisibility is instantly an albatross and the result is that the comedy sequences fail to inspire or inform.

The screenplay of *Memoirs of an Invisible Man* reiterates how important it is to be seen, to be acknowledged. Yet the film does not build to this realization in any substantive way. It might have been more interesting dramatically for Nick Halloway to be thrilled with his invisibility initially, and then realize how isolating a condition it really is. Instead, there is no arc to the character, no dramatic path which leads Nick to his realization that being seen is important, even necessary. The screenplay is also muddled in its own perception of its central character.

Nick is important to Jenkins because, in the words of Jenkins, "he was invisible before he was invisible." In other words, Nick was already isolated, alone, and unremarkable before the accident at Magnascopic. Yet, strangely, this observation does not jibe with the life of Nick Halloway dramatized by the film's earlier scenes. He is a playboy skier, a *player*. In one of the first scenes he is seen talking on the phone with a ski lodge manager as he reserves a room with a king-sized bed "just in case." This bit of business seems to acknowledge his personal charisma and wealth, two factors that would certainly keep him from being "invisible" to the modern world. A "player" can only be so invisible. Secondly, other characters repeatedly note that Nick Halloway is unique. His secretary (Rosalind Chao) marvels at his ability to bluff his way through an important report. And more pointedly, "Nick's way too narcissistic to kill himself," his friends state in his (invisible) presence. Again, there is a contradiction here: Is the man invisible, or is he narcissistic and smug and thus highly visible?

Secondly, if Nick is supposed to have been "invisible" all along, then invisibility actually brings him visibility. For the first time he is important, even though he cannot be seen. If he was invisible before and he deplored it, now, as an invisible man, he could be a celebrity, a circus attraction, as Jenkins tells him. This idea is highly unappealing to Nick, and yet he states how important it is to be seen, to be acknowledged. What better way than to go on the talk shows? All of these details fail to create a consistent personality for the film's central character.

In a sense, *Memoirs of an Invisible Man* seems to be an attempt to do another *Starman*. It is a film in which a strange man and a tender-hearted woman flee government authorities for fear that the man with the special identity will be tortured and abused by American officials in the name of national security. And again in *Memoirs of an Invisible Man*, Carpenter stresses the thematic point of *Starman*: that love and human connection is the most important thing in life. It is the only thing that makes invisibility bearable, because no one is invisible if he or she is loved. That is a noble point to make, perfectly in keeping with past Carpenter films such as *Prince of Darkness* and *Starman*. Yet too much time is spent on the pursuers in *Memoirs of an Invisible Man*, and the relationship between Nick and Alice must share the spotlight not only with the spy pursuit subplot, but all the invisibility gimmicks. What's more (or less), Chevy Chase's character is not nearly so appealing an outsider as Jeff Bridges was. Where Starman was innocent and open, Nick Halloway is paranoid and dour.

Memoirs of an Invisible Man does have some interesting points. As in *Prince of Darkness*, science is ultimately a failure. The accident which causes Nick's invisibility is comical: A cup of coffee spills on a computer and causes a firestorm of sparks and short circuits. From this random happening, one can easily conclude that Carpenter sees science as a fragile thing on which the smallest or most random happenstance can have dire effects. Secondly, there is a terrific scene two-thirds of the way through the picture in which a kid delivering groceries to Nick acts like a jerk because he thinks that nobody is watching him. This is reminiscent of that old truism: Character is what you have when nobody is watching you. Had the film delved further into this subplot, with Nick as a kind of laconic commentator on human behavior, characteristics and manners, the film might have been a very unique updating of the invisible man mythos rather thoroughly mined in the '30s and '40s in such pictures as *The Invisible Man* (1933), *The Invisible Man Returns* (1940), *The Invisible Agent* (1943), and *The Invisible Man's Revenge* (1944). Instead, *Memoirs of an Invisible Man* treads familiar territory while updating only the special effects set-pieces of invisible men past. Although in one scene, Carpenter restages the

unbandaging of the invisible man as seen in the Claude Rains 1933 picture, it loses its horrific effect here. It is a visual homage, but to little effect. Rains played a madman out to terrify. Chase plays an average man out to maintain his anonymity yet disturbed by his invisibility.

Perhaps the scene that rings most powerfully in the mind after a viewing *Memoirs of an Invisible Man* is a dream-sequence which seems to define the horror of invisibility rather well. Nick dreams of himself as a playboy sportsman. He enters his bedroom to find Alice (Daryl Hannah) waiting for him in a black negligee. As Nick unwraps his robe, he is shocked to see that his *groin* has inexplicably become invisible. This funny and bizarre sequence captures a sense of honesty and fear that the rest of the film never manages to emulate. What Halloway fears in invisibility is the loss of his masculinity. It is an honest assessment, and one that the rest of the film never really follows up on.

A genuine misstep in John Carpenter's career, *Memoirs of an Invisible Man* is a film that finds its director at the mercy of big studios and bigger stars. Although he did his best to bring a Hitchcockian style and grace to the film, it is obvious that he was overruled in certain departments. There is less of John Carpenter in this film than any of his other movie projects. Perhaps this is not a surprise, since the teaming of comedy icons with genre directors tends to have disastrous consequences for everyone. In 1983, Richard Pryor's presence in *Superman III* effectively killed the franchise. Likewise, the Eddie Murphy–Wes Craven 1995 venture *Vampire in Brooklyn* emerged as one of the weakest films in both men's careers. John Carpenter is a victim of the same problem in *Memoirs of an Invisible Man*. The strain of producing a satisfactory adventure while at the same time satisfying the Chevy Chase crowd was a hurdle perhaps impossible to overcome. He was brave, if not foolhardy, for trying.

In the Mouth of Madness (1995)

Critical Reception

"The movie starts out with lots of intriguing ideas, and then sidesteps most of them in order to provide a special effects side show that looks inspired by the *Nightmare on Elm Street* series. *Wes Craven's New Nightmare* ... covers similar ground in a much more original way — and it has better special effects." — Roger Ebert, *The Chicago Sun-Times*, February 3, 1995.

"A clever analysis of its genre, knowingly crafted with conventions, stereotypes and even a few ludicrously cheap scares ... with Carpenter ready, willing and able to shift gears effortlessly between the hoary and the horrific ... the kind of adult horror film that will give new hope to those longing to be scared at movies again." — David E. Williams, *Sci Fi Universe*: "Big Mouth: John Carpenter's Lovecraftian Return to His Roots Marks the Welcome Return of a Master," January 1995, pages 66–67.

"A confused and confusing jumble of high-minded fear and low-brow cheap thrills ... *In the Mouth of Madness* sinks under its own pretensions, trying for a cerebral scare that is not very scary.... Carpenter seems to have been undecided as to what this film should have been." — Rick Garman, *Magill's Cinema Annual 1996*.

"There's plenty of eerie atmosphere in the first hour, as solitary bicyclists keep turning up in the wrong places.... But the second half of the movie is mostly a collage of bloody axes, decaying faces and vague references to an apocalypse that's both overfamiliar and about as frightening as acid indigestion." — Lawrence Toppman, *The Charlotte Observer*: "Horror of *Madness* Turns to Comedy," February 3, 1995.

"What transforms *In the Mouth of Madness* from a fright into a disappointment is its reliance on that old standby: Real versus Imagined.... *In the Mouth of Madness* poses all the obvious questions without encouraging any particular desire to know the answers ... all of which leaves *In the Mouth of Madness* stranded — a minor, oddly whimsical work, its narrative energy scattered and lost in blind alleys. You are left with those few, perfect Carpenter instants when the mood turns palpable, and fear begins to form like ice." — Anthony Lane, *The New Yorker*: "Scare Tactics," February 13, 1995.

"One of John Carpenter's most accomplished works as a director ... a thinking man's horror film which Carpenter directs with an auteristic style. Stark, horrific images are skillfully blended with intriguing ideas about horror writing." — John Stanley, *Creature Features*, Boulevard Books, 1997, page 263.

Cast and Credits

CAST: Sam Neill (John Trent); Jurgen Prochnow (Sutter Cane); Julie Carmen (Linda Styles); Charlton Heston (Jackson Harglow); David Warner (Dr. Renn); Bernie Casey (Robbie); John Glover (Dr. Sapir- stein); Peter Jason (Insurance Fraud Perpetrator); Frances Bay (Mrs. Pickman); Wilhelm Von Homburg (Simon); Kevin Rushton (Guard #1); Gene Mack (Guard #2); Conrad Bergschneider (Axe Maniac); Marvin Scott (Reporter); Katerine Ashby (Receptionist); Ben Gilbert (Young Teen); Dennis

O'Connor (Cop); Paul Brogren (Teen); Sharon Dyer (Homeless Lady); Sean Ryan (Bicycle Boy); Lance Paton (Little Boy); Jacelyn Holmes (Little Girl); Hayden Christenmen (Paper Boy); Garry Robbins (Truck Driver); Sean Roberge (Desk Clerk); Robert Lewis Bush (Man); Louise Beaven (Old Lady); Cliff Woolner (Bus Driver); Deborah Theaker (Municipal Woman); Chuck Campbell (Customer); Carolyn Tweedle (Nurse); Thom Bell (Farmer); Mark Adrians (Window teen); Jack Moore-Wickham (Simon's Song); Group of Kids (David Austerwell, Richard Kohler, Kieran Sells, Laura Schmidt, Kyle Sheehan, Daniel Verhoeven, Kevin Zegers, Katie Zegers); Paul Gordon (Stand-in); Teresa Lovegrove (Stand-in).

CREDITS: New Line Productions Presents a John Carpenter film. *Music:* John Carpenter and Jim Lang. *Executive Producer:* Michael DeLuca. *Associate Producer:* Artist Robinson. *Visual Effects Supervisor:* Bruce Nicholson. *Special Make-up Effects:* Robert Kurtzman, Gregory Nicotero, Howard Berger. *Production Designer:* Jeff Steven Ginn. *Film Editor:* Edward A. Warschilka. *Director of Photography:* Gary B. Kibbe. *Written by:* Michael DeLuca. *Producer:* Sandy King. *Director:* John Carpenter. *Unit Production Manager:* John Danylkiw. *First Assistant Director:* Artist Robinson. *Second Assistant Director:* Adam Druxman. *Stunts:* Lloyd Adams, Randy Butcher, Shelley Cook, Paul Chiu, Rick Forsayeth, Shane Harvey, Jeff Imada, Danny Lima, Risa Litwin, Steve Lucescu, Dwayne McLean, Ken Quinn, Robert Thomas, John Stoneham, Jr., Helen Scott, Alison Reid, Rick Parker, Buck Randal, Bryan Renero, Paul Rutledge, John Stead, Anton Tyukodi, R. Ruddell Weatherwan. *Casting:* Back Seat Casting Associates. *Canadian Casting:* Ross Clydesdale. *Executive in Charge of Production:* Adrianna A. J. Cohen. *Stunt Coordinator:* Jeff Imaga. *Script Supervisor:* Benu Bhandari. *Assistant to John Carpenter and Sandy King:* Karin Costa. *Second Assistant Director:* Stuart Williams. *First Assistant Camera:* Michael Hall, Robert McDonald. *Second Assistant Camera:* Kevan

Dutchak. *Camera Operators:* Richard Scaini, Carolyn Cox. *Gaffer:* Tim Evans. *Co-Gaffer:* Kevin Alanthtaite. *Best Boy Electric:* Brian Montague. *Electricians:* Michael Galbraith, Delroy Jarrett, Robe Conde, Kenneth Wyke. *Rigging Gaffer:* R. L. Hannah. *Key Grip:* Mark Manchester. *Best Boy Grip:* Donald Ferguson. *Dolly Grip:* Michael Kirilenko. *Grip:* Ron Jolevsky. *Rigging Grips:* John Scott MacDonald, Cesare DiGiuliuo. *Sound Mixer:* Owen A. Langerin. *Boom Operator:* Dennis Bellingham. *Art Director:* Peter Grundy. *First Assistant and Director:* Gordon M. Barnes. *Second Assistant Art Director:* Karen M. Clark. *Art Department Assistant:* Scott Morrison. *Illustrator:* Joseph F. Griffith, Jr. *Draftsmen:* Stephen M. Berger, William F. O'Brien. *Set Decorator:* Elinor Rose Galbriath. *Assistant Set Decorator:* Danielle Fleury. *Lead Set Dresser:* Peter P. Nicolakakos, Clive Thomasson. *Set Dresser:* Carlos Caneca. *Prop Maker:* Vic Riglen. *Assistant Props:* Ron Hewitt, Graeme B. Gossage. *Men's Costume Supervisor:* Robert Bush. *Women's Costume Supervisor:* Robin Michel Bush. *Women's Set Costumer:* Delphine White. *Men's Set Costumer:* Derek J. Baskerville. *Additional Costumer:* Ann Tree Newson. *Wardrobe Production Assistants:* Cody Carpenter, Daniel Darces. *Make-up Artist:* Donald J. Mowat. *Hair Stylist:* James D. Brown. *Special Effects:* Martin Malivoire Pictures; Ted Ross. *Dogs:* Alvin Animal Rentals. *Dog Trainers:* Anton Tyukodi, R. Ruddell Weatherwan. *Production Consultant:* Cheryl Miller. *Assistant Production Consultant:* Shelley Boylan-Wakefield. *New Line Coordinator:* Lori Keith Douglas. *Production Supervisor:* Casie Marie Carleton, Siobhan Hegarty. *Production Assistants:* Kwame Parker, Lesley Boylen. *Production Controller:* Paul Prokop. *Production Accountant:* Rachel E. Prentiss. *Production Accounting Assistants:* Tish Johnson, Vikki Dodds. *Location Manager:* Brian Campbell. *Locations, PA:* Greg Holmgren. *Still Photographer:* Shane Harvey. *Unit Publicist:* Ernie Malik. *Construction Coordinator:* Donald Vendewater. *Head Carpenter:* Henry Ilola. *Head Scenic Artist:* Ian

Helms. *Senior Painter:* Robert C. Ramacciotti. *First Aid:* Lisa Greco. *Craft Services:* Starcraft Services, Inc., Tanya Shuster, Mary Nichols. *Caterer:* Film Capers. *Extras Casting:* Scott Mansfield. *Transportation Coordinator:* Neil Montgomery. *Transportation Captain:* Frank Tenaglia. *Head Driver:* G. Savoy. *Drivers:* Jazz G. Helie, Dave Staples, W. Doyle, Michael Doyle, Frank Eldridge, John Muir, Lonre Frederick, Jeff Peebles. *Video Playback:* Donald J. Woods Productions. *Executive in Charge of Post Production:* Joe Fineman. *Post Production Supervisor:* Rick Keeley. *Assistant Film Editor:* Paul C. Warschilka. *Second Assistant Film Editors:* Richard Sellmer, Cary Flungold.

Special Visual Effects: Industrial Light and Magic, a Division of Lucasfilm Ltd. *Visual Effects Producer:* Kim Bromley. *Visual Effects Art Director:* Mark Moore. *Computer Graphics Supervisor:* Carl N. Frederyk. *Computer Graphics Animators:* Evan K. MacDonald, Rob Coleman. *Rotoscope Artists:* Rebecca P. Henkes, Jack Mongovan. *Digital Paint Artist:* Lisa Drostoya. *Digital Composer:* Mark Holmes. *Technical Assistant:* Patrick Neary. *Computer Graphics Assistant:* Ron Brown. *Still Photographer:* Sean Casey. *Film Scanning:* Joshua Pimes, Randall K. Bean. *Optical Supervisor:* Kenneth Smith. *Optical Line-up:* Jennifer Lee. *Optical Camera Operator:* James Lim. *Optical Scanning Coordinator:* Lisa Vaughn. *Visual Effects Editor:* Bill Kimberlin. *CMX Editor:* Mary Serafini. *Assistant Editor:* David Tanaka. *Motion Control Camera Operator:* Ray Gilberto. *Camera Assistants:* John Gazdik, Robert Hill. *Electrician:* Brad Jerrell. *Chief Model maker:* Giovanni Donovan. *Model Maker:* Lorne Peterson. *Executive in Charge of Production:* Patricia Blau. *Production Accountant:* Michael Halsten.

Special Effects, Make-up: KNB. *KNB Crew:* Gino Crognale, John Bisson, David Smith, Mike Trcic, Brian Rae, Shannon Shea, Evan Campbell, Brent Armstrong, Claire Manion, Heidi Snyder, Kathy Clark, Bill Hunt, Kevin McTurk, Karrie Aubuchon, George Engle, Mark Tavares, Doug Noe, Donna Salmon, Jeremy Padow, Heather McKee. *Mechanics:* Jeffrey Edwards, Mark Goldberg, Micki Heussen, Thomas Quinn. *Puppeteers:* Tony Chappell, Mark DeLuca, Katy Limmer, Stacy Smith, Aaron Woods. *Coordinators:* Erin Haggerty, Susan Mallon.

Sound Effects: Weddington Productions. *Supervising Sound Editor:* John Dunn. *Supervising ADR Editor:* Harry B. Miller. *ADR Editor:* Andrew C. Patterson. *Dialogue Editor:* Stephanie Black, Howard M. Neiman. *Sound Editors:* Donald Flick, Matthew C. May. *Foley Editor:* Rick Mitchell. *First Assistant Editor:* Galen Goodpaster. *Assistant Editor:* Damon D. Cohoon. *Sound Design:* John Papisil. *Foley Mixer:* Jeff Courtic. *Effects Mixer:* Ron Bartlett. *Supervising Re-Recording Mixer:* Jeffrey Perkins. *Re-Recording Mixers:* Robert Thirlwell, Ken S. Polk. *Recordist:* Larry Hoki. *Negative Cutter:* Sharon MacGeeney. *Color Timer:* Paul O'Driscoll. *Music Recorded at:* Knobworld. *Titles:* Title House, Inc. *Prints by:* Film House. *MPAA Rating:* R. *Running Time:* 95 minutes.

———

"More people believe in my work than believe in the Bible."— Sutter Cane to John Trent

"Every species can smell its own extinction…. Within ten years, maybe less, the human race will just be a bedtime story for their children … a myth, nothing more."— Trent contemplates the end of the world.

———

SYNOPSIS: John J. Trent is dragged kicking and screaming into a padded cell in an asylum overseen by the not-quite-normal Dr. Sapirstein. Trent claims that he is not insane, a claim echoed by all the lunatics around him in the institution. Soon, a visitor comes to Trent's cell: a dark shadow who warns him that "this is not the end." The figure then vanishes, after insisting that Trent "read the end" of his latest work.

Soon, Dr. Renn, a government appointed psychologist, visits the incarcerated John Trent. Trent proceeds to tell the doctor how he arrived at the asylum. He reveals that he was once a free-lance insurance investigator who pinpointed fraud. His last case, the one that has driven him to this unfortunate state of mind, involved the world-famous, best-selling horror author, Sutter Cane.

It all begins (in flashback) when Trent's sometimes employer/sometimes friend at the insurance company, Robbie, enlists his help one afternoon over a cup of coffee. Sutter Cane has disappeared, while still owing his publisher, Arcane Books, the manuscript of his latest work: *In the Mouth of Madness*. Suspecting that the disappearance was part of an insurance scam or publicity stunt orchestrated by the publisher, Trent takes Robbie's case and begins to learn more about the unusual genre writer. Trent meets Arcane Publishing president Jackson Harglow and Linda Styles, editor of all of Cane's novels. Trent also encounters Cane's agent: a paranoid schizophrenic with an axe who, for some reason, is bent on killing Trent! Despite this incident, Trent still believes the author's disappearance is a publicity stunt, especially since Cane's novels are provoking such hysteria among their readers. To Trent, it's just another pop phenomenon like the hula hoop.

After buying several Cane books at a local bookstore, Trent makes a discovery that seems to confirm his belief. When cut up and arranged in a special sequence, the covers of Cane's novels create a map which pinpoints the location of a secret town called Hobb's End. As Cane had written *The Hobb's End Horror*, Trent is sure this is part of Cane's bizarre publicity stunt. With Linda Styles in tow, he decides to visit Hobb's End to find the missing manuscript and expose Sutter Cane as a fraud.

En route to the New Hampshire hamlet, Trent and Styles discuss Cane's work. Trent thought it was effectively written trash, and Styles was frightened by it because it suggested a different reality where insanity had supplanted sanity as the norm. After a long night drive, in which Styles repeatedly sees a strange bicyclist roaming the deserted highway, their car arrives at Hobb's End, a charming old-fashioned New England town.

After checking in at the Pickman Hotel, an establishment Styles recognizes from Cane's novels, Styles and Trent continue their debate about Cane's work. Styles begins to grow increasingly uncomfortable, expressing the notion that Cane's work is not just fiction, it was *real*. Though Trent dismisses this notion, he and Styles soon find their way to a giant black church, one in which (in Cane's novels) evil supposedly dwells. At the same time, a mob of townspeople arrive at the church looking for their stolen and transformed children. In response, the enigmatic Cane suddenly reveals his presence in the sanctuary and unlooses a group of devil dogs on the mob.

After fleeing the scene, Styles becomes more agitated. What they have just witnessed at the church is a scene from *In the Mouth of Madness*, the book Cane was working on when he disappeared. In that novel, an ancient otherworldly evil was breaking into the human world. The takeover started in Hobb's End with the children, and then proceeded to the rest of the human race.

Stubborn as ever, Trent refuses to believe that reality is mirroring bad fiction. To prove him wrong, Styles goes back to the church and meets with Cane. He forces her to read his book — what he calls "the new Bible" — all the way through. The result is catastrophic: After being exposed to *In the Mouth of Madness*, Styles begins to go insane. When Styles returns to Trent she warns him not to read the book, and she exclaims that she is "losing" herself to madness.

By now even the skeptical Trent is having difficulty explaining away all of these weird happenstances: a painting in the lobby that inexplicably changes composition every time someone looks at it, a hideous multi-tentacled creature dwelling in the basement, and so forth. He attempts to leave Hobb's End,

"I think, therefore you are!" Sutter Cane (Jurgen Prochnow) is the god of a bold new Lovecraftian world in *In the Mouth of Madness* (1995).

but he is confronted by Cane, who demands that the insurance scam investigator deliver his new book, the evil manuscript, to the world at large. Realizing that insanity would consume the world, Trent refuses, but Cane forces Trent's hand. Tearing himself apart like a page in a book, Cane opens a rip into the Stygian otherworld. Up from the depths of a very real Hades come the centuries-old creatures who have been longing to live again through humanity. With the book in hand, Trent flees the church and escapes back into reality.

Upon his return, however, Trent finds that reality is not what it used to be. Although he first dumps the manuscript in the middle of the road and later burns it, it keeps coming back to him like a loyal pet. In fact, Jackson Harglow reports to Trent that the book had been delivered months earlier and that it has been out on the market for seven weeks! Worse, a movie is due to premiere that very weekend! Trent begins to lose his grip on sanity at the same time that a violent epidemic sweeps the civilized world. *In the Mouth of Madness*, by Sutter Cane, is causing its readers to change into horrible monsters. Hoping to stop the horror, Trent takes an axe to the readers of the new book ...

... and ends up in the insane asylum. Dr. Renn does not believe Trent's story of strange transformations and a book that cause insanity, and he leaves the premises. Soon, however, the revolution of evil comes even to the remote institution. As the human world ends and a demonic world begins, Trent escapes his prison and goes to see a nighttime showing of *In the Mouth of Madness*, directed by John Carpenter. He watches himself on screen, debating with Styles (who has been written out of reality) about fiction, fantasy and objective reality. As he watches the terror unfold on the silver screen, Trent begins to change, his humanity slipping away from him, inch by inch.

COMMENTARY: *In the Mouth of Madness* might be considered the fourth (and presumably final) movement of John Carpenter's so-called "cerebral" horror exploration. *The Fog* (1980), *The Thing* (1982) and *Prince of Darkness* (1987), the earlier installments, all suggested the possibility of a world "invaded" by evil. Though science diagnosed the problem (in the case of *The Thing* and *Prince of Darkness*) and the ramifications of these invasions in the earlier films, science was found to be untrustworthy as a method of detecting and destroying evil. Self-sacrifice

(MacReady's, Catherine Danforth's) stopped the onslaught of terror before humanity was destroyed in some instances.

In the Mouth of Madness, by contrast, deliberately exists outside the world of science, and it gives the audience no likable protagonist (and thus no surrogate) who is willing to die to save mankind. On the contrary, the film's "hero," John Trent, gives up his humanity and surrenders to the encroaching evil as easily as he would go to see a matinee. In this film, the last vestige of humanity dies glued to the silver screen as he chortles and chomps on popcorn! Unlike Danforth or MacReady, Trent no longer views man as a species worth saving, and in *In the Mouth of Madness*, man is finally replaced by something else, something evil. All man (represented by Trent) can muster here is cynicism, disbelief, anger, hatred and a nasty ironic belly laugh. It is an ugly view of our race.

Consider John Trent. He is the typical Carpenter anti-hero like Snake Plissken or Napoleon Wilson. He is openly disdainful of everything and everyone. He hates the past (antiques are derided as "old shit"). He disapproves of the horror genre as "trash." Worse, he has no faith in humanity and goes so far as to say, "The sooner we're off the planet, the better." The only thing that Trent does take pleasure in is exposing human beings as frauds, in proving, literally, that "anybody's capable of anything." So hateful and disdainful of man is John Trent that even after his confrontation with evil and Sutter Cane, he is still bothered by humanity's sunshine image of itself. "Oh no, not the Carpenters too!" he croaks as "We've Only Just Begun" is piped into his padded cell. Yet despite Trent's blatant cynicism and misanthropy, characters like him have been effective before in genre films because, essentially, they let mankind see itself from an "outside" perspective.

In 1968, for instance, astronaut and humanity critic George Taylor (actor Charlton Heston — Jackson Harglow of *In the Mouth of Madness!*) traveled to a planet of intelligent simians and found himself in a position to defend humanity from the new social order of the *Planet of the Apes*. Despite his misgivings about man, he mounted his defense brilliantly and the character consequently became one of sci-fi film's greatest protagonists. John Trent, confronted with a new social order, is noticeably *unable* to mount a defense for mankind. He is shattered by the notion that his beliefs are wrong. "We are *not* living in a Sutter Cane novel!" he continues to stubbornly insist, beyond all reason, and finally he takes solace in a lonely insane asylum: the only "safe" place in the whole, insane world.

Thus the misanthropic Trent is not heroic in any traditional sense of that word. He is cowardly. Because Trent's indictments of man remain constant and because he never shifts to defend man's perspective, he remains one of the coldest and most remote of all Carpenter characters. Like the film he inhabits, Trent hates human beings. And, frankly, it is hard for the viewer to accept so total an attack on the species. *In the Mouth of Madness* represents Carpenter's ultimate ennui and irritation with humanity, a far cry from his *They Live* (1988) in which humanity took up arms to bravely reclaim its heritage from another invasion of evil. And, unlike *Starman* (1984), *Prince of Darkness* (1987) or even *Memoirs of an Invisible Man* (1992), there is no love in the universe of *In the Mouth of Madness*. Trent, who makes clumsy and ugly sexual advances on Linda Styles, is incapable of love. So, apparently, is the human race — at least according to Carpenter's vision — and that fact makes *In the Mouth of Madness* a bitter film to swallow. It is by far the least accessible of John Carpenter's films.

Yet, as Birack said in *Prince of Darkness*, the hardest things to hear are those ideas which we don't personally agree with. Despite its dark tone, *In the Mouth of Madness* follows through on all of its nihilistic tendencies with consistency and style. It is not a happy or likable vision of man, but Carpenter has done an extraordinary job with the picture nonetheless. His themes may be difficult to "buy into" if one believes that mankind is worth saving, yet his motion picture is admirable in its relentlessness and internal consistency. Although many critics and viewers found the film confusing and contrary, a closer examination shows that *In the Mouth of Madness* is no more and no less than it claims to be: an apocalyptic story about the end of human life on Earth; a meditation about what it *might* be like to be the last sane human in a world where insanity is the norm. Carpenter himself had a different take. He felt the film was a classic western: a story about a hero who goes in search of someone and ends up learning about himself. While that may be stretching it a little, considering the complexity of *In the Mouth of Madness*, that description nonetheless provides viewers a description to hold in their thoughts as they watch the picture unfold.

Amidst all the criticism of man as a species, Carpenter also hacks away at another interesting theme, one that found vogue in *Wes Craven's New Nightmare* (1994). In *New Nightmare*, Freddy Krueger burst out of his fictional films and into the reality of Wes Craven, Robert Englund, Heather Langenkamp and John Saxon. It was an exercise in self-reflexivity, and at the same time it offered a spirited defense of horror as a genre. In *In The Mouth of Madness*, Carpenter presents a world where fiction and reality are also irrevocably intertwined through Cutter's books and Trent's interpretation of "objective" reality. Carpenter's picture, like Craven's, involves characters in a story realizing that they are, indeed, characters in someone else's story. They think they have an independent life only to find that life is a more complex, a much more Pirandellian notion than they suspected. In *New Nightmare*, the "piece" of which Heather Langenkamp is a part is Wes Craven's script for a new *Nightmare on Elm Street* sequel. In *Madness*, it is Sutter Cane's new novel, titled, of course, *In the Mouth of Madness*, where John Trent dwells. Some audiences found this

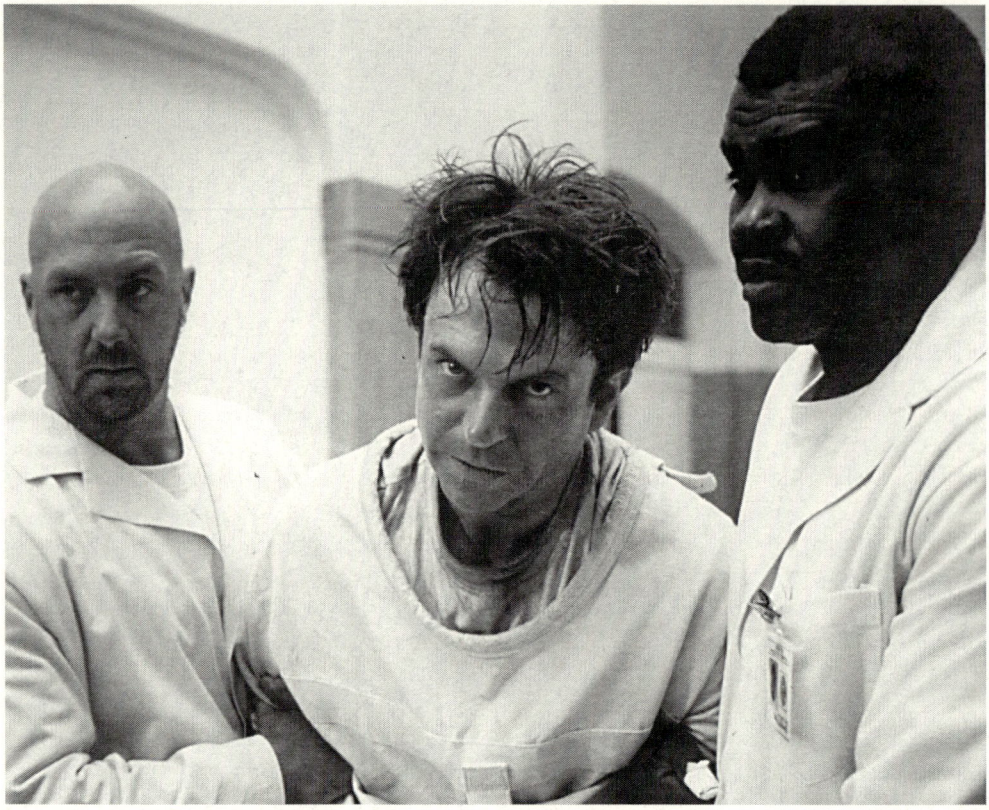

Relegated to an insane asylum, the cynical John Trent (Sam Neill) finds that reality isn't what it used to be in *In the Mouth of Madness* (1995).

conceit confusing in the Carpenter picture because they were asked to revise what they knew to be reality. Which came first, Sutter Cane or John Trent? Was John Trent a "real" person, manipulated by Sutter Cane, or was he a character in a book all along? These questions lent *Madness* a thematic complexity that was interesting, yet simultaneously offputting to audiences in search of a linear horror film.

What Carpenter proves most forcefully with *In the Mouth of Madness* is that the creator of a work of art (whether it be a film or a Sutter Cane novel) ultimately controls that universe. To Roger Ebert, the film violated a set of internal "rules." It made no coherent, logical sense: There was no order to it, only disorder and contradictions. What Ebert may not have seen was that John Carpenter is the Sutter Cane of the film. He is God in the uni-

verse of this film, and he defines the rules, just as Sutter Cane made up his own universe. In the act of creation, the writer can write people "out" (as Cane does to Linda in the film's conclusion), alter plotpoints (Trent delivers the manuscript to Harglow even though he has no memory of it), or define the color of the sky ("My favorite color is blue," Cane asserts, turning the world blue in one stroke). The "Creator" (whether it be God, Carpenter or Cane) shoulders the ultimate control in the universe he creates, and thus the only consistency that matters in that universe is the creator's consistency. So, oddly, *In the Mouth of Madness* is really a film primarily about the creative process, and how "reality" can be twisted, perverted or recreated by authors, directors, and deities. Did God write a book in which we are the characters? Did Sutter Cane?

While tantalizing, this concept is not a particularly new idea. Indeed, Rod Serling handled the same notion in an episode of *Night Gallery* entitled "Midnight Never Ends." That 1971 story asserted that the characters in a play, though they seemed to have individual lives, were actually at the whim of a fickle writer, an invisible God-like creation forever tapping away on an out-of-sight typewriter. *In the Mouth of Madness* falls into the same genre as that vignette: It asks audiences to not only see but understand the mechanisms behind the creative process. The story of *In the Mouth of Madness* makes sense, but only if one looks behind the curtain to see Carpenter manipulating the people, just as Cane manipulates reality within the plot. This plot-point is frequently addressed through Cane's dialogue, such as the lines, "You are what I write" and "I think, therefore you are." Still, this is fairly complex for the average audience hoping simply to be scared by a good yarn.

In *Wes Craven's New Nightmare*, Craven asserted that evil would become loose in society when horror was suppressed by those who thought it was a bad influence. *In the Mouth of Madness* shares that point of view. In Carpenter's picture, evil grows when people lose "the ability to know the difference between reality and fantasy." In other words, all the politicians out there in the world who argue that horror movies cause violence have lost the capacity to see film, even horror film, as literary drama. They "blame" horror films for society's ills, when in fact art tends to reflect society, not vice versa. When books "cause" violence in people, there is already something wrong with those people, and that is the time and the opportunity for the evil to slip through the cracks — back into *our* world. So, where some critics saw Sutter Cane as an indictment of Stephen King, the opposite is actually true. *In the Mouth of Madness* does not attack the Stephen Kings of the world: It attacks those who would suppress the writings of Stephen King for some misguided belief that they will generate violence with their provocative writing.

In the Mouth of Madness is also rather inaccessible to mainstream audiences because it is, basically, a thesis on horror writing and films. Its success depends largely on an audience's knowledge of the genre, and it demands that one bring this knowledge to any reading of it. Obviously, the story is an homage to H.P. Lovecraft, yet would most audiences know who he is, or what he wrote about? Would they understand the nature of Lovecraft's particular brand of evil, of the "undescription?" There are several beautiful Lovecraft-like passages of dialogue in *In the Mouth of Madness*, such as the one which describes the black church in Hobb's End:

> This place had once been the seat of an evil older than mankind and wider than the known universe. It was a place of pain and suffering beyond human understanding.

It is a creepy description, and one that adds to Carpenter's cerebral horror. It is a horror not generated through violence, a musical "stinger," or a supernatural monstrosity: It is a monster purely in the intellectual sense. One has to hear the words, grasp what they describe, and picture the image of that old evil, that Stygian other-universe. Because film is primarily a visual art form, viewers may find it troubling when Carpenter calls on his audience (in this film as in *The Fog*) to listen to *words*, to let the vocabulary wash over them and play on their minds. Again, this is an admirable technique, but it requires two things of the viewer: a knowledge of Lovecraft, and a willingness to be an active participant in the filmgoing process.

To understand *In the Mouth of Madness*, a knowledge of horror is really quite necessary. For instance, the film's structure mirrors that of *Invasion of the Body Snatchers* (1956) in that it opens *in medias res*, at a late point of attack. Like the hero of Don Siegal's paranoid nightmare, John Trent arrives at an insane asylum in a state of panic, screaming about the end of the world. Then the doctors come along and listen to his story, and that story unfolds before the eyes of the audience. The Sutter Cane book, like the extra-terrestrial pods of *Body Snatchers*, is the catalyst which transforms normal human beings into dangerous monsters akin to the *Body Snatchers'* pod people. It is also helpful to know that Dr. Trent's physician, Dr. Sapirstein, is named after the villainous character played by Ralph Bellamy in *Rosemary's Baby* (1968), or that Hobb's End is a name culled from Nigel Kneale's *Quatermass* series, or that Charlton Heston is in the film because of his role as defender of mankind in such end-of-the-world pictures as *Planet of the Apes* (1968), *Beneath the Planet of the Apes* (1970), *The Omega Man* (1971) and *Soylent Green* (1973). Taken separately, each of these details may seem unimportant, but taken together they all add richness to the tapestry of *In the Mouth of Madness*. It is a knowledgeable film which demands that its audience be knowledgeable, and alert.

On a purely visceral level, *In the Mouth of Madness* has its share of non-cerebral horror moments as well. Carpenter is a master at making us jump, and he knows how to generate suspense and terror. Early on, there is a sequence in which Styles spots a young man who is feverishly riding a bicycle on a highway during the middle of the night. It is a scary image because it is one we can all relate to. The idea of being alone at night in a car when a stranger suddenly appears requires no knowledge of the genre: just experience

in day-to-day reality and the unspoken, subconscious language of nightmares. As Styles's car rushes past the cyclist, we get a shot of him in the rear-view mirror and he is bathed in the red hues of the car's taillights for a brief instant before blending irrevocably with the darkness. Was the fleeting image just Styles's dream, her hallucination? Who knows — but virtually everybody has been alone on the road at night and experienced the fear of that unearthly hour when the mind starts to play tricks on itself. When the image of the bicyclist repeats in *In the Mouth of Madness*, it becomes horrific on a full-blown scale: The same "young" bicyclist is now ancient. When he says that Sutter Cane won't let him "out," an image is conjured of this bicyclist riding that same stretch of road for perhaps a hundred years. It really does generate chills.

In the Mouth of Madness is a challenging film. Although filled with grotesque imagery, it tends to be a much more intellectual style of film than Carpenter's early, spare work like *Halloween* or *Escape from New York*. It is deft in its devotion to its theme, but at the same time it is off-putting and sometimes difficult to follow. And since it has no likable lead to take us through this tour of a dark, frightening world, the audience at times feels left behind. *In the Mouth of Madness* is not John Carpenter's best film, but it is one that demands to be respected. A viewer hoping to "get it" should be prepared to sit up straight and pay close attention. And more than one viewing is definitely in order.

Village of the Damned (1995)

Critical Reception

"John Carpenter's best horror film in a long while is one scarifying trip down memory lane. This is a knowing remake of the spooky 1960 English film.... *Village of the Damned* has one of the eeriest opening sequences in horror history, and Mr. Carpenter stages it with relish.... The remake is mostly more sly than frightening…. Mr. Carpenter sticks to re-staging the original story with fresh enthusiasm and a nice modicum of new tricks." — Janet Maslin, *The New York Times:* "Demons' Eye Problems Compound Creepiness," April 28, 1995.

"[The film] benefits from its video release, since the small screen befits this movie's made-for-cable feel…. The only problem is comparing this version with the first: Reeve's hero lacks the fly-in-the-ointment flair of George Sanders in the original. At least Alley scores with her government agent Woman in Black." — J.R. Taylor, *Entertainment Weekly* #296: October 13, 1995, page 86.

"Well-intentioned as it is … something is missing. Perhaps it is that in the nineties filmmakers such as the talented Carpenter are so interested in paying homage to the sixties that all they can do is mimic the original — the film is a bit shallow — as thin and gossamer as the cloud that overtakes Midwich. The lack of depth in the film can be seen in its campy dialogue and its discrepancies." — Kirby Tepper, *Magill's Cinema Annual 1996.*

"Carpenter and screenwriter David Himmelstein retain the main themes of this effective plot, and some of the most memorable scenes…. But they do add a number of new elements — most of which, unfortunately, only serve to muddy the waters. Needless and undeveloped subplots dissipate the clean suspense of the original, and the exponential increase in violence and gore cannot conceal this." — Gary Kamiya, *The San Francisco Examiner:* "The Eyes Have It in Horror Remake," April 28, 1995.

"This remake … is so bad, so unimaginative, so poorly directed, you end up gawking at the screen entranced. What was everyone thinking?… Director Carpenter, who knows how to pile on the gore or at least make us jump … appears to have been on a sedative — or the film was taken out of his hands at the last minute. All the fright moments seem cut short except for the truly appalling emoting. Even Kirstie Alley, whose main battle here appears to be with the bulge … can't cheer us up." — Brandon Judell, *Critics Corner,* 1995.

"Has John Carpenter lost his mind or just his talent?… Carpenter, whose batting average is dipping dangerously low, shows no grasp of character development, plot line or time passage…. As he does all too often, Carpenter insists on using his own overly familiar heart-pulse-and-cheesy-synthesizer score. And please forget the Hitchcock-like cameos, John: I've seen Hitchcock, and you, sir, are no Hitchcock." — Richard Harrington, *The Washington Post,* April 28, 1995.

Cast and Credits

CAST: Christopher Reeve (Dr. Alan Chafee); Kirstie Alley (Dr. Susan Verner); Linda Koslowski (Jill McGowan); Michael Pare (Frank McGowan); Mark Hamill (Reverend George); Meredith Salenger (Melanie Roberts); Peter Jason (Ben Blum); Constance Forslund (Cally Blum); Pippa Peartree (Sarah); Karen Kuhn (Barbara Chaffee); Thomas Dekker (David); Lindsey Haun (Mara); Cody Dorkin (Roger); Trisalee Hardy (Julie); Jessye Quarry (Dorothy); Adam Robbins (Isaac); Chelsea Rene Simms (Matt); Renee Simms (Casey); Danielle Wiener (Lilly); Hillary Harvey (Mara at 1 year); Bradley Wilhelm (David at 1 year); Jennifer Wilhelm (David/Mara at 4 months); Buck Flower (Carlton); Squire Fridell (Sheriff); Darryl Jones (CHP); Ed Corbett (Chief Deputy); Ross Martineau (Younger Deputy); Skip Richardson (Deputy); Sharon Iwai (Eye Doctor;) Robert L. Bush (Mr. Roberts); Montgomery Hom (Technician); Steve Chambers (Trooper #1); Ron Kaell (Trooper

#2); Lane Nishikawa (Scientist); Michael Halton (Station Attendant, Harold); Julie Eccles (Eileen Moore); Lois Saunders (Doctor at Clinic); Sidney Baldwin (Labor Room Physician); Wendolyn Lee (Nurse #5); Kathleen Turco-Lyon (Nurse #3); Abigail Van Alyn (Nurse #1); Roy Conrad (Oliver); Dan Belzer (Young Husband); Dena Martinez (Young Wife); Alice Barden (Woman at Town Hall); John Brebner (Man at Town Hall); Ralph Miller (Villager); Rip Haight/John Carpenter (Man at Gas Station).

CREDITS: *Universal Pictures Presents an Alphaville Production. Casting:* Reuben Cannon. *Music:* John Carpenter and Dave Davies. *Visual Effects Supervisor:* Bruce Nicholson. *Co-Producer:* David Chackler. *Edited by:* Edward A. Warschilka. *Production Design:* Rodger Maus. *Director of Photography:* Gary B. Kibbe. *Co-Executive Producers:* James Jack, Sean Daniels. *Executive Producers:* Ted Vernon, Shep Gordon, Andre Blay. *Based on the book: The Midwich Cuckoos* by John Wyndham *and* the 1960 screenplay by Sterling Silliphant, Wolf Rilla, George Barclay. *Screenplay:* David Himmelstein. *Producers:* Michael Preger, Sandy King. *Director:* John Carpenter. *Unit Production Manager:* Jeffrey Sudzin. *First Assistant Director:* Artist Robinson. *Second Assistant Director:* Christine P. Della Penna. *Stunts:* Bobby Bass, Robin Bonaccorsi, Troy Brown, Kurt Bryant, Hal Burton, Rocky Capella, Steve Chambers, Eugene Collier, Paul Crawford, Laura Dash, Lisa Dempsey, Tom Dewier, Shane Dixon, Jon Epstein, Al Goto, Brian Imada, Jeff Imada, Brad Lackey, Peter Lai, Kevin Larson, Billy Lucas, John Lucasey, Johnny Martin, Mike Martinex, Jeff Mosely, Jim Nickerson, Alan Oliney, Chuck Picerni, Jr., Denny Pierre, Jim Paslof, Mic Rodgers. *Casting:* Back Seat Casting Associates, Sandy King, Cheryl Miller, Peter Jason. *Children's Casting:* Reuben Cannon and Associates. *Casting Associate:* David Giella. *Casting Assistant:* Helen Taylor. *San Francisco and Extras Casting:* Hayes & Van Horn Casting. *Stunt Coordinator:* Jeff Imada. *Script Supervisor:* Benu Bhandari. *Camera Operators:* William Boatman, Dusty Blauvelt, William Waldman. *First Assistant Camera:* Steve Peterson. *Second Assistant Camera:* Brian Kibbe. *Loader:* Ron Peterson. *Gaffer:* Tim Evans. *Best Boy Electric:* Brian Evans. *Electricians:* Jeff Gilliam, Mark A. Lewis, Joseph G. Emanuele, Gary R. McClendon. *Generator Operator:* Ray Appel. *Key Grip:* Harry Rez. *Best Boy Grip:* Jason Rez. *Grips:* Dane Spelman, James Beaumonte. *Sound Mixer:* Thomas Causey. *Boom Operator:* Joe Brennan. *Cableman:* George Reinhardt. *Women's Costume Supervisor:* Robin Michel Bush. *Men's Costume Supervisor:* Bob Bush. *Women's Set Costumer:* Barbara Hartman-Jenichen. *Men's Set Costumer:* Michael C. Lynn. *Key Make-up Artist:* Ken Chase. *Make-up Artist:* Leslie Newcomb. *Key Hair Stylist:* Terry Baliel. *Hair Stylist:* Charlotte A. Gravenor. *Art Director:* Christa Munro. *Set Decorators:* Don DeFina, Rick Brown. *On Set Dresser:* Don Watson. *Set Dresser:* Jody Weisenfeld. *Swing Gang:* Dave Watson, James DiStefano. *Prop Master:* Vic Petrotta, Jr. *Assistant Props:* Kenny Montante, Gary E. Rolof. *Construction Coordinator:* Dwight Williams. *Construction Foreman:* Peter J. Bowman. *Laborer:* Ken Emanuele. *Carpenters:* Sean J. Wright, Ken Olson. *Head Painter:* Teresa Neilson. *Painters:* Bret Deyer, Vola Ruben. *Greensman:* James Burke. *Mechanical Special Effects Coordinator:* Roy Arbogast, Bruno Van Zeeboreck. *Special Effects Assistant:* Keith Urban. *Animals Provided by:* All-Star Animals. *Trainer:* Kathleen Sidjakov. *Production Coordinator:* Cheryl Miller. *Assistant Production Coordinators:* Gina R. Gilberto, Roberta Franklin. *Second Assistant Director:* Charles K. Simmers, III. *Assistant to John Carpenter and Sandy King:* Karin Costa. *Office Production Assistants:* Sean M. Sobczak, Caitlin Phillips. *Set-Production Assistant:* Deanna Stadler, Tracy Lee Eischmann, Sean D. Whitler. *Production Auditor:* Glenn Nicol. *Key Assistant Accountant:* John Alfred. *Second Assistant Accountant:* Elizabeth A. Gray. *Location Manager:* Stefanie Bleet. *Location Assistant:* Russel Draeger. *Studio Teachers:* Christine Bloomingdale,

Lucy MacSwain. *Unit Publicist:* Ernie Malik. *Still Photographer:* Sidney Baldwin. *First Aid:* Christopher Desmond, Paul Crimmins. *Craft Services:* Jimmy's Craft Services. *Caterers:* The Arrangement. *Transport Coordinator:* Ron Hardman. *Transport Captain:* H. Richard Sanders. *Drivers:* Vance Argento, Vaugh R. Bladen, Ben Davis, Felix Ghitescu, Ed Glenn, Gary Hardman, Bill Hogue, Cliff Johnson, Ed Keener, Mike Lowe, David Parker, Richard A. Picconi, Mike Shaw, Gregg Shuman, Murray Staff, Jill Wattles. *First Assistant Film Editor:* Paul C. Warschilka. *Assistant Film Editor:* Ruth Hasty, Michael Mahoney. *Sound Effects Facility:* Weddington Productions. *Supervising Sound Editor:* John Dunn. *Dialogue Editors:* Stephanie Flack, Ron Bartlett. *Supervising ADR Editor:* Julia Evershade. *Foley Editors:* Rick Mitchell, Donlee Jorgensen. *Effects Editor:* Warren Hamilton. *Assistant Sound Editors:* James Murioka, Jeena Phelps, Charles Unger. *Recordists:* Mark Coffey, Matt Beville, Ed Simon, Charlie Ajar, Jr. *Re-recorded at:* Universal Studios Sound Facility. *Re-recording Mixers:* Rick Alexander, Michael C. Caspter, Jim Bolt. *Effects Pre-dub Re-recording Mixer:* Ron Bartlett. *Foley Facility:* Director's Sound. *Foley Assistants:* Paul Holzborn, Bess Hopper. *Foley Mixer:* Jeff Courtie. *ADR Mixer:* Doc Kane. *Loop Coordinator:* Mickie McGowan. *Music Re-recorded and Mixed at:* Cherokee Studios. *Produced by:* The Robb Brothers. *Music Supervisor:* Bruce Robb. *Orchestra Contractor:* John Van Houten.

Second Unit. Second Unit Director: Jeff Imada. *Director of Photography:* Arthur R. Botham. *First Assistant Director:* Christian P. Della Penna. *Second Assistant Director:* Mike Kitchens. *Camera Operators:* Dusty Baluvelt, Jon Kranhouse. *First Assistant Camera:* Vance Piper, John Gazdik. *Second Assistant Camera:* Tony Martin, John Small. *Gaffer:* Jeff Gilliam. *Best Boy Electric:* Joseph G. Emanuele. *Key Grip:* Jason Rez. *Best Boy Grip:* Mark Bolin. *Sound Mixer:* Fred Runner. *Set Costumer:* Paul DeLucca. *Make-up Artists:* Steven E. Anderson. *Hair Stylist:* Donna Dunlop.

Mechanical Special Effects Supervisor: Roy Arbogast. *Special Effects Crew:* Keith Urban, Mike Wood, Richard Wood. *Ambulance:* United Ambulance Service. *Craft Service:* Andrea Record. *Helicopter Unit Pilot:* James Deeth. *Camera Operator:* Jon Kranhouse. *Mechanic:* Doug Postal.

Visual Effects: Industrial Light and Magic. *Visual Effects Producer:* Jacqueline Lopez. *Visual Effects Art Director:* Benton Jew. *Lead Computer Graphic Artist:* Andy White. *Lead Sabre System Artist:* Mark Holmes. *Digital Composing Supervisor:* Dan McNamara. *Visual Effects Editor:* Tim Eaton. *Production Coordinator:* Megan L. Jones. *Sabre System Artists:* Rita Zimmerman, Sheen Duggan. *Sabre Technical Assistant:* Grant Guenin. *Computer Graphic Artists:* Donald S. Butler, Kathleen Beeler, Howard Gertz, Sandra Ford Rapman, Jack Mongovan, Rip Soon Takahashi, Chad Taylor. *Vista Vision Camera Assistant:* John Gazdik. *Digital Timing Supervisor:* Kenneth Smith. *Negative Line-up:* Tim Geideman. *Negative Controller:* Doug Jones. *Assistant Visual Effects Editor:* David Tanaka. *Scanning Operator:* John Whisnant. *Scan Supervisor:* Josh Pines. *Scan Coordinator:* Lisa Van Lott. *Production Assistant:* Andrea Bronzo, Elizabeth Brown. *Computer Graphics Assistant:* Jules Mann, John Torrijos. *CG Senior Production Manager:* Gail Currey. *Video Engineer:* Duncan Sutherland. *Projectionist:* Timothy Greenwood. *Art Department Coordinator:* Jackie Evanochick. *Production Accountant:* Pam Kay. *Communications Engineer:* Dan Howard. *Senior Staff:* Tom Williams, Jeff Mann, Patricia Blau, Jim Morris.

Special Make-up Effects: KNB EFX Group, Inc. *Effects Supervisors:* Robert Kurtzman, Gregory Nicoreto, Howard Berger. *Effects Crew:* Evan Campbell, Shannon Shea, Jeffrey Edwards, Jake McKinnon, Luke Khanlian, Larry Odien, Brian Rae, Karrie Aubuchon, Mark Tavares, Ted Haines, John Bisson, Christopher Robbins, Ron Pipes, Jon Fedele, Rob Hinderstein, Henrik Van Ryein, Nick Morra, Bill Hunt. *Effects Coordinator:* Erin Haggerty. *Live Action Miniatures:* Slagle

Minimotion Inc. *Supervisor:* Pete Slagle. *Director of Photography:* Frank Harris. *First Camera:* Gary Anderson. *Lighting:* Gene Lehfield. *Key Grip:* Rick Tucker. *Model Makers:* Dave Humpert, Greg Tracer. *Set Builders:* Robert Frank, Greg Steffen. *Set Dresser:* June Slagle. *Payroll Services:* Entertainment Partners. *Insurance:* RHH/Ruben Insurance Services, Inc. *Lighting and Grip Equipment:* Hollywood Rental Company, Inc., Matthews Group. *DTS Engineer:* Mark Lewis. *Color:* Foto-Kem Lab. *Negative Cutter:* Sharon McGeeney. *Color Timing:* Mato. *Opticals and Titles:* Howard Anderson Company. *MPAA Rating:* R. *Running Time:* 99 minutes.

"God said let us make man in our own image after our likeness. But image does not mean outer image, or every statue or photograph would be man. It means the inner image, the spirit, the soul ... but what of those in our midst who do not have individual souls or spirits? They have one mind that they share between them, one spirit. They have the look of man but not the nature of mankind."—A suspicious Reverend George contemplates the children of Midwich.

SYNOPSIS: Something silent and colossal flies over the idyllic California town of Midwich early one morning. Dr. Alan Chaffee is awakened by strange sounds, but he dismisses the incident.

It is a big day for Midwich. Frank and his wife, Jill, prepare for a school fair. Frank drops Jill, the school principal, off at the school and then leaves town to pick up a helium tank to inflate the balloons. Elsewhere in town, Cally waits with anticipation for her husband Ben to come home from a foreign trip. Also out of town on this day is Dr. Chaffee, conducting rounds at Butler County Hospital.

At the school fair, everybody mysteriously collapses at precisely 10:00 A.M., slipping into unconsciousness. Upon his return to Midwich, Frank falls unconscious too, and his truck crashes. Frank dies in the blaze. The authorities soon arrive, along with Dr. Susan Verner, to detail this strange phenomenon. It seems the coma zone has a definite boundary: everything existing beyond a certain radius slips into unconsciousness. At the roadblock beyond the zone, Dr. Chaffee arrives, worrying about his wife, who is at home in Midwich.

That night at 6:00 P.M., everybody in Midwich awakens. Everything seems fine, but within days many women in town discover they are pregnant, including Cally (whose husband was not in the country to be the father), Jill, Mrs. Chaffee, and the young Roberts girl, who claims to be a virgin. Dr. Verner gets a grant to investigate the black-out and the pregnancies. She offers all the affected families $3,000 dollars a month to see the pregnancies through, and she finds many takers. There are no abortions in Midwich.

Nine months later, the children of the black-out are all born at the same time. One is born dead, and Dr. Verner hides the corpse before it can be seen by the populace or the medical staff. Time passes and the unusual children start to grow up. They are cruel and unnaturally bright kids. The leader of the white-haired, unemotional children is Alan Chaffee's child, Mara. Using incredible mental powers, Mara forces her mother to scald herself in boiling stew. Later, Mara's mom commits suicide, unable to cope with the thought that her daughter might be a monster. Dr. Verner continues to check in periodically on the children and she soon realizes that they are capable of reading minds, though Verner is able to block their probing brains somewhat. At the Midwich Clinic, an eye doctor inadvertently hurts one of the children, who seem to share a hive mind, and the children strike back in force, blinding the technician with her own eye drops.

As the years pass, the town of Midwich grows more and more afraid of the strange children, but Jill discovers that her son,

David, is not the same as his brethren. He has some humanity within him, and is beginning to understand the concept of empathy. His "partner" in the hive mind was the child who died at birth, and David feels alone. David visits the grave of the dead baby and meets the Roberts girl there. He reads in her mind that she is suicidal, and he feels for her because they share a common loss — the baby was hers. Meanwhile, Jill suggests to Alan Chaffee that he should take the children out of regular school and teach them humanity.

When the town grows increasingly endangered by the powerful children, Alan moves them to a big red barn outside of town, the very barn where they were born. Still, the children manage to commit horrid deeds, killing the school janitor who made harsh comments against them. Bolstered by David's growing humanity, Alan teaches the children about human physiology and human souls. The children seem unreceptive to the concept of the spirit, but they are grudgingly respectful to Dr. Chaffee.

Chaffee and Verner meet. Verner shows Chaffee the baby's corpse, which is hidden in the basement of the Midwich clinic. It is an alien child. Verner then reveals the existence of other "otherworldly" children in Australia, an Inuit community outside of Anchorage, and one on the Turkish-Iranian border. All the births in each community were preceded by black-outs. An alien intelligence apparently implanted the alien embryos in the parents. Verner then asks Alan Chaffee to put this information in the back of his mind, so the children will not learn what he knows.

At the barn, Mara and Jill clash over the right to choose David's path. Mara wants the boy to continue with the children, but Jill is convinced that David is different than the rest of the alien offspring. Still, he joins the other children as they continue to kill members of the community, including Cally's husband, Ben. Elsewhere, Dr. Verner urgently reports that all the other alien colonies on Earth have been destroyed. Accordingly, she

has been told by the government to pack up and get out of Midwich immediately. Alan is unwilling to give up on the children and leave Midwich behind. Although survival is imperative, he feels adaptation, not warfare, is the key to survival. Compassion, he insists to the cold Mara, is what makes humans great. Without feeling, the alien children are just second rate mimics of a superior organism: human beings.

Mara and the other children plan to disperse immediately and form new colonies in a safe haven. The children intend to leave Midwich that night. Alan realizes he cannot let them leave town, and so he plans to end their killing spree. After the children eliminate the town priest, Dr. Verner and others, the police arrive at the barn and attempt to subdue the children. A bloodbath is the result, and the police are brutally murdered by the telepathic children. Chaffee realizes he is humanity's last line of defense. Allowing David to escape, Chaffee returns to the children with a bomb hidden in his briefcase. As they probe his mind, he blocks their efforts by projecting the image of a brick wall. The children tear down that mental brick wall but discover too late about the bomb behind it. Chaffee and the children die when it detonates.

Outside Midwich, David and his mother plan a new life.

COMMENTARY: *Village of the Damned* is John Carpenter's weakest film. This is an unfortunate surprise, since it is based on Wolf Rilla's classic 1960 original, a movie which remains terrifying to this day. That road map was there to follow, but the remake nonetheless fails to generate the sense of dread and terror so notable in the original. Worse, the remake fails to take into consideration 30 years of controversial debate on birth-related topics such as test-tube babies, surrogate parents, abortions, late-term abortions, and abortion pills. The new *Village of the Damned* resolutely fails to speak to this generation about important topics the way that Rilla's film informed an earlier one.

Yet John Carpenter's *Village of the Damned* opens so promisingly. A ghostly shadow from above passes over scenic Midwich. The animals at play in the wild nearby freeze for an instant and then run away, as if aware of the evil from the sky. It is a solid opening that contrasts the beauty of nature and of Midwich with eerie alien whispers and a ghostly shadow that will bring evil to a latter-day Garden of Eden. Even better, Carpenter stages the black-out with real style, and quite a bit of ghoulish humor to boot. When the unconscious townspeople awaken at their school picnic, someone sees that Oliver, who always burns the hot dogs at these functions, has himself fallen on the grill and been overcooked!

So far so good, and the film continues to be competent, even snappy and edgy, as characters are established and the ramifications of the bizarre pregnancies are played out. Cally's husband is away, so she shouldn't be pregnant. The town virgin is also pregnant. These scenes play well, and add to the mystery of the scenario, but there are no new truths here, and all of these developments were part of Stirling Silliphant's original screenplay. It is highly unusual that Carpenter would find no new territory to mine in a story brimming with so many possibilities, especially considering his total reworking of *The Thing* in 1982. There he really had something to say, and his version of the story was almost anti–Hawksian, a riveting exploration of paranoia. In *Village of the Damned*, all of the burning '90s questions surrounding the birth and care of infants is ignored. There is no discussion of medical advances, religious pressure to give birth, the abortion argument, or even the notion of a modern-day immaculate conception. Instead, *Village of the Damned* asks its audience to believe that all the women in a liberal California town — every single one of them — would go ahead and give birth to a possibly inimical child because of a considerable stipend from the Federal government!

A new touch in the film, however, is a common dream sequence that the pregnant women all seem to share (like the prophetic dream-message in *Prince of Darkness*) — a few images in which the women, standing against rolling gray clouds, are blown about by an unseen wind. The suggestion is that this common dream convinces the women, at least subconsciously, to see the pregnancy through. One would think that such a bizarre, ominous set of images would have the opposite effect and send the terrified women to abortion clinics! And would none of the women comment to each other about this rather strange dream? Would they not find it unusual that they all had the same dream at the same time? These questions are all glossed over in the rush to get to the glowing-eyed, defiant alien children. Yet by pushing past these issues, Carpenter overlooks the real horror of the film: the *not knowing*.

The time of the pregnancy should have been drawn out a bit so as to generate some sense of suspense, or at least anticipation. Perhaps Carpenter felt that audiences already knew what would come next (evil children) and that such suspense would not work, but that assumption may have been a mistake. After all, Carpenter re-invented *The Thing* while sticking to the basic scenario (a group of men encounter an alien buried in the ice.) Why could he not have re-invented *Village of the Damned* as well?

Sadly, it is with the development of the pregnancy and the follow-up years as the children grow that *Village of the Damned* loses all sense of believability and style. Not because of the nature of the children; not because of the failure to mine topical issues of concern in America; but because there is literally no effort made whatsoever to suggest the passage of time. At least six or seven years pass during this film, yet none of the adults age a bit. No hairstyles or fashions change in the slightest. Had the movie been thought out a bit more fully, a title scrawl might have been inserted to indicate that the "black-out" occurred in 1988. Carpenter could have put his characters in late eighties automobiles, or perhaps had George Bush giving a speech about "no new taxes" on the television. Then, when the story jumped ahead to the maturing of the children, the screen could have had another *Halloween*-style scrawl reading "1995 — NOW." By so resolutely avoiding issues of time and place, *Village of the Damned* loses all verisimilitude. The earlier film avoided this problem by being filmed in black-and-white in an English village that might appropriately be called timeless. It would look the same from 1950 to 1965. Yet the Midwich of the new *Village of the Damned* is different — or it should be. Carpenter's *Village* seems to take no notice that the world now changes rapidly, and that 1995 would not look the same as 1988.

Village of the Damned has other problems with reality as well. The film seems to believe that everybody in the town of Midwich would go to the same church. Maybe that would be true in the remote English countryside in the early 1960s, but certainly not in California in the 1990s! What about Jewish folks? Or Baptists? Or atheists? Why is the *whole* town Catholic? Again, the film seems to exist in an alternate world determinedly unrelated to the reality the rest of us share.

Another strange choice is to totally recreate the look of the alien children from the first film. They all wear platinum white wigs (which look like wigs) and bland, gray sweaters. Why the heavy wool clothing? Why the gray? These were affectations in the first film that came out of the place and time: the English village in the 1960s. The sweaters were not "alien" apparel, they were the logical clothes for people of that time and place to adorn. The new *Village of the Damned* fails to notice that these affectations are totally out of place in '90s America. Did all the parents get together and decide to buy their children gray clothes? How likely is that in a country filled with so much individualism? These problems could have been mitigated in any number of ways. For instance, it could be established that the children have a differ-

ent body temperature than humans, and that is why they are constantly wearing wool. Or, the film could have established that the children *forced* their parents to buy these strange clothes. Yet not a word of explanation is given, and therefore the details do not mesh to form a believable reality.

Even the scare scenes of the new *Village of the Damned* are hokey. A woman screams as she pours painful eye drops into her eyes — a thoroughly comical image when put to film. Worse, the townspeople go after the children carrying torches (again, a sign that the film does not have a good sense of time: this is not 1495), which of course, gives the children the opportunity to make people light themselves aflame. Even the police bloodbath that closes the film is excessive and unnecessary. It is not realistically staged because, by this time in the plot, the children are clearly established as heartless killers. They have murdered mothers, priests and the school janitor. The police are aware of the children's evil, and yet they do not open fire upon their arrival. Instead, they wait patiently for the children to assemble before them in the front yard of the barn so the children can use their telepathic powers on them. It is nonsensical, and it is not scary because it makes no sense dramatically. The scene's nadir occurs when the children somehow manage to wield their telepathic powers on the helicopter pilot circling above them in the sky. How do they do this? Do they see the pilot? Does he see them? If the "eyes" are the window of their power, as the film's imagery seems to suggest, then logically it is necessary to be present to *see* their evil eyes when one is being manipulated.

Village of the Damned is not all bad. Lindsey Haun is impressive as Mara, the leader of the children. Kirstie Alley is a marvel: icy, witty and filled with both conviction and spicy sarcasm. She brings the film some sense of attitude, which it desperately needs. Christopher Reeve is also sympathetic and human as Dr. Chaffee, if not nearly so charismatic as Sanders in the original picture.

Top: A class picture from Wolf Rilla's *Village of the Damned*, circa 1960. *Bottom:* A class picture from John Carpenter's *Village of the Damned*, circa 1995.

Superman meets Lt. Saavik. Christopher Reeve and Kirstie Alley discuss the alien children in *Village of the Damned* (1995).

Perhaps the bottom line with John Carpenter's *Village of the Damned* is that a remake of a classic is really not a good idea unless one has something new to add to it. John Carpenter does a terrific job of restaging the original film, and generating suspense from the final "brick wall" ending, in which the children attempt to dismantle the blocks Chaffee has built up in his mind. Yet he almost could not help doing a good job in this and other such effective scenes: They were *already* effective and powerful in the source material.

Maybe the problem is simply that Carpenter is too respectful of the original film (and the novel by John Wyndham on which it was based). Maybe he felt he did not have the right to tamper with a classic. As a result, there is nothing particularly new or exciting about *Village of the Damned*. Those differences which do exist are mostly aesthetic. The leader of the children is now a girl; the affected town is in California instead of England; there is more blood and guts in the deadly encounters with the children. The

only genuinely new plot development is the inclusion of a child named David, who is perhaps the only alien with a heart. Because his mate died in childbirth, David is not as much a part of the "hive mind" as the other children, and he feels left out. Sadly, this is only a moderately effective subplot, and though it speaks to the notion of peer pressure as David's mother informs the boy that he can do and be whatever he chooses to do and be, it is still not enough of an inspiration to make the film a success.

A *Village of the Damned* remake needed to speak to the issues that confront America today. What if, for instance, one of the mothers chose to have an abortion (and thereby reflected the individual face of America)? What if *her* baby had been David's mate? Then the act of abortion would have been a central topic of the film instead of just happenstance. David and the others would have wondered what his life would have been like if that individual mother had chosen differently. Likewise, what if modern technology had been able to detect that the children were non-human from the start? How would people have chosen then? Would there have been moral reasons to either go through with, or not go through with, the pregnancies? Or, what if a comparison to the immaculate conception and virgin birth of Jesus had been explicitly made? Or what if the alien nature of the babies had only been discovered in the last trimester, bringing up the possibility of late-term abortions? Obviously, *Village of the Damned* could have been a scary *and* relevant picture if an attempt had been made to update the moral underpinnings of the story. Instead, the film plays like an anomaly: a 1960 film colorized and set in modern America.

The soundtrack to *Village of the Damned* is another exceptional Carpenter composition (with Dave Davies) but even so it only really gets cooking too late. As the end credits roll, the music picks up steam, finally endowing the film with a kind of urgency that was missing throughout the picture, an urgency that suggests the battle is not over and that the alien menace is not really destroyed.

In the Carpenter canon, *Village of the Damned* is the most empty film in evidence. Although humanity is lauded (a far cry from *In the Mouth of Madness*) for emotions such as love, and the final victory is again gained only through self-sacrifice, these touches feel more like remnants from the original film than a legitimate theme which Carpenter felt strongly about.

Ironically, John Carpenter's next film would also be a remake of sorts. Like *Village of the Damned*, Carpenter elected to stay close to the source material of *Escape from L.A.* But he provided that 1996 picture with a satiric spin, proof positive that he had re-thought and re-conceived his original *Escape from New York*. If there were evidence of such thought, or any kind of spin on the original *Village of the Damned*, it would have played a whole lot better. As it stands, this 1995 film is surely a lost opportunity. What could have been a great story about modern morality is instead just a collection of gory set-pieces and recycled '60s ethics.

Escape from L.A. (1996)

Critical Reception

"A go-for-broke action extravaganza that satirizes the genre at the same time it's exploiting it … Carpenter launches a special-effects fantasy that reaches heights so absurd that there's a giddy delight in the outrage. He generates heedlessness and joy … as if he gave himself license to dream up anything.… This is the kind of movie *Independence Day* could have been.… Whose heart is so stony it can resist … Kurt Russell and Pam Grier swooping down from the sky … in an attack on Disneyland?"— Roger Ebert, *The Chicago Sun-Times*, August 1996.

"John Carpenter's *Escape from L.A.* … is filled with … Hollywood in-jokes. These sardonic moments go a long way toward keeping afloat a hopelessly choppy adventure spoof.… It succeeds in being frothily diverting.… But for the most part, the film's horror-movie vision of Los Angeles is surprisingly unimaginative."— Stephen Holden, *The New York Times*, August 9, 1996.

"Every time we've seen this director's name above the title for the past 12 years, excepting the guilty pleasure *They Live*, it's been a sign that we're about to ingest something that's not good for us…. *Escape* is a pathetic sequel…. John Carpenter's *Escape from L.A.* should have happened a long time ago."— Lawrence Toppman, *The Charlotte Observer:* "Escape Sequel May Have You Asking 'What Else Is New?'," August 9, 1996.

"Director Carpenter … veils the story in dim lighting and loud peripheral noises that drown out the dialogue. While the general murkiness creates an appropriately somber mood, it also makes the proceedings hard to follow. Whatever city Carpenter uses for the next sequel, let's hope he at least leaves the lights on."— Ralph Novak, *People Weekly*, August 26, 1996.

"A half-crazed, goofy remake with essentially the same plot … The script by director Carpenter, producer Debra Hill and Russell … is at times muddled and not all the gimmicks work so well the second time around…. But so much of *Escape from L.A.* is a gas … that you should be willing to forgive Carpenter his trespasses. Sort of."— John Stanley, *Creature Features*, Boulevard Books, 1997, pages 168–69.

Cast and Credits

CAST: Kurt Russell (Snake Plissken); A.J. Langer (Utopia); Steve Buscemi (Map to the Stars Eddie); George Corraface (Cuervo Jones); Stacy Keach (Malloy); Michelle Forbes (Braxen); Pam Grier (Hershe); Jeff Imada (Saigon Shadow); Cliff Robertson (President of the United States); Valeria Golino (Tuslina); Peter Fonda (Pipeline); Ina Romeo (Blonde Hooker); Peter Jason (Duty Sergeant); Jordan Baker (Police Anchor); Caroleen Feeney (Woman on Freeway); Paul Bartel (Congressman); Tom McNulty (Officer); Bruce Campbell (Surgeon General of Beverly Hills); Breckin Meyer (Surfer); Robert Carradine (Skinhead); Shelly Desai (Cloaked Figure); Leland Orser (Test Tube); Kathleen Blanchard (Female Narrator); Jacket Mescalino (William Pena); U.S. Cleric Justice (David Perrone).

CREDITS: Paramount Pictures Presents, in Association with Rysher Entertainment, a Debra Hill Production. *Casting:* Carrie Frazier. *Music Composed by:* Shirley Walker and John Carpenter. *Costume Designer:* Robin Michel Bush. *Film Editor:* Edward A. Warschilka. *Production Designed by:* Lawrence G. Paull. *Director of Photography:* Gary B. Kibbe. *Produced by:* Debra Hill and Kurt Russell. *Based on Characters Created by:* John Carpenter and Nick Castle. *Written by:* John Carpenter, Debra Hill and Kurt Russell. *Directed by:* John Carpenter. *Stunt Coordinator:* Jeff Imada. *Stunt Players:* Laura Albert, Roshelle Ashana, John Ashner, Rick Avery, Janet S. Brady, William H. Burton, Jeff Cadiente, Damon Caro, John Casino, Mike Caballos, George Cheung, Phil Chong, Eugene Collier, Paul Crawford, Gregg Dandridge, Jade David, Mary Doest, Gary Davis, Richard Duran, Anne Ellis, Danny Epper, John Esobar, Ramiro Gonzalez, Al Goto, Jeff Greblo, Tom Harper, John Hatelee, Toby Holgun, Norman Howell, Sharon Howell, Brian Imada, Dan Inosanto, Steve Ito, Fredd Jinn, Matt Johnston, John Koy, Brad Lackey, Peter Lai, Steven Lambert, Danny Lee, Leo Lee, Al Leong, James Lew, Brad Martin, Steven Martinez, Dwyane McKee, Wayne Montanio, Bennie Moore, Jr., Jimmy Ortega, Manuel Perry, Stuart Quan, Simon Richee, Vernon Ricta, Mario Roberts, Jimmy N. Roberts, Shawn Robinson, Troy Robinson, Gilbert Rosales, Thomas Rosales, Jr., Debi Lynn Ross, Lori Lynn Ross, Eric Stabenau, Chad Stahalski, Nils Allen Stwear, Ray Sua, Keith Tellez, Chris Thomas-Palamino, Mary Torres, Gary Toy, Dan Turner, Terre Turner, David Wald, Danny Wesels, Danny Wong, Roger Yuan. *Unit Production Manager:* David Witz. *First Assistant Director:* Christian P. Della Penna. *Second Assistant Director:* Martin Jeduka. *Supervisor of Visual Effects:* Kimberly K. Nelson.

Production Supervisor: Alexandra Koch. *Art Director:* Bruce Crone. *Set Decorator:* Kathie Klopp. *Script Supervisor:* Benu Bhandari. *Production Coordinator:* Jeffrey Berk. *Assistant Production Coordinator:* Diane Ward. *Camera Operators:* Jud Kehl, Chris Squires, Leo Napolitino. *First Assistant Photographers:* W. Steven Peterson, Steve Ullman, Dominic Napolitino. *Second Assistant Photographers:* Brian Kibbe, John Stradling, Mark Coyne, Ron Peterson. *Still Photographer:* Robert Zuckerman. *Sound Mixer:* Thomas Causey. *Boom Operator:* Joe Brennan. *Cable Person:* John Agalsoff. *Second Assistant Director:* Jason Roberts. *Property Master:* Bill Macsems. *Assistant Property Master:* Kenny Peterson. *Property Assistant:* Michael Hunter. *Weapons Handler:* Lance Larson. *Lead Persons:* Gary Kudroff, Luigi Muscavero. *Assistant Art Director:* William Hiney. *Set Decorators:* Nathan Crowley, Richard Mays, Christopher Nyshong, Patrick M. Sullivan, Jr., Darrell L. Wight. *Art Department Coordinator:* Carol Kiefer. *Illustrators:* Tim Lawrence, Joseph Muso, Giacommo Chiazza, Len Morganti. *Set Dressers:* Glenn Roberts, John Bevan, Jr., Robert Bleckman, Michael Casey, Larry Cornick, Wayne Fisher, Robert Gray, Kurt Hulett, William S. Maxwell, III, Greg Moore, Nick Rymond. *Chief Lighting Technician:* Norman Glasser. *Assistant Chief Lighting Technician:* George Dunagan. *Lighting Technicians:* Patric J. Abaravich, Thomas J. Embree, Marc Marino, Greg N. Cantrell, Christopher Lama, David E. Hengsteler. *Rigging-Lighting Technicians:* Andrew Carroll, Brian Lovell, Allen Marshal, Steven Merjanian. *First Company Grip:* Charles Saldana. *Second Company Grip:* Jan Gould. *Dolly Grip:* Antonio Carrido. *Grips:* Craig Garfield, Douglas Wall, Charles Wayt, Marc Vollmer. *First Company Rigging Grip:* Bud Heller. *Second Company Rigging Grip:* Bobby Zullo. *Rigging Grips:* James Brusseau, Jack Kohltala. *Assistant Editors:* Vaune Kirby Frechette, Richmond Riedel, Paul Murphy. *Supervising Sound Editor:* John Dunn. *Sound Effects Editor:* Donald Fleck, David Whitaker, John Hulsman.

Sound Design: John Puspisini. *Supervising Dialogue Editor:* David Williams. *Dialogue Editor:* Willy Allen. *Supervising ADR Editor:* Robert Ulrich. *ADR Editor:* Zack David, Joe Dorn. *Supervising Foley Editor:* Christopher Flick. *Foley Editors:* Scott Curtis, Scott Jennings, Ted Caplan. *Assistant Sound Editors:* James Moriaka, Michelle Stirber, Courteney Marvin, Daniel S. Irwin. *Digital Sound Editing:* Paramount Pictures. *ADR Mixer:* Bob Baron. *Foley Mixer:* Randy Singer. *Foley Artists:* Ken Dufva, David Lee Fein, Sarah Monat, Robin Harlan. *Voice Casting:* Barbara Harris. *Re-recording mixers:* Steve Maslow, Ron Bartlett, Michael C. Casper. *Score Conducted by:* Shirley Walker. *Orchestrations by:* Lolita Ritmanis, Michael McCuiston. *Musical Preparation:* Bob Bornstein. *Music Contractor:* The Music Team. *Score Recorded and Mixed by:* Robert Fernandez. *Supervising Music Editor:* Thomas Milano. *Assistant Music Editor:* Jeanette Surga. *Assistant to Ms. Hill:* Chris Svoboda. *Assistant to Mr. Carpenter:* Karin Costa. *Assistant to Mr. Russell:* Jim Petti. *Production Assistants:* Christian Clark, Mauritz Pavoni, Erica Pearce, Benjamin Zara, Jeffrey Howard, Cicely Cambrell, Danny Carter, Angelica Sini, Marcus Tapli, Paul Hackner. *Supervising Make-up Artist:* Marvin G. Westmore. *Mr. Russell's Make-up:* Garry Dannis Luddiard, Jr. *Key Make-up Artist:* Kandace Westmore. *Make-up Artist:* Kaori Turner. *Hair Department Supervisor:* Susan Mills. *Supervising Hair-Stylist:* Linda Arnold-Smith. *Key Hairstylist:* Jill Crosby. *Costume Supervisors:* Robert L. Bush, Llandys Williams. *Assistant Costume Designer:* Juan Lopez. *Unit Publicist:* Patti Hawn. *Construction Coordinator:* John Hoskins. *Location Managers:* Kenneth D. Lavet, David Thornsberry, Gregory Alpert, James M. McCabe, Don Garrison. *Assistant Location Manager:* Valerie Jo Burnley. *Transportation Coordinator:* Kenny Searle. *Special Effects Coordinator:* Marty Bresin. *Special Effects Supervisor:* Dale Ettema. *Special Effects Shop Foreman:* Mark Yuricich. *Special Effects Foreman:* Robert Simonkovic. *Special Effects Make-up:* Rick Baker. *Visual*

Effects Supervisor: Michael Lessa. *Visual Effects by:* Buena Vista Visual Effects. *Action Miniatures by:* Sturber Visual Network, Inc. *MPAA Rating:* R. *Running time:* 101 minutes.

"You may have escaped from New York, but this is L.A. ... and you're about to discover that this fucking city can kill anybody!"— Cuervo Jones to Snake Plissken

---

SYNOPSIS: In the year 1998, hostile forces grow strong inside the United States Immorality reigns inside the country, and particularly in the degenerate city of Los Angeles. A fundamentalist presidential candidate predicts that a gigantic earthquake, representing God's wrath, will ravage the sinful city of L.A. before the millennium has ended.

In the year 2,000, an earthquake of such magnitude does occur, splitting L.A. off from the mainland. The fundamentalist prophet then becomes president for life in the new, Moral United States of America. His first order of business in the White House (relocated to Lynchburg, Virginia) is to sign Directive 17: an initiative which will see all moral degenerates lose their citizenship and be deported to the island of L.A., never to return.

In the year 2013, the president faces a threat when his daughter, Utopia, steals a secret weapon, an all important "black-box," and flees to L.A. A recently arrested criminal, the famous Snake Plissken, is brought to the L.A. Deportation station in hopes that he will succeed in recovering the black box where the official rescue team has failed. The president and his cronies, including Commander Malloy, consider the weapon a matter of national security, but Utopia is expendable. Snake does not wish to accept another state-authorized mission, but he has been purposely infected with a designer virus called Plutoxin 7. It is a fast-acting death warrant that will kill him in eight hours unless he returns with the black box and is provided the antidote.

Unable to decline service, Snake is briefed on his mission. Utopia has fled to L.A. to meet with her cyberspace lover, Cuervo Jones. Jones is a power-mad revolutionary, the leader of a group called the Shining Path. His goal is to re-take America for the Third World. Now, with the black box, he has the means to do just that.

After suiting up in stealth gear, Snake pilots a nuclear submarine to the shores of L.A. His submarine sinks after landing precariously on an unstable pier. Now Snake must find a new escape route from the island while simultaneously accomplishing his mission. As Snake makes his way to Mulholland, he is briefly pursued by a middle-aged surfer, Pipeline, who recognizes him as the famous Snake Plissken. Snake lets the star-struck surfer live, and he heads to the Hollywood Bowl to find the last surviving member of the initial government rescue team. Unfortunately, the would-be rescuer is dead and his corpse is being used for target practice by a bunch of skinhead thugs. Undaunted, Snake goes looking for Cuervo on Sunset Boulevard. He intercepts Cuervo's motorcade, and pursues it on a motorcycle. Snake is taken out of the chase by a deadly assault from Cuervo himself, but Snake survives and continues his quest on foot. He soon meets a tour guide of sorts, Map-to-the-Stars Eddie. Eddie warns him not to go to Beverly Hills, but Snake is running out of time and it is the quickest route to Cuervo's headquarters.

Snake is waylaid in Beverly Hills by the surgeon general of Beverly Hills, a cosmetic surgeon who is cannibalizing the body parts of L.A.'s "normal" denizens so the rich and famous (who have had one too many implants) can continue to appear beautiful. Along with Taslina, a beautiful woman who was deported from the mainland for being a Muslim, Snake escapes. Shortly thereafter, Taslina is murdered in a drive-by shooting. Before long, Map-to-the-Stars Eddie has shown up again, this time driving a fancy car. He shoots Snake with tranquilizer darts and delivers him to Cuervo.

When Snake awakens, he finds himself tied to an exercise machine inside of Cuervo's headquarters. Cuervo now controls the black box, the control device of a weapon called the Sword of Damocles. The remote control can activate a ring of satellites high in orbit. Each satellite is capable of generating an enormous electromagnetic pulse — a blast that could darken either a single tank, a country, of if the world code (666) is pressed, even the entire world itself. Snake watches as Cuervo demonstrates the power of the weapon, shutting down the nation's capital in Lynchburg with an electromagnetic pulse. Cuervo then threatens to shut down all of America if a police chopper does not arrive that night to airlift him out of the Happy Kingdom in Anaheim. With few options remaining, the president agrees to Cuervo's terms.

Snake is then escorted to Los Angeles Stadium, where he is to be the entertainment for the evening. He is forced to play a deadly game of basketball wherein he must make a basket every ten seconds. If he fails, he will be shot immediately. Snake wins the game, scoring again and again until he reaches 10 points. Cuervo is outraged by Snake's victory, but the crowd roars with approval. Snake escapes from the stadium and steals the black box. As he makes off with it through a sewer, he is confronted by Utopia. She is afraid of Cuervo and believes he is just as bad as her father. She asks Snake to take her back to the mainland, but Eddie interrupts the proceedings and shoots Snake in the leg. Snake plummets down a sewer pipe and Eddie returns Utopia and the black box to Cuervo. Snake emerges from the sewer and meets up again with Pipeline, the surfer, who is waiting for the ultimate rush: a killer tsunami that is on the way! After surfing his way through the tsunami, Snake hijacks Eddie and teams up with Hershe, Cuervo's ex-partner in L.A.

In Hershe's headquarters, the Queen Mary, Snake learns that Hershe is an old betrayer from a heist in Cleveland. She used to be a man named Car Jack Malone but now she is a beautiful woman with an exceptionally deep voice. Snake and Hershe iron out their differences, and launch an attack on the Happy Kingdom in Anaheim using makeshift hang gliders courtesy of a gang called the Saigon Shadows. The attack on Cuervo is a success, and Snake, Hershe, Utopia and Eddie attempt to flee L.A. in a government chopper. The chopper takes to the air, but Cuervo blows up the rear section with a missile. Though Eddie survives the fire by jumping out of the helicopter, Hershe is killed. With Utopia at his side aboard the burning chopper, Snake at last brings the helicopter to the mainland. He and Utopia jump from it as it hits the ground and explodes.

Almost immediately, the president demands the return of the black box. Snake wants the antidote to the Plutoxin virus first, but he learns that there is no such thing: it was a ruse designed to make him obedient. When the president orders Utopia to be executed, Snake takes action. He types in the world code, 666, on the Sword of Damocles weapon, and plunges the entire planet Earth into darkness. Now neither the president nor the forces of Cuervo Jones will rule the planet. Better than that, man has the opportunity to start over again, without the fearsome technology that has protected recent dictators such as the president of the United States.

Snake Plissken lights up a cigarette, and welcomes mankind back to the *human* race.

COMMENTARY: Howard Hawks remade *Rio Bravo* as *El Dorado* and *Rio Lobo*. He did it with the same star, the inimitable John Wayne, playing a nearly identical role. He *twice* went over the same thematic territory so expertly covered in the source material (*Rio Bravo*). This re-hash of a good story with the same lead actor and the same writer (Leigh Brackett) is a critical part of the Howard Hawks legend, a piece of his ongoing auteur mystique. Presumably, he saw these films as *one* film, as his return to a theme that, for whatever reasons, he found particularly appealing.

Lifelong Hawks fan John Carpenter, when

Snake Plissken (Russell) swoops down on the Happy Kingdom during the climax of *Escape from L.A.* (1996).

confronted with the assignment to make a sequel to his 1981 cult classic, *Escape from New York*, remembered the example of his idol, and subsequently chose the same road. He remade the original picture, rather than offering a continuation of Snake Plissken's adventures in a new story. Though it takes place in a new city, a new state and a new century, *Escape from L.A.* is very much the same game as its progenitor, the *Rio Lobo* to *Escape from New York*'s *Rio Bravo*. And, again, popular Carpenter star Kurt Russell of *Escape from New York*, *The Thing*, and *Big Trouble in Little China* was back in the lead role.

There are a number of reasons for Carpenter's decision to remake *Escape from New York*. First, a marketing poll conducted by Paramount Pictures suggested that most teenagers did not even know what *Escape from New York* was, let alone the identity of one Snake Plissken. Since this demographic would comprise most of the "new" film's audience, Snake had to be reinvented for generation-next. Secondly, by following exactly, plot-point for plot-point, the moves of *Escape from New York*, Carpenter already had an outline for his new film ready to go: All that was required was a little tweaking and a little updating. Thirdly, like Hawks before him, Carpenter could make a good argument for his status as auteur by ransacking and remaking a past glory. As John Wayne once said about a rerun sequence in his Hawks westerns: "It was great once. It'll be great again!"

So, *Escape from L.A.* premiered in August of 1996 and replayed virtually the same central scenario as *Escape from New York*. Below is a chart listing the similarities between these two franchise pictures:

Plot Point	*Escape from New York* (1981)	*Escape from L.A.* (1996)
The Mission	Rescue a U.S. president	Retrieve a top secret U.S. weapon (and in the process, rescue the president's daughter)
The Locale	New York: An island prison where society's convicts have been deported	Los Angeles: An island where society's undesirables have been deported
"Call/Don't Call me Snake"	Snake's *bon mot* to Hauk (Lee Van Cleef)	Snake's *bon mot* to Malloy (Stacy Keach)
Do the mission or die!	Capsules are inserted into Snake's neck that will explode if he does not return from the mission within a set time.	Snake is infected with the Plutoxin 7 virus which will kill him if he does not return from the mission within a set time.
Life clock	Snake is given a life-clock, and suspense is generated from it "ticking down."	Snake is given a life-clock and suspense is generated from it "ticking down."
It'll get you in, but...	Snake enters the city aboard a glider, which falls off the roof of the World Trade Center.	Snake enters the city aboard a submarine, which falls off a pier.
You can't get there with that.	Snake tracks the president with a life monitor, but it leads him to a drunk bum instead.	Snake tracks the rescue team member with a life monitor, but it leads him only to a corpse.
Hey, I know you!	On the island, Snake runs into an old associate who double-crossed him and has taken on a new name: Brain.	On the island, Snake runs into an old associate who double-crossed him and has taken on a new name: Hershe.
The Texas Switch	Snake switches the critical presidential audio tape with Cabbie's music cassette, "Bandstand Boogie," thus humiliating the president.	Snake switches the critical presidential CD with Map-to-the-Stars Eddie's promotional CD, thus humiliating the president.
Let the games begin!	While on the island, Snake is captured by the bad guys and forced to fight in gladiatorial games.	While on the island, Snake is captured by the bad guys and forced to play a life-and-death game of basketball.
I thought you...	Snake is continually greeted in New York with the phrase, "I thought you were dead!"	Snake is continually greeted in Los Angeles with the phrase, "I thought you'd be taller."
The sacrificial lamb	Snake has a brief flirtation with a beautiful woman (in Chock Full O' Nuts) who ends up being killed.	Snake has a brief flirtation with a beautiful woman (Taslina) who ends up being killed.
It's just a flesh wound.	Snake is shot in the leg (with an arrow) but he still escapes New York and engages in deadly fisticuffs with the Duke.	Snake is shot in the leg (with a gun) but he still escapes L.A. and engages in deadly fisticuffs with Cuervo Jones.

Plot Point	*Escape from New York* (1981)	*Escape from L.A.* (1996)
Screw you, world!	At the conclusion of the film, Snake destroys the cassette tape which could save the world.	At the conclusion of the film, Snake plunges the world into perpetual technological darkness with the Sword of Damocles.

This chart should not be misinterpreted to suggest that *Escape from L.A.* is an uninventive motion picture. On the contrary, John Carpenter has done something extremely clever with this remake. He has put a completely new spin on the earlier adventure while simultaneously returning to all the plot-points from the previous film. For instance, in *Escape from New York*, America is depicted as a police state, but it is the prison which represents the trap, the danger. In *Escape from L.A.*, it is clear that Los Angeles, though decadent, is freer than the continental United States. The mainland is an America of no smoking, no drinking, no foul language, no sex (unless you're married), and no red meat. It is an America where non–Christians, specifically Muslims and atheists, are denied their civil rights because of their beliefs. It is a country where the president, echoing Nazi Germany, talks about issuing his "Final Solution." Thus *Escape from L.A.*, like *They Live*, is a politically and socially relevant picture, instead of just another dystopian adventure. And, as in *They Live*, the right-wing conservative forces in America take it on the chin. The president is a cowardly fundamentalist based wholly or at least in part on Jerry Falwell — hence the reference to Lynchburg, Virginia. Carpenter's world in *Escape from L.A.* is also his ultimate nightmare: Right-wing fundamentalists have taken over the country and killed liberty and freedom.

Additionally, *Escape from L.A.* is clearly designed to be a satire. *Escape from New York* had satiric elements, like the Broadway revue in which the song "Everyone's Coming to New York" was highlighted, but the picture could still be read as a straight adventure. That reading is not possible in *Escape from L.A.* Instead, there is a funny poke at Beverly Hills cos-

metic surgeons, a delightful jab at fickle Hollywood agents (like Map-to-the-Stars Eddie) and humorous attacks on right-wing rhetoric. Even the action sequences are not designed to be serious. In *Escape from New York*, Snake had to fight a deadly battle to the death with one of the Duke's thugs. In *Escape from L.A.* he has to ... make 10 baskets or be shot dead. In *Escape from New York* Snake had to get across a heavily mined bridge before time ran out. In *Escape from L.A.*, he has to surf a tsunami with a wacked-out surfer (Peter Fonda) who warns about the dangers of acid rain. Finally, in the climax, Snake launches an aerial assault on the cinematic equivalent of Disneyland. While these scenes are played straight, they are conceived out of humor. And, amazingly, it all works! *Escape from L.A.* is a truly bizarre film that takes a serious character (a Clint Eastwood knock-off as established by the earlier film) and then surrounds him with utter lunacy based on relevant social issues. It really is like *Escape from New York* on acid.

Though it is, arguably, a brilliant conceit to go back to a classic cult film and redefine the entire concept with humor, this controversial approach is also extremely off-putting to the long-time fans of *Escape from New York*. These folks wanted a *new* story, a legitimate sequel to *Escape from New York* which followed Snake through new territory. That 15-year hope was thoroughly crushed by both Carpenter's repetition of *New York* story elements and his departure into humorous terrain. But again, long-time Carpenter watchers should realize that he does exactly what he wants when he makes a film. He picks projects that appeal to him personally. Apparently, he had no interest in making a straight sequel to a work he had already covered rather thoroughly. Instead, he brought back a be-loved character and a beloved concept and put a whole new, satirical spin on the material. Was Carpenter aware that he was repeating plot elements? Of course. Near the climax of the film, he has Malloy (Stacy Keach) say to Snake: "You know, you're getting very pre-dictable!" What an eloquent way of stating the obvious. Yet, on the same front, Carpenter imbues his old story with new excitement by layering it with satire and social commentary.

Escape from L.A. also features a subplot which was missing from *Escape from New York*. In the remake, there is an impressionable young woman named Utopia. She is the president's daughter and Cuervo's lover. She rails against the "corrupt theocracy of lies and terror" perpetrated by her father, only to realize that Cuervo is every bit the tyrant her father is. Utopia is perfectly named, for she seeks Utopia and is unable to find it. She is thus a surrogate for America's youth (and perhaps Carpenter as well). She is searching for a place on Earth where there is freedom and liberty. Neither the establishment nor the counter-establishment can please her. She thus chooses a third option: Snake Plissken.

When Snake destroys five hundred years of progress and technology, he consequently saves Utopia from the electric chair. His choice to start over is the only choice that can provide for the creation of a real "Utopia." Man must start over, and according to *Escape from L.A.*, *that* is the only answer for Utopia and for mankind.

Escape from L.A. is a funny, well-directed film. The action scenes are amazing, particularly the hang-glider assault on the Happy Kingdom. Although the CGI effects look rather cartoony at points, they are not the point of the picture. Instead, Carpenter is out to once more skewer what he sees as the root cause of America's destruction: the conservative, religious right. Although it flouts audience and fan expectations, *Escape from L.A.* is a rewarding viewing experience if one can recognize the Hawksian nature of it, and buy into Carpenter's funky satire of '90s America. *Escape from L.A.* is a wolf in sheep's clothing. On the surface it appears to be a re-hash sequel of a cult classic, but inside, the film is brimming with anti-establishment energy and an anarchic view of American politics that is hardly typical of "mass" entertainment.

Vampires (1998)

Critical Reception

"Like its blunt title suggests the movie is single-minded and devoid of frills.... It is deliriously bloody and rude.... Though heavy on spooky atmospherics, *Vampires* desperately lacks a new wrinkle.... What keeps *John Carpenter's Vampires* from completely disintegrating is its unnerving, indelible imagery. Carpenter's imagination may not be as fresh as it used to be, but he can still mine the nightmarish power of horrific visuals." — Rene Rodriguez, *Knight Ridder*: "Carpenter's *Vampires* Has Plenty of Blood, Not Much Fun," *Charlotte Observer*, October 30, 1998, page 10E.

"A compendium of mumbo jumbo and claptrap interrupted by vampire hunts, gory deaths, flambéed fiends and a battle to save the world from a better brand of vampire than Bram Stoker imagined, *Vampires* never manages to be either frightening or suspenseful.... Ridiculous without being awful enough to be hilarious, *Vampires* is chock full of exhausted lines." — Lawrence Van Gelder, *The New York Times*: "*John Carpenter's Vampires*: Dad Was Out for Blood, Now Son's a Regular Drip," October 30, 1998.

"What you've really got is a bore.... [It] gleefully wallows in decapitation and bloodletting in the name of marrying the Gothic tradition with the Western genre ... the movie is heavy on sacrilegious stabs at humor.... Woods, his usual weaselly maverick self, is especially vicious and profane to his priest sidekick." — Susan Włoszczyna, *U.S.A. Today*: "Anemic *Vampires* from John Carpenter," October 30, 1998, page 83.

"John Carpenter's *Vampires* bites. How can a movie about vampires ... be so styleless and unsexy?.... [It] has the flat look of *Walker, Texas Ranger* with a little extra sex and violence.... The toothless narrative is so dead that there is no need to take a wooden stake to this sucker." — Michael O'Sullivan, *The Washington Post*: "*Vampires*: A Vein Attempt at Horror," October 30, 1998, page 65.

"Carpenter's knack for horror is undeniable, so his first foray into the bloodsucker genre seems long overdue. *Vampires*—a bracing blend of fright and fun— is worth the wait. There are times when the campy, post-modern *Scream* sensibility of Dan Jakoby's script gets in the way of Carpenter's more provocative conceits, such as an AIDS-era sexual parable involving Jack, Tony, and Katrina." — Peter Travers, *Rolling Stone*, November 12, 1998, page 121.

Cast and Credits

CAST: James Woods (Jack Crow); Daniel Baldwin (Montoya); Sheryl Lee (Katrina); Thomas Ian Griffith (Valek); Tim Guinee (Father Adam Guiteau); Maximilian Schell (Cardinal Alba).

CREDITS: Columbia Pictures and Largo Entertainment Present A Storm King Production. *Producer:* Sandy King. *Director of Photography:* Gary B. Kibbe. *Film Editor:* Edward Warschilka. *Written for the Screen by:* Dan Jakoby. *Based on the Book Vampire$ by:* John Steakley. *Music Composed by:* John Carpenter. *Casting:* Reuben Cannon and Eddie Dunlop. *Director:* John Carpenter. *Art Director:* Kim Hix. *Co-Producer:* Dan Jakoby. *Executive Producer:* Barr Potter. *Costume Design:* Robin Michel Bush. *Special Effects Make-up:* Howard Berger, Robert Kurtzman, Gregory Nicoreto. *Production Designer:* Thomas A. Walsh. *Special Effects:* Darrel D. Pritchett. *Second Unit Director:* Jeff Imada. *Executive Producer:* Barr Potter. *Script Supervisor:* Benu Bhandari. *Unit Production Manager:* Kin Kurumunda. *Makeup:* Jill Cady. *Hair:* Jill Crosby. *Sound Mixer:* Hank Garfield. *Property Master:* Mike Bloze. *Gaffer:* Jack Schlosser. *MPAA Rating:* R. *Running Time:* 108 minutes.

———

"A master vampire able to walk in the sun — unstoppable — unless we stop him!" — Father Adam Guiteau declaims on the obvious.

———

SYNOPSIS: At high noon in the American Southwest, Jack Crow leads a team of scruffy Vatican-funded vampire slayers into a dark, fetid nest of vampires. During the bloody battle inside a dilapidated farmhouse, the vampires are dragged into the sunlight and destroyed, but Jack is disturbed by the absence of the master vampire inside. Later that night, as a victorious Team Crow parties at the nearby Sun God Motel, the much-feared master finally shows his face. The powerful vampire master, Valek, brutally murders Jack's team except for Crow, his right-hand man, Montoya, and a prostitute, Katrina. Unfortunately, Katrina has been bitten (on the thigh) by Valek, and now shares a telepathic link with the vampire. Jack believes that this link will help him locate and destroy the

Jack Crow (James Woods, foreground left) and Montoya (Daniel Baldwin, foreground right) lead Team Crow in *Vampires* (1998).

undead creature responsible for the massacre of his team, but there is a greater danger: Valek knows Jack Crow's name! Crow, Montoya and Katrina just manage to escape the deadly master in the team's white pick-up truck, but Jack is worried that his team was set up by an insider.

While Montoya holes up in a fancy hotel with Katrina, who is rapidly turning into a full-fledged vampire, Jack cleans up the bloody mess at the Sun God Motel, and sets it aflame to hide the evidence of the "undead." He then meets with Cardinal Alba, the Vatican authority who funds his vampire killing expeditions. Jack is assigned a new priest, Father Adam Guiteau, and he learns from Cardinal Alba that Valek is not just any vampire master, he is the original "vampire," the first known vampire in history. In the Middle Ages, Valek was a former priest turned revolutionary who became a vampire when the Catholic Church failed to cleanse his evil spirit in a botched "inverse" exorcism. Now, six hundred years later, Valek seeks a sacred black cross, the cru-

cifix used during his exorcism all those years ago. If the exorcism is finished successfully utilizing the cross, Valek and all his vampire progeny will be invincible, able to survive in direct sunlight. For Jack, this is an unthinkable prospect. He remembers his own childhood, when his father was bitten by a vampire. After his father killed his mother, Jack was forced to kill his own father. He has hated vampires ever since.

While Jack educates Father Guiteau about the real nature of vampires, Katrina begins to experience visions of Valek's bloody activity. She sees in her mind's eye as he travels to San Miguel and kills Father Molina, a veteran priest and scholar in early church history. Before he is killed, Molina is forced to reveal the location of the black crucifix to Valek. Now the race is on between Jack and Valek to possess the all-important cross. Unbeknownst to Jack, Katrina bites Montoya during a violent escape attempt in the hotel, and Jack's right-hand man slowly transforms into a vampire.

Valek is tracked to Santiago, a small ghost town in New Mexico. There, Jack, Katrina, Guiteau and Montoya attempt to cleanse his nest, located in a condemned jail. The attempt is unsuccessful, and Jack is captured by Valek. As night falls, Valek prepares the final exorcism ceremony which will allow him to walk tall in daylight. He ties Jack to a cross, and cuts open his leg. He then drinks Jack's blood: the blood of a crusader. Presiding over the exorcism ceremony is the traitor to Team Crow, Cardinal Alba himself. Alba has lost his faith in old age, and is terrified of death. He has made a deal with Valek: He will complete the exorcism as a priest if Valek turns him into a vampire, an immortal. Although bitten by a vampire, Montoya comes to Jack's rescue along with Father Guiteau. In the final battle, Jack destroys Valek, and Guiteau shoots Alba.

In the aftermath, Jack learns from Montoya that Katrina bit him. Although a vampire killer to his core, Jack allows Katrina and Montoya, who have fallen in love, to flee the scene. He promises to give them a two-day head start before hunting them down. Meanwhile, Guiteau and Jack still have to clean up Santiago of all remaining vampires.

COMMENTARY: It would have been a real pleasure in the closing days of 1998 to report that John Carpenter was back at the top of his filmmaking game. It would have been great to report that *Vampires* lived up to all the "best Carpenter film since *Halloween* hype" being circulated so deliberately throughout the big genre magazines. Alas, such is not the case. *Vampires* (1998) is not a return to greatness, nor is it John Carpenter's comeback film. In the final analysis, it is not a very good movie, or even a good picture within the context of Carpenter's career. On the positive side, *Vampires* is earnest, straight-faced, and serious, all rarities in the post–*Scream* "jokey" horror movie world. On the downside, the picture is strangely distancing and uninvolving, as if Carpenter had purposely intended to direct a picture that audiences would have a difficult time becoming involved in (like *In the Mouth of Madness*). Still, *Vampires* is interesting because, like a master's thesis of his film work, it successfully restates and encapsulates virtually all of Carpenter's common themes and ideas.

Immediately obvious in *Vampires* is the reworking of Carpenter's favorite Howard Hawks template, *Rio Bravo* (already featured in various ways in Carpenter films as diverse as *Assault on Precinct 13, Escape from L.A.* and even *Dark Star.*) Once again, Carpenter's desire to direct a western informs much of a film's imagery, and Carpenter has indeed gone on record as stating that he considers *Vampires,* like *In the Mouth of Madness* before it, a classic western. First and foremost, the Howard Hawks aspect of *Vampires* comes out in the bantering relationship between the two central male characters, Jack Crow (James Woods) and Father Guiteau (Tim Guinee). This relationship borders on the flirtatious (with numerous jokes about sexual arousal, and the equating of wooden stakes with an erect phallus, or "woody"), and it recalls not only the Bishop-Wilson interplay of *Assault on Precinct 13*, but the camaraderie and *joie de vivre* relationship of Sheriff Chance (John Wayne) and Deputy Dude (Dean Martin) in *Rio Bravo.* Like the Chance-Dude relationship, the Crow-Guiteau one is not without its distinct ups and downs. Guiteau must fight hard to earn Crow's respect, and at first the young priest takes some real abuse from the vampire killer. Still, it is easy to see how the played-up violence and more sexually explicit jokes are a logical extension of Hawks's ethos, brought up to date for the '90s.

Another *Rio Bravo* dynamic is reworked in the relationship and details of the Montoya-Crow friendship. They are buddies and comrades too, "men's men" who respect one another. However, their relationship, though built on respect, also has some difficulties. Specifically, Montoya's effectiveness during the latter half of *Vampires* is severely hampered by his so-called "virus," vampirism, just as Dude's effectiveness in the Hawks western is limited by *his* sickness, alcoholism. In both situations, the sidekick recovers sufficiently during the climax to again prove his ultimate worth to his friend and fellow warrior.

Vampire's major set-piece, a battle in a western-style jail, also brings back memories of *Rio Bravo*. In the Wayne film, villain Burdette repeatedly attempts to break into a jail to release his captive brother. In *Vampires*, Crow "liberates" vampires from another jail sanctuary, dragging them outside, into (deadly) sunlight. On a larger scale, *Vampire's* setting is, specifically, the west of *Rio Bravo* and all westerns: glaring hot sun, brutal desert, "ghost towns," and all. As Carpenter intended, the picture is a reflection of the classic American western: a deadly showdown between a bad gang (led by black-garbed Valek) and a good gang (led by Jack Crow).

Vampires is also filled with other typical John Carpenter touches. The film's hero is perhaps Carpenter's ultimate bad-ass, and determinedly unlikable. Jack Crow is so raw, so over-the-top in his hatred of everything, that the audience is virtually *dared* to like him. He is misogynistic, arrogant, brutal, and cynical. He is nastier than Snake Plissken (*Escape from L.A.*) and John Trent (*In the Mouth of Madness*) put together, but, in typical western film fashion, Crow still lives by and is bound by a so-called code of honor. He allows Montoya and Katrina to escape because they covered his ass when he was in trouble. And, like Nada in *They Live*, Crow in *Vampires* comes from a dysfunctional family wherein the authority figure, dear old Dad, was "bad." In *They Live*, Nada's father was physically abusive; in *Vampires*, Jack's father was a vampire who killed his own wife and subsequently caused violence and hatred to be born in his only son. Crow may not be a likable man, but James Woods is phenomenal as the character. Woods is a competent action hero, and a superb bad ass. His high-energy intensity and motor-mouth delivery lends *Vampires* a measure of intelligence sorely lacking in the underdeveloped script.

Carpenter's ever present hatred of authority also runs throughout much of *Vampires*. In Carpenter's vision, the Catholic Church is responsible for the vampire plague. According to the script, all vampires stem from a botched Catholic exorcism held six hundred years earlier. Thus religion itself, the word of God on Earth if you will, is responsible for unleashing a terrible evil on mankind, even though it purports to share hope, faith, and salvation, not terror and destruction. Like *Prince of Darkness*, which established that the Catholic Church had hidden the true nature of Satan and Jesus Christ for several hundreds of years, *Vampires* finds much fault with organized religion in general, and Catholicism in particular. This hatred goes further when the real villain of *Vampires* is finally introduced during the film's climax: Cardinal Alba! As played by Maximilian Schell and imagined by Carpenter, this hypocritical Catholic authority is a man totally without faith. He is a betrayer who is more interested in assuring his own immortality than in practicing or espousing Christian values. He is the opposite of what a priest should be: He is selfish instead of selfless. What Carpenter seems to suggest with this villainous character is that men of God are hypocrites, because in reality they long for the same things the rest of humanity does: immortality, life after death; answers about creation and man's place in the universe. Alba in *Vampires* is a sham because he pretends to be pious and knowledgeable about God's hand on Earth, but is actually far more lost and morally rudderless than the rest of the species.

All of these thematic touches (*Rio Bravo*, hatred of authority, rugged anti-heroes) assure that *Vampires* bears the distinct and unmistakable stamp of John Carpenter's ownership. Perhaps more than any other film in the Carpenter canon, *Vampires* establishes Carpenter's credentials as an auteur, a filmmaker who carries the same ideas, themes, and interests from one project to the next. Contrarily, *Vampires* is the first Carpenter project in some years which does not feature at least a few faces from his standard acting repertory company. In this 1998 epic, there's no sign of Peter Jason, Dennis Dun, Sam Neill, Stacy Keach or Kurt Russell, and that is a real shame. The auteur argument could have been buttressed even further by the presence of familiar Carpenter actors.

As *Vampires* reflects Carpenter's auteuristic tendencies as a horror filmmaker, it also displays his keen sense of imagery and visuals. *Vampires*, like *Village of the Damned,* opens with some remarkably memorable visual flourishes. After a long pan across a western landscape, Carpenter's camera zeroes in like a guided missile (from a racing aerial shot) on the vampire farmhouse nest. This shot suggests the imagery of the Gulf War, wherein camera-bearing missiles slid effortlessly into ever-growing targets like weapons bunkers and warehouses. The racing aerial shot has the same effect here: targeting the location of the enemy, and zeroing in for a "surgical strike" on the site of the film's action.

Then, as Team Crow arrives, Carpenter's editor, Warshchilka, intercuts between close-ups of the intense, sunglasses-bedecked James Woods and the ramshackle front door of the farmhouse where the opening set-piece occurs. Like the previous shot of the fast approach to the farmhouse, both the door and Woods's stone face loom ever larger on the screen, until the sense of anticipation and conflict is almost visceral. Then, the team enters the house, seen from a low angle to accentuate its power.

From there, *Vampires* moves gracefully into the practice and minutiae of vampire-killing, a kind of workaday approach to the vocation, as one vampire after the other is harpooned by Crow and then dragged (via Montoya and a winch on his jeep) into the scorching sunlight.

As *Vampires* depicts the art of vampire slaying, the picture is imbued with an almost documentary-like feel (like *The Thing*), and the audience rapidly becomes familiar with the techniques practiced by Crow and company. Although suspense is sacrificed to present this cinema verité style, a sense of reality is nonetheless heightened by Carpenter's decision to obsess on the details. The intense Woods, the authentically scruffy members of Team Crow, the glistening silver weaponry, and the unusual vehicles all lend a high degree of believability to this fantastic enterprise. This is an especially important distinction because *Vampires* is Carpenter's first and only vampire picture. Before *Vampires*, he openly disdained vampire pictures as being unbelievable and difficult to relate to. He had no desire to make a film about (in the words of Jack Crow) a bunch of romantic figures with "eurotrash" accents who wear "rented formal wear." Therefore, it is vital to Carpenter that the central scenario of his picture, and even the vampires themselves, seem believable and plausible. To accomplish this, he takes a realistic approach to Crow's profession, thus deflecting his own concerns about vampires as well as the audience's.

In all, this opening scene is a perfect introduction to *Vampires*, replete even with a touch of welcome moral ambiguity. In one sequence, the vampire hunters line scorched vampire skulls on the hood of the team vehicle, suggesting grisly trophies like those collected by some American soldiers in Vietnam. Again, this is Carpenter's kind of anti-mythological approach to vampire lore. Crow's men are not heroic Van Helsing types, or lovely martial arts experts like Sarah Michelle Gellar's mythical Buffy the Vampire Slayer. On the contrary, they are callous, whoring, boozing low-lifes. They are real men doing a job, not larger-than-life heroes defending the human race. Team Crow is comprised of pest exterminators, nothing more.

After this artful and unique introduction, however, *Vampires* begins to slide badly into mediocrity. The pacing slows, and over-the-top gore is lingered over during a grotesque "clean up" scene, apparently included for pure shock value.

Some thoughtful critics have argued that Carpenter's films exist in a weird kind of trance state, a mellow but mesmerizing drone.

The heartbeat pulse of the soundtrack, the slow-moving camera, the circuitous dialogue, the precise staging, and other standard Carpenter touches lend many of his film ventures a freaky and memorable rhythm. That rhythm, or drone, depending on preference, is then periodically punctured by moments of pure terror and suspense. Sadly, *Vampires* never gets out of the drone: It is lethargic and flat without any real notable highs or lows. The action scenes fail to inspire dread, terror or even interest, except for one very suspenseful and meticulously edited scene involving an elevator inside the vampire nest. Although it is clear that Carpenter was aiming for "southwestern cool" in *Vampires*, the laid-back pacing causes the horror elements to miss the mark. The lack of horror results in the least frightening Carpenter genre picture since *Christine* (1983), and what one dissatisfied critic disparagingly referred to as "*Harley Davidson and the Marlboro Man* meets *Dracula.*"

Vampires' sleep-inducing pace is not the film's only problem. The script by Dan Jakoby is riddled with surprisingly large lapses in situational logic. In one absurd sequence, for instance, there is a working video monitoring system inside a condemned, rotting jail building (in an abandoned town). Did the vampires leave the closed-circuit system operational just so Jack Crow could stop by and check on their activities? Another flawed premise finds Baldwin's Montoya totally unprepared when Katrina finally goes "vamp" and bites him. Although he knew the transformation was occurring, he apparently did not think to at least muzzle the girl to keep her from attacking him. More important to the film's plot, it is truly a mystery why Alba warns Jack about Valek when secretly he wishes Valek's campaign to succeed. Were Jack really and truly unprepared to face Valek, Cardinal Alba would have a better chance of taking Jack off-guard, capturing him, and winning out in the end. These lapses remind one of the clumsiness of *Village of the Damned* (wherein seven years of story time passed and not one character aged a day). Sadly, *Vampires* is almost as haphazard as that picture, and it fails to keep its details and continuity straight.

On *Mystery Science Theater 3000*, the television series in which Mike Nelson and two robots are forced to watch cheesy genre movies, the 'bot called Crow (no relation to Jack in *Vampires*) occasionally turns to his human companion during a particularly harrowing filmgoing experience and asks, "This movie hates us, doesn't it, Mike?" Were Crow watching *Vampires*, he might ask the same question. Although there is something inherently charming (and maverick) about the politically incorrect *Vampires*, there is also no escaping the conclusion that the audience, and the audience's enjoyment, is truly incidental to this picture. There is no attempt on Carpenter's part to make Jack, his team members, or any of the characters likable. James Woods' Jack is a hateful bastard, railing against everything and everyone, until nobody escapes his raw tongue. Perhaps this hatred-spewing character is admirable because he goes against convention — or perhaps Carpenter has, for once, gone too far. Indeed, James Woods has gone on record saying that he ad-libbed a lot of sequences to amuse Carpenter, but he was the one who was surprised when many of those ad-libbed scenes turned up in the picture's final print. In *Vampires*, it is almost as if Carpenter is saying "screw you" not only to the film establishment which has shunned and ignored him, but to the audience who has so faithfully supported him as well. Although *Vampires* deserves praise for being something other than a Hollywood, by-the-numbers, politically correct horror picture, there is an ugly feeling of contempt running through it as well, and that's hard to take from someone as smart as Carpenter. One wonders if Carpenter's maverick sensibilities have, for once, overbalanced his usually brilliant sense of storytelling.

In toto, *Vampires* is a film with a few fine moments and a couple of neat inspirations. Thomas Ian Griffith is a revelation as Valek, a strong, silent, charismatic villain with real presence. The moment when he attacks Katrina (Sheryl Lee) and sinks his fangs into her luscious thigh is genuinely erotic. Woods is terrific as the controversial slayer, Jack Crow, and Carpenter stages at least two sequences (the opening battle in the nest and the elevator battle in the jail) with real gusto and style. It is fair to assert that in this case at least, Carpenter has gone for style over substance, and *Vampires* is very much a film where a "bad-ass" attitude and texture is fostered at the expense of pace and story.

It is also fair to state that audiences (and this critic too!) want to like both *Vampires* and John Carpenter (who is *not* a bum), but *Vampires* is not the perfect vehicle for such synergy because it goes out of its way to offend, enrage and shock. *The Thing* shocked audiences too back in 1982, but it did so in ways that seemed valid considering the theme and standard operating procedure of its unique, otherworldly protagonist. *Vampires* is nasty, it seems, because somebody, maybe Carpenter, thought that nasty would

equate with cool. There are moments in the film that exist only to establish what a bad-ass, bad-boy Carpenter is — something that is unnecessary considering this maverick's long and highly accomplished film roster. Audiences and reviewers already know he's a maverick dark star and virtuoso technician, so the tone of *Vampires* proves little new. The student of John Carpenter will find plenty to study and revel in here: the anti-authority riffs, the bad-ass attitude of a classic Carpenter anti-hero, the Howard Hawks western motifs, the near-perfect composition and *mise-en-scène*, and so forth, but those looking for the razor-sharp terror of *Halloween*, the paranoia of *The Thing*, the beauty of *The Fog*, the satiric edge of *Dark Star*, the romance of *Starman*, and the ingenuity and wit of *Assault on Precinct 13* will find the elegant touch of the master missing in this venture. John Carpenter is capable of directing a film much more complex, intelligent, and artful than *Vampires*, and one wishes that at this point, 20 years after *Halloween*, he would get on with it.

III

Films Written and Produced by John Carpenter

John Carpenter has been involved in a number of genre films in a capacity other than director. In 1978, his screenplay "Eyes" was revised to serve as the basis for the high-profile, big budget horror-suspense venture *Eyes of Laura Mars.* Although Carpenter was unhappy with the final result, he was gratified to have a Hollywood credit on his resume — an $8 million Faye Dunaway vehicle to boot!

In 1981, John Carpenter succumbed to pressure for a *Halloween* sequel, but instead of directing it, he merely wrote the screenplay and produced the picture. Although, again, he was not happy with the result, the picture was much better than many later *Halloween* pictures such as *Halloween V: The Revenge of Michael Myers* and *Halloween VI: The Curse of Michael Myers.* In 1982, Carpenter contributed his skills as producer to yet another sequel, *Halloween III: Season of the Witch.* The less said about that picture, the better.

In the mid–'80s, however, something interesting happened. John Carpenter became a brand name — almost. Old scripts, long forgotten by Carpenter, were trotted out to serve as the basis for new films. Although these scripts were substantially rewritten, John Carpenter was given "executive producer" credit merely for reading the revised screenplays on New World's *The Philadelphia Experiment* and *Black Moon Rising.*

Though John Carpenter's name can be found on all the films detailed and reviewed below, it is fair to say that none of them are as interesting as films directed by Carpenter himself. Of this bunch, *Eyes of Laura Mars* and *Halloween II* are probably the best films, and *Halloween III: Season of the Witch* is probably the least satisfying. Although there are currently no plans for John Carpenter to serve in the same "brand name" capacity as Wes Craven (*Wes Craven Presents Mind Ripper* [1995], *Wes Craven Presents Wishmaster* [1997], *Wes Craven Presents Carnival of Souls* [1998]), his future as a horror contributor is certainly assured, especially with the financial success of *Vampires* on home video and HBO. Already, his next project as director, *John Carpenter's Ghost of Mars,* has been announced.

Eyes of Laura Mars (1978)

Critical Reception

"On just about any terms — sociological, psychological, romantic, dramatic or thriller —*Eyes of Laura Mars* seems déjà vu. Laura's visions are a variation on the 'killer's eye' gimmick from the 1946 *Spiral Staircase*.... The climactic scene would *like* to be romantic tragedy but the movie by then has wasted too much time."— Donald C. Willis, *Horror and Science Fiction Films II*, Scarecrow Press, 1982.

"Long on trendy settings, high-priced actors and vicious murders, but devoid of narrative thrills ... *Laura Mars* quickly devolves into a prosaic whodunit with a gyp of an ending.... An endless episode of *Charlie's Angels*."— Frank Rich, *Time*, August 21, 1978.

"*Laura Mars* isn't really about anything at all, and the fault is that of screenwriters John Carpenter and David Zelag Goodman. Their script is a model of lazy solutions to interesting problems."— David Ansen, *Newsweek:* "Shudderbug," August 14, 1978.

"*Eyes of Laura Mars* comes to the bone-crushingly obvious conclusion that fashion photography is superficial. It makes the point superficially and at the same time ponderously.... This is a thriller with serious pretensions.... It deals in matters that raise serious questions, it mutters them, and then it drops them like tons of cement.... One pines for more thought."— Penelope Gilliat, *The New Yorker*, August 21, 1978.

"*Laura Mars* is a casualty of the kinky, burnt-out, what's-in-it-for-me '70s ... more mush than memorable. As the film meanders from murder to murder, Laura's horror is explored only superficially.... Faye Dunaway ... is not given the opportunity to act the part.... The result is gloss with little substance."— Rob Edelman, *Films in Review*, October 1978, page 500.

Cast and Credits

CAST: Faye Dunaway (Laura Mars); Tommy Lee Jones (John Neville); Brad Dourif (Tommy Ludlow); Rene Auberjonois (Donald Phelps); Raul Julia (Michael Reisler); Frank Adonis (Sal Volpe); Lisa Taylor (Michele); Darlanne Fluegel (Lulu); Rose Gregorio (Elaine Cassell); Bill Boggs (Himself); Steve Marachuk (Robert); Meg Mundy (Doris Spenser); Marilyn Meyers (Sheila Weissman); Gary Bayer (Reporter); Mitchell Edmonds (Reporter); Michael Tucker (Bert); Jeff Niki (Photo Assistant); Toshi Matsuo (Photo Assistant); John E. Allen (Billy T.); Anna Anderson, Deborah Beck, Jim Devine, Hanny Friedman, Winnie Holliman, Oatty Oja, Donna Palmer, Sterling St. Jacques, Rita Tellone, Kari Page (Models); Dallas Edward Hayes (Douglas); John Randolph Jones, Al Joseph, Gerald Kline, Sal Richards, Tom Degidon (Policemen); Paula Lawrence (Aunt Caroline); Joey R. Mills (Make-up Person); John Sahag (Hairdresser); Hector Troy (Cab Driver).

CREDITS: Columbia Pictures Presents a Jon Peters Production of an Irvin Kershner Film. *Film Editor:* Michael Kahn, a.c.e. *Costumes Designed by:* Theoni V. Aldredge. *Production Designer:* Gene Callahan. *Director of Photography:* Victor J. Kemper a.s.c. *Executive Producer:* Jack H. Harris. *Screenplay:* John Carpenter, David Zelag Goodman. *Story:* John Carpenter. *Directed by:* Irvin Kershner. *Love*

Theme from Eyes of Laura Mars *sung by:* Barbra Streisand. *Words and Music by:* Karen L. Lawrence, John Desautels. *Produced by:* Gary Klein. *Associate Producer:* Laura Ziskin. *Production Executive:* George Justin. *Musical Supervisor:* Charles A. Koppelman. *Gallery Photographs:* Helmut Newton. *Casting Supervisor:* Cis Corman. *Unit Production Manager:* Louis A. Stroller. *Special Photographic Consultant:* Rebecca Blake. *Special Project Assistant:* Susan Landau. *Art Director:* Robert Gundlach. *Assistant Directors:* Louis A. Stroller, Mel Howard. *Second Assistant Director:* Joseph Maimone, Jr. *Music Editor:* Joan Biel. *Sound Editor:* Chuck Campbell. *Assistant Editors:* Paula la Mastra, Trudy Ship, Emily Payne. *Script Supervisor:* Bette Nance. *Camera Operator:* Lou Barlia. *First Assistant Cameraman:* Jack Brown. *Second Assistant Cameraman:* Bruce MacCallam. *Sound Mixer:* Lez Lazarowitz. *Dubbing Mixers:* Robert Knudson, Robert Glass, Don MacDougall. *Special Effects:* Edward Drohan. *Sound Effects Created by:* Neiman Tillar Associates. *Set Decorator:* John Godfrey. *Make-up:* Lee Harman, Vance Gallaghan, Lynn Donohue. *Hairstyles for Ms. Dunaway:* Kaye Pownall. *Hairdressers:* Colleen Callaghan. *Chargeman:* Fred Sanmui. *Project Assistants:* Francine LeFrak, Jerry Jaffe, Hugh Rawson. *Assistant to Mr. Kershner:* Pennfield Jensen. *Wardrobe for Ms. Dunaway:* Bernadine Mann. *Men's Costumer:* James Hagerman. *Women's Costumer:* Marilyn Bishop. *Assistant to Mr. Aldredge:* Donna Tomas. *Property Master:* Walter Stocklin. *Still Man:* Adger Cowans. *Key Grip:* James Finnerey. *Location Auditor:* Vince Martinez. *Unit Publicist:* Vic Heutschy. *Stunt Coordinator:* Alex Stevens. *Production Office Coordinator:* Sheri Leibowitz. *Transportation Captain:* James Giblin. *Gaffer:* James Dolan. Eyes of Laura Mars *Photographs:* Rebecca Blake. *Special Photographic Effects:* James Liles. *Titles:* Cinema Research Corp. *Chem-Tone Negative Processing:* TVC Labs. Filmed in Panavision. "Burn" written and performed by Michaelsek and Oosterveen, produced by Ken Scott, courtesy of CBS Records. "Native New Yorker" performed by Odyssey, produced by Sandy Linzer and Charlie Calello, courtesy of RCA Records. "Shake Your Booty" performed by K.C. and the Sunshine Band, produced by K.C. Finch, courtesy of T.K. Records. "Let's All Chant" performed by the Michael Zager Band, produced by Michael Zager, courtesy of Private Stock Records. "Boogie Nights" performed by Heat Wave, produced by Bobby Blue, courtesy of Epic Records. *MPAA Rating:* R. *Running Time:* 104 minutes.

———————

"I think what Laura is saying with the work is, 'Okay America! Okay world! You are violent! You are pushing all this murder on us. So here it comes, right back at you. And we'll use murder to sell deodorant, so that you just get bored with murder.'" — A model explains the art of Mars to reporters.

———————

SYNOPSIS: Chic New York fashion photographer Laura Mars awakens from a nightmare in which she has watched, through the eyes of a killer, as Doris Spenser, the editor of her new photography book, *Eyes of Laura Mars*, is murdered with an ice pick. Disturbed by the vivid dream, Laura telephones Spenser's house and gets no answer.

Laura goes to the glitzy opening of her photography exhibit at Elaine Cassell's Soho Gallery. She is accosted at the entrance by reporters who tell her that her work, filled with images of sex and violence, is offensive to women. Soon the police also arrive at the exhibit and begin to question people about the murder of Doris Spenser. Mars encounters a young police detective, John Neville, and he calls her work junk. Laura learns of Doris's death and excuses herself from the gallery. She is disturbed, and she wonders if her dream was some kind of psychic experience.

The next day, Laura is back at work, directing a fashion shoot in the middle of a busy Manhattan intersection. During the shoot, Laura experiences a second vision, again seeing through the eyes of a killer. This time the victim is the gallery owner, Elaine Cassell, on the staircase to her apartment. Laura is unable to continue the photo shoot, and she rushes to the scene of the crime.

When Laura informs police that she "saw" the murder, she and her entire entourage are dragged downtown to talk with Detective Neville. He interrogates Laura and shows her crime site photographs that eerily match her own photography work. The kicker is that these murders all took place two years ago, and that the photos have never been published anywhere. Worse, the crimes remain unsolved.

Laura begins to suspect that in some insidious way she is connected to the mind of a psychotic. She began to see images of violence in her work from two years ago, just when these violent crimes began. Neville and Laura visit Cassell's apartment for clues and Laura realizes that Elaine was seeing her (Laura's) ex-husband, Michael, who she believed was living in San Francisco. Neville considers Michael a suspect.

When Laura returns to her apartment, Michael is waiting there. He is worried that he is under suspicion, and he claims that he still loves Laura. He and Laura argue and she gives him 50 dollars cash to get by.

The next morning, Laura finds her agent, Donald Phelps, and her chauffeur, Tommy, arguing about something. Tommy is anxious, and he reveals to Laura that he is an ex-con. He did time for armed robbery and assault with a deadly weapon. Laura asks the two to stop arguing, and goes about her business for the day's shoot in a large, empty warehouse. As she waits for her models to arrive, Laura experiences another vision. This time, she sees someone, the killer, watching *her*. Frightened, she runs through the warehouse and down a long staircase. She runs into Phelps, and sees no further sign of the killer.

During the warehouse shoot, Laura is immobilized again, feeling apprehension and dread. Detective Neville arrives and suggests that she is merely experiencing anxiety attacks because she is overworked. Laura won-

ders if she is hallucinating, but she knows that the corpses rapidly piling up are no delusion. Later, in her upstairs dark room, Laura bonds with the murderer again. She sees him enter the apartment of two models, Lulu and Michelle. He offs each of them, poking out their eyes with an ice pick.

After the funerals of the two models, Neville and Laura realize that they are attracted to each other, and share a kiss in the woods. They fall asleep in her apartment after making love. The next morning, Detective Neville gives Laura a gun, so she can protect herself. That night, Laura goes to Donald Phelps's birthday party. Tommy is there too, and Laura's ex-husband Michael telephones from a laundromat in Brooklyn. He is drunk and suicidal. To get by the police escort outside, Laura and Phelps exchange clothes. Phelps leads the cops away while Laura makes a beeline for Brooklyn. En route, she has yet another vision. Phelps is stalked and killed in the elevator. In a state of shock, Laura wrecks the car and is transported to a hospital.

Days later, John Neville brings Laura home to her apartment from the hospital. They share a tender moment alone, but other police officers interrupt. They believe they have a lead: one of Tommy's playing cards has been found in the elevator where Donald was killed. Neville meets Tommy at his apartment and questions him. Tommy maintains his innocence but grows increasingly uncomfortable as Neville attempts to insinuate that he might be mentally unbalanced. Tommy flees the police and is shot and killed on a busy street. Believing the case is closed, Neville calls Laura on his two-way to tell her to pack her bags. They are going to get out of New York for awhile.

As Laura packs her clothes, she unexpectedly sees another vision. This time, she sees a man murdered in the elevator of her building. Unfortunately, she is not sure who has been murdered: John Neville or Michael. Neville then breaks into the apartment, and soon reveals that he is the crazed killer. He is a schizophrenic with an angry personality, who believes that Laura uses death to sell things. The killer reveals that he was a neglected child and that his mother was a whore who was murdered by a john. In a moment of clarity, Neville's "good" personality emerges and begs Laura to kill him. Reluctantly, Laura kills Neville and ends the reign of the killer. Traumatized, she dials 911.

COMMENTARY: Had *Halloween* not premiered the same year and thoroughly rejuvenated the "stalker" film, *Eyes of Laura Mars* might not look so very dated and unexciting today. Where *Halloween* was inventive in its approach to actors, story, villain, and mounting suspense, *Eyes of Laura Mars* is resolutely uninventive, falling back on ancient Hollywood clichés and depending primarily on artless misdirection rather than the cleverness of its premise. The film is competent, and it boasts a glossy big-budget veneer, but underneath the shining finish, *Eyes of Laura Mars* bears the uncomfortable stench of a studio "star" vehicle. It is more interested in tragic romance than in suspense, and the result is a distinctly lethargic picture in which none of the principals evoke much sympathy.

Eyes of Laura Mars is a very '70s kind of movie, which could have and should have been a good thing. The films of that decade were for the most part experimental, more stylish, personal, and quite liberated in their use of film technique. The seventies was a great period in movie history (at least pre–*Star Wars*). In a visual sense, *Eyes of Laura Mars* takes advantage of all this freedom. It opens not with a murder, nor with the linear beginning of the narrative, but with a startling freeze frame close-up of Faye Dunaway's right eye. The camera pulls slowly back to a shot of both eyes, and then in stark black-and-white this image turns sour, into its negative. Suddenly, Barbra Streisand starts singing a strident pop tune over the visuals, and the screen fades slowly to black. This opening, though it undoubtedly sounds like a campy hoot, is fairly effective. It immediately establishes what is important in the film,

specifically Laura's vision, and then notes how her vision will affect her (the title of the song is "Prisoner"). In other words, the course of the picture will see Dunaway locked in a trap by what her eyes tell her.

This stylish opening is referenced at the close of the picture, as the same freeze frame is shown, again turning into a negative image. Since these images book-end the film, they suggest that the story unfolding in between is merely something flashing before Laura's eyes, a prolonged peek into her life. The book-end images give the film a distinct and interesting context, but ultimately the film fails to forge a connection to those freeze frames. The opening freeze frame, which seems curious, should by the time it appears at the end of the film be fraught with tragedy and meaning. But the film really never generates that notion of love-gone-wrong or the sense that Laura has suffered a debilitating incident that will traumatize her for life. Instead, the images serve solely as book ends, and what is in between hardly seems worth reading.

Irvin Kershner is a wonderful and talented director. He directed the best *Star Wars* film, *The Empire Strikes Back*, and has since done good work with the James Bond film series (*Never Say Never Again*). He brings a real visual flair to *Eyes of Laura Mars*, and ignites many scenes with a distinct and notable perspective. For instance, after the first murder (told with a subjective camera angle), Laura awakens from her nightmare and prowls her apartment. Kershner lenses this sequence in extreme long shot for some good reasons. First, the presence of this woman alone in a huge apartment augments her isolation and visualizes the story's concept that Laura is a lonely woman who has failed in love. Secondly, it immediately notes the vanity of Laura Mars. Her bedroom is crescent-shaped. Behind the bed (which stands alone in the center of the room on a pedestal), the walls are covered in mirrors. In other words, Laura has fashioned in her apartment a haven where all she sees are images of herself. As Laura is an artist who "sees" for a living, this is a noteworthy point to make, and the long-view of the apartment establishes it visually. It also suggests that Laura has, perhaps, been taken with her own self-image as chic photographer, as well as her own celebrity. The mirrored bedroom expresses this characterization in a way that the central performance never quite manages.

Kershner's film also gains positive points for the manner in which it captures New York City. The film was shot on location in Manhattan, and the setting lends an authentic look to *Eyes of Laura Mars*. Dozens of extras mill about behind Laura's exterior photo shoot, and traffic comes to a standstill to gawk at the apocalyptic scenery. For whatever reason, these moments feel real, even though other aspects of the story do not seem to ring true. Where Kershner fails with this picture is not in the images, which are almost continually obsessed with how we see — either through cameras, mirrors, visions, TV monitors, photographs, or the TV news — but in the narrative drive. It fails to engage the viewer, and the lackluster screenplay, which was heavily rewritten after John Carpenter left the project, cannot save the picture.

Many of the film's problems begin and end with Faye Dunaway. She is an excellent actress, no doubt, but she gives a remarkably chilly, mannered performance in this film. She skims only the surface of Laura Mars's personality and resolutely fails to project any vulnerability in the character. Although she reaches heights of hysteria, Dunaway's performance does not express that this woman is terrified for her life, terrified of being alone, or terrified of being involved in the central murders. Because she cannot express this vulnerability, the love scenes in *Eyes of Laura Mars* shrivel before the audience's eyes. She says lines like "I can't control myself," but Dunaway's performance is so tightly controlled, so rigid and unemotional, so glacier-like, that the lines come off as laughable. It is virtually impossible to believe that this woman cannot control *any* element of her life. Had Barbra Streisand played the role as

was originally intended, it is safe to assume that some sense of vulnerability would have been transmitted. Unlike Jamie Lee Curtis in *Halloween*, Faye Dunaway never wins over the viewer to her character's plight. She is too icy to identify with, and Laura's soul remains an unreachable enigma, always slightly beyond the viewer's reach.

Dunaway is not assisted by the screenplay, which calls on her to literally become paralyzed, again and again, at the most awkward situations. This paralysis, caused by her psychic link with the killer, results in a restless feeling in viewers. Laura becomes non-functional when she sees through the eyes of the murderer; she becomes the camera, and thereby a distancing factor for the audiences. Even worse, these scenes of murder and mayhem do not build. Everything is normal, Laura freezes, and the audience gets a close-up of her frightened eyes over and over again. In essence, then, Laura is a kind of early warning system who reveals that the killer is about to commit a crime, and therefore there are no surprises in store for the audience. The same pattern (normality, paralyzed close-up, and then a kill shot with subjective camera) is repeated *ad nauseam* until it seems humorous. As soon as Laura is about to do anything to advance the story (steal a car and rescue her ex-husband, pack her clothes and get out of the city, complete a photo shoot), the film stops in its (and Laura's) tracks with another vision. Rather than propel the story, Laura's visions only keep the film on the same groove throughout its running time.

Eyes of Laura Mars takes a great cast of supporting actors, from Rene Auberjonois, Brad Dourif and Raul Julia to a pre–*L.A. Law* Michael Tucker, and provides each with only enough time on screen to become a plausible suspect. Julia is a sullen, alcoholic ex-husband who has a temper tantrum just bad enough to suggest he might be the killer. Brad Dourif plays an unshaven ex-con who carries a knife to "cut rope and shit." Auberjonois argues with Dourif and Dunaway and wants to continue the photo shoot even while people are dying. Each could be the murderer, but beyond this realization, the audience knows nothing about the characters. They bicker, disappear, reappear and bicker some more, solely to misdirect the audience about the real identity of the murderer. There is nothing wrong with a few red herrings, but *Eyes of Laura Mars* populates its entire film with them.

Had the suspense sequences in *Eyes of Laura Mars* been as stirring as those in *Halloween*, the movie might have worked despite the miscast Dunaway and the overdose of red herrings. Unfortunately, the suspense sequences are oddly abbreviated, and all shot inadequately in the subjective camera angle. Unlike John Carpenter, who filmed only one death in *Halloween* from a first-person perspective, Kershner shoots every death sequence in the same way. The camera rushes in at the victim, the victim turns and screams and is killed (in close-up). This too lends a sameness to the picture, and the subjective camera simply does not work from a realism standpoint. The victims just stand there as the killer approaches, sometimes from ten feet away — and then they scream. They do not fight back. They do not raise their hands in protest. They do not struggle at all. They are like lambs being slaughtered, so it is a little hard to feel sympathy for them. Of course, one can argue that they are being killed by someone they recognize, so they are caught off guard. Then again, the murderer is wearing gloves and brandishing an ice-pick. Acquaintance or not, that should put their defenses up a bit.

The final twist of *Eyes of Laura Mars*, that the killer is Laura's lover, is one that John Carpenter argued vehemently against, and it is easy to see why. Neville is supposed to be schizophrenic, yet his evil personality never breaks through with anybody other than Laura, and only when he wants it to. This is a particularly "functional" brand of schizophrenia, as it does not affect his work or his close romantic relationships. Instead, he just becomes the killer when he has an opportu-

nity to kill, which seems unlikely. Neville's motive for killing all of Laura's friends is also weak. He does not like her work because it glorifies death, so he kills her associates. It makes little sense. Besides, it is finally established that Laura gleans her "violent" imagery not from some inner voice, but from her connection with Neville. What this means, essentially, is that Neville wants to kill Laura for dramatizing what he is thinking. But if he thinks her work is bad for glorifying death, then he must also be bad for glorifying death, since he gave her the idea in the first place!

Despite these faults, some critics have opined that *Eyes of Laura Mars* is actually a rather complex motion picture. In *Eyes of Laura Mars: A Binocular Critique*, Lacy Fischer and Marcia Landy dig deep into the film, which they feel documents

> the relationship between sexual oppression, violence, and pornography and the role of film, television, advertising and photography in producing and reproducing patriarchal idealogy.[1]

Their arguments seem particularly well thought out, but the problem remains that these insights seem more intelligent than the film which generated them. *Eyes of Laura Mars* is rife with issues worth examining. Is violence de-sensitizing people? Are photography and film really art or merely commerce? Is Laura selling violence and murder for moral reasons, or simply to make money? Where do artists' visions come from? Is Laura a sham because her artistic vision belongs to a killer? Does that make her a plagiarist? Is Laura in any way responsible for all the deaths that occur?

These are all provocative questions, but *Eyes of Laura Mars* answers none of them. The audience is left not knowing how to feel because the killer was not affected adversely by Laura's art. He was sick and schizophrenic before Laura began to photograph violent acts. The photography did not make him kill people, his own inner demons did. Perhaps then the film is saying that art imitates life and that the artist exploits the violent to make art. But the question remains, is Laura's photography art? It has lots of tits and ass in it, and it sells well, but what is the statement behind it? At one point in the film Laura declares that she is tired of the physical, spiritual and emotional murder in American society and that she wants others to see it. Why then, does she make it palatable for them? Why does she include beautiful models, provocative nudity, and glamour to teach America a lesson? Why not offer documentary photographs instead?

Eyes of Laura Mars wants to make a coherent statement about violence in our society and our art, but at the same time it wants to tell a love story and a suspense story. The movie itself cannot make up its mind how it feels about the questions it raises. Are viewers supposed to be left with the impression that Laura has brought all of this death on herself with her art? If so, that notion is not transmitted adequately.

Because *Eyes of Laura Mars* does not answer the questions it raises, because it has no emotional center, and because its final revelation seems like a cop-out, the film is not a satisfying viewing experience. It is beautiful to look at, filled with fantastic and provocative images, such as the moment when Tommy Lee Jones stands in front of a broken mirror, side by side with his reflection. For this moment, his schizophrenia is given physical form: One image in the mirror is crystal clear, the other is part of a shattered mirror, like his splintered psyche. Still, the skillfully composed images, the pop seventies soundtrack (which includes "Shake Your Booty" and "Boogie Night") and the authentic New York locations are not enough to make sense out of a film in search of its soul. *Eyes of Laura Mars* is blind to humanity and emotions, content to give viewers only the most surface responses to the most interesting of questions. If Carpenter is unhappy with this film it is because his concept of senseless, faceless evil was eviscerated in an attempt to make a glitzy star vehicle.

Halloween II (1981)

Critical Reception

"Good enough to deserve a sequel of its own. By the standards of most recent horror films, this — like its predecessor — is a class act. There's some variety to the crimes, as there is to the characters, and an audience is likely to do more screaming at suspenseful moments than at scary ones…. The direction and camera work are quite competent, and the actors don't look like amateurs…. And *Halloween II*, in addition to all this, has a quick pace and something like a sense of style."— Janet Maslin, *The New York Times:* "*Halloween II* for Fright Fans," October 30, 1981.

"It's the ultimate in arm-twisting, edge-of-the-seat suspense with murders arriving in ones, twos and threes, all of them horribly anticipated in dark corridors and menacing music."— Archer Winston, *The New York Post*, October 30, 1981.

"As far as suspense goes in horror films, *Halloween 2* is better than most of the 'scare' flicks released in the past 3 years. As a sequel, unfortunately, it comes nowhere near its frightening predecessor."— John Paul Ward, *Films in Review*, December 1981.

"Terrific terror has two requirements: acceleration and humor.... *Halloween II* has none.... *Halloween II* starts and stays at fever pitch. Without relief or variety, this pitch is as numbing as the metronomic regularity with which crabby Michael dispatches his victims."— Joann Rhetts, *The Charlotte Observer*, October 31, 1981.

"*Halloween II* is a retread of *Halloween* without that movie's craft, exquisite timing, and thorough understanding of horror."— Roger Ebert, *Roger Ebert's Home Movie Companion*, Andrews and McMeel, 1993, page 274.

Cast and Credits

CAST: Jamie Lee Curtis (Laurie Strode); Donald Pleasence (Sam Loomis); Charles Cyphers (Sheriff Leigh Brackett); Jeffrey Baker (Graham); Lance Guest (Jimmy); Pamela Susan Shoop (Karen); Hunter Von Leer (Gary Hunt); Dick Warlock (The Shape); Leo Rossi (Budd); Gloria Gifford (Mrs. Alves); Tawny Moyers (Jill); Ana Alicia (Janet); Ford Rainey (Dr. Mixter); Cliff Emmich (Mr. Garrett); Nancy Stephens (Marion); John Zenda (Marshal); Catherine Bergstrom (Producer); Alan Haufrect (Announcer); Lucille Benson (Mrs. Elrod); Howard Culver (Man in Pajamas); Dana Carvey (Assistant); Bill Warlock (Craig); Jonathan Prince (Randy); Leigh French (Gary's Mom); Ty Mitchell (Young Gary); Nancy Loomis (Annie); Pamela McMyler (Laurie's Mom); Dennis Holahan (Laurie's Dad); Nicole Drucker (Young Laurie); Ken Smolka (First Patrolman); Adam Gunn (Young Michael Myers); Roger Hampton (Second Patrolman); Robin Coleman (Medic); Dick Warlock (Third Patrolman); Jack Verbois (Bennett Tramer); Tony Moran (Michael Myers at 23); Kyle Richards (Lindsey); Brian Andrews (Tommy); Anne Bruner (Alice).

CREDITS: Moustapha Akkad Presents a Dino De Laurentiis Corporation Film; a John Carpenter/Debra Hill Production. *Editor:* Mark Goldblatt, Skip Schoolnik. *Executive in Charge of Production:* Nancy Platt Jacoby. *Music:* John Carpenter. *In Association with:* Alan Howarth. *Associate Producer:* Barry Bernardi. *Production Designer:* Michael Riva. *Director of Photography:* Dean Cundey. *Executive Producers:* Irwin Yablans, Joseph Wolf. *Written by:* John Carpenter and Debra Hill. *Produced by:* John Carpenter and Debra Hill. *Directed by:* Rick Rosenthal. *Stunts:* Hill Fransworth, Donna Garrett, Jessie Wayne, Glynn Rubin. *Production Manager:* Jeffrey Chernov. *First Assistant Director:* William S. Beasley. *Second Assistant Director:* Duncan S. Henderson. *Production Assistant:* Geoffrey Ryan. *Location Manager:* Ami Agmon. *Production Coordinator:* Lynne Birdt. *Script Supervisor:* Candy Ann Marcellino. *Production Assistant:* Randi Lynn Chernov. *Camera/Panaglide Operator:* Raymond Stella. *Additional Camera Operators:* Gary B. Kibbe, Douglas Ryan, Jiggs Garcia. *First Assistant Camera:* Clyde Bryan, Case Hotchkiss, Douglas Olivares. *Second Assistant Camera:* Joseph Riggs Murdock. *Sound Mixer:* Tommy Causey. *Boom Operator:* Joseph Brennan, Carl Fischer. *Set Decorator:* Peg Cummings. *Leadman:* Jerry Tirado. *Swing Gang:* Frank M. Furginson. *Property Master:* Daniel Lee Stoltenburg. *Assistant Property Master:* James A. Rathbun. *Property:* Kevin Colnin, Eugene J. Reed. *Propmaker:* Terry G. Feller. *Greensman:* Darrel Huntsman. *Gaffer:* Mark Walthour. *Rigging Gaffer:* Drain M. Marshall. *Best Boy Electric:* Thom H. Marshall. *Electricians:* Terry Marshall, Jr., Steven R. Mathis, Jon Antunovich, Walter Lott, Patrick G. Ralston, Dennis E. Shelton, Ray Thomas, Bobby W. Brown, Norris L. Essex. *Key Grip:* Ronald T. Woodward. *Best Boy Grip:* Kris Krosskove. *Grip:* Joe A. Salamdino, Richard Alexander, Laszlo Horvath. *Make-up Artist:* Michael Germain. *Hair-stylist:* Frankie Bergman. *Still Photographer:* Kim Gottlieb. *Make-up Technician:* John F. Chambers. *Costume*

Supervisor: Jane Ruhm. *Costumer:* Frances Vega Aubrey. *Associate Film Editor:* Michael D. Ornstein. *Assistant Film Editor:* Kimberly K. Ray, Jose Antonio Torres. *Stunt Coordinator:* Dick Warlock. *Negative Cutter:* Brian Ralph. *Special Effects Supervisor:* Larry Cavanaugh. *Special Effects:* Frank Munoz. *Craft Services:* Robert C. Burris, Steve Burris. *Technical Advisor:* Andy Bonin, MD. *Registered Nurse:* Maurice Costello, Jr. *First Aid:* Deborah D. Lee. *Production Illustrator:* Richard M. Sternbach. *Production Accountant:* Art Schaefer. *Production Assistant:* Patricia Klinger. *Casting:* Mary Gail Artz. *Extra Casting:* Susie Johnson. *Construction Coordinator:* Walton Hadfield. *Transportation Coordinator:* Eddie Lee Voelker. *Publicity:* Pickwick, Maslansky, Koeningsberg. *Main Title Sequence:* James Shourt, Shourt Works, Ltd. *Masks:* Don Post. *Sound Concepts:* Cineguild. *Supervising Sound Editor:* David Lewis Yewdall. *Sound Editor:* Walter Hamilton, David Stone, Michael C. Guitierrez. *Dialogue Editor:* Gene Wahrman. *Assistant Dialogue Editor:* Stephen Purvis. "Mr. Sandman" courtesy of Barnaby Records, performed by The Chordettes. *Night of the Living Dead* courtesy of the Laurel Group. *Color:* MGM. Filmed in Panavision. *Titles and Opticals:* Pacific Title. The Dino De Laurentiis Corporation. *MPAA Rating:* R. *Running Time:* 93 minutes.

"In order to appease the Gods, the druid priests held fire rituals. Prisoners of war, criminals, the insane, animals, worse ... burned alive in baskets. By observing the way they died, the druids believed they could see omens of the future. Two thousand years later we've come no further. Samhain isn't evil spirits. It isn't goblins, ghosts or witches. It's the unconscious mind. We're all afraid of the dark inside ourselves."— Dr. Loomis contemplates the nature of evil.

SYNOPSIS: On October 31, 1978, a night of horror continues in Haddonfield, Illinois.

Psychologist Sam Loomis has just shot escaped mental patient Michael Myers six times, but the resilient killer has nonetheless survived the encounter. Myers retreats from the Wallace yard, and he steals a butcher knife from the Elrod kitchen while Mrs. Elrod watches *Night of the Living Dead* on television. Michael Myers then sneaks into another house and kills another Haddonfield resident, young Alice. Elsewhere, the only survivor of the initial Myers massacre, teenager Laurie Strode, is rushed to Haddonfield Memorial Hospital by paramedics Jimmy and Budd. Once there, she is treated by the drunken Dr. Mixter and put into a drugged sleep.

Still looking for Myers, Sheriff Brackett and Dr. Loomis confront a man wearing the same ghoulish white mask as Myers. The trick-or-treater is killed in a fiery car collision, but Loomis suspects the dead man may not be Myers. Then, Brackett learns that his daughter Annie is one of the dead pulled out of the Wallace home. Angry, Brackett accuses Loomis of letting Myers out, and then goes home to console his wife. Deputy Hunt takes over the search for Myers, and Loomis suggests that they adjourn immediately to the coroner's office with a dentist to confirm the identity of the burned corpse.

At Haddonfield Hospital, the nursing staff is unaware that Myers has followed Laurie Strode there. Nurse Karen arrives late and is buzzed in by the overweight security guard, Mr. Garrett. Paramedic Jimmy goes to visit Laurie and begins to develop romantic feelings for her. He informs Laurie that her assailant was Michael Myers, and this knowledge triggers a memory in Laurie's dreams. She remembers an encounter from childhood when her mother informed her that she is *not* her mother. Even worse, she recalls being in an institution visiting a sullen adolescent. Was it Michael Myers?

The phones go dead in the hospital, and head nurse Mrs. Alves sends Janet, another nurse, to inform Mr. Garrett. Garrett leaves the hospital to investigate the telephone pole but he finds evidence of a break-in at the nearby storage building. Myers kills him there, smashing Garrett's skull with a claw hammer.

At the Haddonfield coroner's office, it is determined that the burned-up corpse was only 17 years old. Myers is 21. Soon the body is identified as being young Ben Tramer, a local teen. This discovery means that Myers is still on the loose, so Deputy Hunt and Dr. Loomis head back to the Myers house. When they arrive, they find that the property is being stoned by angry Haddonfield residents. Then, they are informed of a break-in at the Reservoir Road Elementary School, and they head to investigate. At the school, Loomis discovers a drawing of a family, with the Elrods' butcher knife pinned to the representation of the sister. The word "Samhain" is written in blood on the blackboard. Loomis is aware that Samhain is an ancient Celtic Festival referring to the end of Autumn and the beginning of winter — otherwise known as Halloween. Soon, Nurse Marion arrives and informs Loomis that he has been recalled from Haddonfield by the governor and Smith's Grove. A state marshal is waiting outside the school to escort him from town.

Back in the hospital, Nurse Karen and the paramedic Budd meet for an illicit rendezvous. In secret, they proceed to the therapy room and enter the hydrotherapy hot tub together. Michael arrives and kills Budd. He then turns up the heat in the pool and drowns Karen in the scalding water. The grisly murders begin to escalate, and Janet finds Dr. Mixter dead in his office with a needle lodged in his eyeball. Myers kills Janet too, jamming a hypodermic into her eye. Michael tracks Laurie Strode to her room, but she has anticipated his arrival and hobbled to a different room on her broken ankle. Once inside, an exhausted Laurie collapses.

Jimmy and another nurse, Jill, grow concerned because they cannot find Mrs. Alves, Janet, Karen, Budd or Dr. Mixter. Jimmy searches the hospital and finds Mrs. Alves dead in a surgical suite, the blood drained out of her body in an IV tube. Frightened,

Jimmy dashes from the room, only to slip in a pool of blood and fall into unconsciousness. Jill attempts to drive away and warn the sheriff's office, but her car will not start, and her tires are flat. When she looks around, she realizes that all the cars in the lot have flat tires! She runs back inside and finds Laurie, but is stabbed by Myers just as she makes contact.

Myers stalks Laurie through the empty halls of the hospital. She flees down a staircase, into a basement. There she discovers Garrett's body hanging from the ceiling. She escapes Myers in an elevator, and runs out into the parking lot and hides in Jimmy's car. Feeling the effects of a concussion, Jimmy also enters the vehicle. Unable to stay conscious, he falls against the car horn, inadvertently warning Myers of Laurie's location.

While leaving Haddonfield, Marion informs Dr. Loomis about a sealed history file relating to Michael Myers. It seems that Laurie Strode is Myers' younger sister, born two years after he was committed. Realizing that Laurie is again in danger because Myers plans to kill his last surviving sister, Loomis orders the Marshal to turn the car around. He fires a warning shot to make his point, and the car races for the Haddonfield Hospital.

In the parking lot, Laurie crawls away from Jimmy's car. She sees Dr. Loomis arrive and go inside the hospital just feet away, but he does not see her. As Laurie edges for the front door, Myers spots her, and the hunt is on once more. Laurie gets inside, but Myers walks through the locked glass door and keeps coming. Loomis shoots him four times. As Myers collapses, Marion runs outside to use the two-way radio and call for help. Inside, Myers bolts up and murders the state marshal. Cut off from the exit, Loomis and Laurie flee deeper into the hospital as Michael pursues. They find their way into an operating theater. When Loomis is stabbed in the gut with a scalpel, Laurie shoots Myers again, hitting both of his eyes. Blinded, Michael lunges at his two victims. Realizing that the evil must die here, Loomis opens all of the gas tanks in the room. He orders Laurie out of the operating theater, and declares to Michael that "it is time." He flicks on his cigarette lighter and the room explodes. On fire, Myers leaves the blazing inferno, still in pursuit of Laurie. Consumed by the flames, Myers finally collapses.

At last, morning comes to Haddonfield. Ten people are confirmed dead at the hospital, but Laurie Strode is alive. She is escorted from the hospital in an ambulance, and back in Haddonfield, Michael Myers's Halloween mask burns.

COMMENTARY: A sequel is rarely an equal, and *Halloween II* is no exception. It recreates the tricks of John Carpenter's original *Halloween*, but is less generous in the dispensing of the treats. That established, the film is not bad, especially in comparison to *Friday the 13th* and some of the later *Elm Street* films of the 1980s. *Halloween II* is no classic, but it is a respectable job that successfully continues the story of Michael Myers, Laurie Strode, Dr. Loomis and that tortured Illinois town of Haddonfield.

Halloween II opens with a well-composed crane shot in which the camera follows the branch of a tree to reveal the Doyle house, where the tense final moments of *Halloween* occurred. The last five minutes of *Halloween* are replayed in the new film to refresh a viewer's memory (since this film was released before the age of video rentals), and there are some interesting alterations. First off, the angle which shows Michael's young face once Laurie has pulled his mask off is completely excised. Secondly, there is a new exterior shot showing the flare of gunpowder in the darkness of the house as Loomis empties his revolver into Myers. And thirdly, the shot of Michael falling backwards off the ledge has been altered. Strangely, he now seems to be standing *on top* of a railing rather than behind it when he takes the plunge. Another revisionist touch involves Loomis. Now, he now longer notices that Michael Myers's body is missing until he runs down the stairs and rushes outside to the yard. This five-minute recap sequence exemplifies much of both the success and failure of *Halloween II*. Thanks to photography by the talented Dean Cundey and a script by Hill and Carpenter, it looks and feels a lot like *Halloween*, yet some of the specific details are skewed, just not quite right.

On the good side, it seems that great care has been taken to extend the look of the original picture. *Halloween II* opens with a title sequence in the same style as the original, with a jack-o-lantern looming larger and larger on the left side of the frame. As the camera gets closer, however, the pumpkin splits open to reveal a grinning, human skull on the inside wall. This is a different touch, but an acceptable one as it successfully continues the look and feel of the first picture (which also opened with a glowing jack-o-lantern on the left side of the screen). And, in a wonderful bit of cross-film continuity, Annie's corpse — played by Nancy Loomis — shows up for one short sequence. This shows that the crew took real care to make the film seem as if it was really happening on the same night. It would have been easy to keep Annie's corpse under a sheet, or not even show it at all, but instead Loomis was a good sport and came back for this "cameo." The horror movie film festival motif is also continued, with *Night of the Living Dead* playing now on Dr. Demento instead of *Forbidden Planet* or *The Thing*.

On the down side, it is difficult to see how the film crew missed some glaring, incorrect details. For instance, Michael Myers's mask has changed between films. Instead of ratty-looking dark hair, his mask is now decorated with light blonde hair! And Jamie Lee Curtis goes through *Halloween II* wearing a very bad, very obvious wig. She does not look at all as she did in *Halloween*, and so the two movies are a mismatch in that regard.

Still, although it is perhaps impossible for a sequel to perfectly mimic the look of its originator, *Halloween II* manages pretty well. One of the joys of *Halloween*, *Halloween II* and *Halloween III* is that all three films have a unified look (as shot by Cundey) and texture.

Laurie Strode (Jamie Lee Curtis in a bad wig) and Dr. Loomis (Donald Pleasence) go round two with the Shape in *Halloween II* (1981).

This is an admirable quality that is missing from many *Star Trek* sequels (remember how the bridge of the captured Klingon ship inexplicably changed between *Star Trek III: The Search for Spock* and *Star Trek IV: The Voyage Home*?). Lending further continuity between the films, director Rick Rosenthal repeats the subjective camera shots so favored by Carpenter. In *Halloween II*, Myers staggers through an alley, watching as Loomis contacts Sheriff Brackett. Through the whole scene, Myers is heard breathing, but the camera substitutes for his eyes. The only time that the subjective approach proves problematic for Rosenthal is once the action has settled in the hospital. There is a jump cut as Myers goes suddenly from a stairwell to a main hospital hallway. This is pretty much unforgivable since a subjective shot, by its very nature, is representative of human eyes and thus should be uninterrupted. It would be like a person walking down the stairs, but halfway down the steps suddenly finding

himself in another room. Surely the jump cut was used to keep the pacing of the film from flagging, but it is a stylistic miscue.

Halloween II fails to be a great movie primarily in two realms: believability and characterization. Believability is very important to a horror movie's success with audiences, but *Halloween II* makes some fatal errors. For instance, the Haddonfield Hospital has been constructed with what might be called a "smart" door, an entrance that only allows certain characters through it at certain times. Early in the film, it is established that this door is locked, and that the security man, Mr. Garrett, must "buzz" people through if they hope to gain entrance to the facility. Despite this, Michael Myers gets into the hospital unnoticed. Then, he gets out again, kills Mr. Garrett in storage, and gets back in — all without being buzzed in or out! One cannot make the argument that Mr. Garrett left the door unlocked to go search the storage, because at the climax of the picture, Jamie Lee

Curtis runs to the door and she cannot get in. The devil, as they say, is in the details, and *Halloween II* never believably explains how Michael Myers is able to get in and out of the hospital, and back again, without somebody noticing.

The timing of critical events is also a problem for *Halloween II*. Michael Myers escapes the Doyle house, steals the Elrods' knife, kills Alice, and then proceeds to the hospital, where he murders the hospital staff. Yet somehow, he also finds time to break into the elementary school and leave the clue "Samhain" scrawled on a blackboard. When did he do this? How did he cover so much territory in so little time? Remember, this is all supposed to be happening in one night!

The last issue of believability involves the hospital scenario itself. In *Halloween II*, the hallways are dark, the wards are abandoned, and there seems to be no significant second or third shift. Even a small hospital still supports a slew of technicians in the blood bank, the emergency room, the laboratory, specimen processing, histology, client services, and so forth. Where are these behind-the-scenes people? Where are the doctors? Where are the patients? Weirdly, this all-but-abandoned hospital is shown to have a ward filled with infants! Where are their mothers? Logically, they should still be in the hospital, recovering from giving birth. And certainly, it strains believability that there would be no patients in the emergency room on Halloween night. Although one kid is shown to have a razor blade stuck in his mouth, there would surely be other accidents to contend with as well. *Halloween II* never makes the hospital, its central setting, a believable or realistic place, and that fact is catastrophic to the film's overall success.

Characterization is also a stumbling block. Though Donald Pleasence and Charles Cyphers seem to be playing real people again, the new characters invented for *Halloween II* are not very interesting or unique. Budd is a two-dimensional character, both unpleasant and unattractive. He exists solely to be murdered

in the hydrotherapy pool. The rest of the nursing staff is undeveloped throughout the picture as well, and the audience never really gets to know Janet, Jill, Dr. Mixter, Ms. Alves or Mr. Garrett. Pamela Susan Shoop registers strongly as Karen, but this is because the actress has a likable screen presence, not because her character is especially well-written. Of the newcomers, Shoop and Lance Guest fare best, each making a positive impression overall. Still, these characters would not be important if Jamie Lee Curtis had something, anything, to do in *Halloween II*. The slimness of her role here suggests that she is being punished for something. She remains catatonic throughout the film, has little screen-time, and even fewer lines. Although she is stalked extensively at the end of *Halloween II*, viewers never re-connect emotionally to the sweet character that Curtis so expertly essayed in the original film. There is no doubt that Curtis is competent, but she simply has nothing of interest to do in *Halloween II*.

As for Michael Myers, he is but a shadow of his previous shape in this sequel. In the original, he watched and planned his massacre extensively. In the sequel, he walks into a house and kills Alice (a woman whom he has not seen before that moment), on a whim. Where is all the preparation? The fact that Michael now just appears and kills is not only out of character for the killer, it seriously dilutes the suspense. Frankly, much of *Halloween II* is lacking in suspense because Myers appears to a be a guest star in his own film, doing different murderous "bits." He appears and boils one woman's face in a hot tub, he appears and sticks a hypodermic needle in another's eyes. There is no build-up of tension, no structuring of his kills, just isolated gross-out moments. In addition, Myers has become unbelievably complicated in his killing methods in *Halloween II*. He kills Mrs. Alves by putting a tube into her veins and draining her of blood! Are audiences to believe that he is a doctor now? This is especially strange because when Jimmy finds

Mrs. Alves, she is not only leaking blood out of her arm, the tube is neatly sealed to her upper arm with perfectly applied bandages. So Myers not only performed an elaborate operation on her, he packaged up the wound as well! This elaborate method of offing a victim when a scalpel would do just as well diminishes the reality of *Halloween II*.

There is also no hiding the fact that Michael Myers has no real reason to kill any of the medical staff in *Halloween II*. Why not just find Laurie and kill her? Why waste all the time killing people he has not even bothered to observe before this moment? This Michael is more *Friday the 13th*'s Jason than a legitimate follow-up to the Myers throne.

Also disturbing is *Halloween II*'s reliance on the sex and death equation popularized by *Friday the 13th*. Karen and Bud are murdered because he is a jerk and she has violated her responsibilities (leaving the infant ward unattended) to engage in sex in a hydrotherapy pool. They are both offed for their transgressions, but it seems hard to believe that a nurse would so willingly and repeatedly break the rules. How did she get through nursing school if she were really this undisciplined? Probably the most effective part of the hot tub sequence is when Karen, unaware, caresses and kisses Myers's hand. He stands there immobile, accepting the loving gestures in a kind of pleased silence.

Despite all of these problems, *Halloween II* does possess qualities which elevate it above its competitors in the horror genre. The final stalking sequence is exciting and intense, thanks to a combination of the musical score and good direction. The suspense really takes off at the climax of the picture as Jamie Lee Curtis is caught behind elevator doors that close too slowly as Myers approaches, crunching broken glass on the floor as he walks. Had the rest of the film been as intense as the last 20 minutes, this review would look very different. Still, expectations are not high for slasher films. It is quite possible that the adrenaline-inducing nature of this sequence is enough for fans of the genre. That is what they look for, and *Halloween II* does, in the final analysis, deliver that jolt. Rewardingly, Rick Rosenthal has also done a fine job of keeping Michael Myers "invisible," at the fringes of perception (and the frame) again and again. Here his ghoulish shadow is seen behind curtains, and his mask is eerily lit by the light of a fish tank. When more and more horror sequels insist on showing their villains in the open, *Halloween II* maintains Michael Myers's menace by keeping him hidden as often as is possible.

Though short on suspense at points, *Halloween II* is not short on jolts and opportunities to cringe. Michael Myers walking among a bunch of helpless babies in the infant ward is enough to give anybody nightmares. And the sequence where a kid with a boom box unexpectedly walks smack into Myers on a street corner is guaranteed to make one spill the popcorn. As the two pedestrians touch, the *Halloween* theme kicks into high gear, and this movie, for at least a second, feels like John Carpenter's electric original. What differentiates it from the original is that this film lingers on wounds and gore, whereas there was very little blood in *Halloween*. The most sickening moments in *Halloween II* involve a boy (Ty Mitchell of *The Fog*) with a razor blade in his mouth, and Dr. Mixter's repeated bungling of an injection in Laurie's arm. The latter sequence could cause fainting in anyone uncomfortable with needles.

Perhaps the best facet of *Halloween II* involves the decision to incorporate *Night of the Living Dead* not just as an "onscreen" reference, but as a thematic parallel. On a television set, George Romero's film plays out, and in the alleys of Haddonfield it really is the "night of the living dead" as Michael, shot six times, shambles about the neighborhood. Drawing further attention to the fact that Michael is now one of the living dead, he is seen in black and white on one of the hospital monitors, again making a symbolic connection to that classic black and white horror film. In its characters, *Halloween II* also nicely evokes *Night of the Living Dead.*

Jamie Lee Curtis spends much of the film catatonic, useless and in a state of shock, like the character of Barbara (Judith O'Dea) in the Romero film. This may not seem significant, but it proves that *Halloween II* at least has something other than gory murders on its mind.

In the context of John Carpenter's career, *Halloween II* does not seem to be one of his better scripts. It starts off quite well, and has an interesting dialogue about the nature of evil (quoted above the synopsis for the film), but in the final analysis it is neither streamlined nor elegant; it is merely inferior. It also manages to minimize some of the horror of *Halloween*. Viewers learn in *Halloween II*, for instance, that Laurie is Michael's sister. Suddenly, there is a crystal-clear motivation for his spree: He is killing his sisters. Though many people surely wanted just such an explanation, it was surely more frightening when people did not know what Myers wanted, and he was simply a killing machine with no understandable motivations. The whole "sister" subplot is awkwardly inserted in *Halloween II* as well. It is revealed in a nightmare that makes no sense. Since Laurie was born after Michael Myers was committed to an asylum, the only way he could have knowledge of her is if she visited him during his incarceration. And indeed, the dream sequence shows such a visit, with an innocent little girl facing Myers in the asylum. It is not believable, by any standard, that the Strodes would permit their adopted daughter to go in and visit alone the brother who had killed her other sister. After all, they went to all the trouble of sealing Laurie's adoption files so that nobody would know the connection be-

tween Michael and Laurie. So why on earth would they let her go visit him alone? How did she get in the sanitarium to see him if she did not acknowledge her relationship to him? Furthermore, why did her adopted parents even reveal to her that she was related to Myers? If they wanted to keep it a secret, they would not have told her the truth.

A question that many people persist in asking is this: Would *Halloween II* have been better had John Carpenter directed it? There is no point in asking when the fact of the matter is that John Carpenter would *not* have directed this picture. He is on record insisting that having done *Halloween* once, he has no intention of doing it again. Rick Rosenthal did a fair job with *Halloween II*, considering the circumstances and how the film was altered after he delivered his cut. Today, *Halloween II* is regarded as a better sequel than *Halloween III*, *Halloween V* or *Halloween VI*, so Rosenthal's contributions are appreciated by many fans of the series. Of course, he had big shoes to fill. *Halloween* is not only a good film, it is the best film of its kind. The differences in quality between *Halloween* and *Halloween II* roughly approximate those between *2001: A Space Odyssey* and *2010*. The first film is a masterpiece; its follow-up is well-intentioned and competent, but somewhere, the magic got lost.

There is one last interesting trivia note about *Halloween II*. Three of its stars appeared on the first season of the TV series *Buck Rogers in the 25th Century* just prior to filming this sequel. Ana Alicia and Pamela Susan Shoop appeared together in the episode "Vegas in Space," and Jamie Lee Curtis headlined in "Unchained Woman."

Halloween III:
Season of the Witch (1982)

Critical Reception

"The marriage of mysticism and the microchip at the film's heart ... is swamped by the emphasis on maintaining a quota of gory shock effects. Yet the break from the psycho-killer formula is welcome, and there's much pleasing ingenuity on display in the yoking of such disparate models as *Invasion of the Body Snatchers* and ... *Telefon*.... A nice sense of absurdity too, in the throwaway notion of malevolent robotic leprechauns." — Phil Hardy, *The Film Encyclopedia: Science Fiction*, William Morrow, New York, 1984, page 381.

"The concept was chilling as well as campy, but the final film seemed exploitative and diffidently made.... This third sequel was an unlikely and sadistic story not very well told." — Richard Meyers, *The Great Science Fiction Films*, Citadel Press, 1983, page 228.

"Director-writer Tommy Lee Wallace creates a few scary sequences, but an element of fun is missing." — John Stanley, *Creature Features Movie Guide Strikes Again*, Creatures-At-Large Press, 1994, page 170.

Cast and Credits

CAST: Tom Atkins (Dr. Daniel Challis); Stacey Nelkin (Ellie Grimbridge); Dan O'Herlihy (Conal Cochrane); Michael Curry (Rafferty); Ralph Strait (Buddy Kupler); Jadeen Barbor (Betty Kupler); Bradley Schachter (Little Buddy); Garn Stephens (Marge Gutman); Nancy Kyes (a.k.a. Nancy Loomis) (Linda Challis); Jon Terry (Starker); Al Berry (Harry Grimbridge); Wendy Wessberg (Teddy); Essex Smith (Walter Jones); Maidie Norman (Nurse Agnes); John McBride (Sheriff); Loyd Catlett (Charlie); Paddi Edwards (Secretary); Norman Merrill (Red); Patrick Pankurst (Technician); Dick Warlock (Assassin); Martin Cassidy (Watcher); Michelle Walker (Bella Challis); Joshua Miller (Willie Challis); Jeffrey D. Henry (Motel Technician); Michael W. Green (Technician #2).

CREDITS: Universal/MCA and Moustapha Akkad Presents A John Carpenter/Debra Hill Production. *Editor:* Millie Moore, a.c.e. *Executive in Charge of Production:* Jeffrey Chernov. *Special Make-up:* Tom Burman. *Music:* John Carpenter and Alan Howarth. *Associate Producer:* Barry Bernardi. *Production Designer:* Peter Jamison. *Director of Photography:* Dean Cundey. *Executive Producers:* Irwin Yablans, Joseph Wolf. *Produced by:* Debra Hill and John Carpenter. *Written and Directed by:* Tommy Lee Wallace. *Stunts:* Dick Warlock, Loren Janes, Kerrie Cullen. *Unit Production Manager:* Jeffrey Chernov. *First Assistant Director:* Ron L. Wright. *Second Assistant Director:* Scott Ira Thaler. *Casting:* Susan Shaw. *Visual Consultant:* Charles R. Moore. *Location Manager:* Ben-Ami Asmon. *Production Coordinator:* Chip Fowler. *Script Supervisor:* Louise Jaffe. *Assistant to Ms. Hill:* Randi Linn Chernov. *Assistant to Mr. Bernardi:* Carol Rosenthal. *Assistant to Mr. Chernov:* Michele Little. *Assistant to Matt Franco:* David Gersh. *Camera Operator:* Raymond Stella. *First Assistant Cameraman:* Clyde E. Bryan. *Second Assistant Cameraman:* Guy Ladd Skinner. *Second Unit Cameraman:* Steve St. John. *Second Unit Assistant Cameraman:* David Golia. *Still Photographer:* Ronald Batzdorff. *Production*

Sound Mixer: Tommy Causey. *Boom Operators:* Joseph Brennan, Andy Rovins. *Gaffer:* Mark D. Walthour. *Best Boy Electric:* Thom Marshall. *Electricians:* Patrick H. Marshall, Steven R. Mathis, Allen Marshall, Jon Antunovich. *Key Grip:* Ronald T. Woodward. *Best Boy Grip:* Joe A Salamdino. *Dolly Grip:* Laszlo Horvath. *Grips:* Nick Kurges, Richard Babin, Mark Pearson. *Craft Service:* Mark Grech. *Special Effects:* John G. Belyeu. *Special Effects Assistant:* William Aldridge. *Set Decorator:* Linda Spheeris. *Leadman:* William Wright. *Swing Gang:* Greg Lynch. *Property Masters:* James A. Rathbun, Daniel Stoltenberg. *Video Coordinator:* David Katz. *Illustrator:* Carl Aldana. *Costume Supervisor:* Jane Ruhm. *Costumer:* Francis Aubrey. *Make-up Artist:* Ron Walters. *Hair Stylist:* Frankie Bergman. *Stunt Coordinator:* Dick Warlock. *Extra Casting:* Susie Johnson. *First Assistant Editor:* Maurie Beck. *Second Assistant Editor:* Patricia Lee. *Publicist:* Ann Thomson. *Production Accountant:* Larry Hand. *Assistant Accountant:* Lynn D. Ezelle. *Location Assistants:* Kenny Lavet, Bill Cherones. *Construction Coordinator:* Waldon Hadfield. *Propmaker Foreman:* James Walker. *Propmaker:* Terry Feller. *Labor Foreman:* Andrew Flores. *Standby Painter:* Serge Genitempo. *Construction Painter:* Jerry Palermo. *First Aid:* Maurice Costello, Jr., Bernie Granados, Jr. *Caterer:* Bert Jetter. *Transport Coordinator:* Eddie Lee Vollker. *Transportation Captain:* Wayne Roberts. *Drivers:* Tom Thomas, Mario Simon, Ray Appel, Gordon Wiles, Jim Lundin, Tommy Villardo, Chuck Hampton, Dave Pierce, Jim Huffey, Marten Huffey, Steve Grossman, Louis Galliani. *Supervising Sound Editor:* David Lewis Yendall. *Sound Editors:* Warren Hamilton, Colin Mouat. *Dialogue Editor:* Ken Sweet. *Re-recorded at:* Goldwyn Sound Facility. *Re-recording Mixers:* Bill Varney, Steve Maslow, James Cavarretta, Jr. *Post-Production Expediter:* Gretchen Baker. *Animal Coordinator:* Jim Brockett. *Motor Police:* Doug and Bob Laird. *Title Sequence:* John Wash. *Silver Shamrock Commercial:* Sam Nicholson. *Halloween Masks Created by:* Don Post. *Color:* Technicolor. *Filmed in Panavision. Titles and Opticals:* Pacific Title. Creative Mobile Studios. Animation Courtesy of Bakshi Productions, Inc. Special Thanks to: Republic Airlines, Ruxton Ltd, the People of Loleta and Eureka, California. *MPAA Rating:* R. *Running Time:* 99 minutes.

"The barriers would be down, you see, between the real and the unreal, and the dead might be looking in…. Halloween … the last great one took place 3,000 years ago and the hills ran red with the blood of animals and children…. It's time again…. The world's going to change tonight."—Conal Cochrane, explains his motivations to a shocked Dan Challis.

SYNOPSIS: On Saturday night, the 23rd of October, a man runs for his life as a pursuing car relentlessly tracks him down. The frightened man hides in the darkness of a junk yard but is soon attacked by a powerful man wearing a gray business suit. The victim, toy shop owner Harry Grimbridge, escapes his nemesis and runs to a gas station. There he collapses in exhaustion, still gripping tightly a popular Silver Shamrock Halloween mask. The gas station attendant rushes Grimbridge to the hospital and Grimbridge, in shock, warns physician Dr. Challis that "*they are going to kill everyone.*" At first Challis, a divorced father of two, assumes that this warning is just the rambling of a delusional mind. His attitude changes, however, when Grimbridge is murdered in his hospital bed by a bland-looking man in a gray business suit. Challis chases the killer out of the hospital and watches in horror as the assassin enters his car and methodically immolates himself.

The next morning, Dr. Challis meets Grimbridge's daughter, Ellie. She suspects that her father was murdered not by some drug-crazed addict as the police claim, but for some other nefarious purpose. She plans to retrace his last steps before death, and Challis agrees to accompany her on the investigation. Together, they head to idyllic Santa Mira to pick up Grimbridge's supply of Halloween masks from the Silver Shamrock Novelties Factory. Santa Mira, however, is a very strange town. The entire hamlet is run like a corporation by cold-hearted Silver Shamrock CEO Conal Cochran, and video cameras monitor the populace at all times. Ellie and Challis check into a fleabag motel as a married couple, and then investigate the Silver Shamrock factory.

At the factory, Dr. Challis and Ellie are soon met by other "tourists," Buddy Kupler and his family. Buddy is the top Silver Shamrock salesman in the country. Mr. Cochrane graciously escorts the Kuplers, Challis and Ellie on a tour of his mask-making facility, but pointedly refuses to grant access to an area called "Final Processing." While leaving the factory, Ellie glimpses her father's green station wagon tucked away in one of Cochrane's industrial buildings. Now she knows Cochrane and Silver Shamrock were involved with her father's death, but gray-suited businessmen, like the one who immolated himself at the hospital, surround the car.

In another motel room, a mask buyer from San Francisco fiddles with a defective Silver Shamrock mask. She is shocked to learn that the circular Silver Shamrock trademark emblem has a microchip imbedded in it. When the buyer tampers with the chip, it shoots out a blue laser beam and incinerates her face, and disgusting insects crawl out of her mutilated mouth. Silver Shamrock authorities are on the scene immediately and one technician warns Cochran that this incident was a "misfire." Challis overhears the remark and wonders what it could possibly mean.

Cochrane has the whole town bugged, so he is soon aware that Challis has sent a pathologist to examine the ashes of Grimbridge's assassin. Interestingly, she has found nothing organic, only wires and mechanical gears. Soon, a gray-suited minion of Silver Shamrock pays the pathologist a visit, and murders her as well.

While Challis waits to hear back from his friend, Ellie is apprehended and taken to Cochrane's stronghold at the factory. Challis attempts a rescue, but is also captured. Amused, Cochrane shows Challis the entire Shamrock operation, for real this time. His gray-suited assistants are not human at all, but life-size "toys," or androids, that kill at his bidding. Furthermore, the microchips in the Silver Shamrock Halloween masks have microscopic pieces of a stolen Stonehenge rock imbedded inside. Thus the masks are a combination of ancient magic and modern technology. Cochrane calls this unholy union a new form of witchcraft.

Then, Cochrane demonstrates the power of the hybrid microchip to a puzzled Challis. Buddy Kuppler's boy puts on his Halloween mask, and when he watches a television commercial for Silver Shamrock his head breaks open and spews forth a skittering army of hopping insects and slithering snakes. Cochrane plans to duplicate this horrid event for a nationwide audience. On Halloween night, every child with a Silver Shamrock mask, including Challis's two children, will have their brains turned into this fetid, juicy stew of horror while watching the nationally broadcast Silver Shamrock commercial.

As 9:00 Halloween night, the time of the destructive signal, approaches rapidly, Challis rescues Ellie and causes a massive microchip misfire in the factory that kills Cochrane and his technical crew of androids. Challis and Ellie flee Santa Mira and race to warn the world about the deadly television signal. Then Challis discovers that Ellie, like the gray-suited minions of Cochrane, is but an android! As she attacks, he decapitates her and flees to a nearby gas station. He urgently phones the television networks and begs them not to air the Silver Shamrock commercial at 9:00 P.M. Two networks comply with the request, but the third continues to transmit as the clock ticks.

COMMENTARY: To its credit, *Halloween III: Season of the Witch* looks and sounds an awful lot like a John Carpenter film. With

"One more day till Halloween…" A lab tech adorns a deadly Silver Shamrock mask in *Halloween III: Season of the Witch* (1982).

Dean Cundey's camera capturing his particular and notable variety of impenetrable nighttime landscapes, and Carpenter himself contributing his typical pulse-pounding soundtrack, this second sequel feels very much like "the real thing," at least on the surface. Adding to the feeling is the fact that director Tommy Lee Wallace repeats many of Carpenter's favorite stylistic touches. There are the innumerable "stingers" in *Halloween III*, those trademark Carpenter moments in which something malevolent leaps into the foreground of compositions, accompanied by a loud jolt on the soundtrack. There are also several long, slow tracking shots, another hallmark of Carpenter's work. *Halloween III* is not a Carpenter-directed motion picture, but it is a remarkable simulation. Wallace does such a good job of aping Carpenter's *modus operandi* throughout that one wishes he had been called on to direct *Halloween II*. It is obvious he has studied Carpenter's moves.

Sadly, *Halloween III: Season of the Witch* is not a very good film, despite Wallace's conscious homage to John Carpenter's *mise-en-scène*. Although it is a bold step away from the "stalker" milieu of *Halloween* and its many imitators, it is not necessarily a step in the right direction. For what has replaced Carpenter's simple but compelling template (the bogeyman let loose on Halloween) is a confusing, mean-spirited mess with too many plot-holes to be coherent. Part of *Halloween*'s charm was undoubtedly its simplicity of story: Michael Myers came home, after 15 years, to continue his killing spree. In fact, in most of the best horror movies the plot is a linear, uncomplicated one that allows the director to insert his own unique visual style. Consider *Night of the Living Dead* (1968), in which re-animated corpses attack a farmhouse; *The Evil Dead* (1982), in which demons are resurrected in the woods; and *Rosemary's Baby* (1966), in which a woman fears she is carrying the Devil's baby. Each of these pictures features a clean central narrative that is elegant in its clarity and simplicity. Contrast any of those films with *Halloween III*, in which two people find a bizarre town run by an Irish tyrant. Guarded by super-strong androids, actually advanced toys, this megalomaniac is selling Halloween masks to youngsters. The masks carry a combination of Stonehenge rock and computer microcircuitry which at the right time (a television transmission) will cause the children's faces to turn to a mush of snakes and insects. Unlike *Halloween*, *Night of the Living Dead*, or even *The Omen* (1976) and *From Dusk Till Dawn* (1995), the story of *Halloween III* cannot be relayed in a single sentence in any log-ical fashion. Instead, the over-complicated plot raises a number of logistical and dramatic questions.

The town of Santa Mira (named after the town in Don Siegel's *Invasion of the Body Snatchers* [1956]) is a weird industrial factory town reminiscent of Midwich in *Village of the Damned* (1960), Stepford in *The Stepford Wives* (1975), or part of the ongoing British *Quatermass* saga. This setting raises many questions. Are all of the town's inhabitants in on Cochrane's plan to destroy the children of America? If so, why? Are they all descendants of Irish witches? If not, then how can they fail to realize what he is doing, since so many townfolk are employed at the mask factory? Furthermore, have all the town's people been replaced by androids (like *The Stepford Wives*), or are they still human? What about the town's infrastructure? How could the Chamber of Commerce or the police force allow Cochrane's loudspeakers and video-cameras to be put up on every street corner? This is America, after all; wouldn't someone be interested in the civil rights violations occurring in Santa Mira?

The bottom line is that the whole concept of an "evil" town is not sufficiently explored. In *In the Mouth of Madness*, Carpenter returns to the concept of an evil town (Hobb's End), but the concept works there because the town stands on the border separating fiction and reality. Its denizens are the denizens of Lovecraft fiction. Likewise for *The Stepford Wives*, which delineated its town in realistic fashion and saw heroine Katharine Ross learn about the slow process of android replacement. There is no such story clarity in *Halloween III*.

More important in the grand scheme of things is *Halloween III*'s failure to explain anything in terms of character motivation. Why does Cochrane want to kill the children of the country? Just to give all the parents a big "boo?" Just because he is Irish? In the film, when asked this question, Cochrane responds, "Do I need a reason?" On one hand this "motives are incidental" notion may be a forward step towards the landmark *Scream* horror films of the 1990s. On the other hand, it just points out, in this case, that the plot is nonsensical.

In fact, Cochrane's plot really makes no sense for a whole variety of reasons. The first involves the success factor of his plan. Assume for a moment that he is victorious, and that the masks turn all the children of America into that fetid, gooey snake-and-bug stew. *Someone* will certainly put two and two together and realize that Cochrane's masks are responsible, because his company paid for the commercials which caused the transformation. Knowing this, America's enraged parents will, in all likelihood, nuke Santa Mira right off the face of the planet. Why create a dastardly plan that can so obviously be traced back to the source? Furthermore, why draw attention to yourself when you are the dictator of your own little suburb? Cochrane rules Santa Mira with his androids, video cameras and loudspeakers. Why would he mess with a good thing?

Secondly, the plan is totally bogus from a marketing standpoint: The Cochrane Silver Shamrock masks are among the most bland and uninteresting Halloween masks imaginable (a skeleton, a witch, and a pumpkin). What would happen to all the kids who want to go out on Halloween as Batman, or the Power Rangers, or E.T., or Captain Kirk, or Michael Myers, or Wonder Woman, or Superman, or Dracula, or the Wolfman, or Frankenstein, or any other of the myriad all-time favorite Halloween costumes? Even if Cochrane could conceivably corner the market with his unusually simple and uninteresting Halloween masks, there would still be a large percentage of children in America who opted for the aforementioned costumes, thus making Cochrane's plan a failure. What about parents (who would not wear masks)? What about those children who are not watching television at 9:00 P.M. because they are still out trick-or-treating? What about those kids who are in bed already? What about the families that do not celebrate Halloween? What

about the young adults (13 to 16) who have stopped trick-or-treating? Although *Halloween III* tries to make the point through the oft-repeated Silver Shamrock mask commercial that people will buy anything sold on television, the central concept of the film is childish and badly realized.

Halloween III has other problems besides the fact that its central location is hard to swallow and its plan for world domination is unmotivated and nonsensical. The menace in the film comes from the many gray-suited androids deployed by Cochrane. In dramatizing these minions of evil, director Wallace attempts to go for the same kind of faceless horror represented by the white-masked Michael Myers in the earlier *Halloween* films, but that game plan simply does not work here. These men are individuals, and they just look skinny and rather dorky going about their grim business in three-piece suits. Another problem is this: Why do these android men put on black gloves before committing murder? Are they afraid of leaving android fingerprints? Why program these creatures to sneeze and mimic other human behavior, if their faces are always going to be expressionless?

While on the subject of plot inconsistencies, when during the conclusion of *Halloween III* does Ellie (Stacey Nelkin) have time to be replaced by an android? Was she an android all throughout the film (as her line to Challis in the motel, "I'm older than I look" suggests)? If so, then why did she lead Challis to Santa Mira and jeopardize Cochrane's plan? If she is an android, why is she not as bland and waxy as the others? Challis even makes love to her. Would he not notice that she is ... uhm ... different? On the other hand, if Ellie is not an android throughout *Halloween III*, then did the unbelievably efficient Cochrane just happen to have an android replica of her standing by? If instead he built the android on the spot, he must have done it in no more than five minutes, since Challis followed Ellie after she was captured by Cochrane's men. If Ellie was not a robot throughout the entire motion picture, then what happened to the original woman? Is she dead? Captured? Converted? Why does Challis never go back to find her, or rescue her if he suspects she is still alive somewhere?

Lastly, why did Cochrane bother to make an android of Ellie at all? Was he planning for Challis to escape from his lair from the very beginning? If so, why did he bother tying up Challis and putting the evil mask over his helpless head? Furthermore, if Ellie is an android minion of Cochrane, why does she stand idly by and watch Challis destroy the mask-making factory? Instead of stopping Challis when he is jeopardizing the master plan, this super accurate android (down to her decorated fingernails) waits until Challis has escaped. Then, as they drive away to safety, she attacks. Why did she wait? Obviously, this was a ploy on the part of the writer to give the story a final "jump," but like so many things in *Halloween III*, it is not dramatically motivated. On the contrary, this plot point makes not even a modicum of sense.

A list of *Halloween III*'s many problems could conceivably go on forever. The performances are universally bland and unmemorable. The final battle between the Ellie android and Challis is ridiculous (with Ellie's decapitated head sitting in the dirt while her disembodied hand clutches at Challis's neck), as well as overlong. The Stonehenge laboratory set is woefully cheap: A circle of television monitors sitting on everyday metal lattice shelves is not very intimidating or high-tech. The special effects are middling, especially when Cochrane is struck by a blue laser beam from Stonehenge. He turns to stone, apparently (though he looks more like a yummy pie crust), and then he disappears. But to where? Additionally, the sex scene is unmotivated. Ellie and Challis just jump into the sack together, despite the fact there is no real feeling of attraction or chemistry between the two characters (or performers). Also, Challis is seen carrying beer bottles and six-packs, and is shown drinking so often that he comes

off as a raving alcoholic rather than a sympathetic protagonist.

The murders tend to be extraneous as well. The film resorts to killing a pathologist who is not in Santa Mira, and a bum who might have said something politically incorrect to Challis. What do these deaths have to do with the plot? Worst of all, when Challis escapes from Cochrane, the film loses all semblance of realism. In one shot, he throws his mask successfully over a surveillance camera on the ceiling. It catches, of course, and he escapes unseen through an *oversized vent shaft!* As any Trekkie can affirm, the oversized vent shaft is perhaps the worst cliché of bad television science fiction. There is always a giant vent shaft around when you need one. In *Star Trek* the oversized vent shaft saved Captain Kirk in "Dagger of the Mind." In *Space: 1999* it saved Commander Koenig in "The Dorcons." In *Star Trek: Voyager* it was used in "Basics."

On top of all this, *Halloween III* is undeniably mean-spirited: The whole plot concerns an attempt to mutilate and murder innocent children ... something even Michael Myers would never stoop to. In fact, *Halloween III*'s hatred of children is downright weird considering that this film is supposed to be a mass entertainment. The film spends a lot of time on torturing little Buddy Kupler and showing Challis's kids in jeopardy. Although some films have used the children-in-danger plot effectively (*Aliens* [1986], *Shocker* [1989], *Village of the Damned* [1995]), *Halloween III* does not earn the right to be so hateful.

Despite so many flaws, *Halloween III* does manage to feature a few (very few) interesting moments. The title sequence, for instance, is among the most unique moments of the film. A video-game jack-o-lantern is carved on the screen as if by light pen. This is a modernization of *Halloween* and *Halloween II*'s opening credits, in which a real, rather than virtual, pumpkin was carved. This "technology age" pumpkin then harkens back not only to earlier entries and the "trick-or-treat" motif, it suggest the tenets of this particular installment: terror through technology (specifically television). The creepy music, not the original *Halloween* theme, is also electronic, signaling the electronic, artificial nature of the terror to come.

The structure of *Halloween III* is also promising. It is a circular structure, not unlike *Invasion of the Body Snatchers* or *In the Mouth of Madness*. It begins with Ellie's father as he is pursued by evil androids. In a tense, well-directed sequence, he escapes his pursuers long enough to warn the world what is about to happen. By the end of the film, Dr. Challis has found himself at exactly the same spot. He is back to the same gas station, sounding crazy, pursued, and desperate. In a film with few really exciting or valuable moments, this cyclical structure manages to endow the less-than-satisfactory story with a *Twilight Zone* sort of irony. Also welcome is the continuation of the Halloween film-festival motif from *Halloween* and *Halloween II*. In those earlier pictures, characters in the play viewed *Forbidden Planet*, *The Thing*, and *Night of the Living Dead*. In *Season of the Witch*, Challis sits in a bar and watches a commercial for the network broadcast of *Halloween*—a film described in voice-over as an "immortal classic."

Although *Halloween III* is filled with gore and violence, it reaches it pinnacle of creepiness in a well-orchestrated sequence near the film's finale. There is a nice montage of little hands picking up Halloween masks as costumed children from Dayton, Omaha, Baton Rouge, Los Angeles and New York march across various nighttime landscapes. Behind these moving silhouetted figures, a deep orange sky looms menacingly. This is a disturbing image, as the strange little costumed trolls traverse the surface of what could be another planet. For the first time in the *Halloween* pictures, the chill of expectation and anticipation on All Hallow's Eve has been captured beautifully and lyrically. Night has not yet come, only twilight, but the promise of a ghostly evening, from sea to shining sea, captures the universality of the trick-or-treat experience. This brief sequence is too little too late, but it nicely sets a mood of terror before the climax.

Although *Halloween III* is an honest attempt to take the *Halloween* franchise in a bold new direction, it is a failure dramatically and financially. It reminds one of a very bad James Bond film. As the talking villain (Cochrane) takes the captured hero (Challis) through his dark headquarters and evil plans, the universal nature of Halloween has been supplanted by the humdrum predictability of one too many sequels in a tired franchise.

Halloween III: Season of the Witch was so badly received that another *Halloween* film did not follow for six years. That sequel, *The Return of Michael Myers*, ignored the events of the third film — and wisely so.

The Philadelphia Experiment (1984)

Critical Reception

"A fast-moving, action-filled, quite intelligent science fiction film that places emotions over special effects and hardware ... the kind of film that just might attract a cult."— Kevin Thomas, *The Los Angeles Times*, August 3, 1984.

"A mild sci-fi diversion."— Stephen M. Silverman, *The New York Post,* August 1985.

"*Experiment*, written by Wallace Bennett and Don Jakoby, has its moments, but credible performances and an interesting story are not enough to compensate for gaps in logic large enough to sail a battleship through." — Douglas Menville and R. Reginald, *Futurevisions: The New Golden Age of the Science Fiction Film*, Newcastle Publishing, 1985, page 176.

Cast and Credits

CAST: Michael Pare (David Herdeg); Nancy Allen (Allison); Eric Christmas (Dr. Longstreet); Bobby DiCicco (Jimmy Parker); Louise Latham (Pamela); Ken Holliday (Major Clark); Joe Corsey (Sheriff Bates); Michael Currie (Magnussen); Stephen Tobolowsky (Barney); Gary Brockett (Adjutant Andrews); Debra Troyer (Young Pamela); Miles McNamara (Young Longstreet); Ralph Manza (Older Jim); James Edgcomb (Officer Boyer); Glenn Morshower (Mechanic); Vivian Brown (Ma Willis); Ed Bakey (Pa Willis); Vaughn Armstrong (Cowboy) Rodney Saulsberry (Doctor); Stephanie Faulkner (TV Newscaster #1); Michael Villani (TV Newscaster #2); Bill Smillie (Evangelist); Stephan O'Reilly (Punk Rocker); Lawrence Lott (Technician); Clayton Wilcox (Transvestite); Pat Dasko (Newscaster); Pamela Brull (Doris); Richard Jewkes (Technician); Pamela Doucette (Nurse); Deborah Dixon (Nurse); Michael Ruud (Truckdriver); Mary Lois Grantham (Mrs. Waite); Rick Schrand (Mandell); Radar Technician (Brent Laing); Patrick DeSantis (Jim, Jr.); Charles Hall (Commander); David Allen Michaels (Prison Guard); Raymond Kowlaski (Radio Technician); Andrew McCartney (Technician); Anthony R. Nuzzo (Technician); Robin Krieger (X-Ray Technician); Joe Moore (Commander's Buddy); Don Dolan (Driver); Jeffrey S. Smith (Sailor); Tony Farrell (Band Leader); Andrew Bracken (Dazed Sailor); Rudy Daniels (Policeman); Jay Bernard (Engineer); Steve Bachs (First Sailor); Bo Parham (Radio Operator); Harry Beer (Second Sailor); Kerry Lee Maher (Radio Operator); Lawrence Doll (Helicopter Pilot).

CREDITS: New World Pictures and Cinema Group Present a Douglas Curtis Production. In Association with New Pictures Group. *Casting:* Linda Francis. *Special Visual Effects:* Max W. Anderson. *Editor:* Neil Travis. *Visual Consultant:* W. Stewart Campbell. *Director of Photography:* Dick Bush. *Music:* Ken Wannberg. *Associate Producer:* Peg Brotman. *Executive Producer:* John Carpenter. *Story:* Wallace Gray and Michael Janover. *Producer:* Joel B. Michaels, Douglas Curtis. *Director:* Stewart Raffill. *Stunt Coordinator:* Fernando Celis. *Stunt Players:* John Epstein, Monty Cox, Gloria Fioramonti, Ged Ginag, Lee Fraggastis. *Production Manager:* Billy Ray Smith. *First Assistant Director:* Patrick Kehoe, Jeffrey Chernov. *Second Assistant Director:* Gail Joyce Fortmuller. *Art Director:* Chris Campbell. *Production Coordinator:* Coni Lancaster. *Editor:* William Hoy. *Production Auditor:* Amy Rabins. *Camera Operator:* Robert Hayes. *First Assistant Cameraman:* Paul Elliott. *Second Assistant Cameraman:* Steven Finestone. *Key Grip:* Ron McCausland. *Gaffer:* Roger Olkowski. *Costumer:* Joanne Palace. *Makeup:* Annie Maniscalco. *Hair:* Joe Giannone. *Prop Master:* Lee Berglund. *Prop Assistant:* John Carney. *Set Decorator:* Diane Campbell. *Lead Set Dresser:* Terry Kelley. *Assistant Wardrobe:* Marydith Chase. *Casting Assistant:* Jeff Greenberg. *Best Boy Grip:* Phil Broan. *Grips:* David Michaels, Michael Stacks, Dylan Shephard. *Best Boy Electric:* Ben Hausing, Wayne Stroud. *Electricians:* Vincent Contarino, Michael Bolner, Paul Hauser, Ron Sky, Garfield Burke, Nicolas Cline, Michael La Violette. *Transport Captain:* Tom Thomas. *Drivers:* Allan Herendeen, Johnny R. Bartlett, Al Bartoli, Jimmy Dale Holland, Ken Haight. *Generator Technican:* Victor Kloster. *Sound Mixer:* Bob Gravenor. *Sound Man:* James T. Burns. *Location Managers:* Joseph Raffill, Joe Luizzi. *Still Photographer:* M.J. Elliott, Michael Paris. *Unit Publicist:* Al Ebner. *Production Secretary:* Teresa Thomas. *Assistant Auditor:* Michael Donner. *Caterer:* Proud Chef. *Craft Services:* Rudy Daniels. *Production Assistants:* Eric Johnson,

Brent Dowman, Bob Blongiewicz, Randy Stricklin, Phil Strauss. *Second Unit Director:* Max W. Anderson. *Second Unit Photography:* Jonathan Berg. *Second Unit Assistant Camera:* Gary Louzon. *Special Effects:* Special Effects Unlimited. *Special Effects Coordinator:* Larry Cavanaugh. *Special Effects Technicians:* Bob Willard, Steven Lombardi, Bruce Steinheimer, Casey Cavanaugh. *Sound Designer:* David Lewis Yewdall. *Supervising Editor:* John K. Adams. *Dialogue Editor:* Steve Rice. *ADR:* Devon Heffley, Barbara Boguski. *Sound Effects:* Dick LeGrand, Chuck Smith. *Foley:* John Post, Duane Hensel. *Special Visual Effects:* Cinemotion Pictures Incorporated. 1984 by New World Pictures and Cinema Group Venture. *MPAA Rating:* PG. *Running time:* 102 minutes.

SYNOPSIS: In 1943, two young naval officers, David Herdeg and Jimmy Parker, take part in a dangerous experiment. Using Albert Einstein's unified field theory as a beginning, the brilliant scientist Dr. Longstreet has orchestrated an experiment to make American naval vessels invisible to Nazi and Japanese radar. In Philadelphia's harbor, the experiment commences and the U.S.S. *Eldridge* is rendered invisible for a time ... but something goes wrong. The ship and all aboard her suddenly disappear into a glowing time warp. Realizing something has gone wrong, David and Jimmy leap overboard during the experiment, and plummet through a vortex. They land in the year 1984 in a Nevada desert.

In 1984, an aged Dr. Longstreet has been continuing his experiments. This time, he has made an entire town in Nevada disappear. Unfortunately, the presence of the *Eldridge* in the time warp has caused a new vortex to open up in the desert. It is causing severe weather disruptions, and could destroy all life on the planet. A desperate Longstreet and the military attempt to track down Jimmy and David, who may hold the secret to closing the vortex.

Meanwhile, Jimmy and David realize they have traveled through time. After a visit to a highway cafe, they meet up with a woman named Allison. She becomes their tour guide for this new era, and she finds herself attracted to David. Over her best judgment, she agrees to help Jimmy and David escape from the pursuing military officers. During a high speed pursuit, however, Jimmy is injured and the threesome is conveyed to a local hospital. There, Jimmy is struck by an electrical storm and sucked back into the time vortex.

On the run again, David and Allison make for Santa Paul, California, where David's family lives. Once there, David learns his father has died, and that Jimmy has somehow managed to return to 1943. He is now an old, married man with an adult child. David attempts to question Jimmy about the time travel experience, but his friend has grown unstable from the shock of it all. He just wants to be left alone.

The military continues to pursue David and Allison, and finally the intrepid Major Clark catches up with them. In custody in Nevada, David meets up again with the scientist who orchestrated the experiment. A repentant Dr. Longstreet reveals to David that the out-of-time sailor must return to the ever-expanding vortex and shut off the *Eldridge*'s generator. That is the only way to close the rift in the space-time continuum. If David is successful, the *Eldridge* will return to 1941, and the Nevada town will re-materialize in 1984. If David fails, he could be lost in time and space for eternity.

David and Allison have fallen in love, but David agrees to undertake the dangerous mission. Garbed in a spacesuit and helmet, he is propelled into the coruscating vortex.

Once inside the time vortex, David accomplishes his mission. The town and the ship are returned to their respective time zones, and David returns to 1984 to continue his relationship with Allison.

COMMENTARY: The year 1984 saw a resurgence of the time travel adventure in low budget science fiction cinema. Before he became King of the World, director James Cameron brought a malevolent traveler from

Time enough for love: Nancy Allen and Michael Pare in *The Philadelphia Experiment* (1984).

the future to the present in the watershed Schwarzenegger flick, *The Terminator*. Conversely, New World Studios picked up an old John Carpenter script idea from Avco Embassy and brought a kinder, gentler traveler (Michael Pare) from the past to the present in Stewart Raffill's *The Philadelphia Experiment*. Unfortunately, it is the Cameron film, not Stewart Raffill's, which remains the more memorable experience.

There is nothing really wrong with *The Philadelphia Experiment*, except that it looks and feels like a typical low-budget production from the 1950s. Where *The Terminator* had a taut script, a great concept, a sense of style, and a fast pace, *The Philadelphia Experiment* is such slow, muddled going that it defies all attempts at focus and concentration. The film's central problem is that it has no idea where it is really going. Indeed, John Carpenter left the project as a creative force because he felt that after he set up the accident with the ship, it was impossible to resolve the story. Consequently, once Michael Pare's lead character has arrived in the 1980s, he runs from the authorities, but for no real reason. He knows all along that if he is to survive, he must return to the vortex and the missing ship. Since he knows this, all of the chase sequences and even the romance with the lovely Nancy Allen (*Carrie* [1976], *RoboCop* [1987], *Out of Sight* [1998]) are just filler until he decides to stop running, turn around, and face his fate. The movie could have been over in a half hour if Pare's David Herdeg had not decided to play a variation on David Janssen's *The Fugitive* and gone running cross-country.

Herdeg and his love, Allison (Allen), meet by random chance, and fall (unbelievably) in love on what amounts to an extended, but overall purposeless "road trip." The threat in this case is a nebulous one: a vortex that is sucking up our atmosphere, and there is no real interesting villain. *The Philadelphia Experiment* also bears some resemblance to Carpenter's *Starman* in that it is a science fiction road trip, but in this case the characters are not so realistic. What made *Starman* so interesting was the Jenny Hayden character portrayed by Karen Allen. She was a woman who had lost everything and lived in a world of images. She found redemption and hope through her encounters with a messiah-like alien being. In *The Philadelphia Experiment*, Nancy Allen has a part of lesser substance. She is kidnapped at a diner and grows to love her kidnapper for unknown reasons (except that he's cute). The final freeze-frame of *The Philadelphia Experiment* shows Herdeg and Allison locked in a romantic embrace, an image which suggests the picture was supposed to be a love story. However, the love story aspect of this adventure seems forced, and as all true romantics know, the best love stories end tragically. In *Titanic*, lovely Leo and Kate Winslet are separated, but Rose (even as an old lady) is sure that his heart does go on. In *Starman*, Karen Allen's Jenny Hayden was forced to say good-bye to her alien love, and the audience left the theater weeping. *The Philadelphia Experiment* plays more like an old '30s serial: A hero jumps into danger, falls in love, defeats the bad guy (in this case a weather vortex) and comes back to claim his prize — the woman he loves. It is not necessarily bad, just fairly uninspired.

Although Michael Pare and Nancy Allen both do their best with the material, the script fails not only them, but the other actors as well. Professor Longstreet, the man responsible for the accidents in the past and the present, is an ambiguous character — but not ambiguous in a good way. The audience is never certain if he is a good man who made a bad mistake or an opportunist who made the same mistake twice in his bid to be successful. Barely any screen time is devoted to this character so he remains a cipher, a piece to be maneuvered and manipulated according to plot necessity rather than an identifiable human being.

What *The Philadelphia Experiment* would like to be about is its central debate: Is the past or the present better? To Raffill's directorial eye, the world of the '80s is ugly and garish, bright and superficial. He gives us close-ups of bright lipstick, dyed hair, and slutty '80s clothes at several points. He shows Michael Pare encountering transvestites and punk rockers. He shows Ronald Reagan on the television and makes the point that the president is a B movie actor. He contrasts that view of an ugly present with the muted, casual world of the past. The 1940s are filled with humor, dance (in the night club), navy blues, comforting nights, and more. At the end of the film, Pare's character has the choice between returning to his past or staying in the future. He chooses the future, because he has found love there, and *The Philadelphia Experiment*'s ultimate point is perhaps that only love makes a difference, whereas setting is unimportant. Better to be a permanent fish-out-of-water and know real intimacy with another person than be stuck forever alone in one's own time. While this is an admirable, human and believable conclusion to the film, its impact is blunted by the repetitive car chases, foot chases, and pyrotechnics.

Since *The Philadelphia Experiment* plays like a modern-day B movie, it is helpful that real naval equipment was utilized throughout the picture to carry the story. Also rather successful is Raffill's direction of the 1940s sequence which opens the film. Although it might have been more effective lensed in black-and-white, a sense of time and place is nicely established through a conjunction of music, makeup, hairstyles, costuming, and a voice-over radio broadcast telling of the Allied war effort. Raffill is also good with the chase aspects of the picture, particularly Pare's flight through a two-story restaurant. Unfortunately, these superb action sequences tend to take away from the personal nature of the story. And, again, since David is running away for no good reason, the chases are just well-orchestrated time-killers.

The Final Countdown (1979) was another picture in the vein of *The Philadelphia Experiment*. In that movie, the nuclear aircraft carrier *Nimitz*, commanded by Kirk Douglas, went backwards in time through a vortex and ended up at Pearl Harbor in 1941. In many ways, that film is a better one, because it focuses on the real issues involved: can the past be changed? Is it right to change it? As it also features a disappearing ship, it is also a better exploration of the alleged Philadelphia experiment that so inspired John Carpenter in the late seventies. Once the accident occurs on the *Eldridge* in *The Philadelphia Experiment*, the ship is all but dropped from the adventure, a detail of minimal importance.

Even in the final journey of David Herdeg through time, an animated light show reminiscent of the Stargate sequence in Stanley Kubrick's *2001: A Space Odyssey*, *The Philadelphia Experiment* fails to generate any real suspense, any real *frisson*. Instead, this special effects moment tends to remind one of the time-traveling special effects of the low-budget BBC TV series *Doctor Who*.

It is unnecessary to go into further detail about *The Philadelphia Experiment*'s failings. It is an average, uninspired motion picture that is, perhaps, not a bad way to spend two hours on a dull evening. No classic, the picture at least proved a stepping stone for some of its writers and actors. Michael Pare went on to work with John Carpenter in *Village of the Damned* (1995), and Dan Jakoby penned *Lifeforce* (1985), the Tobe Hooper remake of *Invaders from Mars* (1986) and *Vampires* (1998) among other high-profile genre efforts.

In retrospect, John Carpenter was right about *The Philadelphia Experiment*. At its core was a good idea, but as a film, there just was not much to hold onto.

Black Moon Rising (1985)

Critical Reception

"First rate ... Superbly paced, shrewd, witty and imaginative ... A good, unpretentious genre thriller." — Bill Kelley, *Cinefantastique* Volume # 16, Number # 2: "*Black Moon Rising*," May 1986, page 50.

"This is a mindless dingbat movie that relies on all the old clichés for whatever thrust the limpid, often dismally moronic script fails to provide: unwatchable violence, savage beatings, noise and high-speed car chases…. Not recommended for anyone with either acrophobia or good taste."—Rex Reed, *New York Post*, January 10, 1986.

"The aim is for a high-tech movie. Whether you find it to be high-tech or high dreck depends … on your automotive prejudices. Speaking personally, get me back in the slow lane."—Mike McGrady, *Newsday*, January 10, 1986.

"Close to the quintessential Grade-B movie—fast, funny, sexy and thoroughly diverting."—Ralph Novak, *People Weekly*, January 27, 1986.

Cast and Credits

CAST: Tommy Lee Jones (Quint); Linda Hamilton (Nina); Robert Vaughn (Ryland); Richard Jaeckel (Earl Windom); Lee Ving (Ringer); Bubba Smith (Johnson); Dan Shor (Billy Lons); William Sanderson (Tyke Thayden); Keenan Wynn (Iron John); Nick Cassavettes (Luis); Richard Angarola (Dr. Melato); Don Opper (Frenchie); William Marquez (Reynoso); David Pressman (Kid at Grocery Shop); Stanley DeSantis (The Mover); Edward Parone (Mr. Emilio); Al White (Maintenance Man); Bill Moody (Windbreaker Man); Townsend Coleman (Waller); Dalton Cathey (Maitre D'); Frank Dent (Tech #1); Steve Fifield (Tech #2); Dave Adams (Foreman); Lana Lancaster (Ryland's Receptionist); E.J. Castillo (Mechanic #1); Peterson Banks (Mechanic #2); Rudy Daniels (Officer); Carl Ciarfalio (Ringer's Man #1); Don Fulford (Ringer's Man #2); Vincent Pandoliano (Man in Cul-de-sac); Dough MacHugh (Casino Security #1); Eric Trules (Casino Security #2); Lisa London (Redhead).

CREDITS: New World Pictures Presents a Douglas Curtis and Joel B. Michaels Production. A Harley Cokliss Film. *Casting:* Linda Francis, c.s.a. *Production Designer:* Bryan Ryman. *Special Visual Effects:* Max W. Anderson. *Editor:* Todd Ramsay. *Director of Photography:* Misha Suslov. *Music:* Lalo Schifrin. *Screenplay:* John Carpenter, Desmond Nakano, William Gray. *Story:* John Carpenter. *Producer:* Joel B. Michaels, Douglas Curtis. *Directed by:* Harley Cokliss. *Stunts:* Greg Gault, Debbie Evans, Pete Antico, Michael Haynes, Dennis Scott, Bud Ekins, Polly Burson, Chuck Hart, Carey Loftin, Gary Davis, Beau Gibson, J.N. Roberts, Randy Hall, Monty Cox, Dan Plum, Gloria Fioramonti, Steve Blalock, Phil Adams. *Production Manager:* George W. Perkins. *First Assistant Director:* Betsy Magruder. *First Assistant Camera:* Michael E. Little. *Production Coordinator:* Coni Lancaster. *Production Accountant:* Rachel Talalay. *Gaffer:* Jack Cochran. *Key Grips:* Dylan Shephard, Dan Zarlengo. *Costume Designer:* Jack Buehler. *Make-up and Hair Design:* Annie Maniscalco. *Location Manager:* Tim Healey. *Special Prop Design/Propmaster:* Roger Holzberg. *Script Supervisor:* Connie Papineau. *Sound Mixers:* Jonathan Stein, Steve Nelson. *Stunt Coordinator/Black Moon Driver:* Bud Davis. *Second Unit Director:* Douglas Curtis. *Still Photographer:* Michael Paris. *Production Secretary:* Lisa Lange. *Best Boy Electricians:* Anthony Beverly, Michael Harnden. *Electricians:* Chantal Jacobs, Dima Suslov, Doug Olson. *Best Boy Grip:* Bradford Scott. *Grips:* Anthony Caldwell, Erik Highman. *Assistant Make-up and Hair:* Sheri Short. *Key Costumer:* Stephanie Meltzer. *Wardrobe Assistant:* Kerry Mellin. *Assistant Property Master:* Ron Woods. *Property Assistant:* John A. Keim. *Boom Operators:* Barry Bookin, Walter Gorey, Jr. *Special Effects Coordinator:* Larry Cavanaugh, Bruce Steinheimer. *Special Effects Assistant:* Al Bartoli, Casey Cavanaugh. *Second Assistant Camera:* Paul D. Hughen. *Third Assistant Director:* Josh King. *Assistant Art Director:* Miles Ciletti. *Set Decorator:*

Aleka Corwin. *Assistant Editor:* Wendy Phifer Mate. *Apprentice Editor:* Phil Reznik. *Associate Casting Director:* Jeff Greenberg. *Assistant Auditor:* Michael Way. *Assistant Location Manager:* Marshall Moore. *Rigging Gaffer:* Michael Bolner. *Camera Loader:* Gregory Vanger. *Set Dressers:* Barbara Metzenbaum, Sarina Rotstein, Jim Ransohoff, Steve Olsen. *Leadman:* Robin Petyon. *Swing Gang:* Steven Adams, Christine Lomaka, Alfonso Peres Pardo. *Storyboard Artist:* Len Morgant. *Special Effects Props/Electronics:* Brent Scrivner. *Extras Casting:* Complete Casting Services, Inc. *Consultant:* Richard Kendall. *Transportation Consultant:* Tom Thomas. *Transportation Captain:* Russell Delia. *Drivers:* Jimmie Holland, Craig Scott. *Product Van Driver:* Mike Clark. *Honeymoon Driver:* Brick Graham. *Black Moon Mechanics:* Howard Faulkner, Paul Thomas. *Assistant to Tommy Lee Jones:* Lubka Jacobs. *Assistant to Mr. Cokliss:* Margie Waller. *Craft Services:* Kathleen Campbell. *Catering:* Cinema Catering, Peyton Kirkpatrick, Michael Bonfiglio. *Product Assistant:* Todd Connolly, Rik Converse, Robert Crane, Leo McKenzie, Vince Onker, Allyson Scheu, Reed Shelly. *Special Visual Effects:* Cinemotion Pictures Incorporated. *Visual Effects Camera:* Jonathan Seay. *Visual Effects Second Camera:* David Stump. *Optical Supervisor:* Beth Block. *Printer Operators:* Betz Bromberg, George Lockwood. *Animation Camera:* Joshua Cushner. *Special Rigging:* Stephen Small, Lindell Wolf. *Miniatures:* Michael Novotny. *Unit Publicist:* David Gibbs, Dennis Davidson and Associates. *Set Construction:* Time and Space. *Construction Coordinator:* Yerna Bagby. *Construction Assistants:* Imy Quinn, Luca Prosseda, Michael Stone. *Sound Design:* David Lewis Yendall. *Sound Effects Editor:* R.J. Palmer. *Dialogue Editor:* Steve Rice. *Foley Editor:* F. Hudson Miller. *Sound Engineer:* Jon Evans. *Foley Artist:* John Post. *Re-recording Mixers:* Ray West, Joseph Citarella, Charles "Bud" Grenzbach. *Additional Arrangement Performed by:* Brian Banks, Anthony Martinelli. *Music Editor:* Dan Carlin, Sr. *Assistant Music Editor:* Elizabeth Algarin. *Music Supervisor:* Frank Capp. *Orchestration:* Gary Stockdale. *Voice Casting:* Barbara Harris. *Negative Cutter:* Diane Jackson. *Color Timing:* Bob Raring. *Insurance:* Buckley Norris/Albert G. Ruben. *Completion Guarantor:* The Completion Bond Company, Robert Mintz. *Video Playback:* Ruxton, Ltd. *Titles and Opticals:* Pacific Title. *Special Effects:* Special Effects Unlimited, Inc. *Color:* CFI. *Prints:* Technicolor. *Eastman Color:* Kodak. *Locations by:* Filmtrucks. *Camera Systems:* Clairmont Camera. *Motor Homes:* Florian Enterprises, Jeff Pandeli, Darrell Pandeli. *Black Moon Designed and Built by:* Bernard Beajardin in Association with the University of Concordia, Montreal, Canada. "Sleeping with the Enemy" written by Chari Brandon and Jack Littlejohn, performed by Chari Brandon. *Special Thanks to:* Jeff Schechtman, Apollo Computer Inc., Michael Sciulli, Philip Neale, Steve Weber, Arco Center, Coldwell Banker, Norland Properties, Digital Equipment Corp., Levolor-Lorentzen, Inc., Laser Sound, Instructional Technology Services, Time Systems, Inc., Cardkey Systems, Inc., Masland Carpets and Allied Chemical Corp., Lindsey and Hall, Inc., National Performance Center, Bayless Stationers, National Motorsports, English Leather, Calendar Girls Pageant, Kristina Garan, Heidi Gardner, Lisa Stofflet, George Houraney, Larry Joseph, Jack Scanlon. Sculptures and Prints in Ryland's office after the work of Eduardo Paolozzi by kind permission of the artist. Filmed on location in Hollywood. *MPAA Rating:* PG. *Running Time:* 100 minutes.

SYNOPSIS: Sam Quint, a freelance operative working for the U.S. Government, breaks into the Accounting Division of the Lucky Dollar Corporation and steals a valuable audio tape critical to an ongoing Federal investigation. After the theft, alarms blare, and Quint is pursued by Lucky Dollar's gun-for-hire, his old competitor Marvin Ringer. Quint escapes his pursuers in his Cherokee but realizes that the security men are still hot on his trail. At a nearby gas station, he hides the vitally important audio tape in the rear of a new car prototype called "Black Moon." The unique vehicle runs not on gasoline, but on hydrogen, and it can accelerate up to 325 miles per hour. Quint narrowly escapes another close encounter with Marvin Ringer, but realizes he must now also recover the cassette and turn it over to his government employers. The Black Moon is being shown off at a fancy Hollywood bar called "The Betsy," and Quint hopes to retrieve the tape there.

Quint's plan is ruined, however, when a car thief named Nina beats Quint to The Betsy and steals the Black Moon from under the nose of its inventors and Quint. The inventors, ex–NASA scientists, have tied up all their money and dreams in the car, and are desperate to retrieve it in time to turn it over to an Italian manufacturer. Quint chases Nina through Los Angeles, but she escapes. Later, Quint sees an unmarked truck pulling away from a warehouse close by and deduces that it could be hiding the Black Moon. On a hunch, he follows the truck to twin glass towers. One skyscraper is completed, and its partner is under construction. Both buildings are run by a wealthy man named Ryland, who is actually running a very expensive car theft ring. Ryland's towers are impenetrable, and protected by expensive security tools. With only 72 hours left to turn the audio cassette over to the Feds, Quint teams up with the Black Moon inventors to crack the car ring's mammoth fortress.

Seeking help, Quint visits an old friend, Iron John, who helped build Ryland Towers. Iron John reveals that the towers were built over an unused sewer, and Quint thinks he might know a way in. Still, he needs inside help. He tracks down Nina in a night club and they begin a passionate romance. Quint asks her to help him steal back the Black Moon. Nina, who has no love for Ryland even though he found her on the streets and gave her a second chance, agrees to help.

Aware that Quint is snooping around

where he does not belong, Ryland begins playing for keeps. His thugs murder Iron John and one of Black Moon's inventors. Quint is also tracked down by his nemesis Marvin Ringer, who beats him up badly. Nina tends to Quint's wounds, but there is no time to relax: It is time to steal back the Black Moon.

Quint engineers the daring break-in, using the unfinished tower as the entrance to the more secure completed tower. Of course, this entrance requires Quint to perform a dangerous maneuver between the roofs of both buildings. Nina is apprehended by Ryland, who has secretly videotaped her having sex with Quint. Furious and jealous, he orders her interrogated.

After Quint has crossed from the roof of the unfinished building to the upper floors of the completed skyscraper, he rescues Nina and they make for the Black Moon. They try to drive out of the building, but iron bars lower in front of the vehicle, trapping it inside. Forced to take another route, Quint drives the spectacular vehicle into a freight elevator, and it goes all the way up to one of the top floors. Ryland is waiting for them there, but Quint and Nina refuse to surrender. Quint then uses the Black Moon's secondary boost to fly the vehicle through a plate-glass window. The Black Moon effortlessly jumps the gap between towers and escapes unharmed into the unfinished building!

Though Ryland is dead, struck down by the Black Moon on its jump between buildings, Quint and Nina face new dangers from Marvin Ringer, who has shown up once to more to claim the Lucky Dollar audio tape. Ringer and Quint fight it out, and Quint emerges victorious. The inventors of the Black Moon get their car back, the Feds get their tape, and Quint swears it is time to retire.

COMMENTARY: It is rather enjoyable to look back at *Black Moon Rising* today, and watch how its star, Tommy Lee Jones, has honed his acting skill and on-screen charisma

Before he was a "man in black," Tommy Lee Jones was Quint in *Bad Moon Rising* (1985).

in a decade and a half. The opening, pre-title sequence of *Black Moon Rising* perfectly captures the Jones mystique as the actor goes through a *Mission: Impossible*–style plot, sasses an inexperienced convenience store robber, and generally displays his wit and superiority. By the by, all this happens in a scene that serves no real dramatic purpose in the film as a whole. Nonetheless, this fun initial sequence ends with a weak one-liner ("That boy's got a bad attitude") and a shit-eating grin from Tommy Lee Jones. In other words, where the script fails to be intelligent, or even funny, Jones steps in slyly and endows the material with more than the obvious. He may be headlining inherently weak material, but he sure gives it his all. From these few moments, it is easy to see how the "Gerard" persona Jones perfected in *The Fugitive* (1993) and *U.S. Marshals* (1998) was born. Today, few stars are Jones's equal, and

he has been seen in everything from *Batman Forever* (1995) to *Men in Black* (1997)

That little bit of starmaking aside, *Black Moon Rising* still plays much like a low-rent James Bond picture of '80s vintage. The frenetic action on-screen is accompanied by jazzy, fast-paced music from Lalo Schifrin, the artist who composed the memorable theme to *Mission: Impossible* in the late '60s, and the uninspired plot concerns a high-tech urban car theft ring operating out of a twin skyrise development. *The Man from U.N.C.L.E.* himself, Robert Vaughn (post–*Superman III* [1983]) is on hand as the Bondian villain: a wealthy but corrupt businessman. Like Max Zorin (Christopher Walken) in *A View to a Kill* (1985) or Gert Frobe in *Goldfinger* (1964), Vaughn not only gets to make dire threats to the film's protagonists, he gets to spring cute little traps on his bad guy associates. Instead of dropping a cohort out of a blimp or

Linda Hamilton took time between *Terminator* assignments to play a beautiful car-thief in *Black Moon Rising* (1985).

Equipped with turbo thrust, secondary thrust, and a slick aerodynamic shell, this sleek craft is the hackneyed plot's central bone of contention. Everyone wants to know: Who will own the Black Moon? For viewers who are into that sort of thing, all of the myriad car chases, crashes, and action scenes will be most welcome. For others, this caper film will fail to satisfy to any significant degree. Like the car it services, *Black Moon Rising* is a well-crafted engine that runs just fine. Sadly, there's not much to see under the hood. It is all too typical of the empty-headed entertainment of the 1980s, and it is mired down in escapes and captures, escapes and captures, *ad nauseam*. With the emphasis on gadgets, vehicles and action, this is a movie without much of a human soul, though Hamilton and Jones remain engaging throughout.

crushing him in the trunk of a car, however, Vaughn leads his associate to an elevator where he is murdered. It is one more cliché "Bond" moment in a film filled with them.

Linda Hamilton, post–*Terminator* and pre–*King Kong Lives* (1986), also drops in as the stereotypical "Bond girl," but she manages to imbue her role with a fetching kind of innocence and charm, despite her big '80s style hairdo. Like Tommy Lee Jones, she is better than the material, which is derivative as much of Glen Larson's television show *Knight Rider* (1982–85) as it is of a James Bond flick. Like Jones, Linda Hamilton would reach stardom in the '90s, in pictures such as *Terminator 2: Judgment Day* (1991) and *Dante's Peak* (1997).

As has been written elsewhere, the real star of *Black Moon Rising* is the titular vehicle.

It would be tempting to look at Quint (Jones) as another of John Carpenter's disenfranchised protagonists. Here we have a man with loyalty to nobody (like Snake Plissken, Napoleon Wilson, John Nada), and plenty of cynicism (like John Trent or Jack Crow). Yet Quint is not so much a down-and-outer as a skeptical loner: a secret agent who realizes the authority he is currently reporting to is no better than the bad guys he helps to bring down. He is anti-hero lite. He's just bad enough to be likable, not bad enough to be a walking, talking affront to the establishment, like Snake Plissken. The rest of the film is not "from the mind of John Carpenter," as the ads claimed, it is just exploitation of one of the director's many old ideas. Remember, Carpenter earned a credit on this film *simply for reading the script*. Any deep analysis of it for Carpenter themes would thus be unwarranted.

Like *The Philadelphia Experiment, Black Moon Rising* is not a bad film, it is just a typical B-grade movie. Still, with Tommy Lee Jones, Linda Hamilton, Richard Jaekel (*Starman*) and Keenan Wynn (*Laserblast* [1978]) doing the enjoyable thesping, there are worse ways to spend a couple of hours.

IV

John Carpenter on Television

For much of his career, John Carpenter was openly disdainful of television. He even referred to it on more than one occasion as "talking furniture." Consequently, he resisted opportunities to direct episodes of *The Twilight Zone* revival of 1985, though fellow genre directors such as Wes Craven, Jeannot Szwarc, Peter Medak, Tobe Hooper, Rick Rosenthal, and William Friedkin all found safe haven there. Additionally, Carpenter's sequel to *The Fog*, to be written by Dennis Etchison, was also briefly considered as a television film project before Carpenter pulled out of the project.

Although his scripts for two westerns were translated to the small screen in the early '90s, Carpenter has only directed two genre television ventures in his 25 year career: *Someone's Watching Me!* (1978), which was released theatrically in Europe as *High Rise*, and the Showtime special *John Carpenter Presents Body Bags* (1993), which was designed to appeal to the same crowd as HBO's *Tales from the Crypt* (1989–1996) series. In the non-genre milieu, Carpenter directed the smash-success *Elvis* in 1979.

Someone's Watching Me! (1978)

"A tense psychofilm made for television … a more interesting exercise in suspense than its more renowned theatrical brother … Carpenter's treatment … packs a nice surprise punch with its clever twist on the Hitchcock model."—John McCarty, *Psychos — Eighty Years of Mad Movies, Maniacs, and Murderous Deeds.*

"Owes much to Alfred Hitchcock's *Rear Window* for its voyeurism and per-secution paranoia ... written-directed by John Carpenter, who again distills the finest essences of the suspense-horror story.... This also works as a parable about modern-day hazards of city living, but just taken for what it is, it's a better-than-average effort."—John Stanley, *Creature Features*.

Cast and Credits

CAST: Lauren Hutton (Leigh Michaels); David Birney (Paul Winkless); Adrienne Barbeau (Sophie); Charles Cyphers (Gary Hunt); James Murtaugh (Leone); Grainger Hines (Steve); Len Lesser (Burley Man); John Mahon (Frimsin); J. Jay Saunders (Police Inspector); Michael Laurence (TV Announcer); George Skaff (Herbert Stiles); Robert Phalen (Wayne); Robert Snively (Graves); Jean LeBouvier (Waitress); James McAlpine (Slick Man); Edgar Justice (Charlie); John J. Fox (Eddie).

CREDITS: Warner Bros. Presents. *Director:* John Carpenter. *Executive Producer:* Richard Kobritz. *Producer:* Anna Cottle. *Teleplay:* John Carpenter. *Director of Photography:* Robert B. Hauser. *Editor:* Jerry Taylor. *Music:* Harry Sukman. *Assistant Director:* Phil Barber. *Associate Producer:* Anna Cottle. *Running Time:* 91 minutes (120 with commercials).

SYNOPSIS: Lovely and independent Leigh Michaels leaves behind a love affair gone bad and moves to Los Angeles. Once there, she gets a job as a television director and rents a high rise apartment filled with wall-sized windows that look out on the city and other high rise buildings. The same beautiful windows which allow her to peer out at the world, unfortunately, also permit the world to peer *in* at her. Before long, a man who has become obsessed with Leigh starts to stalk her, sending her letters, mailing gifts, and even telephoning. Leigh is unable to convince the police that her "secret admirer" is dangerous, and so with the help of a lesbian friend named Sophie she sets out to learn more about her opponent.

Leigh soon learns that her Peeping Tom nemesis occupies the apartment directly across the way from her own home. He thus has a perfect view inside her apartment. When Sophie breaks into the killer's apartment, Leigh is astonished to watch the killer creeping up and murdering Sophie in her very own apartment. In a final battle, Leigh must come face-to-face with the deadly voyeur who has turned her life into a living hell.

COMMENTARY: Shot before *Halloween*, but released afterwards, *Someone's Watching Me!* is the production that perhaps forever associated John Carpenter with the master of suspense, Alfred Hitchcock. Since it premiered at about the same time as *Halloween*, the two films were viewed by most critics as companion pieces. Critics and scholars thus placed Carpenter in the category of suspense/horror director since both of his '78 films (like *Psycho* [1960]) concerned women endangered by lunatics. If one adds the Carpenter-penned *Eyes of Laura Mars*, that makes three of a kind.

In point of fact, Carpenter has always been more of a Howard Hawks aficionado than a Hitchcock one. Still, it is easy to see how *Someone's Watching Me!* led to the perception that Carpenter was one of the young students who was part of the post–Hitchcock generation, like Spielberg or DePalma.

The similarities to Hitchcock are indeed startling almost immediately in *Someone's Watching Me!* The dramatic set-up, that of a murderer and a voyeur with a telescope sharing a strange link, recalls *Rear Window* (1954). The notion of the deranged psychokiller comes from Hitchcock's most shocking and memorable feature, *Psycho*. And even the opening credits of *Someone's Watching Me!*, featuring traveling animated lines (which looked like horizontal and vertical bar graphs) intersecting one another, recalled the opening Saul Bass sequence of *North by Northwest* (1959). Though that last touch was reportedly the idea of Carpenter's producer, Richard Kobritz,[1] not Carpenter, it added immeasurably nonetheless to the perception that *Someone's Watching Me!* was a film of Hitchcockian proportions.

Unfortunately, *Someone's Watching Me!* has not been rerun on broadcast television in some time, and it is not yet available for purchase or sale on VHS. Still, many critics, including John McCarty, have insisted that it is actually better than *Halloween*. That's quite a feat, so if John Carpenter fans feel inclined to launch any particular campaign (besides for a sequel to *The Thing*), the release of *Someone's Watching Me!* on videotape or DVD would surely be a good one to undertake.

Someone's Watching Me! features several members of the early Carpenter repertory company, including Adrienne Barbeau and Charles Cyphers.

John Carpenter Presents
Body Bags (1993)

Cast and Credits

CAST: "The Morgue": John Carpenter (Coroner); Tom Arnold (Man #1); Tobe Hooper (Man #2).

"The Gas Station": Robert Carradine (Bill); Alex Datcher (Anne); Peter Jason (Gent); Molly Cheek (Divorcee); Wes Craven (Pasty-Faced Man); Sam Raimi (Bill — Dead Attendant); David Naughton (Pete); Buck Flower (Stranger); Lucy Boyer (Peggy); Roger Rooks (TV Anchorman).

"Hair": Stacy Keach (Richard); David Warner (Dr. Lock); Sheena Easton (Megan); Dan Blom (Dennis); Attila (Man); Kim Alexis (Woman); Greg Nicoreto (Man with Dog); Deborah Harry (the Nurse).

"Eye": Mark Hamill (Brent); Twiggy (Cathy); John Agar (Dr. Lang); Roger Corman (Dr. Bregman); Charles Napier (Manager); Eddie Velez (Player); Betty Muramoto (Librarian); Bebe Drake-Massey (Nurse); Sean McClory (Minister); Robert L. Bush (Man); Gregory H. Alpert (Technician).

CREDITS: John Carpenter Presents *Body Bags*. *Written by:* Billy Brown and Dan Angel. *Music:* John Carpenter and Jim Lang. *Director of Photography:* Gary Kibbe. *Production Designer:* Daniel A. Lomino. *Editor:* Edward A. Warschilka. *Executive Producers:* John Carpenter, Sandy King, Dan Angel. *Co-producer:* Dan Angel. *Producer:* Sandy King. *"The Gas Station" Directed by:* John Carpenter. *"Hair" Directed by:* John Carpenter. *"Eye" Directed by:* Tobe Hooper. *Unit Production Manager:* Peter L. Berquist. *First Assistant Director:* Artist Robinson. *Second Assistant Director:* Christine P. Della Penna. *Casting:* The Backseat Casting Company. *Camera Operator:* Gordon Paschal. *First Assistant Camera:* Jeff Norvat. *Second Assistant Camera:* Brian Kibbe. *Loader:* Lisa A. Guerriero. *Video Operator:* Joe A. Unsinn, III. *Script Supervisor:* Hope Williams. *Gaffer:* Jon Timothy Evans. *Best Boy Electric:* J.R. Richner. *Electricians:* John Owens, Joe Garcia, Al Hood. *Key Grip:* Harry L. Rez. *Best Boy Grip:* Mark A. Bolin. *Second Grip:* Craig Pfeiffer. *Company Grip:* Jack Bauer. *Sound Mixers:* Mark Bovos, James S. Larue, Robert Allen Wald. *Boom Operator:* Scott Sherline. *Cableman:* Jeffrey A. Humphreys. *Set Decorator:* Cloudia Rebar. *Leadman:* Jason Bedig. *Swing Gang:* Gary Breuer, Scott M. Anderson. *Propmaster:* William W.

King. *Assistant Props:* Norman "Pepe" Tuers. *Men's Costuming Supervisor:* Robert Bush. *Women's Costuming Supervisor:* Robin Michel Bush. *Set Wardrobe:* Robert Iannacone. *Make-up Artists:* Greg LaCava. *Hair Stylist:* Carolyn L. Elias. *Coroner's Make-up:* Rick Baker; Cimovation, Inc. *Sound Effects:* Howard Jensen. *Hair Creature Stop Motion:* Effects Associates, Inc. *Hair Creature Digital Animation:* Garden of Allah. *Special Make-up Effects:* KNB Group, Inc.; Robert Kurtzman, Greg Nicoreto, Howard Berger. *Assistant Film Editor:* Paul C. Warschilka. *Apprentice Editor:* Angela Lucky. *Stunt Coordinators:* Jeff Image, Henry King, Tony Brubaker. *Supervising Sound Editor:* Anthony R. Milch. *Sound Editors:* Donald J. Warner, Jr., John Kwaitkowski, Hector Gika, Jay Nierenberg, Joseph Holsen, Shaun Sykora. *Assistant Sound Editor:* Rickley Dumm. *Supervising ADR Editor:* Becky Coblentz. *ADR Editor:* Lee Lemont. *Sound Effects Recordist:* Gary Blufer. *Sound Effects Coordinator:* Blake Marion, John Michael Fonaris. *Sound Editing:* Soundstorm. *Re-recording:* International Recording Corporation. *Supervising Re-recording Mixer:* Jeffrey Perkins. *Re-recording mixer:* Kurt Kassalke. *Recordist:* Larry Hoki. *ADR Recording Mixer:* J.P. Westen. *Foley Recording Mixer:* Bruce Bell. *Extras Casting:* Rainbow Casting. *Assistant to John Carpenter and Sandy King:* Karin Costa. *Production Accountant:* Elizabeth Braela. *Production Coordinator:* Cheryl Miller. *Assistant Production Coordinator:* J. Matt Merritt. *Location Manager:* Kenneth D. Lavett. *Assistant Locations Manager:* Gregory Alpert. *Still Photographer:* Elliott Marks. *Unit Publicist:* Steve Rubin. *Construction Coordinator:* Michael S. Wright. *Construction Foreman:* Frank Leasure. *Propmakers:* Curtis B. Jones, Steve Morey, Todd K. Jensen. *Labor Foreman:* Todd R. Livingston. *Paint Foreman:* Craig Nyce. *First Aid:* B.J. Smith. *Craft Services:* Jesse W. Quiroz. *Transport Coordinator:* Ron Hardman. *Transport Captain:* Harold Davis. *Drivers:* Timothy Abbatoye, Mike Berdrow, Peter P. Chittell, Kenneth L. Hardman, Bob L. Hendrix, Maxwell Johnson, Gary E. Kincaid, Harold G. Muehlig, William Prevatte, Sherman Raney, Lanny Scaletta, Raymond Van Holtan. *Production Assistants:* Steve Dellerson, Michael Salver, Paul Sterling, Gary Conway. *Negative Cutter:* Sharon McGeeney. *Music Recorded at:* Knobworld. *Titles:* Pacific Titles. *"Almost Cut My Hair" Written by David Crosby, Performed by Crosby, Stills, Nash, Published by Stay Straight Music. Executive in Charge of Production:* Steven Hewitt. *MPAA* Rating: Made for TV. *Running Time:* 103 minutes.

SYNOPSIS: On a slow night in the city morgue, a ghoulish coroner recounts three tales of horror and death.

In the first story, a college student studying psychology starts her night job at an isolated gas station just outside Haddonfield. The lovely Anne is shown the ropes of the job by Bill, a nondescript, pleasant co-worker. After he leaves for home, however, Anne must contend alone with drunks, winos, and homeless strangers. Worse than that, she is soon pursued by a vicious serial killer who has been murdering innocents in Haddonfield. To Anne's horror, she discovers that the man she assumed to be Bill is actually the devious fiend. As Anne attempts to survive her night of horror, a client who left behind his credit card proves to be the unlikely hero of the adventure.

In the second of the coroner's stories, a man named Richard faces a grave problem: He is losing all of his hair. Convinced that he will be old, unattractive and useless to society without hair, Richard becomes obsessed with growing more. He tries the traditional brush-over, a new, flamboyant cut, hairpieces, and even black spray-paint to cover his bald spot. Richard's salvation finally arrives in the form of Dr. Lock and his clinic. Dr. Lock has perfected an experimental technique which he promises will grow hair. Richard signs up, and awakens the morning after the procedure to discover he has long, luscious hair. Richard's joy turns to horror, however, when his hair will not stop growing. When Richard cuts some of his new "hair," he discovers an even more disturbing secret: His hair seems to be alive! When Richard returns to Dr. Lock for an explanation, the unusual doctor reveals all. Lock is an alien being, and his people are born in a small, defenseless state. They require special nourishment to survive — nourishment that can only be found in the human brain. The hair transplant has actually been a ruse to incubate the small, hair-like serpent creatures in Richard's head. Now, the vain Richard's mind will be devoured by the creatures squirming within his scalp.

In the third of the coroner's stories, a professional baseball player is badly injured in a car accident just as he is about to make the transition to the majors. Although Brent survives the wreck, he loses an eye. He is given an eye transplant, and for awhile everything seems fine. Soon, however, Brent experiences hallucinations and delusions. He sees all kinds of grotesque murders and graphic violence. Then, he begins to experience the urge to kill those around him, including his wife. When Brent questions his friendly doctor about this, he understands the nature of the problem: His new eye once belonged to a homicidal maniac.

COMMENTARY: *Body Bags* is essentially a lark, and it should be viewed and reviewed in that vein. Mostly, *Body Bags* represented an occasion for John Carpenter and his directorial cohorts in the genre business, such as Wes Craven, Roger Corman, Tobe Hooper, and Sam Raimi, to cut loose and have a good time. The cast was also a collection of familiar faces: Mark Hamill, David Naughton, Peter Jason, Buck Flower, Deborah Harry, and even John Agar. Carpenter's goal in doing this picture was to tell three horrific and amusing horror stories in the vein of the old William Gaines E.C. Comic Books *Vault of Horror* and *Tales from the Crypt*. So, the television event was both tribute and celebration, and indeed, those are the feelings that are most evident throughout the picture. It is a fun movie not to be taken too seriously or analyzed as "deep" and "meaningful."

John Carpenter has some clever fun in "The Gas Station," an adventure which finds a night-worker (Alex Datcher) at a gas station outside of Haddonfield being terrorized by a psycho-killer. In this story's penultimate moment, Carpenter re-stages, shot-for-shot, the final battle royale of *Halloween*. This time, it is Alex Datcher in the foreground instead of Jamie Lee Curtis, and a wicked Robert Carradine in the background instead of Nick Castle's the Shape, but the composition and effect is the same. Although some might be bothered at Carpenter's wholesale recycling of his famous *mise-en-scène*, like *Escape from L.A.* it actually fits in with Carpenter's Hawksian qualities. Just as Hawks went back and re-staged the same sequences again and again in similar films, and even featured the same "Hawks woman" in virtually every motion picture he directed, so will Carpenter occasionally go back to his early days and re-film something in nearly identical fashion. The church of *Prince of Darkness* substituted for the abandoned police station of *Assault on Precinct 13*, the city of L.A. substituted for New York in *Escape from L.A.* and in *Body Bags* the great composition of *Halloween* is punctuated to make the terror of "The Gas Station" almost tangible. If it ain't broken, don't fix it!

"The Gas Station" is also probably the scariest of the three stories presented in *Body Bags*. It makes excellent use of its location: a multi-building gas station which seems to exist in the middle of nowhere, in the midst of a seemingly unending night. As is typical for Carpenter, he is able to plug in to the audience's fear of being alone at night, without any possibility of rescue or escape. Datcher is pretty much a prisoner out there at that station throughout the story, and Carpenter maintains tight framing around her face for much of the vignette. He then contrasts those intense close-ups of Datcher with lots of long, silent shots of the gas station. By playing these contrasts, giant human fear against the forbidding vastness of a nowhere night time, Carpenter generates considerable

**Under the ghoulish makeup, John Carpenter is your host in the mortuary for his 1993 anthology,
John Carpenter Presents Body Bags (1993).**

suspense. Although comedic elements do enter the picture with Robert Carradine's campy, over-the-top portrayal of a serial killer, "The Gas Station" is one story that nonetheless has some energy and kick to it.

"Hair" is a different animal all together. This story represents another of John Carpenter's modes. "The Gas Station" was a paean to his early days of spare, lean horror like *Halloween* or *The Fog.* "Hair" looks and feels a bit more like a mid–1980s Carpenter picture. It has some similarities to *They Live,* particularly in that a malevolent alien race is, unbeknownst to the populace, feeding off the people of Earth. As in *They Live,* there is also some wonderful and humorous social commentary as John Carpenter pokes fun at infomercials (with David Warner hilariously reading a Teleprompter, his eyes darting from left to right and back again) as well as the pervasive vanity of today's television culture.

Richard, the hero of "Hair," is a man who believes that everything will be great so long as he has long, healthy hair. He has no self-worth so long as he is balding. Much of the story's duration is thus obsessed with comedy as Richard adorns a bad toupee and spray paints his bald spot black. Then the horror kicks in when he gets his hair — and it won't stop growing. When it is revealed that the alien hair is actually feeding on Richard, the story has made its didactic point: Be careful what you wish for! In this case, Richard's obsession with what's atop his head has made him neglect what's in it. He wasn't thinking, and soon he won't be breathing either.

The final story is Tobe Hooper's "Eye," and any analysis of it would surely belong in a study of that director's career. "Eye" is a more traditional horror story than "Hair" but a little less spare than "The Gas Station." It falls squarely into the tradition of the *Hand of Orlac* (1924), *Hands of a Stranger* (1962), *The Hand* (1981), *Body Parts* (1991) and the *Night Gallery* episode "The Hand of Borgus Weems." In each adventure an appendage or organ (usually a hand belonging to a serial killer) is grafted onto an innocent man who has suffered an accident. In the case of "Eye," it is Mark Hamill's ocular orb which sees all manner of disgusting, gory crimes after the transplant (performed by John Agar.) Like the other two *Body Bags* stories, "Eye" is solidly cast with genre names and well directed by the master of a very different horror style from Carpenter, but it lacks the element of fun so prevalent in both "The Gas Station" and "Hair." Because Brent (Mark Hamill) comes perilously close to murdering his family, and because his visions are so grotesque (and bloody), it is hard to take this particular story lightly. Still, the notion was to produce a grab-bag of horror fulfilling all kinds of genre requirements, and in that regard, *Body Bags* succeeds.

Throughout *Body Bags*, John Carpenter performs as "our host," the decaying and disgusting mortician. Like the Cryptkeeper, the Old Witch or the Vault Keeper of E.C. Comics, Carpenter portrays a rather ghoulish character who makes very bad puns about the dead, whom he refers to as "the arriving departed." As the mortician, Carpenter also shows unhappiness with the number of natural deaths in his morgue, and he even washes down his dinner with a nice glass of formaldehyde. As host of the proceedings, Carpenter seems to have a good time, and the audience is likewise rewarded. *John Carpenter Presents Body Bags* is by no means a "serious" work, but it is a highly entertaining one, and worthy of seeing just to get a feel for Carpenter in each phase of his directing career. Whether you enjoy him as master of suspense ("The Gas Station") or horror director with a social conscience ("Hair"), *Body Bags* is an opportunity to see this director just cut loose and have fun. He has certainly earned the opportunity.

V

Epilogue: We Are Transmitting from the Year 1999...

It was a moment of pure joy for those Howard Hawks aficionados who had watched his film career for so many years and longed for the director to achieve some kind of official recognition in America for his unique and consistent talent. And who better to present his Academy Award to him behind the podium than his friend and star of choice, John Wayne? It was a great moment for Hawks fans and for American cinema...

If one is inclined to view John Carpenter as a latter-day Hawks and Kurt Russell as a contemporary John Wayne, the question must be asked: Will that scene onstage at the Oscars ceremony be re-staged with the modern players? Will filmgoers, in years to come, see a white-haired Carpenter quietly accept a golden statue in honor of his notable work and his many years in the industry?

Alas, it is a highly doubtful possibility at this writing, at least for the near future. For Carpenter to win an Academy Award, as a director of a specific film or for a "lifetime achievement," would require a Herculean leap that most Hollywood players are not quite ready to make. Simply put, they'd have to take John Carpenter's work seriously. As this book has, hopefully, established at least in part, there is certainly plenty to appreciate in each and every one of Carpenter's motion pictures from the strictly visual to the thematic. However, there is still that unfair label to contend with, that ugly left-over from the release of *The Thing* in the summer of 1982; that "pornographer of violence" stereotype which still haunts John Carpenter with more determination than Michael Myers himself.

No matter how skilled a director Carpenter remains, horror is not now, nor has it ever been, a respected genre. Its position as the black sheep of film types stands pat despite the efforts of Kevin Williamson, Wes Craven, Tobe Hooper, Robert Wise, William Friedkin, John Carpenter and a host of others over the years to craft stylish and meaningful pictures in the milieu of fear. Although Carpenter, more than Craven or Hooper, has been able to escape "horror" through sidesteps to action (*Assault on Precinct 13*) and science fiction (*Starman*, *They Live*), the horror-director label remains tethered to his neck. And as long as he is associated with it, the Hollywood establishment will be slow to recognize his talents as a latter day auteur. Indeed, it has only been in the last three to four years that some critics have begun to see *The Thing* as a masterpiece, a fact immediately obvious to those who had opted to see it over *E.T.* back in '82.

If Carpenter has a legacy as a filmmaker, it is not merely that he was responsible for creating *Halloween*, the most profitable independent feature film for over a decade, and *The Thing*, and 1975's best science fiction film, *Dark Star*, and 1984's best science fiction film, *Starman*; nor is it that he created a franchise with *Halloween* or *Escape from New York*. Instead, he will be remembered primarily for his desire to do things his own way. John Carpenter makes the films he wants to see when the rest of Hollywood is assembling and manufacturing heartless and soulless "blockbusters" like *Godzilla* (1998) or *Armageddon* (1998). No matter the subject of a Carpenter film, it invariably features his spin, his ethos, his individuality in every regard: music, editing, camerawork, language, psychology, themes. In a world of computer-generated special effects, agent-generated stars, and box office–generated sequels, this throwback to individuality is a rare gift and a welcome role model for the filmmakers of tomorrow. The maverick who took on the Reagan administration before it left office with *They Live*, who took on the Catholic Church in *Vampires*, who has adapted Stephen King and paid homage to Kneale, Lovecraft, and Hawks, will ultimately be remembered for his willingness to buck the cookie-cutter trend of blockbuster filmmaking and his fearless desire to be his own man. *Vampires* may not be the best of Carpenter's films, but it stands proudly as a beacon of individuality compared to *Godzilla*, *Armageddon*, and other movies which talk down to audiences and offer generic, whitebread and politically correct "thrills." Like Haddonfield's famous mass murderer, Michael Myers, the maverick spirit of John Carpenter is unkillable and unstoppable.

Appendix A:
Some Directing Opportunities John Carpenter Has Turned Down

John Carpenter is a fascinating film artist, and an absolute individual. He rigorously applies his own special criteria and film background to any movie project that crosses his desk. Most of all, he makes movies that *he* would like to see, that he would personally enjoy.

Although this approach has produced many great films over the years, it has also effectively kept John Carpenter well out of the Hollywood mainstream. In his more than 25 year career, he has turned down many prestigious projects which eventually became monster hits for their respective studios. Below is a list of prominent film projects that Carpenter turned down, as well as the reasons why he did so:

1. *Star Trek: The Motion Picture* (1979)
   because: he did not think he could bring anything of value to the material.

2. *The Fan* (1981)
   because: he did not want to do another slasher picture after *Halloween* and *Someone's Watching Me!*

3. *Top Gun* (1985)
   because: he did not like the script.

4. *The Golden Child* (1986)
   because: he liked *Big Trouble in Little China* better.

5. *Tai Pan* (1986)
   because: he did not want to spend that much time overseas, away from home.

6. *Fatal Attraction* (1987)
   because: he saw it as a yuppie version of Clint Eastwood's *Play Misty for Me* (1971).

7. *Exorcist III* (1990)
   reason unknown

8. *Halloween H20* (1998)
   because: he had already been there and done that.

Appendix B:
Slasher Films That Followed
John Carpenter's *Halloween*

In the wake of *Halloween* (1978) every director with a camera and $100,000 in his pocket set out to make a slasher picture that could cash in on the success of John Carpenter's seminal horror film. Although good, successful films always inspire numerous offspring (witness *The Black Hole* [1978], *Message from Space* [1979], *Starship Invasions* [1978] and *Star Crash* [1978] after *Star Wars* [1977]; and *Galaxy of Terror* [1981], *Intruder Within* [1981], *Horror Planet* [1981], *Forbidden World* [1982], and *Creature* [1984] after *Alien* [1979]), John Carpenter has nonetheless often been accused and attacked outright by conservative elements of American politics for being a "pornographer" of violence. He has been blamed for all the slasher films that followed *Halloween*, when in fact he should be honored for making a stylish film that has survived the test of time and become a classic film even outside the world of horror.

On a more pragmatic note, Carpenter should be appreciated for turning an invest-ment of $300,000 into a pot of cash worth $85 million and still counting. Although imitation may be the sincerest form of flattery, it is probably this commercial success, rather than John Carpenter's critical success, that most of the films listed below truly attempted to emulate. Following, in alphabetical order, is a roster of "slasher" pictures that followed fast on the heels of *Halloween's* low-budget success in the late '70s and early '80s:

> *Alone in the Dark* (1982)
> *April Fool's Day* (1986)
> *Blade in the Dark* (1983)
> *Blood Lake* (1987)
> *Blood Rage* (1979)
> *The Bloody Birthday* (1980)
> *Bloody New Year* (1987)
> *Boogeyman* (1980)
> *The Burning* (1982)
> *Christmas Evil* (1980)
> *Curtains* (1982)
> *Cutting Class* (1989)

Death Screams (1982)
Death Valley (1981)
Don't Answer the Phone (1981)
Don't Go in the House (1980)
Don't Go in the Woods (1980)
Don't Look in the Attic (1981)
Don't Open the Door (1979)
Don't Open till Christmas (1984)
Dorm That Dripped Blood (1981)
Double Exposure (1981)
The Driller Killer (1979)
Eyes of a Stranger (1980)
The Fan (1981)
Friday the 13th (1980)
Girls' School Screamers (1984)
Graduation Day (1981)
Happy Birthday to Me (1981)
He Knows You're Alone (1981)
Hell Night (1982)
Hide and Go Shriek (1987)
*Hollywood Strangler Meets the
    Skid Row Slasher* (1979)
House on Sorority Row (1983)
Humongous (1982)
The Initiation (1982)
Just Before Dawn (1982)
The Killer Instinct (1981)
The Last Horror Film (1982)
Madman (1981)
Maniac (1980)
Mortuary (1981)
Mother's Day (1980)
My Bloody Valentine (1981)
New Year's Evil (1982)
New York Ripper (1981)

Night School (1980)
Open House (1987)
Pieces (1983)
The Prey (1980)
Prom Night (1980)
The Prowler (1981)
Road Games (1982)
Schizoid (1980)
Silent Night, Deadly Night (1984)
Slaughter High (1985)
Sleepaway Camp (1983)
Slumber Party Massacre (1982)
Sorority House Massacre (1985)
A Stranger Is Watching (1982)
Terror Train (1980)
To All a Goodnight (1980)
Too Scared to Scream (1983)
The Toolbox Murders (1979)
Trick of Treats (1982)
The Unseen (1980)
Visiting Hours (1981)
Watch Me When I Kill (1981)
When a Stranger Calls (1979)
You Better Watch Out (1980)

If the above-listed films are the illegitimate children of *Halloween*, then the recent spate of *Scream* inspired stalker pictures (*Scream 2* [1997], *I Know What You Did Last Summer* [1997], *Disturbing Behavior* [1998], *Urban Legend* [1998], *I Still Know What You Did Last Summer* [1998]) might be termed the grandchildren. Whatever you call them, all of these recent films also owe a measure of debt to John Carpenter's classic original.

Appendix C:
The John Carpenter
Repertory Company

One of the many qualifications for the title "auteur" is that a film director works with the same performers again and again, as if somehow those performers represent an extension of the director's personal ethos. John Carpenter has adhered to this theory in his film career, and worked with a "stock" repertory company again and again. Below is a list of performers who have become John's Carpenters arms and legs.

1. Kurt Russell (*Elvis* [1979], *Escape from New York* [1981] *The Thing* [1982], *Big Trouble in Little China* [1986], *Escape from L.A.* [1996])
2. Donald Pleasence (*Halloween* [1978], *Escape from New York* [1981], *Halloween II* [1981], *Prince of Darkness* [1987])
3. Jamie Lee Curtis (*Halloween* [1978], *The Fog* [1980], *Halloween II* [1981])
4. Charles Cyphers (*Assault on Precinct 13* [1976], *Halloween* [1978], *Someone's Watching Me!* [1978], *The Fog* [1980], *Escape from New York* [1981], *Halloween II* [1981])

5. Nancy Loomis (*Assault on Precinct 13* [1976], *Halloween* [1978], *The Fog* [1980], *Halloween II* [1981], *Halloween III: Season of the Witch* [1982])
6. George "Buck" Flower (*The Fog* [1980], *Escape from New York* [1981], *Starman* [1984], *They Live* [1988], *Body Bags* [1993], *Village of the Damned* [1995])
7. Peter Jason (*Prince of Darkness* [1987], *They Live* [1988], *Body Bags* [1993], *Village of the Damned* [1995], *Escape from L.A.* [1996])
8. Tom Atkins (*The Fog* [1980], *Escape from New York* [1981], *Halloween III: Season of the Witch* [1982])
9. Adrienne Barbeau (*Someone's Watching Me!* [1978], *The Fog* [1980], *Escape from New York* [1981], *Blood River* [1991])
10. Nancy Stephens (*Halloween* [1978], *Halloween II* [1981], *Escape from New York* [1981], *Halloween H20* [1998])

A group of semi-regular performers, with two films each in the company, includes Darwin Joston (*Assault on Precinct 13, The*

Fog), Ty Mitchell (*The Fog, Halloween II*), Victor Wong (*Prince of Darkness, Big Trouble in Little China*), Dennis Dun (*Prince of Darkness, Big Trouble in Little China*), Sam Neill (*Memoirs of an Invisible Man, In the Mouth of Madness*), Stacy Keach (*Body Bags, Escape from L.A.*), Mark Hamill (*Body Bags, Village of the Damned*), Harry Dean Stanton (*Escape from New York, Christine*), David Warner (*Body Bags, In The Mouth of Madness*), Keith David (*The Thing, They Live*), Susan Blanchard (*Prince of Darkness, They Live*) and Robert Grasmere (*Prince of Darkness, They Live*).

In a behind-the-scenes capacity, an avid John Carpenter viewer should watch to see how many times Dean Cundey, Debra Hill, Donald Morgan, Daniel Lomino, John Lloyd, Lawrence Paull, Alan Howarth, Shirley Walker, Eddie Lee Voelker, Mark Walthour, Tommy Lee Wallace, Joe Brennan, Robin Bush, Jeff Imada, Roy Arbogast and Sandy King show up during credits for his films.

Appendix D: Recurring Characters in the Films of John Carpenter

If the films of John Carpenter are viewed together as part of one giant tapestry, certain people, characters and archetypes appear again and again. His heroes are almost continuously authority-hating anti-hero crusaders, the women in his pictures are often reflections of Angie Dickinson in *Rio Bravo*, and the villains either represent the evil of "authority," or a kind of mad-dog faceless evil which attacks relentlessly and always in superior numbers. Below is a listing of the characters who are dramatized most frequently in Carpenter's film pantheon:

The Rugged Anti-Hero with an Anti-Social Bent

1. Napoleon Wilson in *Assault on Precinct 13* (1976)
2. Snake Plissken in *Escape from New York* (1981) and *Escape from L.A.* (1996)
3. R.J. MacReady in *The Thing* (1982)
4. Jack Burton in *Big Trouble in Little China* (1986)
5. John Nada in *They Live* (1988)
6. John Trent in *In the Mouth of Madness* (1995)
7. Jack Crow in *Vampires* (1998)

The Hawksian Woman

1. Leigh in *Assault on Precinct 13*
2. Leigh Michaels in *Someone's Watching Me!* (1980)
3. Stevie Wayne in *The Fog* (1980)
4. Maggie in *Escape from New York*
5. Gracie Law in *Big Trouble in Little China*
6. Holly Thompson in *They Live*
7. Styles in *In the Mouth of Madness*
8. Dr. Verner in *Village of the Damned* (1995)

Evil, Crazy, or Dishonest Authority Figures

1. The six co-conspirators of *The Fog*
2. The American president in *Escape from New York*

3. Blair in *The Thing*
4. Arnie's mother in *Christine*
5. Fox in *Starman*
6. Holly Thompson, yuppies, politicians and Republicans in *They Live*
7. Jenkins in *Memoirs of an Invisible Man* (1992)
8. Dr. Verner in *Village of the Damned*
9. The right-wing Republican president in *Escape from L.A.*
10. Cardinal Alba in *Vampires* (1998)

The Wild Bunch (a gang of villains who attack en masse, almost without thought)

1. Street Thunder in *Assault on Precinct 13*
2. Blake's avengers in *The Fog*
3. The Crazies in *Escape from New York*
4. The "possessed" street people in *Prince of Darkness*
5. The seven masters in *Vampires*

The Buddy or Sidekick (possible enemy who becomes friend and "equal" to the anti-hero)

1. Lt. Bishop in *Assault on Precinct 13*
2. Childs in *The Thing*
3. Wang in *Big Trouble in Little China*
4. Frank in *They Live*
5. Father Guiteau in *Vampires*

Appendix E:
Rating John Carpenter

John Carpenter's many films (as director) are rated below from most to least satisfying, but there remains a significant problem with any such tally. Many of the films in Carpenter's filmography are quite good, but not quite good enough to rate among his best works. *Escape from New York*, *Starman*, and *They Live*, for instance, are ranked #6, #7, #8 respectively. This puts them well down the list, although by most critical standards each film would surely rank as very good one.

In fact, rating Carpenter's films is a very difficult task, and there is no real consensus about which of his films are best. For example, *Big Trouble in Little China* has a substantial cult following whose proponents would surely place it near the top of his filmography. Additionally, Carpenter's more mainstream phase in the 1980s could result in *Christine* and *Starman* rating higher on some lists than his brilliant but admittedly less accessible films such as *Dark Star* and *Assault on Precinct 13*. Furthermore, how is one to rate *In the Mouth of Madness*, a film that is gaining adherents as the years go by,

and looks to be making a *The Thing*–style resurgence in mass popularity?

The list below reflects this author's personal choices of John Carpenter's best films, and one can tell from a quick scan of the roster that there is a real bias here towards his more challenging early (1974–1982) work. Others may feel differently, but any student of cinema hoping to gain a familiarity with Carpenter's work would probably be best served by a viewing of the top four films on this register. One can hardly go wrong with the paranoia and "in your face" intensity of *The Thing*, the suspense of *Halloween*, the genre-busting of *Assault on Precinct 13* and the thematically rich *Dark Star*. Only the theatrical films directed by Carpenter are rated, so one will not find *Someone's Watching Me! Halloween II*, *Eyes of Laura Mars*, *Halloween III: Season of the Witch*, or *John Carpenter Presents Body Bags* on the list.

1. *The Thing* (1982)
2. *Halloween* (1978)
3. *Assault on Precinct 13* (1976)
4. *Dark Star* (1974)

5. *The Fog* (1979)
6. *Escape from New York* (1981)
7. *Starman* (1984)
8. *They Live* (1988)
9. *Prince of Darkness* (1987)
10. *Big Trouble in Little China* (1986)

11. *Escape from L.A.* (1996)
12. *In the Mouth of Madness* (1994)
13. *Christine* (1983)
14. *Vampires* (1998)
15. *Memoirs of an Invisible Man* (1992)
16. *Village of the Damned* (1995)

Notes

I. A History and Overview of John Carpenter's Career

1. Wells, Jeffrey. *Films in Review*: "New Fright Master John Carpenter." April 1980, page 218.

2. O'Bannon, Dan. *Omni's Screen Flights, Screen Fantasies*. Edited by Danny Peary. "The Re-Making of *Dark Star*." Dolphin Books, 1984, page 148.

3. Mitchell, Blake, and James Ferguson. *Fantastic Films* Collector's Edition # 17: "John Carpenter, Natch!" Blake Publishing Corp., July 1980, page 20.

4. Van Hise, James, and Dennis Fisher. *Starlog* # 57: "Ron Cobb: From *Dark Star* to *Conan*—Imagination at His Fingertips." April 1982, page 30.

5. Sunden, Ed II. *Fantastic Films* Special Edition # 22: "An Exclusive Interview with Ron Cobb, Preproduction Artist on the SF Movie *Alien*." February 1981, page 51.

6. Swires, Steve. *Films in Review*: "Leigh Brackett," 1975.

7. Wood, Robin. *Howard Hawks*. Doubleday, 1968, page 42.

8. Nilsson, Thomas, and Steve Biodrowski. *Cinefantastique* # Volume 22, Number #3: "The Return of John Carpenter." December 1991, page 5.

9. Rosenthal, David. *New York*: "Rated 'H' for Horror." February 1980, page 2.

10. Lofficier, Randy and Jean-Marc Lofficier. *The Bloody Best of Fangoria*, Volume # 5: "John Carpenter: Of Fogs and Things." 1986, page 17.

11. Ferrante, Tim. *Fangoria* # 79: "The Rage of Aquarius." December 1988, page 54.

12. Swires, Steve. *Starlog* # 41: "John Carpenter's *Escape from New York*, High Adventure in the Future." December 1980, page 30.

13. Medved, Harry and Michael Medved. *The Golden Turkey Awards*. A Perigee Book, 1980, pages 90–91, 94.

14. Wells, Jeffrey. "New Fright Master John Carpenter." *Films in Review*, April 1980, page 219.

15. Mitchell, Blake, and Ferguson, James. *Fantastic Films* Volume # 3, Number # 1: "The Fog." May 1980, page 41.

16. Weaver, Tom. *Starlog* # 132: "Janet Leigh: Mistress of Menace." July 1988, page 96.

17. Maronie, Samuel J. *Starlog* # 45: "On the Set with *Escape from New York*." April 1981, page 29.

18. Swires, Steve. *Starlog* # 49: "The Stars of *Escape from New York*, Kurt Russell & Adrienne Barbeau: Survivors of the Future." August 1981, pages 17–18.

19. Maronie, Samuel J. *Starlog* # 46: "From *Forbidden Planet* to *Escape from New York*: A Candid Conversation with SFX & Production Designer Joe Alves." May 1981, page 50.

20. Swires, Steve. *Starlog* # 48: "John Carpenter." July 1981, page 76.

21. Swires, Steve. *Starlog* # 59: "John Carpenter Directing *The Thing*." July 1982, page 27.

22. Swires, Steve. *Starlog* # 57: "Bill Lancaster on Scripting *The Thing*, or 'The Bad News Beast.'" May 1982, page 16.

23. Garris, Mick. *Fangoria* # 21: "Landis, Cronenberg, Carpenter: A Panel Discussion of Fear on Film." August 1982, page 26.

24. Swires, Steve. *Starlog* # 58: "An Interview with Cinematographer Dean Cundey." June 1982, page 38.

25. Carlomagno, Ellen. *Fangoria* # 21: "Rob Bottin and *The Thing*." August 1982, page 16.

26. *Starlog* # 141: "The Great American Curmudgeon: Wilford Brimley." April 1989, page 16.

27. Swires, Steve. *Starlog* # 100: "John Carpenter: Success & Failure in Hollywood, Part II." November 1985, page 46.

28. Thompson, William B. *Starlog* # 81: "Alan Dean Foster, Master of the Novelization." April 1985, page 53.

29. Weaver, Tom. *Starlog* # 174: "Things Change." January 1992, pages 36–37.

30. Naha, Ed. *Starlog* # 63: "Kurt Russell has SomeTHING on His Mind." October 1982, page 50.

31. Warren, Bill. *Starlog* # 141: "Nigel Kneale: The Quatermass Addendum, Part Three." April 1989, page 70.

32. Horsting, Jessie. *Stephen King at the Movies*. A *Starlog* Signet Special, 1986, page 36.

33. Broadwater, Cynthia. *Daredevils* # 13: "*Starman*." November 1984, page 10.

34. Greenberger, Robert. *Starlog* # 90: "Karen Allen, Beloved of John Carpenter's *Starman*." January 1985.

35. Swires, Steve. *Starlog* # 92: "John Carpenter on *Starman*." March 1985, page 20.

36. Swires, Steve. *Starlog* # 109: "John Carpenter: Kung Fu, Hollywood Style." August 1986, page 13.

37. Wiater, Stanley. *Dark Visions: Conversations with the Masters of the Horror Film*. Avon Books, 1992, page 21.

38. Swires, Steve. *Starlog* # 125: "John Carpenter's Guide to Hollywood Survival." December 1987, page 13.

39. Jones, Alan. *Starburst* Volume 10, Number 9: "John Carpenter *Prince of Darkness* Exclusive *Starburst* Interview." May 1988, page 12.

40. Shapiro, Marc. *The Bloody Best of Fangoria* # 7: "Donald Pleasence Is Not a Madman." February 1989, page 53.

41. Fourzon, Pamela. *Cinefantastique* Volume 16, Number 2: "*Big Trouble in Little China*." May 1986, page 53.

42. Swires, Steve. *Starlog* # 136: "John Carpenter & the Invasion of the Yuppie Snatchers." November 1988, page 37.

43. Shapiro, Marc. *Fangoria* # 78: "Run! Run! Run for Your Life! *They Live*!" October 1988, page 22.

44. Shapiro, Marc. *Starlog* # 171: *"Memoirs of an Invisible Man."* October 1991, pages 41–42.

45. Shapiro, Marc. *Starlog* # 178: "I'm Invisible and You're Not." May 1992, pages 7–9.

46. Salisbury, Mark. *Starburst* Special # 14: "John Carpenter." 1992/93 pages 17–19.

47. Biodrowski, Steve. *Cinefantastique* Volume 24, Number 3/4: "Tales from the Morgue: *Body Bags.*" October 1993, page 113.

48. Jones, Alan. *Cinefantastique* Volume 26, Number 2: "John Carpenter, Directing *In the Mouth of Madness* à la H.P. Lovecraft." February 1995, page 44.

49. Williams, David E. *Sci-Fi Universe* # 4: Memoirs of Madness." December/January 1994, page 45.

50. Walters, Jean. *Sci-fi Universe* # 4: "Julie Carmen: Mouthful of Madness." December/January 1994, page 67.

51. Kilday, Greg, and Anne Thompson. *Entertainment Weekly* # 312: "To Infinity and Below." February 2, 1996, page 32.

52. Lamanna, Dean. *Cinescape* Volume 1, Number 3: "The Maw, the Scarier." November 1994, page 60.

53. Kilday, Greg, and Anne Thompson. *Entertainment Weekly* # 312: "To Infinity and Below." February 2, 1996, page 32.

54. Beeler, Michael. *Cinefantastique* Volume 27, Number 11/12: "Carpenter Gets Bicoastal—*Escape from L.A.*" July 1996, page 8.

55. *Cinescape* Volume 2, Number 8: "Summer Movie Preview." May 1996, page 39.

56. *Cinescape* Volume 2, Number 8: "Summer Movie Preview." May 1996, page 39.

57. Chrissinger, Craig W. *Fangoria* # 176: "Vatican Versus *Vampires.*" September 1998, page 27.

58. Spelling, Ian, and Anthony C. Ferrane. *Fangoria* # 172: "Kevin WIlliamson's Latest: New *Halloween* and More." May 1998, pages 8–9.

59. Golder, Dave. *SFX*: "LA Story." November 1996, page 55.

II. The Films of John Carpenter

1. Von Gunden, Kenneth, and Stuart H. Stock. *Twenty All-Time Great Science Fiction Films.* Arlington House, Crown, 1982, page 190.

2. Wollen, Peter. *Signs and Meaning in the Cinema.* Indiana University Press, 1972, page 86.

3. Bywater, Tim, and Thomas Sobchack. *Introduction to Film Criticism: Major Critical Approaches to Narrative Film.* Longman, 1989, page 72.

4. Telotte, J.P. *American Horrors: Essays on the Modern American Horror Film*: "Through a Pumpkin's Eye: The Reflexive Nature of Horror." University of Illinois Press, 1987, page 122.

5. Hogan, David J. *Dark Romance: Sexuality in the Horror Film.* McFarland, 1986, page 252.

6. Clover, Carol J. *Men, Women and Chainsaws: Gender in the Modern Horror Film.* Princeton University Press, 1992.

7. Peary, Danny. *Cult Movies.* Delacorte Press, 1981, page 126.

8. Dika, Vera. *Games of Terror: Halloween, Friday the 13th and the Films of the Stalker Cycle.* Fairleigh Dickinson University Press, 1990, page 51.

9. Guerrero, Eduard. *Journal of Popular Film and Television,* Volume #18: "AIDS as Monster in Science Fiction and Horror Cinema." Fall 1990, pages 87–93.

10. Doherty, Thomas. "Genre, Gender and the *Aliens* Trilogy." *The Dread of Difference: Gender and the Horror Film*, University of Texas Press, 1996, page 191.

11. Crane, Jonathan Lake. *Terror and Everyday Life: Singular Moments in the History of the Horror Film*. Sage Publications, 1994, page 137.

12. Gerani, Gary, and Tom Schulman. *Fantastic Television: A Pictorial History of Sci-Fi, the Unusual and the Fantastic*. Harmony Books, 1977, page 101.

13. Thonen, John. *Cinefantastique*, Volume 30, Number 7/8: "John Carpenter: Cinema of Isolation." October 1998, page 71.

14. Dietrich, Bryan. *Journal of Popular Film and Television*: "*Prince of Darkness*/Prince of Light." Summer 1991, pages 91–95.

III. Films Written and Produced by John Carpenter

1. Fischer, Lacy, and Marcia Landy. *American Horrors: Essays on the Modern Horror Film*. "*Eyes of Laura Mars*: A Binocular Critique." University of Illinois, 1987, page 63.

IV. John Carpenter on Television

1. Wells, Jeffrey. *Films in Review*: "New Fright Master John Carpenter." April 1980, page 222.

Bibliography

Badley, Linda. *Film, Horror, and the Body Fantastic*. Greenwood Press, 1995.

Bywater, Tim, and Thomas Sobchack. *Introduction to Film Criticism: Major Critical Approaches to Narrative Film*. Longman, 1989.

Clover, Carol J. *Men, Women and Chainsaws: Gender in the Modern Horror Film*. Princeton University Press, 1992.

Clute, John. *SF: The Illustrated Encyclopedia*. Dorling Kindersley, 1995.

Crane, Jonathan Lake. *Terror and Everyday Life: Singular Moments in the History of the Horror Film*. Sage Publications, 1994.

Dika, Vera. *Games of Terror: Halloween, Friday the 13th and the Films of the Stalker Cycle*. Fairleigh Dickinson University Press, 1990.

Ebert, Roger. *Roger Ebert's Movie Home Companion, 1993 Edition*. Andrews and McMeel, 1993.

Hardy, Phil. *The Film Encyclopedia: Science Fiction*. William Morrow, 1984.

Hogan, David J. *Dark Romance: Sexuality in the Horror Film*. McFarland, 1986.

Grant, Barry Keith. *The Dread of Difference: Gender and the Horror Film*. University of Texas Press, 1996.

King, Stephen. *Danse Macabre*. A Berkeley Book, 1981.

McCarty, John. *Psychos: Eighty Years of Mad Movies, Maniacs, and Murderous Deeds*. St. Martin's Press, 1986.

Menville, Douglas, and R. Reginald. *Future Visions: The New Golden Age of the Science Fiction Film*. Newcastle, 1985.

Meyers, Richard. *S-F 2: The Great Science Fiction Films from* Rollerball *to* Return of the Jedi. Citadel Press, 1983.

Moore, Darrell. *The Best, Worst and Most Unusual: Horror Films*. Publication International, Ltd., 1983.

Peary, Danny. *Cult Movies*. Delacorte Press, 1981.

Pinedo, Isabel Cristina. *Recreational Terror: Women and the Pleasures of Horror Film Viewing*. State University of New York Press, 1997.

Stanley, John. *Creature Features: The Science Fiction, Fantasy, and Horror Movie Guide*. Boulevard Books, 1997.

_____. *The Creature Features Movie Guide Strikes Again*. Creatures at Large Press, 1994.

Tudon, Andrew. *Monsters and Mad Scientists: A Cultural History of the Horror Movie*. Basil Blackwell Ltd., 1989.

Von Gunden, Kenneth, and Stuart H. Stock. *Twenty All-Time Great Science Fiction Films*, Crown, 1982.

Waller, Gregory A., editor. *American Horrors: Essays on the Modern American Horror Film*. University of Illinois Press, 1987.

Wiater, Stanley. *Dark Vision: Conversation with the Masters of the Horror Film*. Avon Books, 1992.

Williams, Tony. *Hearths of Darkness: The Family in the American Horror Film*. Associated University Presses, 1996.

Zinman, David. *Fifty Grand Movies of the 1960s and 1970s*. Crown, 1986.

Periodicals

Cinefantastique

Cinescape

Daredevils

Famous Monsters of Filmland

Fangoria

Fantascene

Fantastic Films

Films In Review

Gorezone

Sci-Fi Entertainment

Sci-Fi Universe

SFX

Starburst

Starlog

Twilight Zone Magazine

Index

Numbers in **bold** indicate photographs.